The Human Geography of Tropical Africa

T4-AHW-257

The Human Geography of Tropical Africa

Reuben K. Udo
Professor of Geography, University of Ibadan, Nigeria

HEINEMANN EDUCATIONAL BOOKS (NIGERIA) LTD
IBADAN

HEINEMANN EDUCATIONAL BOOKS
LONDON   NAIROBI

Heinemann Educational Books (Nigeria) Ltd
Head Office: PMB 5205, Ighodaro Road, Ibadan
Phone: 62060, 62061   Telex: 31113   Cable: HEBOOKS, Ibadan

Area Offices and Branches:
Ibadan Ikeja Akure Benin Ilorin Owerri Enugu Uyo
Port Harcourt Jos Maiduguri Makurdi Zaria Kano Minna

Heinemann Educational Books Ltd
22 Bedford Square, London WC1B 3HH
PO Box 45314, Nairobi

EDINBURGH MELBOURNE AUCKLAND
HONG KONG SINGAPORE KUALA LUMPUR
NEW DELHI KINGSTON PORT OF SPAIN

Heinemann Educational Books Inc.
4 Front Street, Exeter, New Hampshire 03833, USA

British Library Cataloguing in Publication Data
Udo, Reuben K.
    The human geography of tropical Africa.
    1. Anthropo-geography—Africa, Sub-Saharan
    I. Title
    909   GF28.A/
    ISBN 0-435-95919-0

    ISBN 978 129 517 1 (Nigeria)

Set in 10/11pt Apollo
Printed in Great Britain by
BAS Printers Limited, Over Wallop, Hampshire

Contents

Contents

List of Figures

List of Plates

List of Tables

Acknowledgements for Plates

Mike Abrahams/Network, 7.2;
Christie Archer, 2.1;
Alan Hutchison Library, 6.4, 6.6, 7.3, 9.4, 9.5, 10.1, 10.2, 11.1, 11.2, 12.1, 12.4, 13.2, 14.3, 14.4, 14.5, 14.6, 18.1;
International Defence and Aid, 5.2;
The Mansell Collection, 17.1;
D. W. Phillipson, 8.1;

John Topham Picture Library, 6.5, 8.3, 15.2, 15.3, 15.4, 15.6, 16.2, 18.2, 19.1, 19.2, 19.3;
Reuben K. Udo, 1.2, 2.4, 4.1, 7.1, 9.1, 9.2, 9.3, 9.6, 11.6, 13.1, 15.1;
Sheila Unwin, 1.1, 1.3, 1.4, 2.2, 2.3, 2.5, 4.2, 6.1, 6.2, 6.3, 8.2, 8.4, 11.3, 11.4, 11.5, 13.3, 14.1, 14.2, 16.1, 16.3;
C. James Webb, 3.1, 3.3, 3.4, 3.6.

Preface

The Human Geography of Tropical Africa is written for students preparing for the General Certificate of Education (Advanced Level). The volume is also suitable for use by students in Advanced Teachers' Colleges, Colleges of Education and undergraduates taking courses on Africa or African Studies.

There are five sections, the first of which, A, considers aspects of the physical environment. Both the relatively static aspects such as relief, drainage and climate as well as the more dynamic aspects such as soils, diseases and pests are discussed as a necessary introduction to enable a fuller understanding of the many human problems of development which feature in the remaining four sections. Section B discusses aspects of the traditional societies including land tenure systems, population growth, distribution and migration as well as the consequences of rapid urbanization.

Sections C and D consider respectively primary economic activities such as agriculture, fishing and mining, and secondary as well as tertiary activities such as manufacturing, transport and trade. The last section, E, covers aspects of the political geography of tropical Africa, starting with the legacies of the slave trade and of European colonial rule and ending with the issues involved in the economic integration of the new states of tropical Africa.

That section of Chapter 1 dealing with the geological history of tropical Africa has benefited greatly from comments and suggestions from Dr S. W. Peters, a geologist at the University of Ibadan. I am grateful to him for his help.

The maps were drawn by Mrs Anne Aderogba, Mr D. S. Faoye and Mrs C. M. Babarinde of the Department of Geography, University of Ibadan, Ibadan.

Reuben K. Udo
University of Ibadan

Introduction

Tropical Africa is that part of the African continent lying approximately between the Tropics of Cancer and Capricorn. The more precise definitions of this immense landmass differ considerably from one writer to another. Thus Kimble (1962) defines tropical Africa as the area bounded by the southern limit of the Sahara desert in the north and by the Limpopo Valley in the south. Kimble's 'natural' boundaries, like the Tropics of Cancer and Capricorn, cut across some countries such as Mauritania, Mali, Algeria, Namibia and Botswana. They are therefore unsuitable boundaries for our purpose, since statistical data on population, production and trade are usually given for political units rather than for regions bounded by natural features like rivers, deserts or mountain ranges. Many authors tend to define their northern and southern boundaries of tropical Africa in relation to international boundaries.

A cursory survey of the literature on tropical Africa confirms that only a few authors agree on the number of countries that constitute this massive land area. A few examples compared with our definition will suffice. In this volume, we define tropical Africa as the entire continent of Africa excluding Lesotho, Swaziland and the Republic of South Africa in the south, and Egypt, Libya, Tunisia, Algeria, Morocco and Western Sahara in the north. Morgan (1977) further excludes Namibia, while Etienne Van de Walle's (1968) definition adds Namibia and Mozambique to our list of countries to be excluded. *The Atlas of Tropical Africa* by Davis (1973) covers an even more restricted area. Finally the reader will notice that the size of tropical Africa in Pierre Gourou's well-known *The Tropical World* (5th ed. 1980) is comparatively very small. This is so because Gourou was in fact writing on humid tropical lands.

Tropical Africa, as defined in this study, covers a total area of about 23 million sq. km. or about 76 per cent of the area of the African continent. The total population of 338·45 million in 1980 represented about 73·40 per cent of Africa's population. There is a remarkable variety of landscapes ranging from the rugged highlands of the Ethiopian massif to the almost featureless plains of central Botswana, and from the dry arid wastes of eastern Mauritania to the vast swampy lands that constitute the Niger Delta. The cultural environment is even more varied, since each of the 600 or more ethnic groups, who live in tropical Africa, occupies a distinct contiguous territory, speaks its own language and has different customs and taboos.

The grouping of this large number of distinct ethnic groups into the existing 37 countries of tropical Africa has been achieved through the 'balkanization' of Africa by European powers during the closing years of the nineteenth century. Each country is made up of at least four ethnic groups, while some countries are inhabited by more than fifty. National integration remains a thorny problem in many countries although all attempts to alter the colonial boundaries of tropical Africa have so far failed. European colonization has also had the effect of reducing the number of official languages adopted by the countries of tropical Africa to under ten, English, French and Swahili being the most widely used official languages.

At the end of the Second World War in 1945, the only independent countries in tropical Africa were Ethiopia and Liberia. Fifteen years later, by 1960, almost every country in West and Central Africa had attained political independence, and in 1980 the only colonial territory in tropical Africa was Namibia. This is a remarkable record of political change in view of the fact that, for most countries, independence was achieved without bloodshed. However, most of the countries turned out to be too small both in land area and especially in terms of the total population. Lack of skilled man power and capital as well as a high degree of indiscipline have combined to hinder meaningful economic development. The result is that the governments of most countries have been unable to satisfy the ever rising expectations of their peoples.

Thus in spite of the fact that tropical Africa has extensive reserves of rich deposits of iron ore, phosphate, copper, chrome, industrial diamonds and crude petroleum, the world's largest potential hydro-electric power, and a very long growing season, the region remains the most undeveloped of the under-developed world. Many years after the attainment of political independence, control over the extraction and marketing of most minerals still remains in the hands of foreign companies, mostly European and American. The same situation applies in respect of manufacturing and even in the commercial sector in many Francophone countries. The entrenchment of foreign companies in these sectors has resulted in the drainage of revenue, in the form of profits, exorbitant personal allowances to expatriate staff and generous tax concessions, away from the African countries where such revenue is needed.

Currently the most disturbing aspect of the economy of tropical African countries is in respect of the agricultural sector which still employs more than 70 per cent of the labour force. A serious and worsening food deficit situation exists in most countries, notably Senegal, Upper Volta, Zaïre, Burundi, Botswana, Mozambique, Ghana, Nigeria, Angola and Somalia. In a few cases the food deficit situation is caused by local supply problems, but in most countries the main cause is low output of the farmers who still use primitive farm implements. Many poor countries have therefore had to spend a considerable proportion of their meagre foreign exchange earnings to purchase staple foods like rice, maize (for poultry feeds), sugar and flour; all of which are being cultivated locally, but in insufficient quantities. Throughout the 1970s the food import bills for tropical Africa exceeded £1,000 million sterling (₦2,000) every year, with many countries spending over 15 per cent of their total import expenditure on food. The prospects in the 1980s are not much brighter: the population of tropical Africa is increasing at a faster rate (2·7 per cent) than food production (1·2 per cent).

Industrial crop production has also declined considerably in some countries, and even in those countries where there is no absolute decline in production, the supply has been increasing more slowly than the demand. Nigeria, formerly a major exporter of palm oil and groundnuts, has since 1972 become a net importer of these commodities. In the past, the diversion of labour from food crop farming to industrial crop production was considered to be a major cause of the food-deficit situation in many rural areas. Today the industrial crop sub-sector itself suffers from loss of labour as more people migrate from the rural areas.

The manufacturing sector has made considerable progress in many countries since independence, but there is as yet no industrial nation in tropical Africa. Light industry accounts for about 70 per cent of the total production by value, and in most countries the factories are still owned and manned by expatriates from Europe, North Africa or Asia. Government protection of virtually every manufacturing company has tended to encourage inefficiency and the production of shoddy goods, some of which carry fraudulent labels of country of manufacture. The absence so far of large integrated iron and steel works, except in Zimbabwe, has proved a major setback towards effective industrialization.

The slow pace of development during the two decades ending in 1980 was partly due to political instability in many countries. In a few countries the situation degenerated so much that it resulted in a civil war. Unfortunately this phase of the political evolution of tropical Africa is still with us, and may even continue for the rest of this century. This is so because the root cause of political instability in contemporary tropical Africa is not really the multi-ethnic character of each country but the high level of indiscipline amongst the people. Indiscipline in tropical Africa today manifests itself in various forms, the most obvious being the deplorable attitude to work, lack of patriotism and widespread corruption. The indigenous contractor who builds a poor road after 'buying' a highly inflated contract, for example, is neither disciplined nor patriotic. His life-style, like that of the more greedy politician and merchants, has contributed to general dissatisfaction amongst the poorer members of the society. Such people therefore constitute a threat to peace and stability in the society.

Some 27 countries of tropical Africa experienced one or more military coups between 1960 and 1972. The causes given for these major disturbances vary considerably although such causes can be traced to general indiscipline even among members of the armed forces. It is this indiscipline that has resulted in the leaders of self-proclaimed corrective regimes being more corrupt than those whom they removed from office. Fortunately an increasing number of these military rulers are quitting the stage for good. The task for the future is to prevent the military from coming back to power. The most effective way to do this is to pursue policies that will raise the level of literacy and the standard of living of the vast majority of our peoples.

Four macro-regions are recognized in this volume. These are East Africa, West Africa, Central Africa and southern tropical Africa. The definitions of these macro-regions are as in Table 5.3. East Africa for example covers a much more extensive area than the former British East Africa which was made up of Kenya, Uganda and Tanzania. But southern tropical Africa is equivalent to the whole of southern Africa except Lesotho, Swaziland and the Republic of South Africa.

References

Davis, H. R. J. (1973), *Tropical Africa – An Atlas for Rural Development*, University of Wales Press, Cardiff.

Gourou, P. (1955, 5th ed. 1980), *The Tropical World*, translated by E. D. Laborde, Longman, London.

Kimble, G. H. T. (1962), *Tropical Africa*, Vol. I, 'Land and Livelihood', abridged ed., Doubleday and Co, New York.

Morgan, W. B. (1977), 'Food Supply and Staple Food Imports of Tropical Africa', *African Affairs*, journal of the Royal African Society, London, vol. 76, no. 303, pp. 167–76.

Walle, Etienne Van de (1968), 'The Availability of Demographic Data by Regions in Tropical Africa', in J. C. Caldwell and C. Okonjo (eds.), *The Population of Tropical Africa*, Longman, Harlow, pp. 28–33.

Section A
The Physical Environment

1   Structure, Relief and Drainage

In comparison with Europe or North America, Africa has a relatively simple structure and relief. This is explained by the fact that most of the continent consists of an ancient and rather stable plateau of very old hard rocks which have not been affected by major earth movements since Precambrian times, that is about 570 million years ago. The African plateau, which really consists of several plateau surfaces, is therefore noted for the almost complete absence of recent folded mountains such as are to be found in the Alps of southern Europe, the Rockies of the Pacific coast of North America or the Himalayas of south-central Asia. There are, however, two small areas of fold mountains in the Atlas region of north-west Africa and in the Cape Province of South Africa, both areas of which are outside tropical Africa. The Atlas mountains are really a southward extension of the European Alps and are of a more recent age (about 65 million years old), while the Cape fold mountains belonging to the Carboniferous period are estimated to be 310 million years old. The geology and relief of these two regions are therefore much more complicated than other parts of the continent.

Apart from the Atlas Mountains and a few restricted coastal areas of recent sedimentary rocks, the African continent consists of a Precambrian crystalline massif of very old hard rocks generally referred to as Basement Complex rocks. The rocks which consist mainly of granites, gneisses and schists form the solid foundation of the continent, although they outcrop on the surface in only about one-third of the continent. The other two-thirds of Africa is covered by sedimentary rocks consisting of marine and continental deposits, which overlie the Basement Complex rocks in such areas as the Lake Chad Basin, western Senegal, the Zaïre Basin and the Kalahari Basin. The marine deposits were laid down during the series of marine invasions in which sea water covered extensive areas of Africa, especially during the Paleozoic (or Primary) Era. The outline of the sequence of these marine invasions along with major geological events and the associated geological formations are presented in the following discussion.

Geological history

The Precambrian Era

Our starting point is the Precambrian Era which appears at the bottom of Table 1.1. The early Precambrian was characterized by extensive metamorphism and localized folding which is thought to have been very intense in some areas such as the north of Lake Victoria. Because of the long period of exposure to erosion, the folds and other irregularities in Basement Complex rocks have since been planed down. As a result such areas are characterized by extensive plains and plateaus which often cut across the structure. Precambrian Basement Complex rocks are exposed as shields which are almost entirely crystalline and highly mineralized especially in southern Ghana, Liberia, Katanga and the Witwatersrand in South Africa. The Older Granites of Nigeria, the large expanse of granitic terrain in central Tanzania and the Gneiss Complex of northern Uganda belong to this Era.

Some Precambrian rocks consist of ancient sedimentary formations which show numerous traces of life in the form of bacteria and algae. The Precambrian sediments found in the Barbeton Mountain district of Swaziland and the Transvaal contain the oldest known organic remains – about three billion years old. Other Precambrian sediments including shallow marine deposits occur in the Bulawayo area of Zimbabwe as well as in southern Ghana, Upper Volta and Mali.

The Precambrian ended after a period of extensive glaciation which affected much of Africa south of the Equator. The Precambrian tillites found in the Zaïre Basin and the Transvaal have been identified as hardened boulder clays formed during this period of glaciation. Minerals associated with these very old hard rocks of the Basement Complex include diamond, gold, copper, tin, manganese and uranium.

The Paleozoic Era

The consolidation of the African Basement Complex ended in the early Paleozoic during the Pan-African Orogeny when most of the continent was uplifted. Granites, and metamorphosed and folded basement rocks of this age are common in the West African shields and in East Africa. A long period of erosion of the uplifted landmass preceded the marine invasion of the western Sahara by the Cambrian sea which originated from the north-west and extended south through the Zaïre Basin into the Kalahari. Consequently Paleozoic sedimentary rocks are largely confined to northern Africa, the Zaïre Basin and the south-west of southern Africa. Whereas the rather thin Paleozoic sedimentary cover overlying the Basement Complex in the Sahara is of marine origin, the Zaïre Basin and South Africa were areas of predominantly continental sedimentation. The Zaïre Basin contains thick Paleozoic continental beds, but in South Africa the much thicker sandstones of the lower Paleozoic Table Mountain Series, and the overlying Karroo System contain marine and tillite beds.

During the Ordovician period which lasted for about 60 million years, much of West Africa and the Sahara was submerged. The coarse sandstones and red beds deposited in these inundated areas were derived mainly from sediments originating from areas uplifted during the Pan-African Orogeny. Extensive deposits of such sediments occur around the Ahaggar Mountains as well as in Togo, Ghana and the Republic of Benin. In Morocco where the Cambrian sea still existed, shallow water limestones and red beds accumulated in the Moroccan Anti-Atlas while deep water sediments were laid down in the High Atlas. The late Ordovician was marked by extensive glaciation which deposited tillites in the Algerian Sahara, the Anti-Atlas, Sierra Leone and Ghana.

The Silurian period was marked by widespread marine transgression in the Sahara during which fossiliferous black mud accumulated in Senegal, Guinea, Niger and areas further north. This transgression was perhaps related to the melting of late Ordovician ice sheets. Evidence for the withdrawal of the Silurian sea exists between the Ahaggar and Tibetsi Mountains in eastern Niger, where Silurian beds are discordantly overlain by Devonian-Carboniferous sandstones and fossiliferous shale and limestones which attest to a renewed marine transgression. Devonian sandstones occur in western Sudan while on the present coast of Ghana fossiliferous marine beds suggest the influence of another Devonian sea which probably came from the west through Brazil.

Marine conditions during the Carboniferous and Permian periods were restricted to North Africa because the late Carboniferous saw the northward retreat of the sea, leaving behind some gulfs and lagoons in Morocco and Algeria. Estuarine sediments of the lower Carboniferous occur along the coast of Ghana between Cape Coast and Dixcove. Most of the Carboniferous sediments of northern Africa, however, belong to the late Carboniferous when continental conditions had replaced the earlier marine conditions. Important outcrops of these continental sediments include the Voltaian sandstone in Ghana, Togo and the Republic of Benin, and similar formations in Mauritania, Senegal, Mali and Guinea. The late Devonian-Carboniferous earth movements which caused the uplift from which

these sandstones were derived are referred to as the Hercynian Orogeny. The Mauritanid foldbelt which runs from Guinea to the Spanish Sahara was formed during Hercynian tectonic movements.

In southern Africa, the late Paleozoic sediments which consist of basal tillites, sandstones, shales and coal measures are mostly continental. The Karroo System which is over 10,000 m thick in South Africa covers vast areas in southern Africa and extends as far north as the Equator where it is considerably reduced in thickness. Towards the end of the Carboniferous period, almost all of southern Africa was subjected to extensive glaciation by ice-sheets which might have covered the ground for a longer period than the Pleistocene ice-sheets of Europe and North America. This glaciation also affected South America and India and the late Paleozoic tillites in the three continents justify the assembly of Africa, South America and India into the supercontinent, Gondwanaland. In parts of South Africa, scratched rocks and *roches moutonnées* have been identified in areas where glacial sediments have been removed by erosion or stripped off in quarries. The glacial Dwyka tillites of Cape Province have been identified as lithified boulder clays of late Carboniferous age. Southern Africa was still under ice-sheets when one of the few violent earth movements that have affected Africa occurred, resulting in intensive folding of the rocks in south-west Cape Province. The ranges of hills running parallel to the coast south of the Great Karroo of South Africa are erosional remnants of these folds.

The Paleozoic Era ended with the Permian period when the formation of the lower Karroo beds which started during the late Carboniferous period continued. These beds contain rich coal deposits in South Africa, Zimbabwe and Tanzania. The Permian period also marks the beginning of a long interval of standstill during which the African landmass remained above sea level and was subjected to prolonged denudation and deposition of the products of subaerial erosion.

The Mesozoic Era
During the early Mesozoic, which started with the Triassic period, there was no marine sedimentation except along the Atlas Mountains and in southern Tunisia. The formation of extensive clay bands with gypsum and salt in North Africa continued along the margin of the ancient Mediterranean Sea. The sediments of the upper Karroo in southern Africa were associated with continental subaerial erosion and deposition. The end of the Triassic was characterized by intense basaltic volcanic activity in Morocco and in West Africa and southern Africa. Extensions of these basaltic lavas covered parts of the Karroo formation of southern Africa, including the Basutoland massif where

Table 1.1   Geological history and rock formations

Era	Periods & duration in years	Epoch & duration in years	Years before present	Major events
Cainozoic	Quaternary	Holocene		Continental and marine alluvial deposits in inland Niger Delta, middle Zaïre Basin, Botswana, coast of Mozambique and Niger Delta amongst other areas.
		Pleistocene	1,800,000	Alternating wet and dry phases. Dry valleys and underground water in the Sahara. Formation of Lake Chad Basin. Renewed volcanic activity in West and East Africa. Stone tools and other evidence of early man.
	Tertiary	Pliocene (3,200,000)		Faulting, downwarping and uplift in East Africa created the Great Rift Valley, the Lake Victoria Basin and drainage truncation. Intensive volcanic activity and formation of volcanic mountains and lava plateaus.
		Miocene (17,000,000)		Marine conditions restricted to the Mediterranean coastlands. Formation of limestone in Cyrenaica, and the East African coast.
		Oligocene (15,000,000)		Formation of Red Sea depression. Marine limestone formed in Tanzania and Somalia. Lignite deposits near Onitsha and Asaba.
		Eocene (17,000,000)		Volcanic activity in Jos Plateau, Kenya, Cameroun and Biu Plateau. Formation of Atlas Mountains. Niger Delta begins to form.
		Paleocene (11,000,000)	65,000,000	Retreating continental seas and massive sedimentation especially north of the Equator.
Mesozoic	Cretaceous (72,000,000)			Extensive marine invasion of Africa by sea water extending from the Mediterranean into the Sahara. Inland extension of Gulf of Guinea by way of the Benue Valley. Formation of Enugu coalfield.
	Jurassic (59,000,000)			Break-up of Gondwanaland resulting in the isolation of Africa. Marine invasion of East African coastlands and separation of Malagasy from mainland. Formation of Younger Granites.

Table 1.1 (cont.)

Era	Periods & duration in years	Epoch & duration in years	Years before present	Major events
Paleozoic	Triassic (30,000,000)			Formation of Upper Karroo and of extensive clay bands with gypsum and salt in the Sahara. Volcanic activity in South, North and West Africa.
			230,000,000	
	Permian (55,000,000)			Formation of Lower Karroo beds continued along with formation of rich coal deposits in South Africa, Tanzania and Zimbabwe.
	Carboniferous (65,000,000)			Marine conditions during Lower Carboniferous in North Africa. Sediments largely of continental origin. Hercynian Orogeny – formation of the Mauritanid mountain chain in north-west Africa. Glaciation in southern Africa. Cape folds formed.
	Devonian (50,000,000)			Marine invasion of Libya, the Sahara and western Sudan. Limestone and sandstone of the age occur on the coast of Ghana near Accra.
	Silurian (45,000,000)			Extensive marine invasion of the Sahara and Guinea coastlands. Continental sedimentation in Zaïre Basin, Tanzania and South Africa followed by intensive folding.
	Ordovician (60,000,000)			Marine invasion of north-west Africa. Glaciation in the Sahara. Ordovician sandstones occur in Guinea, Mali, Volta Basin and north-west Ethiopia.
	Cambrian (70,000,000)			Sedimentary formation of conglomerates, limestones, sandstones and volcanic veins in Mali, Mauritania and Namibia. Marine invasion of western Sahara and Kalahari Basin. Extensive glaciation of continent.
			570,000,000	
	Precambrian			Glaciation of Africa south of the Equator. Extensive metamorphism and restricted folding. Oldest known fossilized unicellular algae formed in Swaziland and Mali.

5

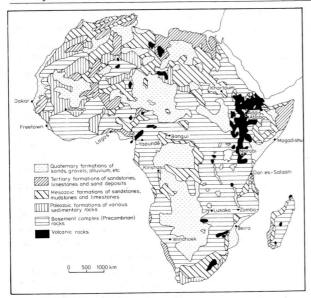

Fig. 1.1 The surface geology of Africa

the lavas attain a thickness of about 200 m. Triassic-Cretaceous granites and volcanic rocks are represented in the Younger Granites Province of Cameroun, the Jos Plateau and Niger.

Intensive subaerial erosion continued throughout the Jurassic when almost the entire continent was reduced to a plain, remnants of which have been identified as the 'Gondwana' erosion surfaces of Africa. Examples include the Jos Plateau, the Nyika Plateau of Malawi and parts of the Basuto mountains. The Triassic salt beds of Morocco which pass southward into other thick salt beds of early Jurassic age in the Spanish Sahara and Senegal are overlain by extensive middle and late Jurassic marine beds. This expanding marine influence in coastal West Africa was caused by the separation of eastern North America from West Africa and the formation of the present North Atlantic Ocean Basin. The Jurassic period is also associated with the break up of Gondwanaland, the hypothetical super-continent which was made up of all the southern continental landmasses of Africa, South America, Antarctica, India and Australia. This event, which resulted in the isolation of Africa, was followed by marine invasion of the East African coast during which Somalia and the south-eastern part of the Ethiopian massif were submerged, while Malagasy probably separated from the African mainland. Jurassic marine sediments are therefore restricted to the coasts of Tanzania, Kenya, Somalia and western Malagasy.

The separation of South America from western Africa was marked by uplift and Rift Valley formation in the

Jurassic, followed by the outpouring of extensive plateau basalts in south-west Africa. The Jurassic–early Cretaceous continental red beds which occur mostly in the subsurface in the coastal basins of Ivory Coast, Ghana, Benin Republic, south-western Nigeria, Cameroun, Gabon, Congo Republic, and Angola accumulated in lakes and river valleys along these rifts. These deposits, which have been penetrated during recent oil exploration drilling in these basins, are overlain by thick salt beds from Angola northward to Gabon. The salt beds of middle Cretaceous age pass upward into marine deposits. Salts were formed when the sea made limited entry into the grabens. With the final separation of South America from Africa in the middle Cretaceous, about 105 million years ago, the South Atlantic Ocean was established, and fully marine sedimentation ensued.

In the interior of West Africa the long period of standstill and denudation which started during the Permian period was terminated by submergence and extensive flooding of the Sahara in the middle Cretaceous. A shallow and warm gulf stretched all the way from the ancient Mediterranean Sea through Algeria and Mali and formed an inland sea in the Sahara similar to the Black Sea or the Baltic Sea. From the Gulf of Guinea in the south another sea stretched north-eastward along the Benue valley and terminated somewhere in Borno State. Recent palaeontological and sedimentological data suggest that contrary to previous belief, the Cretaceous Saharan Sea and the Benue Sea did not merge into one continuous seaway that stretched from the Mediterranean to the Gulf of Guinea.

The oldest sedimentary rocks in Nigeria belong to the Cretaceous period; and in the Enugu-Abakaliki area as well as in the lower Benue valley, these sedimentary beds show mild folding. The coal at Enugu in Nigeria and the associated sandstones and shales were formed at this time. Continental and lagoonal sandstones with plants and crocodile remains as well as important deposits of limestone associated with the Saharan Sea, occur in various parts of the Saharan region including Sokoto in north-western Nigeria. Elsewhere in East and southern Africa, marine Cretaceous rocks are also found near the coasts of Kenya, Tanzania, Mozambique, Natal and Cape Province.

The Cainozoic Era

During the Cainozoic Era, the African continent experienced several turbulent movements which resulted in the formation of the Atlas Mountains in the north-west and the Great Rift Valleys in eastern Africa. The Tertiary deformations affected only a few regions while the greater part of the continent witnessed uplift and the gradual shrinking of the Cretaceous continental sea and marine sedimentation. The Tertiary started with the Paleocene Epoch when remnants of the Saharan Sea were confined to Sokoto in north-western Nigeria, western Niger, Mali and North Africa. Marine sedimentation continued throughout the coastal areas of Africa.

The Eocene Epoch experienced widespread uplift of the Basement Complex and volcanic eruptions in Ethiopia, Arabia, Somalia, Kenya, the Jos and Biu Plateaus of Nigeria and the Cameroun Highlands. The proto Red Sea depression formed in the late Eocene and early Oligocene was accompanied by volcanism. It was also during the Eocene that the powerful earth movements which created the Alpine mountain system affected north-west Africa. Being very rigid, the African landmass resisted the violent thrusts from southern Europe, thereby restricting their effects to the formation of the Atlas Mountains from sediments which had piled up in the Mediterranean Basin since the beginning of the Mesozoic Era. Widespread continental sedimentation and laterite formation took place in the interior of Africa from Eocene times onwards. The Niger Delta began to form during this time.

Marine conditions became even more restricted during the Oligocene Epoch when marine limestones continued to form along the Mediterranean continental shelf. Other areas of marine sedimentation during the Oligocene included Somalia and Tanzania where similar limestone deposits occur. In West Africa, continental conditions existed, except in a few places, along the coast. The thick beds of sand and clay with lignite seams in Benin, Owerri and Onitsha Provinces of Nigeria were formed in coastal lagoons and swamps left behind by the retreating sea.

Extensive limestone deposition continued in the Cyrenaica district of Libya and parts of northern Algeria during the Miocene. In East Africa, the early Miocene was a period of extensive peneplanation when much of the area was reduced by about 300 m (1,000 feet) below the earlier surface. Parts of this bevelled surface have been preserved and protected from further erosion by extensive lava flow which originated from the eastern Rift Valley, an event which was accompanied by volcanic fissure eruptions. Volcanic activity also occurred during the Miocene in Goree and the Dakar district of Senegal where extensive basalts still survive. The plateau sands of the Zaïre Basin and the Kalahari also belong to the Miocene Epoch.

The early Pliocene was also a time of crustal stability, but rifting and volcanic activity continued in East Africa. Much of eastern Kenya and Tanzania, away from the Rift Valley, were reduced to plains at this time while the Miocene sedimentary cover in Uganda was heavily incised by rivers which flowed from western Kenya through the site of Lake Victoria to join the Zaïre River

system. This early Pliocene erosion cycle was terminated by large-scale structural instability which started during the middle Pliocene and which completely changed the landscape and drainage patterns of East Africa. The earth movements which caused this instability resulted in the downwarping and downfaulting which created the eastern and western Rift Valleys and the Lake Victoria depression. The downfaulting and subsidence which caused the Rift Valleys were accompanied by strong uplifting of the shoulders of the Rift Valley to form extensive ranges of highlands such as the Mitumba Mountains which constitute the western border of Lake Tanganyika. The headwaters of the Zaïre River in Uganda and western Kenya were truncated by the uplifts, resulting in drainage reversal and the subsequent filling up of the Lake Victoria depression. Volcanic activity continued within and near the eastern Rift Valley to produce the large central volcanoes of Mount Kenya (5,202 m), Mount Kilimanjaro (5,963 m), Mount Elgon (4,321 m), and Mount Meru (4,565 m), as well as extensive lava plateaus.

In West Africa, the region of the Middle Niger around Timbuktu in Mali consisted of a series of freshwater lakes which continued into the Quaternary period. Continental conditions also prevailed in other parts of West Africa and indeed in the rest of the continent excepting along the Mediterranean coastlands, where marine beds exist in Egypt, Tunisia and Algeria. Pliocene limestone deposits occur in Angola and Zanzibar.

The early Quaternary period otherwise referred to as the Pleistocene Epoch is associated with extensive glaciation in Europe and North America. In Africa, the Pleistocene Epoch was characterized by alternating wet and dry phases. The origin of some dry valleys in West Africa, including the wadis of the southern Sahara as well as some river terraces, is linked with these climatic changes. In East Africa, the wet phases caused considerable advances of the glaciers that still cover the highest mountains; while the rivers all over Africa spread out sheets of fine alluvium which helped to smooth out irregularities in the relief.

It was also during the Pleistocene Epoch that the waters of the upper Niger were captured by the rejuvenated middle Niger. The large underground water resources of the Sahara accumulated during the wet phases of the Pleistocene while the extensive sand dunes of both the Sahara and the Kalahari deserts were produced during the dry phases. Pleistocene uplift in north-eastern Nigeria, Chad and Niger Republic supplied sediments to a central depression, the Lake Chad depression, the water level of which fluctuated considerably during the wet and dry climatic phases of the Pleistocene. Numerous ephemeral lakes also formed in the depressions formed by faulting, downwarping and lava damming in the East African Rift Valleys.

The Pleistocene also featured renewed volcanic activity in West and East Africa. Lavas and well-preserved volcanic cones associated with the Pleistocene abound on the Jos Plateau, the Cameroun Highlands, East Africa and Malawi. The two volcanoes of the Mamelles in the Cape Verde peninsula belong to the Pleistocene and it was the basalt flow from these volcanoes that formed Almadi Point which is Africa's most westerly point. Pleistocene formations in Africa are rich in stone tools and other evidences of the early man.

Climatic changes during the Pleistocene also created raised beaches in various parts of the African coast. These changes continued into the Recent or Holocene period in which we live and it is thought that the inland Niger Delta and the Lake Chad basin are currently experiencing a relatively dry period. The main events of the Holocene consist of extensive continental and marine deposition in such areas as the inland Niger Delta, the Zaïre Basin, Botswana and the coastlands of the Niger Delta and southern Mozambique.

We end this review of the geological history of Africa by recalling the fact that Basement Complex rocks outcrop over one-third of Africa. The remaining two-thirds consist of sedimentary deposits of various geological periods. Outside the Atlas and the Cape of Good Hope districts, these sedimentary layers have remained generally horizontal and without folding. The tabular appearance of the relief in these vast sedimentary areas of the continent is therefore largely due to this horizontal structure.

Relief and major landforms

The major relief features of tropical Africa are a close reflection of the geological history presented in the previous section. A simplified relief map of the continent (Fig. 1.2) reveals that on the basis of elevation, there are two Africas: High Africa in the east and south, and Low Africa in the north and west. Tropical Africa, and indeed the whole continent, is characterized by a narrow coastal plain, an equally narrow continental shelf and a number of plateau surfaces which represent the major cycles of subaerial erosion and immature drainage. Four major relief areas are distinguished and these are 1. the coastline and coastal lowlands, 2. the interior lowlands, 3. the interior high plains and 4. the highlands.

The coastline and coastal lowlands
Africa has a remarkably straight coastline which is free from deeply penetrating indentations. There are no well-defined peninsulas, nor large estuaries, and

Fig. 1.2 High and low Africa

offshore islands are very few. The character of the coastline may be explained partly by faulting and partly by continental uplift of an essentially solid landmass of very old hard rocks. The long period of structural stability dating back to the end of the Primary Era has also helped to smooth the coastline through the formation of deltas, sand bars and lagoons. Natural harbours are therefore so few and far between that it is common to find coastal stretches of over 1,500 km in which there are no natural harbours. Many African countries therefore have had to expend large sums of money in constructing artificial harbours such as those of Tema (Ghana), Point Noire (Congo Republic) and Abidjan (Ivory Coast).

Evidence of drowning or submergence exists along a few stretches of the coastline such as between the Saloum estuary in Senegal and Cape St Ann in Sierra Leone where many river estuaries have been submerged to produce the ria coastlines of Gambia, Guinea-Bissau, Guinea and Sierra Leone. Other stretches of drowned coastline along the Atlantic coast include eastern Ivory Coast, the coastline of the Bights of Benin and Bonny, extending from the Volta Delta in Ghana to the eastern end of the Niger Delta, the coastlines of Cameroun and of Gabon. Along the Indian Ocean coast, the most extensive area of drowning occurs along the coastline of Kenya and Tanzania where a rise in sea level during the Holocene (Recent) period drowned many old river courses to form the existing coastal creeks. Mombasa Island was formed at this time. Extensive silting is currently taking place along the estuaries, creeks and lagoons of these drowned coastlines which are characterized by mudflats and mangrove forest vegetation.

Raised beaches are also a common feature of sections of the coastline of tropical Africa and have been attributed to earlier fluctuations in sea level during the alternating wet and dry phases of the early Quaternary Era. For example, the rise in sea level which resulted in the drowning of the East African coast of Kenya did not attain the very high levels of previous phases of inundation. In consequence, many raised beaches and abandoned cliffs are conspicuously displayed in appropriate locations along the coast, for example, the raised beaches along the coast of Mombasa and on both sides of Kilindini Harbour and the abandoned cliff-line which overlooks the Oceanic Hotel in Mombasa (Ojany and Ogendo, 1973). The raised beaches of the Freetown Peninsula of Sierra Leone, which lie below the 45 m contour, were also formed at about the same period as those of the Mombasa coast. In the Freetown area the raised beaches appear below the cliffs fronting the sea coast as well as along the lower reaches of the numerous rivers that drain the area (Gregory, 1970). Raised beaches also occur along the coast of Namibia from Conception Bay to the south of Port Nolloth.

Pl. 1.1 The raised beach and abandoned coastline overlooking the Oceanic Hotel, Mombasa

Rocky cliffs and promontories occur along some stretches, notably along the Freetown Peninsula and parts of the coast of western Ivory Coast and Ghana. The most extensive stretch of rocky coast extends from the Namibia port of Luderitz to just north of the Orange River mouth, where the very rugged rocky coast is characterized by high cliffs and many small islands (Wellington, 1955, p. 149). Occasional rocky outcrops also occur along the Indian Ocean coast north of

Quelimane in Mozambique, but the dominant relief features of this coastline right up to the Red Sea are coral reefs, which also fringe the shores of islands along the coast.

In those parts of tropical Africa where desert conditions extend to the coast, the coastlines are generally very smooth and are bordered by sand dune belts. The coasts of Mauritania, the Cayor district of Senegal, and the Namib Desert coast between the Cunene River and the port of Luderitz are fronted by sand dune belts behind which lie narrow inland depressions or lagoons which have been wholly or partly cut off from the sea. The longest stretch of low-lying, straight and inaccessible coast which is fronted by sand dunes is the Indian Ocean coast of Somali Republic which extends south into north-east Kenya.

The descent from the coast to ocean depths is generally abrupt all over tropical Africa, the 200 m (about 100 fathoms) submarine contour rarely being more than 30 km from the coast. The continental shelf is therefore very narrow except in a few areas such as the region of the Zaïre River mouth and the area between Cape Verde and Cape St Ann.

As is the case with the continental shelf, the coastal lowlands of tropical Africa are generally narrow except in a few areas such as the coastal plains of Mauritania and Senegal, south-eastern Nigeria, southern Mozambique and the central coastlands of Somali Republic where the coastal lowlands stretch inland for about 160–240 km. Elsewhere, the coastal plains, which have a general elevation of not more than 200 m, rarely extend beyond 80 km from the coast. The characteristic landforms of the coastal lowlands include lagoons and swamps which give way further inland to gently undulating dissected plains. The swampy Niger Delta is characterized by meandering water channels, high levées and numerous oxbow lakes. Abandoned beach ridges constitute the dominant landforms of the outer perimeter of the Niger Delta while the islands of solid red earth in the region of Port Harcourt provide evidence of drowning of this section of the coast. The Zambezi Delta displays similar features to the Niger Delta except that coral reefs occur on the outer banks of the distributaries.

In Mauritania and northern Senegal, the coastal lowlands are covered with extensive coastal dunes which are usually parallel to the shore and often rise to an elevation of over 30 m. River courses in the area have been interrupted by the dunes, behind which they form a string of lagoons and marshes called *seyane* in the St Louis area. In the more humid areas of Senegal, the coastal dunes are fixed and covered with scrub, but north of Nouakchott the dunes become mobile and the landscape more open. Coastal mobile sand dunes, which often cover areas as wide as 30 km, are also common

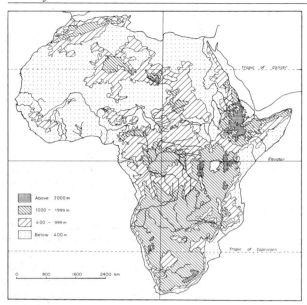

Fig. 1.3 Relief and drainage

along the arid coastlands of the Somali Republic. The extensive dune belt which extends from the coast of Natal to the north of the Zambezi mouth is however characterized by fixed sand dunes which often rise to over 100 m and which are usually covered with low spiny bushes.

The interior lowlands

Apart from a few locations in the Sahara Desert, the interior lowlands are higher in elevation than the coastal plains, their general elevation ranging from 200–400 m above sea level. The rise from the coastal plains, through these lowlands to the high plains, is through a series of steps, each of which marks the end of one and the beginning of another cycle of erosion. The rivers descend these steps in rapids and falls. The interior lowlands are very extensive in Low Africa, especially West Africa and the Zaïre Basin. In East and southern Africa, these lowlands are restricted in extent, being no more than narrow extensions of the equally narrow coastal plains.

Interior lowlands such as the Chad Basin, the inland Niger Delta and the central Zaïre Basin, which are basically products of prolonged sedimentation, may be distinguished from lowlands such as the Cross River Plains, the scarplands of south-eastern Nigeria, the Oyo Plains of Nigeria and the western lowlands of Niger Republic, which are products of subaerial erosion. The landscape of the lowlands of deposition consists of vast featureless plains, the monotony of which is relieved in some localities by sand dunes or fossil dunes covered

with scanty vegetation. The lowlands produced by erosion exhibit similar relief forms although some of them, such as the Oyo Plains, are developed on rocks of the Basement Complex while others, such as the scarplands and the Cross River Plains, are developed on sedimentary rocks. Inselbergs or erosional survivals which appear here and there all over the plains are the commonest landforms. They are characterized by very steep sides and are usually dome-shaped except where a capping of lateritic ironstone gives rise to flat-topped inselbergs. Gently sloping fringing rock-cut pediments are usually associated with inselbergs developed on old hard rocks of the Basement Complex although these pediments are not always obvious in the inselbergs found in some areas, including the Oyo Plains of Nigeria. Inselbergs occur singly or in groups, and in areas of Basement Complex rocks they may be found in various stages of disintegration (Plate 1.2).

The origin of inselbergs is still a subject of controversy amongst geomorphologists. The most reasonable theories attribute their formation to slope retreat or to sub-surface exhumation of rocks. Inselbergs are generally associated with semi-arid and savanna landscapes but many inselbergs also occur in the high forest areas such as the Idanre and Akure districts of Ondo State in Nigeria. In many parts of tropical Africa these isolated hills provided defensive sites for refugee settlements during the period of the slave trade.

Pl. 1.2 A typical inselberg in Nigeria

A number of other interesting landforms occur in the scarplands of south-eastern Nigeria. These include the elongated sandstone ridges of the Udi–Nsukka Plateau which rise steeply for about 90 m above the plateau surface and the impressive east-facing Enugu escarpment which rises almost vertically for 200 m above the Cross River Plains. In many locations the sandstone

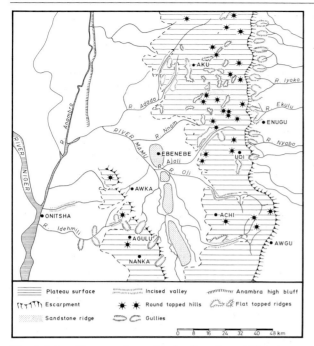

Fig. 1.4 Landforms and scarplands of south-east Nigeria

ridges have been broken up to form a line of flat-topped hills usually separated by dry valleys. The slopes of the Enugu escarpment are heavily dissected by numerous steep-sided small valleys or gullies which drain into the Cross River Plains. Other landforms of the scarplands include the limestone caves at Ogbunike near Awka and the Agulu Lake which was formed by sandbanks blocking the mouth of a tributary stream. The destructive but beautifully carved erosion gullies at Nsudde, Agulu and Nanka constitute one of the most impressive landscapes in tropical Africa.

The interior high plains

In Low Africa, the interior high plains have a general elevation of 400–1,000 m as compared with a general elevation of 1,000–1,500 m in High Africa. The high plains of Hausaland in Nigeria and the interior plateau of Sierra Leone belong to the high plains of Low Africa while the central plateau of East Africa and the Kalahari Basin belong to the high plains of High Africa. Whatever their elevation or location, the high plains consist of extensive level landscapes. In the high plains of Hausaland and the central plateau of East Africa, both of which are developed on very old hard rocks, the characteristic landscape consists of wide plains crossed by mature streams which flow in broad shallow valleys. This monotonous scenery is diversified by numerous inselbergs which rise abruptly above the plains.

The interior plateau of Sierra Leone is also developed on old hard rocks which consist predominantly of granite. Much of the plateau surface is covered with lateritic crust above which rises a large number of inselbergs. A number of bigger and elongated hill masses, which the local people call mountains, are also characteristic of this region. Prominent among these are the Loma Mountains, the Sula Mountains, which contain large reserves of iron ore, and the Wara Wara Mountains.

In the case of the Kalahari Basin which covers over 1,640,000 sq km, the entire area is covered with a thick mantle of sand. The sandy waste is broken here and there by the outcropping of rock floors which attain considerable heights in various parts of northern Botswana including the Ghanzi district and the Chobe National Park area where the rocky Gubatsa and Goha Hills are located. Prominent rock outcrops also appear in the area to the south-east of the Makarikari depression and along the valley of the Linyanti River which drains the far north of Botswana. Sand dunes and fossil sand hills rising to a maximum height of about 90 m are common in the central parts of the basin. In many districts of the southern Kalahari Basin, the dune crests are separated by small depressions or pans which overlie limestone and decaying vegetation. These pans contain water during the rainy season, but are dry during the much longer dry season of the year.

The highlands

All land areas having an altitude of over 1,500 m are considered to be highlands in High Africa. In countries like Ethiopia, Kenya and Tanzania some of the highlands rise to elevations of over 4,000 m. In each of these countries, the highlands are usually treated as separate geographical regions, not just because of their altitude, but because of the cool, moist and healthy climate that the altitude induces and also because of the wide coverage of volcanic rocks which weather to form soils which are much more fertile than soils in other parts of these countries. The highlands of Low Africa possess either all or almost all of these attributes, although their altitude, which is between 1,500 and 2,000 m, is generally much lower. Another common characteristic of the highlands is that they descend steeply to meet the surrounding high plains and furthermore, they form the source of many fast-running streams which flow through their slopes in very deep narrow valleys.

The most extensive highland areas occur in East Africa and Ethiopia. The dominant relief features of the East African Highlands are the Great Rift Valleys and the great volcanoes which occur either within the floors or on the margin of the Rift Valleys. The East African Rift Valley system starts in Syria and forms the Jordan

Pl. 1.3 Highland view in Malawi with Mt Mlanje in the background

Valley, the Dead Sea, the Gulf of Akaba and the Red Sea. It penetrates into Africa by way of the Awash Valley of Ethiopia and on leaving Ethiopia, it divides into two main branches which are separated by the Lake Victoria depression. The eastern branch passes through Kenya and Tanzania, enclosing Lake Turkana and a string of smaller lakes, while the western branch, which encompasses Lakes Albert, Edward, Kivu and Tanganyika, forms the border between Zaïre on the one hand and Uganda, Rwanda, Burundi and Tanzania on the other. The two branches join again just north of Lake Malawi and leave the continent by way of the Shire and lower Zambezi Valleys.

In parts of Kenya the Rift Valley is up to 60 km wide while the fault scarps are 500–1,000 m in height. Since the faulting occurred in a series of parallel faults, the sides of the main valley are stepped. Young volcanic cones and plugs appear within the valley floor; the more important ones include Menengai (2,280 m), Suswa (2,357 m), Silali (2,355 m) and Langonot (2,776 m). The tops of these cones have all been blown off to form craters, the Menengai crater being so large that it passes for a caldera. The highest elevations are generally along the margins of the highlands and include the four great volcanoes of Africa, Mount Kilimanjaro (5,963 m), the highest mountain in Africa, Mount Kenya (5,202 m), Mount Meru (4,565 m) and Mount Elgon (4,321 m). The summits of these mountains are covered with snow all the year round.

The Ethiopian Highlands form the most extensive area of mountainous country in tropical Africa. The base consists of a high plateau surface with an average altitude of 300 m supporting numerous high mountains with peaks above 4,000 m. The main branch of the Great Rift Valley divides the highlands into two unequal parts, namely, the Ethiopian massif which occupies most of western Ethiopia and the much smaller Harar massif along the eastern flank of the Rift Valley. The walls of the Rift Valley are very steep especially along the line joining Alamata to Dabra Sina where the walls of the faults rise abruptly to about 2,000 m from the Danakil Plains. The main massif slopes gradually westwards towards the Nile Basin while the general elevation declines southwards. Among the high mountain groups rising above the level of the high plateau are the Simen Mountains whose highest peak, the Ras

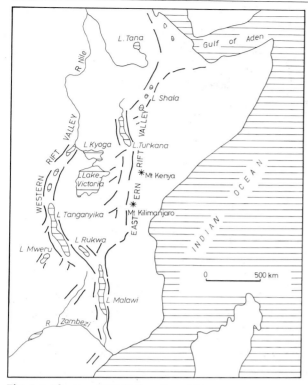

Fig. 1.5 The Great Rift Valley, East Africa

Daschau, is 4,620 m; the Choke Mountains, where the Talo Peak (4,413 m) is located; and the Mendebo Mountains of the Harar massif where the Batu Peak (4,307 m) is located. None of these peaks has permanent snow cover. Both the surface of the plateau and its slopes are deeply incised by valleys with vertical walls, while the floor of the Rift Valley contains many small lakes.

The highlands of south-central and southern tropical Africa are more dispersed and much smaller in extent. They include the eastern Highlands of Zimbabwe, the Bie Plateau of Angola, the Windhoek Highlands of Namibia and the highlands of northern Zambia and the Katanga Province of Zaïre. The eastern Highlands of Zimbabwe consist of a belt of rugged country about 300 km long, its highest point being the Inyangani Peak (2,596 m). The more extensive Bie Plateau of Angola has many more high peaks and constitutes the hydrographical centre of the country. Its western slopes descend into the coastal plains through a series of steep slopes, separated by narrow erosion surfaces. Low mountains of quartzite, granite inselbergs and extensive rocky surfaces characterize the desert highlands of Namibia which are bounded in the west by a sharply defined escarpment. The Katanga Highlands have a much more level topography so that the watershed which forms the boundary between Zaïre and Zambia is hardly perceptible.

In Low Africa, the most prominent highland areas include the Cameroun–Adamawa Highlands, the Jos Plateau, the Fouta Djallon Highlands and the Sahara Desert Highlands of Ahagger, Tibetsi and Darfur. All the highlands show evidence of recent volcanic activity which has given rise to many interesting landforms. In the Cameroun–Adamawa Highlands and the Jos Plateau, for example, there are numerous volcanic cones which have well-preserved craters, some of which contain crater lakes. In addition a long period of laterization, during which the lava flow from these cones was buried under a capping of ironstone, followed by surface erosion, has given rise to numerous flat-topped hills or mesas on the plateau base of these highlands. All the highlands are heavily dissected by permanent streams or by dry valleys formed during the wetter phases of the Quaternary Era.

Drainage characteristics

Extensive saucer-shaped depressions such as the Chad Basin, the middle Niger Basin, the Zaïre Basin, the Lake Victoria Basin and the north Kalahari Basin cover vast areas of both High and Low Africa. Some of these basins are areas of inland drainage with no outlet to the sea, while others, such as the Zaïre Basin, have a very restricted outlet to the sea. As a general rule these basins are enclosed by higher land areas which have much

Fig. 1.6 Inland drainage basins

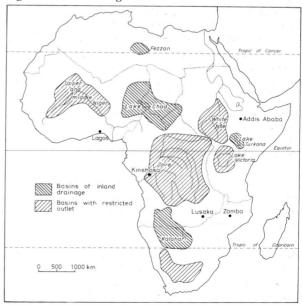

Pl. 1.4 Lake Victoria

steeper slopes on the seaward sides and rather gentle and hardly perceptible slopes on the inland sides. The result is that the usually shorter and faster-flowing coastal streams are characterized by deeply incised gorge-like valleys while the sluggish streams which flow into these inland depressions usually do so through broad open valleys, except the streams originating from the Ethiopian Highlands and the East African Highlands. Through the process of headward erosion, the coastal streams have progressively encroached upon and captured the headwaters of some of the inland flowing rivers.

River capture is a very common phenomenon in tropical Africa and its regular occurrence has been greatly facilitated by the imperceptible character of most African watersheds which in many places consist of ill-defined gently sloping surfaces, rather than prominent hills or ridges. The capture of the upper Niger by the lower Niger at Goa and the capture of the Enyong Creek by the Imo River near Umuahia are good examples. Another good example is the capture at Rocadas of the upper Cunene River of Angola by the lower Cunene which flows into the Atlantic Ocean. Formerly the upper Cunene flowed from the Bie Plateau into the Etosha Pan inland drainage basin but following the capture, the water resources of the basin have been greatly reduced. A similar situation is expected to occur

in the Lake Chad Basin if the imminent capture of the Logone by the upper Benue is not prevented. The loss of the Shari–Logone waters to Lake Chad, which receives about three-quarters of its waters from the Shari–Logone system, would adversely affect current irrigation and ranching projects in the Chad Basin. It can be inferred from the last two examples that river captures in tropical Africa have had the effect of depriving the drier interior of the little water which it has.

Lakes

All the saucer-shaped depressions either contain lakes or did so in the past. The lakes associated with them are very shallow even when they are as extensive as Lake Chad (2 m deep). Furthermore, the extent and level of the waters of these lakes vary considerably according to the season and often, as in the Kalahari, some of the shallow lakes have since been reduced to swamps or disconnected patches of brackish water. The deepest lakes in tropical Africa are found in the East African Rift Valleys where Lake Tanganyika, the world's second deepest lake (1,435 m) is located. The largest lake in tropical Africa is Lake Victoria which has an area of 83,000 sq km, that is, about six times the area of Lake Chad (14,000 sq km). Lake Victoria is, however, only 80 m at its deepest as it lies within a relatively shallow crustal depression separating the two main branches of the Great Rift Valley and not within the Rift Valley itself.

A large number of crater lakes exist in the areas of recent volcanic activity, but these are usually not as extensive as the increasing number of large man-made lakes associated with multi-purpose river basin development projects. The large man-made lakes include Lake Volta (8,500 sq km), Lake Kariba (5,200 sq km), Lake Cabora Bassa (2,800 sq km) and Lake Kainji (1,200 sq km).

Dry valleys
Another important feature of tropical African rivers is that most of them are dry for most of the year while the volume of the few large and permanent rivers fluctuates considerably with the seasons. Dry valleys are particularly numerous in the savanna areas, and in the semi-arid and arid areas these valleys remain dry for several years. Dry valleys are also common in wetter areas, such

Fig. 1.7 The course of a hypothetical African river

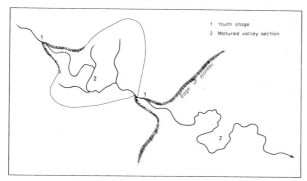

as the Udi–Nsukka Plateau, and are covered with thick layers of sandstones or limestone. In the drier savanna areas, the dry valleys are easy to recognize owing to the gallery forest vegetation which they support. The origin of dry valleys in semi-arid and arid areas has been attributed to river action in a period of more humid climate as well as to the action of flash floods. In the more humid areas, dry valleys are clearly caused by the porous nature of the surface rocks which permits the continuous flow of water only during the heavy rains of the rainy season. Many dry valleys are also associated with the phenomenon of river capture discussed earlier (p. 14).

Rapids and waterfalls
Another interesting characteristic of tropical African rivers is the alternation of 'youth' sections with their steep-sided V-shaped valleys and 'mature' sections with their open flat-bottomed valleys. The 'mature'

sections of the valleys are of course associated with the various erosion surfaces, while the 'youth' sections occur along the slopes which separate these erosion surfaces. The numerous rapids and waterfalls which interrupt the course of most tropical African rivers usually occur at the head of the youth sections of the valleys, that is, at the knickpoints associated with the various erosion surfaces. The River Niger, one of the largest rivers, displays these alternating sections of youth and maturity very clearly. Starting from the Fouta Djallon Highlands, the Niger flows through narrow valleys before entering the open Macina Plains of the inland delta region. The river then passes through another 'youthful' section by flowing through the gorge between Say and Goa where the capture of the upper Niger occurred. Below the town of Say, the Niger Valley opens up into another 'mature' section. This phenomenon is repeated several times further downstream, at other constriction points, including Kainji, Itobe and Onitsha, before the Niger finally enters the sea. A bottle-neck topography (Fig. 1.7) results.

Rapids and waterfalls constitute a serious impediment to the navigation of African rivers in much the same way as the fluctuations in volume hamper the use of these rivers for the production of hydro-electric power and for navigation. The navigational problems created by the numerous falls and rapids of the Zaïre River are probably the most notorious. Some of the major falls of the upper reaches of the Zaïre include the Cornet Falls, the Kuibo Falls, with a descent of over 30 m, the Kibombo and the Stanley Falls. Between Stanley Pool and the head of the Zaïre Estuary at Matadi the river falls nearly 270 m over a distance of 240 km by a series of cataracts collectively referred to as the Livingstone Falls. The great potential of these falls as a source of energy has often been stressed, but at the same time they constitute a troublesome and expensive hindrance to navigation.

Rivers flowing in two directions
Finally we come to the rather curious and interesting drainage system of south-west Uganda. Before the formation of the Lake Victoria depression in the Miocene to early Pliocene period, the area was drained by westward flowing rivers from western Kenya through the Ankole and Buganda Provinces of Uganda to join the Zaïre River system. Following the formation of the Rift Valleys and the downwarping which produced the Lake Victoria depression, the headwaters of the Zaïre in Uganda were truncated, resulting in drainage reversal and the consequent formation of Lake Victoria by the now east-flowing rivers. Later, a gentle uplifting of the area between the western Rift Valley and Lake Victoria produced a situation whereby

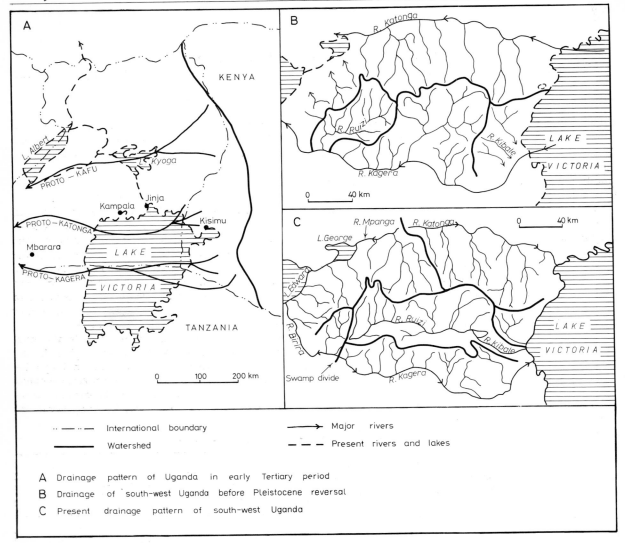

Fig. 1.8 The drainage of south-west Uganda

sections of the rivers then flowing eastwards into Lake Victoria were slightly raised to form water divides. The curious situation today is that these low and imperceptible watersheds are themselves under water or are swamps from which water flows both to the east to join Lake Victoria and to the west to join the Rift Valley lakes of Edward and Albert (Doornkamp and Temple, 1966). A good example of rivers flowing in two directions is the River Katonga which flows eastwards to join Lake Victoria just north of Bukakata and westwards to join Lake Edward through Lake Kiru. Another good example is the River Kagera which flows eastwards through northern Tanzania to join Lake Victoria and westwards to join Lake Edward.

References

Doornkamp, J. C. and Temple, P. H. (1966), 'Surface Drainage and Tectonic Instability in Part of Southern Uganda', *Geographical Journal*, 132, pp. 238–52.

Gregory, S. H. (1970), 'Landforms of the Freetown Area', *Sierra Leone Geographical Association*, Occasional Paper, no. 2, pp. 9–15.

Morgan, W. T. W. (1973), *East Africa*, Longman, London.

Ojany, F. F. and Ogendo, R. B. (1973), *Kenya: A Study in Physical and Human Geography*, Longman, London, p. 43.

Wellington, J. H. (1955), *Southern Africa, A Geographical Study* – vol. I: *Physical Geography*, Cambridge University Press, Cambridge.

2   Climate, Vegetation and Soils

Climate is the average weather, or day-to-day atmospheric conditions, over a given area. In tropical Africa, the association between climate and vegetation is so close that the natural vegetation zones replicate, almost without any alteration, the major climatic zones. The direct influence of climate through deep weathering and leaching, and its indirect influence through the vegetation cover on the profile and humus content of the soil is also considerable. In addition the vegetation cover protects the soil from accelerated soil erosion and helps to regulate the moisture content of the soil. Indeed, the relationship between soil and vegetation is so close that some of the major soil groups, such as rain forest soils and desert soils, are named after the corresponding vegetation zones.

Climate

Because of its latitude, tropical Africa feels the full influence of the sun throughout the year, except in parts of High Africa where there is a considerable lowering of temperatures by altitude. The effect of relief on rainfall in High Africa is also clearly brought out in East Africa and Ethiopia where the interior highlands receive much more rain than the coastal areas. In Low Africa on the other hand and especially in West Africa the climate of a place is generally determined largely by its distance from the sea. Thus, Freetown, on the coast, receives the full influence of the rain-bearing south-west monsoon and therefore records a total annual rainfall of 3,505 mm spread over eight months of the year. Timbuktu, on the other hand, is hot and dry for most of the year because it is about 1,300 km from the sea.

In tropical Africa we talk of the dry season and the rainy season; not summer, autumn, winter or spring. Some areas however have four seasons, namely the long dry season, the main rainy season, the short dry season and the short rainy season, while most areas have just two seasons, the dry season and the rainy season. In all cases it is the rainfall rather than temperature that determines the season of the year in tropical Africa. In fact, since the temperature is high throughout the year, rainfall is the most important element of climate as far as agriculture is concerned. In most areas success or failure depends on the amount, distribution and reliability of

the rainfall. Furthermore, in many rural areas which are located far away from water courses, rainwater remains the most important source of water for both man and beast.

Rainfall distribution and seasons

Some important general features of the rainfall shown in Table 2.1 and Figs. 2.1 and 2.2 can be listed as follows:
1. The coastal areas, with the exception of the Accra dry belt, receive more rain than the immediate interior districts. In West Africa, for example, there is a general decrease inland in the amount of rain from about 3,050 mm per annum along the coasts of Sierra Leone and Liberia, and the Niger Delta, to under 250 mm in the areas north of latitude 15°N.
2. The effect of relief, resulting in higher total annual rainfall for inland areas like the Kenya Highlands, the Ethiopian Highlands and the Jos Plateau. In Kenya, for example, Garissa, which is located on the eastern plains at a distance of about 260 km from the coast, receives about 280 mm of rain every year. By comparison, the

Fig. 2.1 Mean annual rainfall

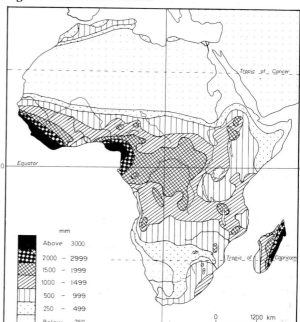

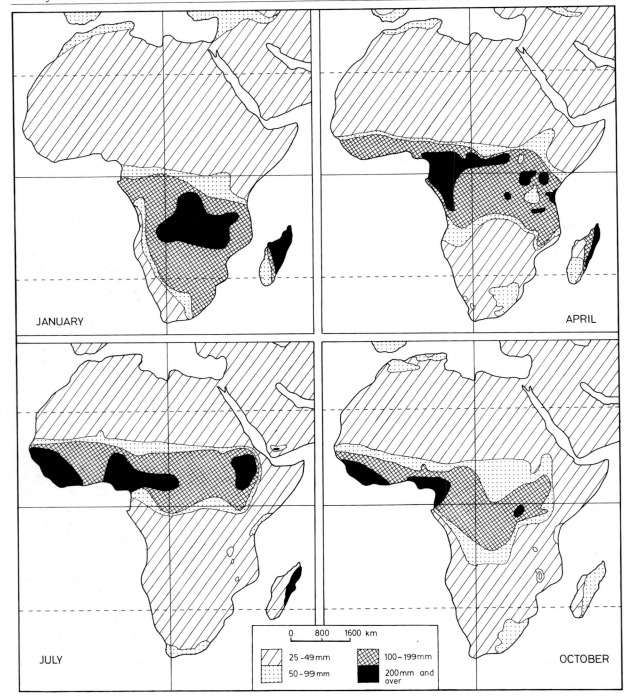

Fig. 2.2 Seasonal distribution of rainfall

town of Kericho, on the Kenya Highlands, receives over 1,835 mm even though its distance from the sea coast is more than 630 km. Both Garissa and Kericho are on almost the same latitude.

Pl. 2.1 Lake Turkana in the Rift Valley

3. The rainshadow condition of the Kenya section of the eastern branch of the Rift Valley which has only 162 mm of rain at Lodwar, near Lake Turkana, increasing southwards to 384 mm at Magadi, near the Kenya border with Tanzania. By comparison the towns of Marsabit and Nairobi on the eastern part of the Rift Valley have 817 mm and 830 mm of rain respectively while Kitale and Kericho, which are located west of the Rift Valley, have 1,132 mm and 1,837 mm of rain respectively.

4. The Accra dry belt which raises many questions for the geographer: the rainfall increases immediately north of the coastal dry belt. There are two common explanations for this dry belt:

a. the alignment of the coast in a direction parallel to that of rain-bearing winds, in contrast for instance to the situation along the Sierra Leone coast where the south-west winds meet the coast at right angles;

b. the upwelling of cold water resulting from the meeting in this neighbourhood of the cold Benguela current and the warm Guinea current, which cools the winds passing over the water and thereby causes fogs instead of rain along the coast.

You may come across a few other explanations, but it is well to bear in mind that the matter has not yet been satisfactorily settled.

5. The very scanty rainfall of the Namib Desert and the extension of desert climate along the coast almost to the mouth of the River Zaïre. The situation is attributed to the cold Benguela current which causes fog and low clouds resulting in fine drizzle instead of rain. Port Nolloth, for example, has 85 days of fog compared with about two days at Durban on the Indian Ocean coast.

6. The varying length of the rainy season; this decreases inland from the coast in West Africa where most areas in the forested south have about seven months with at least 100 mm of rain as compared with less than three months in the far north. In East Africa, on the other hand, the number of months with at least 100 mm of rain increases inland from four months along the coast to about seven months in the Kenya Highlands and the Lake Victoria districts.

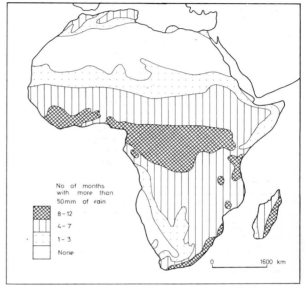

Fig. 2.3 Length of the rainy season

7. Areas which have a two-maxima rainfall regime as opposed to those which have a one-maximum regime. In West Africa the two-maxima regime occurs in the south where the wettest months are June and October while the short dry season occurs in August. The west and north have a one-maximum regime with September as the rainiest month. In East Africa, the two-maxima regime occurs around Lake Victoria, the Kenya Highlands and eastern Kenya. The rainy seasons of eastern Kenya are March to May and October to December. North-west Kenya, like most of south-central and southern tropical Africa, has a one-maximum regime. In Malawi the rainy season lasts from October to April with a short break in December, thereby producing a double-maxima regime.

Other aspects of the rainfall

There are several facts about the character of the rainfall, such as its reliability and intensity, which cannot be readily read from maps or tables. Our definition of the climate of a place should remind you that the rainfall figures in Table 2.1 are averages taken over many years. Considerable monthly and annual variations occur in most stations. This is particularly true of the northern parts of West Africa where annual variations of up to 50 per cent are common. Large variations also occur all over East Africa, caused partly by topographical contrasts and partly by the distribution and presence of large bodies of water such as Lake Victoria and the Indian Ocean (Ojany and Ogendo, 1973).

Considerable delays occur in the onset of the rains resulting in delayed cropping or scorching of seeds planted in expectation of them. Once they start they are often so heavy, with fierce thunderstorms, that they wash out the newly planted seedlings and damage the roofs of thatch houses. A night storm may blow down tree trunks across roads, thereby impeding traffic for many hours. The intensity of the rainfall in West Africa at the beginning of the rainy season is so great that during the thunderstorms as much as 35 mm may fall in one hour. Towards the middle of the rainy season, the intensity of the rain decreases so much that along the coast, it may drizzle throughout the day. Daily maximum falls of over 250 mm have been recorded in East Africa, notably at Entebbe (280 mm in May 1958), Kilifi, near Mombasa (288 mm in May 1947) and at Vanga on the south Kenya coast (375 mm in October 1953).

Temperature

A study of the temperature figures in Table 2.1 and in Fig. 2.4 will confirm some of the following facts about the temperature conditions in tropical Africa.

1. Temperatures remain high throughout the year and for most stations there is little seasonal variation. In East Africa, for example, the seasonal variation rarely exceeds 5°C. In the south of West Africa the mean daily temperature remains around 27°C throughout the year except during the rainy season when the temperatures are cooler, owing to the cooling effects of the rains and the fact that cloud cover curtails the amount of insolation.

2. In Low Africa, higher day temperatures are recorded in the interior, except in highland areas such as the Jos Plateau, the Guinea Highlands and the Mambila Plateau, all of which have lower temperatures compared with the surrounding lowlands. In High Africa, on the other hand, the day temperatures decrease with distance from the coast because of the higher altitudes of the interior plateaus and highlands.

3. The diurnal range increases with distance from the sea, especially in West Africa where the far north has clearer skies and does not benefit from the moderating influence of the sea. During the harmattan, which is a cool dry wind from the Sahara, the pattern of diurnal variation in the western and eastern Sudan, as well as in

Fig. 2.4 Monthly mean temperatures for January and July

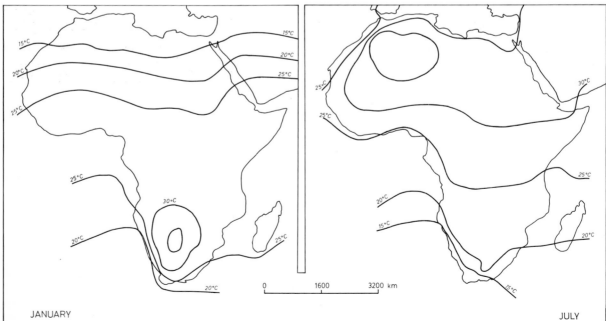

Table 2.1 Temperatures (°C) and rainfall data for selected stations (mm)

Station	Elements	Jan	Feb	Mar	April	May	June	July	Aug	Sept	Oct	Nov	Dec	Year	Climatic type
WARRI															
6·0 m (20 ft)	Temp. max.	31	33	33	33	31	30	28	28	29	30	32	31	31	Equa-
5°31′N	Temp. min.	22	22	23	23	23	22	22	23	22	22	22	24	23	torial
5°44′E	Rainfall	32·5	52·5	132·5	225	270	372·5	385	295	427·5	427·5	110	10	2,655	
KINSHASA															
325 m (1,066 ft)	Temp. max	30	31	31	32	30	28	27	28	30	30	30	30	30	Sub-
4°20′S	Temp. min.	22	22	22	22	22	19	17	18	20	22	22	22	21	equa-
15°15′E	Rainfall	127·5	139·4	180·5	208·6	133·5	4·9	1·0	3·5	32·5	136·5	235·5	170·5	1,374·5	torial
BOUAKE															
338 m (1,110 ft)	Temp. max.	33	34	35	35	33	31	29	29	30	31	32	33	32	Humid–
7°41′N	Temp. min.	21	22	22	22	22	21	21	21	21	21	21	21	22	tropical
5°02′W	Rainfall	10	37·5	102·5	145	132·5	150	80	115	205	130	37·5	25	1,170	
KANO CITY															
472 m (1,549 ft)	Temp. max.	30	32	36	38	37	35	31	29	31	34	34	31	33	
12°02′N	Temp. min.	13	16	19	22	24	23	22	21	21	20	17	14	19	Dry–
8°32′E	Rainfall	0	0	2·5	7·5	67·5	112·5	200	310	127·5	12·5	0	0	840	tropical
DAKAR															
32 m (105 ft)	Temp. max.	28	28	28	27	28	31	31	31	31	31	31	28	29	Dry–
14°39′N	Temp. min.	18	18	18	18	20	23	25	24	25	24	23	20	22	tropical
17°25′W	Rainfall	0	0	0	0	0	30	87·5	260	142·5	42·5	5	0	567·5	coast
KAYES															
56 m (183 ft)	Temp. max.	35	38	41	44	43	40	34	32	33	35	38	34	37	
14°24′N	Temp. min.	17	19	22	25	28	26	24	23	23	23	18	18	18	Sahel
11°26′W	Rainfall	2·5	0	0	0	25	95	157·5	237·5	185	42·5	0	0	745	
AGADEZ															
520 m (1,706 ft)	Temp. max.	28	33	42	42	44	44	41	39	41	41	34	32	38	
16°59′N	Temp. min.	10	12	21	21	25	24	23	23	23	20	15	12	18	Desert
70°56′E	Rainfall	0	0	0	0	5	7·5	50	92·5	17·5	0	0	0	172·5	
ADDIS ABABA															
2,451·6 m (8,083 ft)	Temp. max.	23	24	25	25	25	23	20	20	21	22	22	22	23	
9°02′N	Temp. min.	6	7	9	10	9	10	11	11	10	7	4	5	8	High-
38°42′E	Rainfall	16	44	70	86	95	136	282	294	192	21	15	6	1,257	land
EQUATOR															High-
2,762 m (9,065 ft)	Temp max.	20	21	21	19	18	17	16	16	18	19	19	18	18	land
0°11′S	Temp. min.	8	8	8	9	9	8	8	8	8	8	8	8	8	equa-
35°33′E	Rainfall	33	34	72	168	142	123	163	205	111	53	63	53	1,222	torial

western Kenya, becomes more complicated. In East Africa, the Rift Valley and the adjoining highlands have a large diurnal range of over 20°C.

4. Along the coasts of Mauritania, Senegal, Gambia and Angola there is a curious situation, which is that the rainy season's mean daily temperatures are higher than the dry season's temperatures. The temperature figures for Dakar and Luanda confirm this. It is thought that the low temperatures in the dry season are caused by the cooling effect of the cool Canary and the cold Benguela currents and by the sea breezes blowing across them.

5. In West Africa the mean daily temperatures for January decrease northwards. Thus, in the west Conakry has a mean temperature of 27°C compared with 23°C for Dakar. The figures for the eastern district stations are 30°C for Zungeru and 26°C for Zinder while the figures for the central district stations of Tamale and Timbuktu are 27°C and 21°C respectively. It is therefore erroneous to say that in West Africa the interior is always hotter than the coastal areas. It is true, however, that in July the temperatures increase northwards.

6. The effect of the highlands in East Africa is such that in some districts the mean temperature of the coldest month falls to 18°C, with the result that the climate ceases to be 'tropical' in Koppen's classification, which defines such areas as warm temperate rain climates. This change occurs at an altitude of about 1,650 m and it is significant that during the colonial period land over 1,500 m was regarded as climatically suited to European settlement (Morgan, 1973, p. 35).

Winds and ocean currents

Two groups of air masses dominate the climate of tropical Africa. These are the north-east group of tropical air masses which mostly affects areas lying north of the Equator except in East Africa where the north-east tropical maritime air mass penetrates south of the Equator; and the south-east group of tropical air masses. The meeting point of both groups of air masses is called the Inter-Tropical Convergence Zone (ITCZ). The ITCZ moves north and south according to whether the north-east air masses or the south-east air masses are dominant. In West Africa the ITCZ rarely reaches the coast and since the rain falls only in those areas of West Africa lying south of the ITCZ, several sections of the coast have rain almost all through the year.

In January, when the noon rays of the sun are vertical over the Tropic of Capricorn ($23\frac{1}{2}$°S), a low pressure region extends over Central Africa from the area just north of the Equator, while a high pressure region occurs over the Sahara. In consequence, three main air masses move southwards from the Sahara and the Arabian Desert. These are the western north-east tropical maritime air mass or the north-east trades, the north-east tropical continental or the harmattan and the

eastern north-east tropical maritime air mass or the north-east monsoon which affects the areas east of the Rift Valleys. At this time the ITCZ lies very close to the coast of West Africa from where it turns south-east across Gabon, Zaïre and Botswana. The dominant wind over West Africa and East Africa at this time is the harmattan which is also referred to as 'Egyptian air' in East Africa. Those parts of tropical Africa which lie south of the ITCZ are at this time of the year under the influence of the south-east trades which blow over South Africa but are deflected along the Atlantic coast north of the Orange River into a south-west wind which blows over the Benguela current into Namibia and western Angola.

In July, when the sun is vertical over the Tropic of Cancer, the major low pressure area over the Gulf of Oman and Baluchistan in south-west Asia extends as a vast shallow trough to cover the Sahara while a high pressure area exists over the south Atlantic in the region of latitude 20°S. At this time the ITCZ, which started to move northwards in February, is located just south of latitude 20°N. The dominant air masses affecting tropical Africa at this time originate from both the south Atlantic and the south Indian Oceans and are carried towards the Equator by the south-east trades of the two oceans. The eastern half of Central Africa and East Africa south of the Equator come under the influence of the moist south-east tropical maritime air mass from the Indian Ocean, which on crossing the Equator is deflected into a south-west wind over Uganda, northern Kenya and the Horn of Africa. A branch of this Indian Ocean air mass passes over South Africa to the Atlantic Ocean where it is deflected north of the Orange River into a south-west wind which blows along the coast extending from Namibia to the Zaïre River mouth.

The south-east tropical maritime air mass, originating from the south Atlantic, is deflected on crossing the Equator into the moist south-west monsoon which dominates the climate of all parts of West Africa lying south of latitude 20°N. It is this wind that brings heavy rain to the coastal areas of West Africa. The ITCZ reaches its inland limit over the Sahara in August and remains stable for a few weeks before starting to move towards the south. These few weeks of stability are usually associated with the short dry season which occurs in parts of West and East Africa.

The harmattan

The harmattan is a cold, dry and very dusty north-east wind which blows from the Sahara towards the Equator at a velocity of 16–24 km per hour. It begins to blow in November and continues till March in East Africa. In West Africa its influence along the coast rarely lasts for more than two weeks, but in the north it blows for

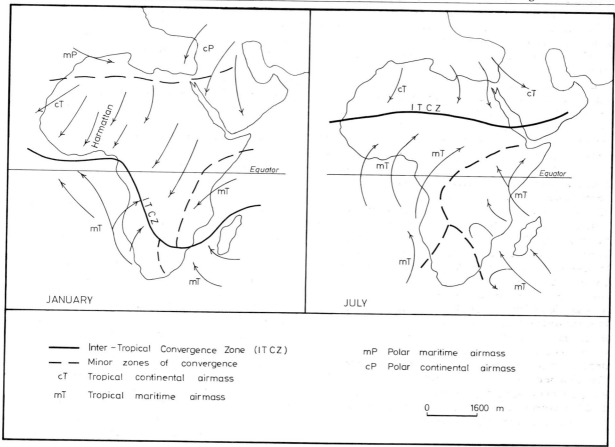

Fig. 2.5 Wind systems

about three months. The dryness and coolness which characterize the harmattan season provide a great contrast to the hot humid weather of the southern parts of West Africa. Although some people consider harmattan weather to be pleasant and healthy, there are several unpleasant features associated with it, such as desiccated and cracked lips, skin (and furniture), the spread of dust all over the house, and a greater occurrence of cerebrospinal meningitis.

Other winds

Along the coasts the two seasonal winds are sometimes replaced by sea and land breezes. Sea breezes blow during the day from a much cooler sea surface to replace air expanding from a warmer land surface. Their effect is felt most between 3–5 p.m. Land breezes, on the other hand, blow from land to sea between the hours of 10 p.m. and 8 a.m. The effect of sea breezes is usually restricted to a maximum range of 16 km from the coast. Land and sea breezes are also very prominent and regular along the shores of Lake Victoria.

In the highlands of High Africa topography dominates the pattern of airflow and may give rise to marked rainshadows. On clear nights strong katabatic winds are common in many localities including the Rift Valleys.

Ocean currents

The currents along the coasts of tropical Africa are the cool Canaries current, the warm Guinea current and the cool Benguela current on the Atlantic coast; and the warm Agulhas and East African coast current along the Indian Ocean coast.

As a factor of climate, ocean currents influence climatic conditions in an area through the winds blowing over them. Winds blowing over a warm current are usually moisture-laden while winds blowing over cold currents usually have a cooling effect on the coast and bring about the formation of fog rather than rain. Both the frequent fogs occurring along the coast of Mauritania and the desert condition along this coast are attributed to the influence of the cool Canaries current. The cooling effect along the northern Mauritania coast during the summer month of August is caused by the fact that the surface temperature of the sea is about 21°C while the arid interior records a temperature of over 40°C.

The east–west Guinea current with a surface temperature of about 27°C is a warm current which brings excessive heat and humidity to the coast between Banjul and Cape Lopez. The dry climate along the coast of Accra is also thought to be caused, at least partly, by conditions created as a result of the meeting of the cold Benguela current and the warm Guinea current.

South of the Equator on the Atlantic coast is the cool Benguela current, the climatic effects of which are more prominent than those of the Canaries current. The surface sea temperature along the coast of Namibia is below 15°C all through the year. This results in a cool foggy sea coast, almost all of which has a desert climate.

A great contrast exists along the Indian Ocean coast which has warm ocean currents. The temperature of the waters off this coast is comparatively high, ranging from about 27°C at the Equator to 20°C off the coast of southern Mozambique. The sea temperature off Maputo (Laurenço Marques) on the east coast is therefore about 5°C higher than the temperature off the west coast town of Luderitz which is on about the same latitude as Maputo. The Mozambique coast has the south-flowing Agulhas current while the East African coast has an equally warm current. However, the coast north of the Equator is relatively cool, resulting in the formation of frequent fogs and arid conditions along the coast of the Somali Republic.

Relative humidity

What makes the climates of tropical Africa, especially those of Low Africa, so unpleasant is the high relative humidity rather than high temperatures. The relative humidity is the ratio between the amount of water vapour actually held in the air and the maximum possible amount at that temperature. It is a measure of the dampness of the atmosphere and is usually expressed as a percentage.

As a general rule, the relative humidity is highest in the morning and evening, the minimum value being about midday. Stations nearer the coast usually have higher relative humidity and for all stations the relative humidity is always higher during the rainy season. The main reason for this is that during the rainy season most coastal areas are under the influence of rain-bearing winds which have a relative humidity of about 100 per cent. As with the rainfall, the seasonal variation in relative humidity is much greater in the interior than on the coast. The average annual daily relative humidity at Lagos, for example, is 98 per cent at 8.00 a.m. and 73 per cent at 1.00 p.m. while the corresponding figures for Kano City are 60 per cent at 8.00 a.m. and 32 per cent at 1.00 p.m. Higher relative humidities and much greater diurnal variations are recorded in the highlands of East Africa as compared with the Jos Plateau of Low Africa. The figures for Nairobi, for example, are 95 per cent in the morning and 52 per cent in the afternoon, while the corresponding figures for Jos are 69 per cent and 39 per cent respectively.

Climatic regions

Fig. 2.6 is a simplified map of the climatic regions of Africa. The six climatic regions found in tropical Africa are: 1. equatorial, 2. humid-tropical, 3. dry-tropical, 4. Sahelian, 5. desert and 6. highland.

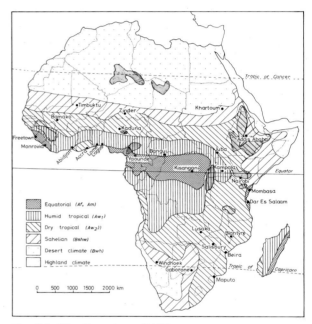

Fig. 2.6 Climatic regions of Africa

Equatorial regions (Af, Am)

There are two types of equatorial climate in tropical Africa. These are the Central African type (Af) which is characterized by constant heat, high relative humidity and well-distributed rainfall, for example, of about 2,655 mm at Warri; and the Guinea coast type (Am) which is similar to the Af type, except that the rainfall, of about 3,510 mm at Freetown, is much heavier during the northern summer months when the South-west Monsoon is the dominant prevailing wind. The Central African type, which occurs between latitude 5°N and 5°S, starts from southern Nigeria and extends to the Zaïre Basin. Temperatures are high all through the year, the mean maximum for each month being above 25°C. The rainfall, which occurs mainly in afternoon thunderstorms, is heavy and continuous throughout the year. It is the uniformity and monotony of the constant succession of hot-wet months that distinguish this climatic type from others. The Guinea coast type (Am) occurs along the coastal areas extending from western Guinea to the eastern Ivory Coast. Temperatures are uniformly high as for the Af type except that both the diurnal and annual range are greater. Unlike the Central African type, which receives mostly convectional rainfall, the Guinea coast type derives most of its rain from the South-west Monsoon.

Humid-tropical regions (Aw₁)

This climatic region has a clearly marked dry season and a rainy season. The total annual rainfall of about 1,170 m for Boauke is less than for the equatorial region although the morning relative humidity is as high as in areas with equatorial climates. The humid-tropical climate is found in its ideal form in areas north of the Equator where it is called the Guinean type. Bouake in the Ivory Coast is located within this region. Temperatures are uniformly high as in the equatorial region, although the mean monthly maximum temperatures and the mean monthly minimum temperatures are respectively higher and lower compared with the equatorial climatic type. It follows that both the diurnal and the annual range are greater.

In the high plateau area of Katanga and Angola, the humid tropical climate is slightly modified by altitude and oceanic influence. Temperatures remain uniformly high but are not excessive and the rainfall is generally lower than in areas located in Low Africa.

Dry-tropical regions (Aw₂)

This climate, usually called the Sudan type, affects the most extensive area in tropical Africa. North of the Equator it is basically a continental climate but in East and Central Africa it is greatly modified by oceanic influences and altitude respectively. In West Africa, where this climate is found in its ideal form, the rainy season is shorter (about five months) compared with the Guinean (Aw₁) type. The annual total rainfall is 500–1,000 mm, but there is considerable variation from year to year. The onset of the rains, normally in May, is rather unreliable especially in the northern half of the region and may lead to crop failures. Both the diurnal and the monthly temperature range are much greater than in the regions already described. The relative humidity at 8.00 a.m. is low, particularly in the dry season, rising at Kano City from about 37 per cent in January to 94 per cent in August which is the rainiest month (310 mm).

South of the Equator, the dry-tropical climate is both continental and oceanic since this climatic region extends south from Tanzania to cover Zambia, Malawi, Mozambique, Zimbabwe and parts of Angola. Along the coast of Mozambique, temperatures are high throughout the year, although not as excessive as at Kano City. Curiously, the highest mean annual temperatures occur during the rainy-season months of December to April when the figures hover around 28°C. The total annual rainfall of 1,000 mm is slightly higher than for Kano City. Further inland, the highland station of Zomba in Malawi displays the same temperature characteristics except that the effect of the highlands results in much cooler temperatures of about 23°C during the hottest months (October to January). The rainy season lasts from November to March or April and the total annual rainfall is usually high at about 1,400 mm, being more than one-and-a-half times the rainfall figure for Kano City.

Sahel (Bshw)

This type of climate is found in Mauritania, Mali, Niger, Chad, the Republic of the Sudan, eastern Kenya and the southern Somali Republic. In southern Africa it is found in Botswana, Namibia and along the coast of Angola. It has a rainfall of between 250 and 500 mm which comes during the three rainy-season months of June, July and August in West Africa or January, February and March in southern Africa (Windhoek). Mean annual temperatures of over 38°C are common during the rainy season, but there is a considerable lowering of temperatures to about 32°C during the dry season when the harmattan blows. High diurnal and annual temperature ranges are characteristic both in West Africa and in southern Africa where the mean monthly temperatures are much lower.

Desert (Bwh)

The desert or Saharan climates occur in areas with less than 250 mm of rain. There is no rainy season, since the little rain that falls can come in any month of the year. In certain areas it may not rain for several years. Temperatures are very high, especially in the southern interior districts of the Sahara Desert where afternoon temperatures may exceed 43°C. Both the diurnal and annual temperature ranges are high. Along the coasts of Mauritania and Namibia, both of which are affected by ool currents, both the mean monthly temperatures and the annual temperature ranges are much less.

Highland

Ethiopia has the most extensive area under highland climate. Other areas are the Fouta Djallon Highlands, the Cameroun–Adamawa Highlands, the Jos Plateau, Ruanda–Burundi and the East African Highlands. In all cases, the effect of the highlands is to lower the temperature and increase the rainfall compared with the surrounding plains. The climate of a particular highland area, such as the Kenya Highlands, is therefore a modified type of the climate of the climatic belt in which the highland is located. The mean monthly temperatures for the Equator (Kenya), which is located just south of the town of Equator at an altitude of 2,762 m, for example, hover around 13°C throughout the year. The uniformity and monotony of the rather low mean monthly temperature as well as the very small annual range of only 2·5°C confirm that Equator town has a highland equatorial climate. Further confirmation is given by the fact that like the true equatorial climate, Equator town receives some rain all the year round.

In Ethiopia there are three main altitudinal climatic zones: the Quolla, the Woina Dega and the Dega. The Quolla, which has an upper limit of 1,830 m, consists largely of valley bottoms which are hot, damp and sheltered from winds. The Wiona Dega or 'wine highland' extends from 1,830–2,500 m and is generally warm and healthier. The total rainfall of this zone is however much higher, resulting in considerable dissection of the steep slopes. The Wiona Dega has very good soils which are intensively cultivated since it attracts a high density of population. The last and highest zone is the Dega or highland, which is the cool area above 2,500 m. Cultivation on the Dega is possible up to an altitude of 3,600 m beyond which the Dega becomes too cold and receives too much rain to permit successful settlement.

Vegetation

The close relationship which exists between climate and vegetation in tropical Africa is most obvious in West Africa where the main vegetation belts, like the climatic regions, are arranged in a west–east direction. The reason for this is that rainfall is by far the most single important factor influencing the natural vegetation of tropical Africa. This fact is best confirmed by comparing the map of annual rainfall (Fig. 2·2) with the vegetation map (Fig. 2·7).

Other factors which influence the vegetation of tropical Africa are man, altitude and soil or edaphic conditions. We shall examine briefly how these factors operate.

The human factor has worked mainly through the clearing and burning of bush in preparation for cultivation, through overgrazing and through bush burning for hunting. Many woodlands have also been destroyed through the cutting of trees for timber, firewood, yam sticks and building poles. So great is the influence of man that today vast areas of high forests have been replaced by secondary forests or tree-crop plantations of rubber, cocoa, oil palm and kolanut trees.

Altitude is an important factor which modifies the vegetation of highland areas in much the same way as it

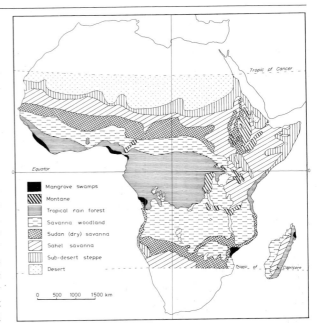

Fig. 2.7 Natural vegetation

modifies the climate. The vertical arrangement of vegetation belts in the Cameroun Mountains (Low Africa) and Mt Kilimanjaro (High Africa) are shown in Figs. 2.8 a and b. The high altitude grassland of the Bamenda Highlands provides good cattle grazing in an area where the surrounding lowland supports forest vegetation. The case of the Ethiopian Highlands is presented in the section on montane vegetation (p. 29).

River valleys and other areas which are waterlogged for several months do not support forest vegetation. Grassland vegetation occurs in some areas such as the Sobo Plains of the Bendel State of Nigeria, which are located in the rain forest belt. Areas with lateritic soils (see below, p. 31) located in the forest belt support grassland vegetation since the compact nature and impermeable character of laterite does not support tree growth. Gallery forests found along dry valleys or along the valleys of seasonal streams in grassland areas are also caused by soil conditions. Usually soils along these valleys retain more moisture compared with soils in the nearby uplands, hence the greater concentration of trees along such valleys.

Vegetation types

The vegetation of tropical Africa falls into seven main types. These are 1. swamp and other coastal vegetation, 2. tropical rain forest, 3. savanna woodland or derived savanna, 4. Sudan or dry savanna, 5. Sahel savanna or thorn scrub 6. Saharan and 7. montane.

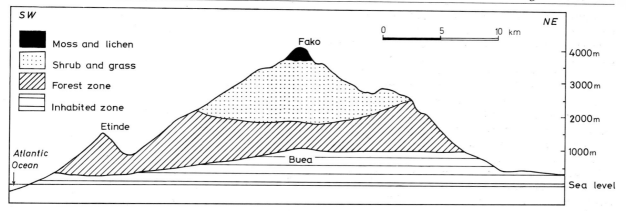

Fig. 2.8a Montane vegetation zone, Cameroun mountains

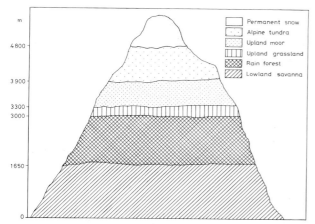

Fig. 2.8b Mt Kilimanjaro

Swamp and other coastal vegetation

Along the coasts of West and East Africa, groves of coconut palms with a light or no undergrowth overlook the waters of the Atlantic and Indian Ocean respectively. In several places, such as Popo Island (south of Badagry), Bonny Island and the Kwale–Kilifi coastal area of Kenya, the extent of this vegetation has been increased as a result of the establishment of coconut plantations.

In West Africa an extensive stretch of saltwater swamps in which mangroves make up the main vegetation appears immediately behind the coconut corridor. As shown in the vegetation map, the belt of mangrove swamps is not continuous. The width varies greatly from 1·5 km in the Lagos area to over 30 km in the Sapele area of the Niger Delta. Plate 2.2 shows a typical mangrove swamp. The tallest trees, exceeding 20 m, appear in the centre of islands and peninsulas that

Pl. 2.2 A mangrove swamp in East Africa

characterize mangrove areas, although the densest growth of entangled roots and branches is found along the banks of the numerous water channels.

Mangrove wood makes excellent fuel which burns easily even when it is fresh. It is not readily attacked by termites and is used for building, mining props and railway sleepers. The bark and fruit are rich in tannin

27

and during the pre-colonial and early colonial periods the bark was sometimes burnt to produce salt.

Further inland, beyond the reach of tidal water, mangroves give way to freshwater plants. This is the freshwater swamp zone which is most extensive in the Niger Delta. The most important plant in the zone is the raffia palm which supplies palm wine, taken fresh or fermented for distilling local gin. House building materials obtained from the raffia palm include palm fronds, used as rafters as well as for constructing the walls, piassava for tying up the wooden framework of the walls and roofs, and the leaves which are used for making roofing mats. A considerable amount of piassava is also exported to Europe where it is used for making brushes and brooms. The oil palm tree and a few rain forest trees such as iroko and the oil bean tree also grow in freshwater swamps.

Pl. 2.3 The Ituri rain forest in Zaïre

Tropical rain forest

The densest vegetation cover, consisting of evergreen forests of tall trees, with an undergrowth of lianas and other climbing plants, occurs in areas having equatorial and humid-tropical climates. It is called the tropical rain forest and is restricted to those parts of the Zaïre Basin, West Africa, Central Africa and the eastern coasts of Malagasy, which receive a minimum of 1,500 mm of rain and have a rainy season of not less than eight months. The tallest trees are over 40 m high; but there are two other distinct layers of trees – a medium layer about 30 m high and a lower layer below 15 m. In areas where the rain forest has remained untouched for several decades, the top canopy may become so closely interlocked that the rays of the sun are completely prevented from reaching the ground, so that the ground remains damp and almost void of undergrowth (Plate 2.3).

Although large stretches of the forest are not penetrable because of dense and tangled growth of trees and climbing plants, the African rain forest is not as dense as that of the Amazon Basin. It is characterized by small forest clearings which represent the site of existing or abandoned villages. The rain forest is rich in economic trees such as iroko, mahogany, sapele wood and walnut; but the stands of marketable species are widely scattered, making exploitation expensive. Exploitation is also difficult because the bases of many of the tree trunks are fluted by winged buttresses rising up to 3 m from the ground.

In parts of the eastern states of Nigeria where there is great demand for farmland, the rain forest has since been replaced by the oil palm bush. The oil palm tree is an important economic crop and is usually preserved when the bush is burnt in preparation for farming. High forest vegetation, however, survives in the few forest reserves of this area.

Savanna woodland or derived savanna

Savanna woodland or the tree savanna, as it is sometimes called, is the most extensive vegetation type in tropical Africa. It consists of a mixture of trees and grass, trees being very numerous in sparsely settled areas. In West Africa, the tree savanna is known as the Guinea savanna while the local name in East and Central Africa is *miombo* woodland. In areas where the rainfall can support a forest vegetation the tree savanna is usually described as derived savanna, since it is a product of the continuous destruction of high forest by farmers. A greater part of the tree savanna is, however, a product of local climatic conditions since the rainfall in most areas is either too scanty or not sufficiently widely distributed to support high forest vegetation.

Tall grass and other tall herbaceous growth form a continuous cover over large areas, but there are also well-established woodlands of trees of up to 15 m high. The more important trees of the Guinea savanna include the fan palm, shea butter, dry-zone mahogany and the tamarind; while those of the *miombo* woodlands belong mostly to the *Brachystegia* family. These trees grow very long tap roots and have thick barks which serve as protective covers from the annual dry-season fires. All trees in this vegetation zone shed their leaves in the dry season when water is scarce.

Gallery or fringing forests are a characteristic feature of woodland savanna areas. They are found along water courses where the soil is usually moist, and rarely cover more than 12 m on either bank. Forest outliers which, like the gallery forests, have a greater tree density are also common on rocky hills.

Sudan or dry savanna

This is characterized by fewer trees, while the grass becomes shorter compared with the tree savanna. The

Pl. 2.4 Baobab trees in Sudan savanna, near Sokoto, Nigeria

main cattle belt of West Africa lies in this zone. Indeed the bush fires which sweep across vast areas of the Sudan savanna towards the close of the dry season are usually caused by cattle rearers, whose aim is to hasten the sprouting of fresh grass for feeding their animals.

A wide variety of acacia trees appears all over the Sudan savanna, especially in West Africa where this vegetation is sometimes described as acacia grasslands. The dominant tree species in East and Central Africa is the mopane tree, which has given the name mopane savanna to the vegetation in these areas. Other important common trees include the shea butter, the African locust bean, the silk cotton and the baobab. These are all fire-resistant trees and their stems are usually burnt and twisted. Only a few of these trees exceed 12 m in height.

Traces of the natural vegetation, consisting of greater stands of trees, are found along water courses and uncultivated hill slopes. Villages are usually embedded in tree groves and, in general, an island of woodland in the open grassland or *kurmi*, as the Hausa call it, represents a village or hamlet or the site of an abandoned settlement.

Sahel savanna
This type of vegetation consists of thorn bushes and small trees which grow under dry conditions. The vegetation is rather scanty and even during the rainy season the grass cover never forms a continuous carpet. Large areas of bare sand separate tufts of short grasses and bushy trees which are about 5–10 m high (Plate 2.5). The Sahel savanna extends right across the northern part of West Africa from Mauritania through Mali, Niger and Chad to the Sudan. It is also found in

parts of Ethiopia, the Somali Republic, Kenya, Tanzania and Botswana.

The characteristic tree is the acacia, of which several varieties grow. Some of these trees, especially *Acacia senegal*, produce gum Arabic, which is an important item of trade. A few date palms begin to appear in this zone while large groves of dum palms are very common. In West Africa, the far north of this zone consists of more stunted grass as well as widely scattered bush up to 3 m tall and shrubs which rarely exceed 1 m in height. This is the semi-desert or sub-desert steppe. Semi-desert vegetation also occurs in the Somali Republic and in parts of Namibia.

Desert
Desert vegetation appears in areas having less than 250 mm of rain per annum. Almost all the desert areas of tropical Africa are in the Sahara hence this type of vegetation is usually described as Saharan. A small area of desert vegetation also appears along the coast of Namibia, where, as in the Sahara, most of the landscape consists of bare surfaces of sand, pebbles and rocks.

Although the true desert receives occasional rain once in several years, desert vegetation is largely restricted to the oases and to areas where the water table is near the surface. The oases support a permanent vegetation of dates and permanent settlement where crops like wheat and millet are grown under irrigation. Perennial shrubs and small trees grow in areas with underground watercourses. Such plants usually have thorns instead of leaves. The Sahara also has a vegetation of herbs which begin to grow immediately after a rainstorm and live for only a few weeks.

Montane vegetation
Just as highland areas have higher rainfall but lower temperatures than the surrounding lowlands, their

Pl. 2.5 Elephants grazing in Sahel savanna, Kenya

vegetation also differs with an increase in altitude. Thus in Ethiopia, the vegetation of the highlands differs considerably from the open acacia woodlands of the plateau, where the main areas of forest vegetation consist of eucalyptus plantations. In the highlands, the hot and wet Quolla climatic zone supports up to a height of 1,830 m a dense forest vegetation of mostly juniper trees and euphorbia plants. The vegetation of the warm Wiona Dega zone which lies between 1,830–2,500 m consists of temperate or mountain grassland similar to grassland on the Obudu Plateau of the Cameroun–Adamawa Highlands. The predominant species in this temperate grassland are of the *Pennisetum* family, although sedges and rushes as well as species of *Eleusine*, *Setaria* and *Digitaria* are also common. In the cool and highest regions of the Dega which lie above 2,500 m, the vegetation consists of alpine grassland with scattered stands of wild olives and juniper trees.

In Kenya, where the Sahel savanna is the predominant type of vegetation, the most extensive areas of high forest are the montane forests of the Kenya Highlands. The relief effect on vegetation is also obvious in Low Africa even though the highlands are not high enough to produce the whole range of montane vegetations found in the East African mountains or the Ethiopian Highlands. The Jos Plateau, for example, which is located in a grassland region, has forest vegetation on the windward slopes and grass vegetation on the plateau surface.

Soils

The close relationship between soil types, climate and vegetation zones which we referred to in the introductory paragraph of this chapter (p. 17) can be confirmed by comparing the generalized soil map of tropical Africa (Fig. 2.9) with the maps showing climatic regions (Fig. 2.6) and vegetation (Fig. 2.7). Climate is probably the most important factor in the formation of tropical African soils. It influences soil formation largely through temperature, which affects the rate and depth of weathering, and through rainfall, which is responsible for the leaching of soluble products in the soil. (Leaching is the process whereby clay particles and soluble salts are continuously carried down into the ground by percolating rainwater.) In general, therefore, deep soils are associated with areas of high rainfall and high temperatures, although shallow soils are found in areas underlain by laterite, since laterite is highly resistant to weathering. The other factors of soil formation are:

1. The parent material from which the soil is formed. This may consist of weathered materials from Basement Complex rocks, volcanic lava or sedimentary rocks, or of sand and other deposits brought by wind or running water. The parent material usually determines the physical appearance and the chemical composition of the soil. For example, parent materials derived from rocks such as granites and sandstones, which have a high quartz content, give rise to sandy soils, while those derived from lava, which has a low quartz content, produce clayey soils.

2. Topography, which affects not only depth and physical character of the soils but also the water content and the rate of soil loss through erosion. On very gentle slopes, soils tend to be marshy or poorly drained while steep slopes have very thin soils. Deep soils are usually formed in undulating areas.

3. Living organisms which, when they die, add considerable organic matter to the soil. In addition to protecting the soil from rain wash, the vegetation recirculates plant nutrients by extracting them from the depths and depositing them on the surface in the form of leaf fall. Worms, burrowing animals and termites are also important in mixing up organic remains in the soil.

4. Time, which is an important factor affecting the maturity and fertility of soils. Youthful soils are usually shallow and have a high content of undecomposed weatherable materials, little profile development and many characteristics of the parent material.

Fig. 2.9 Soil types

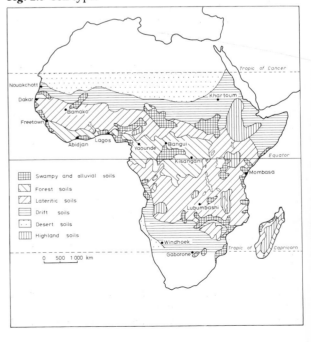

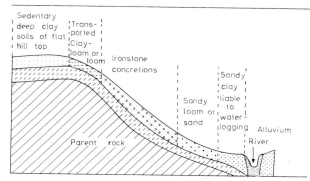

Fig. 2.10 Soil catena

Soil catena

The term catena is used to describe the arrangement of soil types developed along a sloping hillside from the top of the hill (watershed) to its base (valley). Different topographic forms also produce different catenas. Fig. 2.10 illustrates a soil catena in the cocoa belt of south-west Nigeria. The top of the hill is relatively flat so that erosion is slight, thereby permitting the formation of deep clay soils derived from weathered crystalline Basement Complex rocks. Lateritic soils form on the lower slopes which are affected by fluctuations in the level of the water table. Further down the slopes, the soils consist of sandy loams and sand, while poorly drained sandy clay soils form in the valley.

Main soil groups

The five major soil groups of tropical Africa are shown in Fig. 2.9. There is a considerable variety of soil types within each group and the map presents a very generalized picture. The five groups are 1. swampy and alluvial soils, 2. forest soils, 3. lateritic soils, 4. loess soils and 5. desert soils.

Swampy and alluvial soils

Along the coast the soils are sandy and impoverished through leaching. This is the main reason why the sandy beaches and ridges fronting the sea are not cultivated. A more extensive area of swampy soils which support mangrove vegetation separates the coastal sands from the waterlogged silts of the inland freshwater swamps. The coastal swamps suffer from an oversupply of water from rain and rivers. In Sierra Leone and Guinea these soils are used for growing swamp rice. The inland Niger Delta freshwater swamps are also used for rice production.

Forest soils

Soils in this group are usually rich in humus derived from heavy leaf fall in the forest. Unfortunately these soils are heavily leached because of the heavy rainfall.

Under cultivation, forest soils soon lose their fertility, which is concentrated in a thin top layer. This is why it is necessary to rest the soil under bush fallow for as many as twenty years to compensate for three years of continuous cultivation (Finck, 1973, p. 18). Reduced fallow periods prevent the re-establishment of the original humus level, resulting in soil impoverishment and poor crop yields.

Lateritic soils

Lateritic soils form along gentle slopes or plateau surfaces, stripped of tree cover. A marked dry season alternating with a wet season is a necessary condition for formation. During the wet or rainy season mineral salts, mainly compounds of iron and aluminium, are carried down into the ground by leaching. At the same time the rise in water table during this season helps to cause an upward migration of iron and aluminium salts. The result is a concentration of these salts in a restricted zone. In the dry season the soil waters are brought to the surface by evaporation, leaving behind insoluble compounds of iron and aluminium in slag-like concretions. This is laterite.

Under plant cover laterite is soft and heavy but when exposed to the atmosphere it becomes so hard that it appears as a rock. It is this quality that makes laterite suitable for making dirt roads as well as for building walls of houses. Occasionally, laterite may be rich enough in iron or aluminium to form the ore for these minerals. However, lateritic soils are of little value for agriculture since root growth and development in these soils is very limited (Gourou, 1980).

Much of West Africa, Tanzania, Uganda, Central Africa and Malagasy are covered with lateritic soils. In West Africa the major areas of lateritic soils occur outside the forest belt and south of the desert–Sahel boundary. They are usually cultivated if better soils are not available.

Loess soils

A fairly broad belt of chestnut steppe soils extends from northern Senegal across the north of West Africa to the southern shores of Lake Chad and continues to southern Sudan. Loess-type soils also occur in the western Somali Republic, southern Angola and Botswana. These soils are developed in a grass environment and are similar in texture to the prairie soils of North America. The parent materials consist mostly of loess or fine sand brought downwind from arid zones. The soils are comparatively fertile, but are not fully utilized because of the low rainfall in the areas where they occur.

As the vegetation becomes thinner, these soils change colour from dark brown to light brown, indicating a decrease in the humus content. Thus while the southern loess soils of northern Nigeria support good crops of cotton, maize and rice, the sandier lighter soils of the desert borderlands seem more suitable for groundnut and millet cultivation.

Desert soils

Wind action and occasional flash floods in the desert have the effect of sorting out soil parent materials into rocky areas, dune areas with sandy materials and playa floors with silt and clay. Since there is little rainwater for downward leaching, calcium carbonate and soluble salts usually accumulate within the upper horizon of desert soils. There are, however, some desert soils which are not saline. Irrigation projects are usually restricted to areas with non-saline salts since many crops, including cotton, millet and guinea corn, cannot thrive well on saline soils. In tropical Africa it is the shortage of water rather than the presence of salts in the soils that is the major limiting factor in cropping desert soils.

Other soils

A wide variety of soils occurs in the highland areas of Ethiopia, East Africa and Angola, amongst others. Often these soils are very fertile since they are developed on deeply weathered and well drained lava parent materials. Dark-brown or black clayey soils with deep cracks occupy large areas of the Chad Basin and the White Nile Basin of Sudan, where they are sometimes called black cotton soils, although cotton is rarely grown on them. The black soil of the Accra plains is peculiar in that, unlike most black soils, it is not fertile. This is largely because the soil owes its dark colour not to decayed vegetable matter, but to the mineral content of its parent material.

Soil erosion

Soil erosion takes place when the rate of soil loss far exceeds that of soil formation. This is accelerated soil erosion as distinct from natural erosion. It is usually started off as a result of human interference through farming, grazing or road-making. Thus soil erosion is largely associated with areas of great population concentration. Other important factors which help to increase the rate include the steepness of the slope, the torrential character of the rainfall and the texture and structure of the soil.

There are two main types of soil erosion: sheet erosion and gully erosion. Sheet erosion, by wind or running water, takes place on gently undulating surfaces which have been stripped of much of their vegetation. This type of erosion is particularly common on the plateau surfaces of savanna and Sahel regions. The soil loss may expose the roots of grasses as is the case on the Udi Plateau of Nigeria.

The most spectacular and probably the most destructive type of soil erosion is gully erosion which has assumed catastrophic dimensions along the east-facing

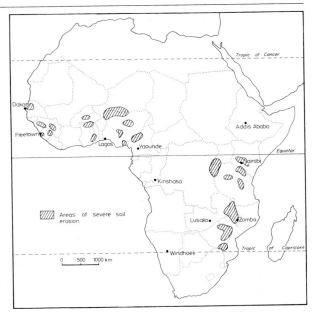

Fig. 2.11 Areas of severe soil erosion

escarpments of the scarplands of south-eastern Nigeria. Other areas which have been badly affected by gully erosion include the over-farmed districts of Kikuyuland in Kenya, the slopes of the Fouta Djallon and the districts around Sokoto and Ouagadougou. In the Awka and Udi districts of south-east Nigeria, gully erosion has destroyed so much farmland that the local people have had to migrate to farm in other parts of the country. Some gullies in these districts started when rainwater became concentrated along footpaths leading to scarp foot springs, where the people obtain water for drinking and other domestic use. Poor methods of farming, such as making mounds and ridges along the slopes of a hill instead of along the contours have had the same effect as footpaths in initiating gullies. The vast quantity of sand removed from these gullies is deposited in other low-lying areas which are also rendered useless for cultivation.

Soil conservation

The aim of soil conservation is to retain the fertility of the soil and its structure thereby preventing soil erosion. A system of farming in which no fertilizer is used impoverishes the soil and weakens its structure, making it less resistant to soil erosion. The traditional African systems of land-use have their built-in protective devices against soil erosion, the chief of which is to leave the land under bush fallow for many years. Mixed cropping and the avoidance of steep slopes also help to check soil erosion. But in areas where there is great demand for farmland, the fallow periods have been reduced from over ten years in the past to about three years, while steep slopes are now commonly cultivated without terracing.

Efforts to check soil erosion and help the soil to regain its fertility include the following measures:

1. Preventing any form of cultivation in areas now affected by gully erosion. In the Agulu district of south-east Nigeria, for example, villages close to the gully heads have since been evacuated while impoverished land has been put out of cultivation.
2. Building soak-away pits along the shoulders of footpaths and roads so that rainwater is trapped through diversion ditches and prevented from washing away the soil.
3. Planting fast-growing shrubs like *Acioa barteri* (*icheku* in Ibo or *akan* in Ibibio) and the cashew tree; the heavy leaf fall from these plants is expected to supply humus to help reclaim the soil. This is a form of afforestation.
4. Contour tillage, which involves cultivating across a slope. This method is widely adopted in Ethiopia, Central Africa and parts of southern Africa.
5. Terrace cultivation in which flat, step-like shelves are cut into hillsides and mountain slopes. In the Maku district of south-east Nigeria, the terrace walls are fortified with blocks of concretionary ironstones, the width of the terraces varying from 4·5 to 9 m.
6. Strip cultivation in which the field is laid out in a strip pattern, with the strips sometimes following the contour. The strips are usually arranged alternately or in a repeating sequence for crop rotation, with the inclusion of fallow strips. Strip cultivation is therefore used as a means of controlling both wind and water erosion as well as a method for effective crop rotation. The strips are usually made across, rather than parallel with, the prevailing wind direction in order to serve as effective wind breaks. In eastern Zaïre, east–west strips measuring 100 m wide and 1·6 km long are planted using a crop rotation system based on rice, maize and beans for the first three years, after which cassava is planted before the land reverts to fallow.
7. Gully reclamation, whereby small dams are spaced at intervals of 6–10 m along the gully to impede water flow. Gully dams are made with logs, straw, stakes, wire netting or earth, each of which may be reinforced with rocks.

References
Finck, A. (1973), 'The Fertility of Tropical Soils Under the Influence of Agricultural Land Use', *Applied Science and Development*, I, pp. 7–31.

Gourou, P. (1980, 5th ed.), *The Tropical World*, Longman, London, pp. 13–24.

Morgan, W. T. W. (1973), *East Africa*, Longman, London.

Ojany, F. F. and Ogendo, R. B. (1973), *Kenya: A Study in Physical and Human Geography*, Longman, London.

3 Pests, Diseases and Health Problems

Pests and diseases are important elements in the physical and cultural environments of tropical Africa. They impose a major constraint on the process of improving the standard of living since most crops are affected by one or more of them, as are beasts and men. Indeed, in parts of tropical Africa, the destruction of crops by pests may be greater and more disastrous than losses due to unreliable rainfall. Animal pests and diseases have also constituted a major setback to successful animal husbandry in the greater part of tropical Africa, thereby making it difficult in most countries to produce enough meat to satisfy local demand. And, of course, there are numerous problems posed by the high incidence of various types of human diseases, some of which are peculiar to tropical lands.

In this chapter we consider the major pests and diseases of tropical Africa with particular reference to the ways in which they affect the development of the economy of the region. The underdeveloped state of the economy of tropical Africa has often been attributed to the menace of pests and diseases and the inability of local technology to cope with this menace. Fortunately, it is now possible to control the spread of most pests and diseases, and some have already been eradicated.

Pests and diseases have affected the economic and social development of tropical Africa in the following specific ways:

1. The quantity and quality of farm produce are reduced. Large quantities of food crops, notably maize, rice and tomatoes, are destroyed by pests and fungal diseases as well as by locusts. Most industrial crops, including cocoa, tobacco and cotton, also suffer from pests and fungal diseases to the extent that a loss of up to 40 per cent of the normal yield may occur when fungicides are not applied. Furthermore, the quality of harvested crops deteriorates considerably in storage as a result of damage caused by pests, which attack crops like maize, rice and beans.
2. The quantity and quality of meat and other animal foods derived from domesticated animals are also greatly reduced. This happens to be a more serious problem since the main cause of malnutrition in tropical Africa is not an inadequate supply of food but a deficiency of animal protein.
3. Food shortages, notably of starch and animal protein, resulting partly from the menace of pests and plant diseases, have created a situation in which large sums of money are expended on food imports, even though no less than 70 per cent of the population of tropical Africa is engaged in agriculture. It is indeed embarrassing that Nigeria, for example, should import maize from the United States of America in order to support her poultry industry. It is equally absurd that in 1978 the price of one chicken in Lagos was equivalent to that of four in New York!
4. Periodic famines have been caused by food shortages occasioned by the ravages of plant pests and diseases. Often those who survive the famines become easy victims to a number of diseases because their resistance has been greatly lowered as a result of poor feeding.
5. Infants suffer most from retarded development caused by protein deficiency. Kwashiorkor, a common killer disease amongst infants, is also caused by a lack of adequate protein, and often those children who recover become physically and mentally retarded for life.
6. A poorly fed man is an inefficient worker, and the poor performance of workers in tropical Africa is partly due to the low nutritional content of food commonly eaten.
7. The numerous tropical diseases, especially malaria, have a debilitating effect.
8. The cost of controlling and eradicating pests and diseases which affect plants and animals, as well as of preventing and curing human diseases, is a great drain on the meagre resources of the governments of tropical African countries.

Pests, diseases and the tropical environment

It is now an established fact that the variety of pests and diseases in tropical lands is much greater than in other parts of the world. In addition to local diseases, a number of imported diseases including measles, whooping cough and hepatitis have been introduced from temperate lands. It is not surprising, therefore, that tropical countries are considered to be less healthy than temperate ones. Indeed much of tropical Africa was for a long time referred to as the 'white man's grave', because of the high morbidity and mortality rates amongst European explorers, missionaries and traders during the nineteenth and early twentieth centuries. The deaths continued to be attributed to the 'insalubrious climate' even after it had been established that they were caused mainly by malaria, which is transmitted by mosquitoes. Permanent European settlement in tropical Africa was therefore restricted to those districts, which, because of their high altitude, have a temperate type of climate. Today, the widespread use of air conditioners has made it possible to create temperate climates in many offices and homes in tropical Africa.

It is important to emphasize at this point that only a few of the diseases now commonly referred to as 'tropical' are confined to the tropics for purely climatic reasons. Many of these diseases were formerly common in temperate regions but have since been eradicated, while others still appear occasionally. The disappearance of malaria and other diseases from temperate countries suggests that there are other factors, in addition to climate, which facilitate the survival and spread of pests and diseases in tropical Africa. These factors include such other aspects of the physical environment as the terrain and the vegetation, as well as aspects of the social environment such as living habits and housing conditions, educational status and income levels.

Starting with climate, we note that the basic characteristics of tropical climates are high temperatures throughout the year and an abundant and regular supply of moisture during the rainy season. The winter season, when growth is highly restricted in temperate regions, is absent in tropical lands, and so trees and pests multiply even during the dry season once water is made available by irrigation. Mosquitoes breed readily in stagnant waters formed by rainwater that is trapped

Pl. 3.1 The malaria-carrying *anopheles* mosquito

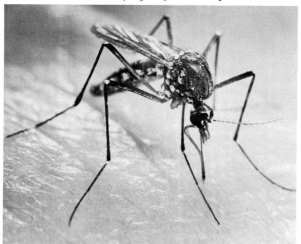

in depressions, as well as in rainwater collected in abandoned containers like broken pots, cans and disused calabashes. Malaria and filariasis, both of which are found all over tropical Africa, are therefore more prevalent in the wetter coastal areas and in the densely forested belt along the Equator. Drier areas of the Sahel and Sudan savanna, which are under irrigation, also provide suitable habitats for the carriers of these diseases and for other pests.

Excessive rainfall has been associated with a drastic fall in cocoa output in various parts of the tropics since very poor harvests usually occur during the years of heaviest rainfall. The main cause of poor cocoa yields in such years is, however, the black pod disease, a fungus which attacks cocoa pods and pod stalks, and whose spread is greatly favoured by heavy rainfall and high humidity. In Nigeria the loss due to this disease is estimated to be about ₦15 million per year. It is controlled by spraying infected trees with fungicides.

A number of human diseases such as measles, smallpox and cerebrospinal meningitis are also associated with the climate. Often, as in the case of cerebrospinal meningitis, the effect of the climate is indirect. This particular disease occurs during the harmattan season when people sleep crowded together in poorly ventilated mud huts to avoid the extreme cold and dust storms which occur during the night. Under such living conditions the disease spreads easily.

Aspects of the terrain which affect the breeding and spread of pests and diseases include drainage and vegetation. Extensive swamps and other areas of stagnant water, including the coastal creeks and lagoons, as well as dammed lakes, provide suitable habitats for mosquitoes and are therefore heavily infested with malaria. Dams and irrigation channels, such as those found in the Gezira, in the Bacita sugar estate and numerous other irrigation schemes, as well as fish ponds, provide breeding places not only for mosquitoes but also for snails which are the main hosts for bilharzia parasites (see p. 40). Another deadly disease associated with riverine environments is river blindness (onchocerciasis) which is caused by a parasitic worm transmitted by the female of the fly vector, *Simulium damnosum* (see p. 42) (Hunter, 1966).

The tsetse fly, which carries the parasites that cause *trypanosomiasis* in cattle and sleeping sickness in man, is associated with forest and wooded savanna vegetation and is widespread all over the humid tropical areas of Africa. In the open savanna regions the fly is restricted to fringing forests and may be eradicated or controlled by destroying such vegetation. It is the heavy infestation of the Guinea savanna belt by these flies that has made it difficult for cattle and horses to survive in the southern parts of West Africa, the Zaïre Basin and parts of Angola and Tanzania.

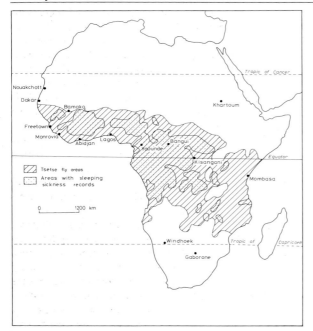

Fig. 3.1 Tsetse fly areas and distribution of sleeping sickness

Field experiments have confirmed that the incidence and spread of the tsetse fly can be controlled through the effective and permanent occupation of wooded countrysides. This is where the density of the rural population becomes relevant since a minimum threshold population is required to tame and control a given environment. In Nigeria, for example, the menace of the tsetse fly is much less in the wetter but more densely populated south-eastern districts of Owerri, Umuahia, Ikot Ekpene and Abak where the forest cover has since been replaced by oil palm bush, as compared with the drier but very sparsely settled Middle Belt districts of Kontagora, Abuja, Bida and Nasarawa which support wooded savanna vegetation. In these Middle Belt districts and in many other parts of tropical Africa, it was the heavy loss of population during the period of the slave trade that brought about the regeneration of extensive woodlands which provide the necessary habitat for the tsetse fly in areas where the fly had previously been kept under control. The result was that the remnant population had to abandon some village sites because of their inability to tame the environment and thereby control the tsetse fly.

The social environment plays a very important part in the incidence and spread of diseases, which are much influenced by the conditions under which people live and work. These conditions are themselves governed by the educational status, the income levels and the culture of the people. The disappearance of some

diseases in Europe following the rise in living standards, improved housing and the introduction of social welfare services, confirm that the most effective way to combat communicable (infectious) diseases is to initiate development programmes aimed at reducing the rate of poverty and illiteracy amongst the people. It is when windowless huts are replaced by well-ventilated houses, when pipe-borne water is provided so that people no longer have to bathe in and draw water from streams and irrigation channels, and when adequate arrangements are made for the disposal of solid and liquid wastes in the villages and towns, that fewer people will suffer from cerebrospinal meningitis, cholera, dysentery, river blindness and flea-borne diseases.

Plant pests and diseases

Pests are troublesome or destructive creatures such as insects, mice, snails and some birds. Plant pests, such as grasshoppers, locusts, worms and some larger animals, may directly attack plant shoots, seeds or tubers, thereby causing reduced yields or even death. Other pests, notably insects, act as disease vectors which take up and pass on various diseases, mainly in the form of viruses, to plants while feeding on their leaves. Leaf mosaics in cassava, yams and tobacco, for example, are transmitted by insect vectors.

Grasshoppers are one of the most destructive plant pests in tropical Africa. They occur in large swarms, covering vast areas and are very destructive to plant leaves, including food crops. These grasshoppers breed during the early months of the dry season and constitute a serious menace to crops raised in irrigated fields as well as to mature cassava plants, the leaves of

Pl. 3.2 A close-up view of the locust, one of the plagues of Africa

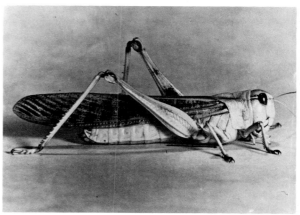

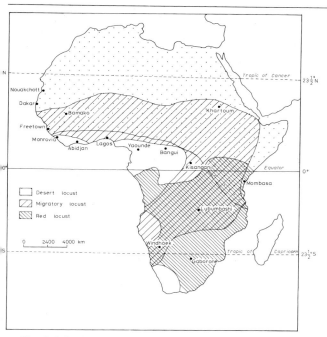

Fig. 3.2 Locust areas

Legend:
- Desert locust
- Migratory locust
- Red locust

0   2400   4000 km

which are completely eaten. Fortunately they disappear suddenly as soon as the rains start and do not therefore do any damage to wet-season farms. However, the locust, which generally affects large areas, breeds during the rains in West Africa and is by far the most destructive and most dreaded type of grasshopper. Locust swarms may be very large, covering up to 5,200 sq km, and some species travel great distances of over 1,600 km, eating every green leaf and shoot along their path. The African migratory locust, for example, which originates from the marshes of the middle Niger floodplains, migrates to all parts of West Africa and even as far as East and Central Africa. Locust plagues have been known to cause severe famines in parts of tropical Africa. Fortunately the incidence of such plagues has been greatly reduced since the end of the Second World War, thanks to the measures taken by the United Nations and other international bodies to control locusts.

Birds are another category of pest causing a lot of damage to maize, millet and guinea corn fields. In Gambia and the Cameroun Republic, baboons still destroy many food crops. Various types of worm also attack and destroy maize, yams, okra, tomatoes and other food crops, while some bush animals such as the grass cutter, the bush rat and the bush pig, eat cassava and yam tubers before they are ready to be harvested.

Stem borers are another set of plant pests which have caused extensive damage to a variety of both food crops and industrial crops. Cereal crops such as maize, rice and millet, and tree crops including coffee, oil palm and kolanut, all suffer from stem borers which sometimes destroy the crops at the seedling stage. The stem borers of maize are the larvae of moths which lay their eggs between the leaf-sheath and the stem. Loss of yield is greatest with late maize planted towards the end of the rainy season, but the loss can be greatly reduced by the application of insecticides.

In addition to causing physical destruction of plants and seeds, some plant pests act as disease vectors which transmit virus diseases from one plant to another. These plant diseases are generally grouped into three broad categories, namely virus, fungal and bacterial diseases.

Most food crops and industrial crops grown in tropical Africa suffer from some form of virus disease, which usually affects the leaves by destroying the green matter and thereby reducing the rate of photosynthesis. The leaf spots, which affect cassava and yams, causing the plants to be stunted, and leaf mosaics, which alter the colour of the leaves of groundnuts, cassava, tobacco, yams and several other crops, are all caused by viruses. However, the most notorious and destructive plant virus disease in tropical Africa is the swollen shoot which affects mostly tree crops, notably the cocoa tree. Swollen shoot is an example of a plant virus disease transmitted by an insect pest, the mealy bug, which feeds on the sap of trees. The disease results in falling leaves, loss of fruit and the eventual death of the tree. Unfortunately, spraying with insecticides is not effective and the only way to combat its spread is to cut down diseased trees, a rather expensive remedy which is not very popular with small-scale farmers. The disease was first reported in Ghana in 1936 and later spread into the Nigerian cocoa belt (Varley and White, 1958).

On the whole, fungal diseases attack a larger number of crops and are more widespread. This is why losses due to fungal diseases are much more substantial even though these are more amenable to treatment than virus diseases. A common fungal disease which has recently spread all over tropical Africa is the groundnut rust caused by the fungus *Puccinia arachidis Speg*. Although the disease was reported in Russia as far back as 1910 it was first encountered in the tropical African country of Zimbabwe only in 1974. Within eighteen months it had spread to Zambia, Kenya, Tanzania and Mozambique, and in 1976 it was first reported in the Borno State of Nigeria. The disease attacks the leaves of groundnuts which eventually curl up and fall off (Akrokoyo *et al.*, 1977). Other crops which are commonly attacked by rust include maize and millet.

One of the best-known fungal plant diseases in tropical Africa is the black pod disease which affects the cocoa tree and is found in all cocoa-producing areas.

The disease attacks cocoa pods and pod stalks from where it spreads to the tree itself. In West Africa, which is still the most important cocoa-producing area in the world, black pod has caused a great deal of damage in Nigeria whereas the Ghana cocoa belt has suffered more from swollen shoot disease (Oyenuga, 1967).

Fungal diseases are largely responsible for the poor yields of cotton in various parts of tropical Africa, especially in the wetter areas. The commonest of these diseases are anthracrone which affects the bolls, the stems and the leaves, and grey mildew which causes whitish spots on the underside of the leaves. Other common fungal diseases include black root rot which causes a lot of damage to cow peas, tobacco and groundnuts, and wilt, the most destructive groundnut disease, which attacks the stem of groundnut plants especially in the wetter parts of tropical Africa.

Compared with virus and fungal diseases, bacterial plant diseases are less widespread and less destructive. One of the common bacterial diseases is angular leaf which affects the leaves of the cotton plant. Another common bacterial disease is bacterial blight which causes the leaves of guinea corn to turn yellow, especially in the wetter parts of tropical Africa.

Animal pests and diseases

The tsetse fly is the most widespread animal pest in tropical Africa. Fourteen species of the fly have been identified and these have been classified in four major groups: *Glossina palpalis*, *G. morsitans*, *G. fusca* and *G. brevipalpis*. All varieties transmit trypanosomes which cause sleeping sickness, nagana, souma and baleri. *Trypanosoma brucei* or nagana affects mostly cattle and

Pl. 3.3 The tsetse fly, carrier of *trypanosomiasis*

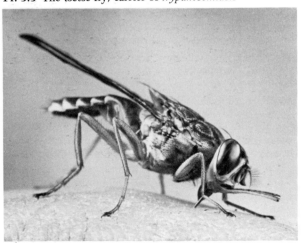

is largely responsible for the inability of the larger zebu-type cattle and horses to survive in the high forest zones. *T. pecaudi* or baleri affects mainly horses and dogs while *T. dimorphon* or souma attacks cattle, horses and smaller animals. Sleeping sickness or *T. gambiense* affects human beings. All varieties of the fly thrive in wooded environments which provide the necessary shade and coolness for rest and breeding. *G. morsitans*, however, tolerates drier conditions and is therefore much more widely distributed and is found even in altitudes of up to 1,500 m (UNESCO, 1975, pp. 276–7).

Other common pests include ticks, which cause damage to the skin, sometimes producing wounds and abscesses, as well as causing such diseases as tick fever, gall sickness and rikettsiosis. Lice are a very common pest affecting horses, cattle, dogs, cats and sheep; each animal has its own species of lice. Fleas attack mostly dogs and cats causing considerable skin irritation.

Among the common animal diseases of tropical Africa, *trypanosomiasis* is one of the most widespread. When transmitted by tsetse bite, the trypanosomes affect the bloodstream, lymph nodes and central nervous system often resulting in death. The disease has caused great economic loss amongst some cattle-rearing communities and has significantly reduced the quantity of animal protein available for the human population. Another very deadly but less common cattle disease is rinderpest or cattle plague which attacks all types of cattle including the *muturu* and *N'dama* of the forest zones. It is a highly communicable disease which also attacks wild animals such as bush pigs and antelopes. Diseased animals have a high fever and suffer from loss of appetite within the first few days of contracting the disease. These symptoms are followed by profuse diarrhoea and dysentery resulting in progressive dehydration and emaciation followed by coma and eventual death.

Rabies attacks mostly dogs and wild animals including the wolf, fox and jackal and is often communicated to man through dog bites. Rabies is a disease of the central nervous system and usually results in spells of madness followed by death.

Tuberculosis and bovine pleuro-pneumonia are also among the communicable diseases which mainly affect cattle. Outbreaks of both diseases are common in cattle markets as well as along cattle tracks in regular use by nomadic cattle herders. Cattle and other domestic animals suffer from several bacterial diseases including anthrax and blackquarter. Anthrax occurs throughout the world and all animals are susceptible to it. The most commonly affected animals are goats, sheep, cattle, horses, dogs and cats, which usually acquire the disease by grazing on contaminated pastures, or by eating contaminated food. Human beings sometimes become infected through handling wool, hides or the carcasses of diseased animals. Bloody discharges may occur from the nose, mouth and anus of affected animals and pregnant animals often abort. The acute form of anthrax results in death within two days and the dead animal becomes rapidly bloated with blood oozing out from the natural body openings.

The commonest domestic animal in tropical Africa is the native chicken although modern exotic poultry has been widely adopted in most countries since the early 1960s. Poultry diseases which sometimes assume epidemic proportions include fowl cholera, fowl typhoid, fowl pox and newcastle disease.

Human diseases

In spite of the great advances made in medical science and the increasing number of hospitals and health centres, the people of tropical Africa still experience much preventable suffering through various diseases such as malaria, bilharzia, cerebrospinal meningitis, river blindness and kwashiorkor. Often the patients in hospital wards do not respond readily to treatment because their bodies are weak from undernutrition. As Buchanan and Pugh (1955) have rightly pointed out, disease, malnutrition and low agricultural productivity (resulting partly from plant and animal pests and diseases, and partly from low output by under-nourished farmers) form a vicious circle. It is against this background that we now proceed to discuss some of the more common and debilitating diseases in the region.

For the purpose of simplifying our discussion, we adopt three broad categories of common diseases. These are 1. diseases due to poor sanitation, 2. diseases carried by insect pests and 3. diseases caused by malnutrition.

Diseases due to poor sanitation

Many diseases, still rampant in rural and low-income residential urban areas in developing countries, including tropical Africa, are largely due to primitive living conditions. Some of these diseases also existed in pre-industrial Europe, but have since been eradicated, and a few of them are also disappearing in those areas of tropical Africa where houses have replaced huts and where piped water has been provided. Diseases within this category are all communicable and can be controlled by observing simple rules of hygiene. Some of these, such as yaws, smallpox, measles and leprosy, are basically skin diseases while others, notably dysentery and cholera, are intestinal. There are also others, such as cerebrospinal meningitis, which affect the brain and spinal column.

Yaws was formerly very common in all rural areas

with little water, especially in the equatorial zone of tropical Africa, but has now been virtually eradicated. It is transmitted by direct contact with the open wounds of an affected person and a large number of villagers may contract it in areas where it is endemic. In 1955, for example, the proportion of people suffering from yaws in the southern parts of Nigeria varied from 16–37 per cent (Buchanan and Pugh, 1955). Yaws affects mainly children and is very painful and disfiguring. Fortunately it is readily curable with suitable drugs, notably penicillin, and once a patient recovers he is immune for life.

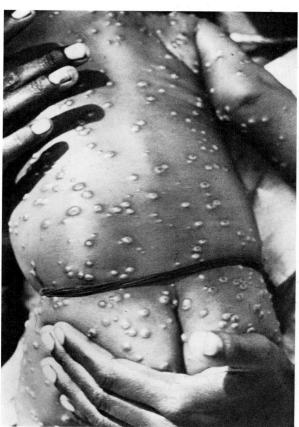

Pl. 3.4 A child suffering from smallpox, now officially eradicated

Smallpox was, until recently, another common disfiguring disease affecting parts of tropical Africa and even the developed countries, with its frequent epidemic outbursts. In years of serious epidemics, smallpox often resulted in extensive loss of life, while some of those who survived lost their sight or became pockmarked. Smallpox has now been eradicated over much of tropical Africa thanks to the mass vaccination of schoolchildren during the 1940s and of the general public in the 1950s and 1960s. Occasionally, however, localized outbursts of the disease still occur and one of the methods adopted to stamp it out is the routine vaccination of new-born babies.

Measles, a virus infection, is still a killer of children in many parts of Africa, but once recovered a child is immune for life. Transmission of the disease is largely through the inhalation of infective spray from patients in the catarrh stage of the disease (Davey and Wilson, 1965, pp. 94–5).

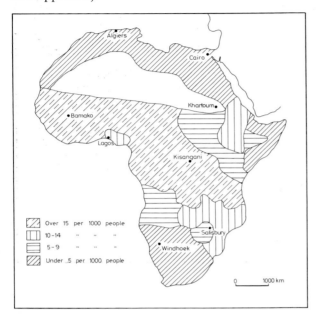

Fig. 3.3 Distribution of leprosy

Leprosy, a chronic communicable disease which is transmitted by direct contact, is endemic in Africa. It was also endemic in temperate zones, where it has since been eradicated. In the early 1940s the number of lepers in Nigeria was as high as 400,000 while the figure for the former French Equatorial Africa was put at about 22,000. The incidence of the disease appears to be particularly high in these two areas, and indeed in other parts of Africa, because while lepers are isolated and kept in leper settlements or segregated villages for treatment in some areas, they move about freely in others. As a rule, leprosy is more common in communities with a very low standard of living and on the whole children and adolescents are more susceptible.

Amongst the more serious intestinal diseases, dysentery and cholera are the most widespread not only in tropical Africa but also in other low-income areas where people tend to live crowded in pre-industrial cities or in shanty-town suburbs of modern cities. The incidence of dysentery is so common that it ranks second only to

malaria as the major health hazard in Africa. Dysentery usually results from eating contaminated food, such as raw vegetables, or from drinking contaminated water. Cholera occurs less frequently but generally assumes epidemic proportions when it erupts. Cholera epidemics have been reported in various parts of Africa in recent years resulting in several thousand deaths. It is basically a water-borne disease and can be prevented by maintaining a high standard of personal and environmental hygiene. Uncollected heaps of rubbish and careless disposal of human waste, characteristic of the core areas of most traditional towns, have been largely responsible for the frequent outbursts of cholera epidemics in African countries.

Bilharzia or *schistosomiasis* occurs mostly in West and East Africa as well as in Egypt and the Sudan. It is very common in settlements located near rivers or lagoons and has become endemic in areas of important irrigation schemes or hydro-electric power schemes such as the Gezira, the Volta Dam and the Bacita sugar estate. Thousands of cases are reported every year in Zaïre, Chad, Gabon and Nigeria; and in the 1940s, up to 76 per cent of people living in the lagoon town of Epe in Lagos State were affected by the disease (Adejuwon, 1978). The bilharzia parasite penetrates the skin while a man wades through the water, or the disease is contracted from the drinking of contaminated water – a situation which could be avoided were piped water to be provided.

Other important killer diseases associated with poor sanitation include cerebrospinal meningitis and tuberculosis. Outbreaks of cerebrospinal meningitis, during which thousands of people die, occur almost every year in the northern parts of West Africa and in Central Africa during the dry season (see p. 35). The mortality is probably higher than for other common diseases since death often occurs during the first two days of the attack.

Tuberculosis occurs in all parts of the world, but in the developed countries the incidence of, and mortality resulting from, the disease have declined. In tropical Africa, as in other Third World countries, tuberculosis is still widespread, especially in West and southern Africa. The disease is readily transmitted by inhaling the tubercule bacilli which occur in the saliva or cough discharges of infected persons. Infection may also result from the transfer of the bacilli to the mouth on fingers, such as when feeding a baby the African way or even through infected feeding bottles. The social customs of African communities such as eating with fingers from a common plate, smoking a common pipe and the general low standard of hygiene amongst some communities favour the spread of tuberculosis (Davey and Wilson, 1965, pp. 101–3).

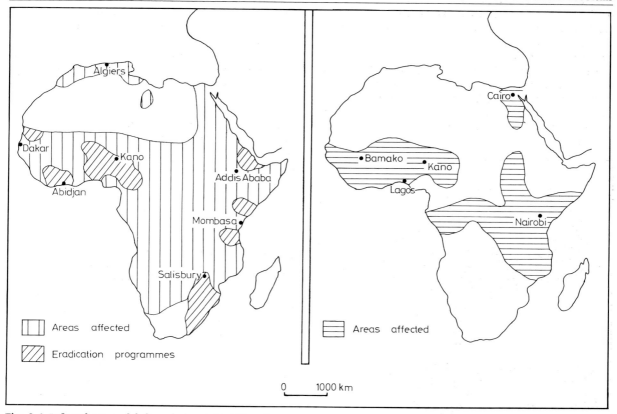

Fig. 3.4 Infested areas of, left, malaria; right, bilharzia

Diseases carried by insect pests

A large number of diseases are carried by mosquitoes but the most common in tropical Africa are malaria, yellow fever and filariasis. Malaria, which is transmitted primarily by the *anopheles* mosquito, is endemic all over Africa and is by far the commonest disease in tropical Africa. It is a notorious killer of infants and it is not exaggerating to say that virtually every person in the region has suffered from malaria at one time or another. Indeed most people contract the disease repeatedly, often more than four times in a year. In Nigeria, reported cases exceed 400,000 every year. Malarial patients become physically and mentally weak and are unable to perform normal duties. It is therefore a major cause of loss of man-hours in offices as well as on the farm.

Yellow fever is endemic in that part of tropical Africa lying between latitudes 15°N and 15°S. It is primarily a virus infection of monkeys and is transmitted to man by the *Aedea aegypti* mosquito, which also conveys it from man to man. Yellow fever epidemics are common in urban areas, affecting people of all ages, but those who have been attacked acquire a lifelong immunity.

Compared with malaria, the number of deaths from yellow fever is insignificant (Davey and Wilson, 1965, pp. 136–43).

Sleeping sickness or human *trypanosomiasis* is caused by the *T. gambiense* parasite conveyed to man by tsetse fly bites. It is largely confined to that part of tropical Africa lying south of latitude 10°N and is usually fatal if untreated. As a rule, sleeping sickness occurs mainly in sparsely settled wooded rural areas where the population is so small that it cannot effectively deforest the area by regular cultivation, thereby helping to destroy the habitat of the tsetse fly. During the colonial period a number of villages were transferred from infested riverine areas of French Equatorial Africa to new and healthier sites. In Zambia, the sleeping sickness epidemic resulted in the mass evacuation of people from riverine villages which were burnt down to prevent people returning to settle there. The displaced villagers were settled in larger villages on the plateau. However, the amalgamation of several villages was not popular and most villagers subsequently deserted these 'government villages' (Kay, 1964).

Another insect-borne disease which is common in

41

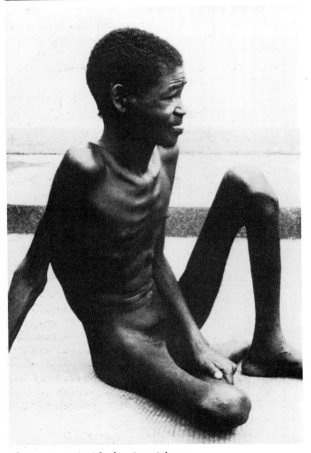

Pl. 3.5 A man with sleeping sickness

riverine areas is river blindness (*onchocerciasis*), a chronic non-fatal filarial disease which eventually causes blindness. The disease is endemic in the grassland areas of West and East Africa, and in recent years the building of dams, notably the Volta Dam, has resulted in the extension of *onchocerciasis* along the main rivers of tropical Africa (UNESCO, 1975, p. 289). The main vector of the disease in West Africa is the 'black fly' (*Simulium damnosum*), but in East Africa and the Zaïre Basin the dominant fly species is the *S. neavei*. The flies usually bite on the legs injecting micro-filariae worms into the skin. After a few months, a heavily infested skin begins to thicken and subsequently the micro-filariae spread to other parts of the body including the face and eyes, causing blindness (Davey and Wilson, 1965, pp. 199–200).

Diseases caused by malnutrition

Starvation or undernutrition which occurs periodically is still common in tropical Africa and is usually caused by crop failures from lack of rain, flooding or pest damage. Undernutrition causes swelling of the feet and legs as well as anaemia and starving persons are often mentally disturbed. Obesity or overnutrition, which is caused by consuming more food than is required, is not as common as in the developed countries. There are, however, indications that obesity will become a major nutritional problem in the future since it is generally considered to be 'evidence of good living' in Africa and therefore adds prestige to the individual. Severe obesity often leads to difficulty in moving about and excessively fat people are more susceptible to diabetes, high blood pressure and varicose veins (Latham, 1973, pp. 95–8).

The most serious cases of nutritional disease in tropical Africa are, however, not caused by starvation or obesity but by malnutrition which has become a major public health problem in the region. Malnutrition is caused by the lack of essential food factors such as protein and vitamins in the diet. Common diseases associated with malnutrition include kwashiorkor, marasmus, rickets and endemic goitre. Kwashiorkor is caused by protein deficiency in food given to children after they have been taken off the breast and affects children mostly between one and three years of age. It is a very serious disease causing delayed growth, swelling of feet, hands and face, hair and skin changes and may result in death if not treated (Latham, 1973, pp. 120–4).

Marasmus is also an infant disease, especially common during the first year of life, and is associated with calorie deficiency. It is a form of starvation arising from an inadequate supply of breast milk or of manufactured baby foods. Some misguided middle-class parents are known to buy very expensive synthetic milk which they overdilute for the purpose of economy, thereby unwittingly starving their babies. Affected babies fail to grow and lose weight. In severe cases the limbs become emaciated, the ribs are prominent and the eyes sunken. Adults also suffer from protein-calorie malnutrition which often leads to anaemia, dry, scaly skin and hair changes (Latham, 1973, pp. 130–8).

Rickets results from calcium deficiency in the body and affects mostly infants and young children. Children suffering from rickets sometimes appear plump and well-fed with a characteristic potbelly. The disease affects the bones, which remain soft and weak, resulting in more deformities as soon as the child begins to walk. Bow legs are the commonest manifestation, but knock-knees may also occur. In the more serious cases the spine is affected. Fortunately most African children are spared from the misery of rickets because of the abundant sunshine and the fact that they are very scantily clothed. Indeed the incidence of rickets is reported to be highest amongst children who are overclothed and those who are often tied to their mother's back for long periods so that their skins are not adequately exposed to sunlight (Latham, 1973, pp. 112–15).

Compared with rickets, the incidence of endemic goitre is more common in tropical Africa. The main cause of the disease is lack of iodine in the diet. It affects both children and adults, especially females at puberty and during pregnancy. Patients with goitre have a swollen thyroid, a gland which is situated in the lower front part of the neck. In severe cases the swelling becomes very large and unsightly and in these instances the only way to cure the patient is by surgery. Children who suffer from goitre grow very slowly and are generally mentally dull while children whose mothers have goitre are often deaf or dumb and may be mentally retarded (Latham, 1973, pp. 140–4).

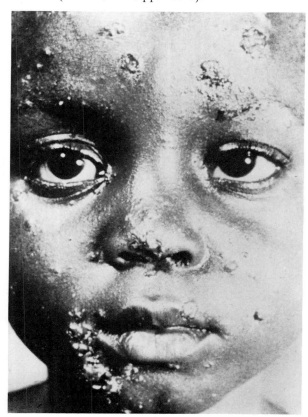

Pl. 3.6 Child diseased with yaws

Diseases, health and economic development

There is a common saying amongst most African peoples that 'health is wealth'. The people of tropical Africa are therefore fully aware of the importance of good health and the need to eradicate disease. Unfortunately many of them still associate some diseases with either evil spirits or the actions of their enemies. The high incidence of poverty and the generally low standard of living combine with ignorance to create a situation in which communicable diseases are still rampant. Many hospitals and dispensaries have been built in each country, particularly since independence, and in some countries the number of doctors has increased considerably. However, owing to the rapid increase in population, the doctor–population ratio is still low and often the hospital dispensaries are without drugs. Efforts to improve the health situation should therefore be directed largely towards mass measures for the control and prevention of diseases.

Enough evidence has been presented in this chapter to show that the high incidence of various diseases has adversely affected the process of economic development. The review of diseases associated with malnutrition indicates that children who have suffered from some of these diseases cannot compete favourably in schools and are unlikely to grow into healthy efficient workers either on the farms or in offices. The weakening effect of a malaria attack, for example, has been responsible for low output of work in offices, and malaria has often been cited as the main cause of absenteeism from work. The eradication of mosquitoes will therefore bring about a more effective labour force, just as the eradication of the tsetse fly will benefit cattle raising.

The health situation today has improved considerably since independence. This is largely because a fast developing economy has made more money available for people to spend, thereby making it possible for them to build spacious and well-ventilated houses instead of huts. As more and more people become educated, a sizeable proportion of the population will be in a position to support piped water, electricity and good houses. It is then that the common diseases, which have since been eradicated in the developed countries of the world, will also disappear from tropical Africa.

References

Adejuwon, J. O. (1978), 'Pests and Diseases', in J. S. Oguntoyinbo, O. O. Areola and M. Filani (eds.), *A Geography of Nigerian Development*, Heinemann, Ibadan, p. 107.

Akrokoyo, J. O. *et al.* (1977), 'Groundnut Rust in Nigeria', *Samaru Miscellaneous Paper 68*, Zaria, pp. 1–4.

Buchanan, K. M. and Pugh, J. C. (1955), *Land and People in Nigeria*, University of London Press, London, p. 56.

Davey, T. H. and Wilson, T. (1965), *Davey and Lightbody's Control of Diseases in the Tropics*, H. L. Lewis and Co. Ltd, London.

Hunter, J. M. (1966), 'River Blindness in Nangodi, Northern Ghana', *Geographical Review*, 56, pp. 398–416.

Kay, G. (1964), 'Aspects of Ushi Settlement History: Fort Rosebery District, Northern Rhodesia', in R. W. Steel and R. M. Prothero (eds.), *Geographers and the Tropics: Liverpool Essays*, Longman, London, pp. 235–60.

Latham, M. C. (1965), *Human Nutrition in Tropical Africa*, FAO, Rome.

Oyenuga, V. A. (1967), *Agriculture in Nigeria*, FAO, Rome, pp. 96–7.

UNESCO (1975), *Teacher's Study Guide on the Biology of Human Populations in Africa*, Unesco Press, Paris.

Varley, W. J. and White, H. P. (1958), *The Geography of Ghana*, Longman, London, p. 160.

Section B
Peoples, Societies and Social Change

4 Traditional Societies, Land Tenure and Rural Settlements

Cultural prejudices, like food habits, are not easy to change. It is therefore not surprising that many people in the northern continents still consider Africa to be the 'dark continent' and are more knowledgeable about the Pygmies of Zaïre or the Bushmen of Botswana who are very few in number and not typical of African societies. At the same time they know very little and may not even be interested to know about the more typical and more numerous groups such as the Yoruba, Ibo, Kikuyu and Hausa, and are surprised to see modern apartment buildings or factories in tropical African cities. What is more disturbing and pathetic is the fact that many young Africans, who still depend mostly on books written in Europe and America, also accept, without much questioning, views expressed about other parts of Africa by foreign writers. Fortunately an increasing amount of enlightened literature is now available on the traditional societies of tropical Africa. However, much of what is written is not readily accessible to schoolteachers and children, hence the need to present a brief review of traditional African societies in the first part of this chapter.

When Africans talk about tradition they refer to social and cultural institutions and ways of doing things which they consider to be indigenous. Many of these institutions were discredited as barbaric by Christian and Muslim missionaries and some were proscribed by the colonial governments. The last twenty years have seen a considerable cultural revival to the extent that even the established churches have been obliged to modify their modes of worship to include some elements of African culture in order to maintain a threshold population in their congregations (see p. 81). On the other hand, western influences have considerably modified some aspects of African traditions. Indeed in some urban areas and among some sections of the societies, the political wind of change which started in the 1950s and resulted in the independence of most countries in the 1960s was accompanied by a cultural change. Today, however, the vast majority of people in tropical Africa still live in rural areas and have therefore witnessed few of these changes. A basic understanding of African traditional life is therefore essential for a proper assessment of the problems faced by governments and people in their efforts to create a modern society in the various countries of tropical Africa.

Kinship, genealogy and territoriality

Although the peoples of tropical Africa belong to more than 300 different ethnic groups, each of which has its own language, customs and taboos, and usually occupies a distinct and contiguous territory, there are a number of basic social features which apply to most, and sometimes all, of these ethnic groups. Indeed some of these features apply to all pre-industrial societies, past and present, in other parts of the world.

Traditional society in tropical Africa is organized into kinship groups called 'lineages' by anthropologists. The lineage consists of all the descendants of one ancestor who is often legendary amongst the larger groups. The lineage is described as a patrilineage if the descendants of the common ancestor are related and inherit property through males, and as a matrilineage where relationship and inheritance are through females. Descendants of the common ancestor by both male and female links are called agnates. The lineage group usually constitutes an exogamous unit, and it frequently holds property in common, such as an oil palm bush.

The vast majority of ethnic groups in tropical Africa, especially those who live north of the Equator, are patrilineal. Occasionally, as is the case with the eastern Ibo clans of Ohafia and Abiriba in Nigeria, small matrilineal groups may be found amongst a predominantly patrilineal people. There is, however, a wide belt of concentrated matrilineal groups which extends from Angola in the west, through Zambia to Mozambique in the east. Under the matrilineal system of descent, the mother's brother or maternal uncle is obliged to assume responsibility for the training of his sister's children. This curious system appears to be associated with a high incidence of marital instability in the society and certainly does not conform to traditional African thinking about the role of the father and property inheritance generally. There are also a few smaller ethnic groups such as the Yako of the Cross River State of Nigeria, the Nuba of Kordofan Province of Sudan, and the Herero people of Namibia who have a double descent system in which an individual is a member of both the patrilineal and matrilineal descent groups.

A close relationship exists between territorial and kinship organization. Often, for a given clan or sub-ethnic group, settlement units such as the compound (homestead), the hamlet, the village and the village-group ('town') are essentially varied categories of kinship associations. In consequence, it is usually territorial–kinship relationships, rather than morphology and functions, that form the basis of defining a settlement, as Jones had in mind in describing Ibo society. He observed that Ibo social structure is 'based on a theory of agnatic descent which regards each village-group as a patri-clan, descendants of a common ancestor, and its component villages and their sub-divisions (the ward, hamlet, compounds) as maximal, major and minor lineages of this clan' (Jones, 1949). The village in Ibo society is thus the maximal lineage of the clan, while the hamlet and the compound are respectively the major and minor lineages.

The territorial–kinship relationship is presented diagrammatically in Fig. 4.1, where VG stands for the village-group, which usually occupies a large and seldom compact area of land. The unity of the village-group depends on a common name, usually that of a mythical ancestor, a common territory and common customs and taboos. Amongst some ethnic groups such as the Ibo of Nigeria, the village-group is the highest traditional political and social unit. In pre-colonial days, the village-group had limited social links with other similar groups although there were considerable economic links through periodic markets. From the apical ancestor, the founder of the VG, the founders of the villages were descended, V_1, V_2 and V_3, each of which has its own distinct territory within the territorial limits of the VG. Each village in turn is made up of smaller units, H_1, H_2 . . . H_9 which may be a hamlet with a defined territory or just a residential ward of the village in societies where the people live in large compact villages.

As a general rule the village has a greater degree of unity than the village-group. This is particularly true of the politically decentralized or so-called stateless societies such as the Ibo, Ibibio and Tiv of Nigeria. Green has described the position of the Ibo as follows:

the village-group may be considered as a whole in certain respects, but it is the village which for most practical purposes, manages its own affairs. Within the village, authority is dispersed among groups rather than centralized in any one individual or body. . . The extended families composing the village themselves paddle their own cause in many matters . . . and although the whole village considers itself theoretically a kinship unit, in fact, the sentiment of kinship wears thin outside the bonds of the extended family . . . (Green, 1941)

The political system among the more centralized groups is certainly different, but much of Green's observation about kinship also applies to such groups as the Edo of Nigeria or the Ashanti of Ghana.

There are a few less organized ethnic groups to which the territorial–kinship relationship does not apply. One such group is the Tonga of southern Zambia who are also found in Zimbabwe, where they are known as Batonka. Among the Tonga, the clan (VG) is not named after a first ancestor, but after an animal, such as the leopard, a plant or an historical event! The result is that members of the clan cannot easily trace their genealogies to a common ancestor. Unlike other African clans, the Tonga clan does not occupy a discrete and contiguous territory but is dispersed in such a way that local neighbourhoods are inhabited by people from many other clans. A Tonga clan therefore consists of people bearing a common name but dispersed widely over the ethnic territory. Clansmen claim vague kinship to one another and are forbidden to intermarry.

The decentralization and apparent lack of order in the spatial arrangement of the clan also extends to the

Fig. 4.1 Genealogy and territoriality

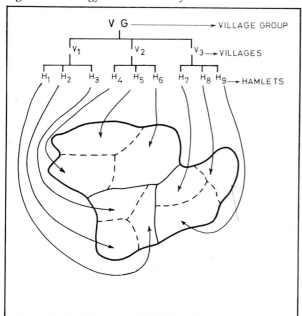

village. Traditional village settlement in tropical Africa normally consists of people who can trace descent in one or other line from a common ancestor; but not so the Tonga village. This is made up of a group of adult Tonga males and their dependants, who have come from different clans and who are registered as tax-payers under a single village headman. There is no blood relationship, characteristic of most African villages, and generally the Tonga village is very unstable since the members can readily choose to transfer from one village to another. Indeed, during the colonial period, any person who was able to induce nine other taxable males to settle on a new site with him was readily accorded recognition as a village head (Allan *et al.*, 1948, p. 35).

The family and the compound

The nuclear or immediate family consisting of a man, his wife and children is the primary group of modern society. It is characterized by a common surname, a common habitation and some economic provision shared by all members of the group. In traditional African society, as in any other pre-industrial society, the basic social group is not the nuclear family but the extended or patriarchal family. The extended family consists of a man (the patriarch), his wife or wives, the families of their sons, and sometimes the families of younger brothers who have not yet established their own compounds (homesteads). The extended family is not only a social but also an economic unit with common property. Traditionally the power of the head of the family is absolute and the wife or wives, as well as other members of the extended family, are socially and economically subordinate to the head. Extended families are also characteristic of other pre-industrial societies and were prevalent in the feudal societies of medieval Europe.

New members of the extended family belong to the group by virtue of birth or marriage (wives). As a rule, a wife marries into the family even though she is in reality married to only one male member. This is why other family members often refer to a young bride as 'our wife'. It is also common practice on the death of a husband for the head of the family to ask a widow to

Pl. 4.1 A typical homestead in the Sudan savanna

choose any other male member as her husband. However, the widow may decide to marry outside the family and when that happens, the new husband is required to refund the bride-price originally paid on the woman to the family of the deceased husband.

Like other aspects of traditional life, the extended family is undergoing some change similar to that which occurred in Europe and other areas which had pre-industrial societies in the past. The rapid rate of urbanization and the spread of a western type of education are the two major agents of change which involve the gradual displacement of the extended family by the nuclear family. The economic situation in the colonial and post-colonial period has tended to make young people less dependent on their elders. The highly educated young people, most of whom live in urban areas, have largely rejected the subordinate roles which traditional society imposed on them and have become rather 'rebellious', as some elders put it. It is, however, the 'rebellion' of young women, an increasing number of whom 'now wear trousers meant for men', that is most distressing to the more conservative elders.

The case against the extended family as presented by the younger generation is that it kills individual initiative because of the subordinate position of young people to the family head and to elderly people in general. It is also argued that the system tends to inhibit the social advancement of the more progressive and successful members of the extended family who are expected to care for less progressive and even indolent members. Thus a well-paid company executive or civil servant who agrees to operate within the system is obliged to spend his income on distant relatives so that he cannot invest his money as savings. Those who support the system argue that it is the only way to provide some form of social security in societies where the state has not yet provided for unemployment, sickness and old age. They also argue that the extended family system, in which a brother is his brother's keeper, has contributed significantly to the training of younger members in schools and the professions since most African governments have so far been unable to provide free education even at the primary level.

The extended family lives in a compound which consists of a cluster of houses or huts and is usually referred to by the name of its head. A young man who has just built a house for himself and his wife may also refer to it as his compound. In reality such an isolated house is the nucleus of a compound since other buildings may shortly be put up to house the wives (if he marries a second wife), to store grain and to shelter domestic animals. The population of a compound can therefore range from two persons to over 120 people. Indeed, amongst the Ohafia Ibo of Nigeria the compounds, which are usually very closely built up, may contain more than 400 persons. Amongst some ethnic groups, the compound is surrounded by a mud wall or a fence of live sticks or grass thatch, and has only one official entrance (Fig. 4.2, p. 50). Each enclosed compound has an open space, part of which is used as a vegetable garden. The immediate surroundings of the compound are usually cultivated every year.

In some ethnic territories, each compound has one or more reception huts or houses, located close to the entrance into the compound, and entry into a large compound is often through the main reception hut. As a rule, the arrangement of living huts within the compound reflects the closeness of blood relationship between adult male members of the extended family. Thus amongst the Tiv of Nigeria, for example, 'a man lives closer to his full brother than he does to his half-brother, and closer to his half-brother than to his father's brother's son' or cousin (Bohannan and Bohannan, 1962, p. 17). In recent years, an increasing number of young men have preferred to build modern houses outside the compound enclosure. The size of traditional compounds has therefore become smaller over the years and in some localities, the large traditional family compound no longer exists.

Traditional and contemporary land tenure systems

There are several definitions of the term land tenure. In this book we adopt the definition which considers land tenure to be 'the fabric of rights and obligations which comprise the tripartite relationship between man, land and society'. It is this definition that best reflects the often-quoted statement of a Nigerian traditional ruler, the Elesi of Odogbolu, who while appearing before the West African Lands Committee set up by the British Colonial Government submitted as follows: 'I conceive land to belong to a vast family of which many are dead, few are living and countless members are still unborn.' This traditional view that land belongs to the whole community – the living, the dead and generations yet unborn – is applicable to almost all the peoples of tropical Africa. The implication is that in traditional societies, land cannot be permanently alienated, whatever the circumstances, although land can be pledged. Today, in spite of the changes which have affected the society and the economy, it is still considered an abominable act to sell a piece of land in which one's parents or grandparents were buried.

Traditional land tenure systems
Under the traditional land tenure systems, which are commonly referred to as communal land tenure, the land belongs to the village, the village-group or the

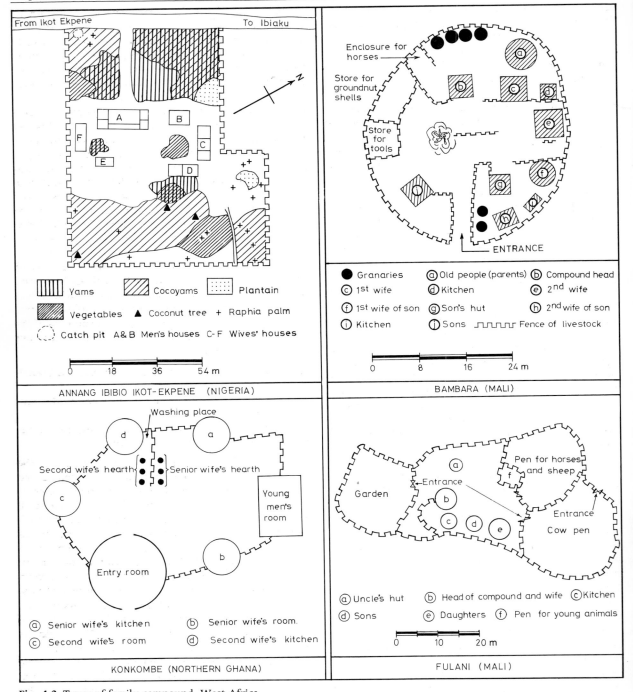

Fig. 4.2 Types of family compound, West Africa

clan. The right of the individual to use the land derives from his membership of the community. All aliens are excluded except when given special permission to use the land by heads of families in the village or clan. Furthermore, the title to land by members of the community is purely usufructuary and land which is no longer in use by the individual reverts to the community. Outright sale of land is prohibited. Under this system, each member of the community is entitled to as much land as he needs to cultivate for the purpose of sustaining his family. There is therefore no landless class under the traditional system of communal land tenure.

The traditional ideas that land belongs to the community and that every member has a right to as much land as he wants to cultivate remained good as long as there was sufficient land for everybody. This system continues today in many sparsely settled areas where land is still abundant. However, in the densely populated areas pressure on farmland 'has made it more or less impossible for one central authority to control individual land tenure . . .' (Bridges, 1939). This is the situation in parts of Okigwi Division of Iboland in Nigeria where Green notes that the absence of communal control over land 'accords with, and reacts on, the democratic, pluralistic nature' of the social organization (Green, 1941). Unlike in the past, ownership and control of land in this very densely populated part of Nigeria 'are dispersed rather than concentrated, just as is authority in general social affairs'. In such areas, land has now become a marketable commodity, although sales are still largely restricted to members of the village-group or clan.

Modifications to traditional land tenure systems because of land shortage are recent and very localized since much of tropical Africa is still very sparsely populated. By comparison, the changes caused by the spread of Islam and the subsequent imposition of Islamic land law have affected a larger area and population. The imposition of colonial rule in tropical Africa also brought about marked changes in traditional land tenure systems, especially in those countries where large areas of land were alienated and set aside for settlement by immigrants from Europe. The disturbance of traditional land tenure by the spread of Islam appears to be restricted to those areas, such as parts of the northern states of Nigeria, where Islam was imposed through conquest. In other Islamicized areas, including parts of Yorubaland, land tenure was not affected probably because a section of the community adopted Christianity while others remained adherents to traditional African religions.

In those areas where Islamic law was imposed by conquest, the degree of disturbance which occurred in the local land tenure systems is not certain. We know,

however, that the bulk of land conquered by Muslim warriors in Africa fell into the category of *kharaj* lands; and that there are two classes of *kharaj* lands, namely *wakf* and *sulh*. *Wakf* lands consist of areas captured by force and therefore constituted into state lands by Muslim rulers. The original owners of the land were however allowed to remain on the land on payment of *kharaj* as rent. By contrast *sulh* lands consist of areas acquired under treaty, a sort of protectorate. In this case the original owners of the land continued to retain their rights of occupation but were required to pay *kharaj* in the form of tribute. In practice almost all lands in Muslim controlled areas, especially in West Africa, were in the *sulh* category because, as Thompson and Adloff (1958, p. 345) have rightly observed, even the most unscrupulous Muslim conqueror recognized that conquest gave him no right to ownership of the soil.

Changes in land tenure in the colonial period
During the colonial period traditional African land tenure systems suffered a major shock from which they have never recovered. The shock took different forms in different territories, depending on the policies of the metropolitan powers. In this section we shall consider briefly three types:

1. Outright nationalization of land, for example, French West Africa;
2. Alienation of African land for European settlement, for example, Kenya;
3. The emergence of individual ownership in various territories such as Nigeria and Ghana.

Among such peoples as the Yoruba, the Bemba, the Ashanti, the Mossi or the Bini, who have a centralized political system in which the paramount ruler is considered sacred or divine, the ruler is said to hold all land in the state or kingdom 'in trust for the people'. French policy of total nationalization of land in her African territories rested largely on the erroneous assumption that the land which the African paramount ruler held in trust for the people belonged to the ruler. Hence the argument that France, as the successor to the African rulers, had acquired sovereign rights over all land in her protectorates. It was the same line of argument that Lugard adopted when in 1901 he told the Fulani rulers of the Sokoto/Gwandu Empire that the rights to the land which the Fulani had acquired from the people by conquest had automatically passed to the British following the defeat of the Sokoto Caliphate by British troops. In the process of administering the former northern Nigeria, the British proceeded to extend this land policy over the whole territory, even though parts of the territory had not been conquered by the Fulani. In Portuguese territories, which were officially considered to be overseas provinces of

Portugal, as well as in Belgian Africa, all lands belonged to the state, although certain lands were preserved for African cultivation through a system of land reserves (Bailey, 1969). Outright nationalization made it easy for government to grant land in the form of concessions to European planters. The local people were, however, free to cultivate the land more or less under traditional systems of tenure in Native Reserves on condition that the state could dispossess them of such land if, for instance, a valuable mineral was discovered.

Secondly, traditional African land tenure systems were affected by the permanent alienation of land in High Africa for the purpose of European colonization. This land was completely lost to the original African owners whereas Africans were still in a position to cultivate their land in areas where land was nationalized by the colonial power. This second type of shock was greatly resented not only by African rulers but also by the people, and eventually led to armed revolt in Kenya and Zimbabwe. Moreover the permanent alienation of land for European settlement in Kenya and Zimbabwe was contrary to the declared British principle of the paramountcy of native interests, which British colonial officers faithfully invoked to support their refusal to grant concessions to European planters seeking to establish tree-crop plantations in Nigeria and Ghana.

The third type of shock was the emergence of individual title to land resulting in the complete collapse of traditional land tenure systems in some parts of tropical Africa. This development occurred largely in areas where the colonial powers had decided to apply the system of indirect rule, and where there was little interference with the traditional systems of local government. The emergence of individual title to land was therefore not directly caused by the colonial administrators, but rather a result of inevitable social changes that accompanied the imposition of European rule. The ways in which this third shock came about is the subject of the next section.

Individual land tenure

We observed earlier that in the very densely settled parts of Iboland, traditional communal land tenure has since broken down and that land has now become a marketable commodity. We also noted that this particular area belongs to one of the so-called stateless societies of tropical Africa where authority in general social affairs is highly decentralized. However, the emergence and rapid spread of individual land ownership is neither restricted to 'stateless' societies nor to very densely populated areas where farmland is in short supply. Individual land ownership has become very common even in areas where traditional rulers still claim divine rights, including the right to hold the land

'in trust for the people'. This is the position today in Yorubaland, in the ancient Kingdom of Benin, in Kikuyuland and amongst the Ganda of Buganda.

The new economic order which came with the colonial administration played a major role in the emergence of individual land tenure. The introduction and rapid expansion of industrial crops, especially tree crops, and the increasing pressure of population on land in the very densely settled areas resulted in shortage of farmland. Village heads and elders found it increasingly difficult to meet individual demands for more farmland. As a result, people resorted to farming a piece of land for longer periods than is permissible and consequently came to claim outright title to such land. People who were short of money proceeded to pledge their land and some even sold their holdings. The spread of individual title to land in such areas is therefore a result of the decline in the authority of traditional rulers following their inability to fulfil one of the basic principles of traditional land tenure which stipulates that a member of the community is entitled to as much land as he requires for the purpose of maintaining his family. The wide adoption of a money economy also contributed to the trend.

Tree-crop farming, as a specific example, is inconsistent with traditional communal land tenure. Traditionally, tree crops such as coconut, oil palm and kolanut trees belong to the man who planted them or to his descendants. If a man plants a grove of oil palm trees, for example, on land 'shown' to him by his grandmother, it is only the crops that belong to him, not the land. At the same time the *de jure* owner of the land cannot claim ownership of the tree crops and is obliged to buy them if he wishes to remove the trees from his land. In order to prevent this situation of *de facto* ownership of land by tree-crop planters who have no title to land, many people refuse to allow migrant farmers to cultivate tree crops on land leased to them. For the same reason, village elders do not normally allow people to establish large tree-crop farms on communally held land. It is also the desire to avoid the risk of having their perennial crops cut off when a piece of community land is required for public use that makes tree-crop farmers prefer to purchase their farmland outright.

We end this discussion of land tenure systems by listing the various types of land ownership which may be found in contemporary tropical Africa.

1. Private ownership – which may be by inheritance or through purchase, and which is largely alien to traditional African ideas about land. Private ownership of land is on the increase and appears to fit the developmental needs of today.
2. Family land – which belongs to an individual and the

Pl. 4.2 Farmer's house in Tanzania – note banana trees in the background

right to which devolves on all his children. Amongst some ethnic groups, such as the Edo of the ancient Kingdom of Benin, family land is inherited by the eldest son of the deceased, to the exclusion of other children, that is if the 'founder' of the family died intestate and if the intestacy is governed by customary law. A man may, however, partition his land amongst his male children before he dies. Furthermore, in many parts of tropical Africa brothers, sisters and uncles, who are traditionally regarded as members of a deceased's family, are not so recognized for the purpose of sharing family land.

3. Stool land – usually restricted to areas with centralized traditional political systems such as Ashanti, Buganda, Mossi ethnic territory, the Kingdom of Benin and Yorubaland. Stool land is normally inherited by the holder of traditional chieftaincy to which the land is associated. In reality the paramount ruler who 'holds all land in trust for the people' has rights only over stool lands and lands which he may have acquired before appointment to the stool.

4. Communal land – which may belong to the village or the clan. Among some groups, such as the Tonga who

are a cattle-owning people, all uncultivated land is subject to common rights of pasturage. In areas where land shortage has brought about the predominance of individual land ownership, the only areas of communal land are the village squares, bad bush where wicked people are buried and possibly the market squares.

5. State land – which consists of land acquired compulsorily by government or land donated by communities and individuals to government for public use. A substantial area of land in urban centres, including residential districts for government officials, industrial estates and university institutions are located on state land.

6. Unoccupied land – which includes wasteland and forest reserves. Most forest reserves belong to government and therefore constitute a class of state land. Large areas of land which have not yet been settled are in effect communal land and it is wrong to refer to such land as no-man's land since there is no land which has not been claimed by one group or another.

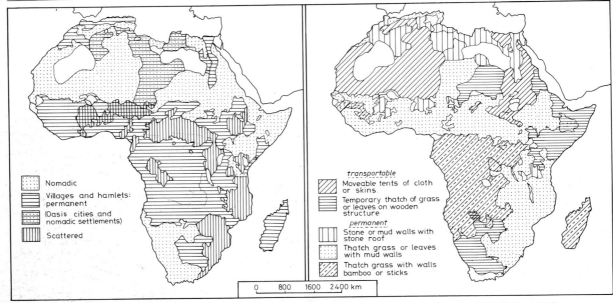

Fig. 4.3 Types of rural settlement (left) and habitat (right) (after *Biology of Human Populations*, UNESCO, p. 342)

Rural settlements

The great majority of the people of tropical Africa still live in rural settlements consisting of small hamlets and villages. The compound which houses the family is the basic unit of settlement and some of its basic character-istics have already been presented in this chapter. A collection of compounds occupied by people who claim common ancestry constitutes the hamlet or village, depending on the size of the settlement. It is important to remind ourselves at this point that it is usually the territorial–kinship relationship and not morphology that defines a settlement unit. Thus an administrative village may consist of isolated compounds scattered all over the territory occupied by a group of people who claim a common ancestor, so that there is no village formation whatsoever. Rural settlements therefore consist of a wide range of groupings of compounds which vary from very closely nucleated or compact villages and hamlets to widely dispersed and scattered compounds.

In the discussion which follows, we are concerned with settlements that are permanent in the sense that their occupants are not nomads. We are, however, aware that members of some ethnic groups such as the Tuareg, the Cattle Fulani and Masai are nomadic cattle rearers who live in temporary settlements which they abandon as soon as local supplies of grazing and water are exhausted.

Why are some settlements closely nucleated while others are widely dispersed? Is the dispersed rural settlement a primary or secondary form of land occupation in rural areas? What are the advantages and disadvantages of each mode of habitation in the pre-industrial situation in which tropical Africa finds itself today? What is the reasoning behind recent attempts at village integration in parts of tropical Africa? These and similar questions will engage our attention in the remaining pages of this chapter.

The nucleated village is the common type of rural settlement all over tropical Africa. It is found in both forest and grassland areas and appears to provide the most suitable arrangement for the smooth operation of the traditional block-farming system, which features the periodic cultivation of different sections, or blocks, of the village territory. The emergence and survival of the nucleated village was also necessary for defence and amongst some ethnic groups, especially in the grassland environment, each large village was surrounded by thick walls of clay. In extensive swampy areas such as the Niger Delta, the shores of Lake Chad and the inland delta region of Mali, closely nucleated villages are typical on the limited areas of land not liable to seasonal flooding. The widespread occurrence of nucleated village settlements, which is also typical of many other pre-industrial societies, has tended to make people accept them as the normal and rational form of settlement in traditional Africa. At the same time the occurrence of dispersed and scattered compounds has attracted considerable attention and speculation con-

Pl. 4.3 A Masai woman outside her *manyatta* made of mud and cow-dung

cerning their origin and functioning.

Dispersed settlements have often been associated with the highly segmented or decentralized political systems found amongst the so-called stateless societies of tropical Africa. The Tonga people of Zimbabwe, who have a decentralized political system, for example, live in 'villages' which consist of compounds scattered widely over the village territory. The Tiv people of the middle Benue Valley in Nigeria also live in compounds which are scattered over the countryside, Tiv political organization is also highly decentralized. Indeed the degree of decentralization is such that, amongst the Tiv, there is no position of leadership attached to any lineage. According to Bohannan and Bohannan (1962, p. 33) 'the only Tiv group of which one could say "there must be someone responsible" is the compound which is the residential unit of the family or extended family.' We have already noted the ultra-democratic and pluralistic nature of Ibo social organization and the fact that in parts of Iboland, ownership and control of land are dispersed, just as is authority in general social affairs. It is significant that extreme dispersal of compounds is characteristic of those rural districts of Iboland where individual land holding has since displaced the traditional communal land tenure system.

The occurrence of dispersed settlements in areas where the indigenous political system is centralized is also common. The association of dispersed settlements with decentralized political systems cannot therefore be sustained. The Mossi of Upper Volta and the Wolof of Senegal live in dispersed rural settlements even though they both have a highly centralized political system. The Mossi rural landscape, for example, consists of very scattered compounds loosely connected and grouped socially rather than morphologically, into villages. Indeed in the very densely settled parts of Mossi territory it is difficult to tell where one village begins and another ends, a situation which is also replicated in the very densely settled Ibo areas of southern Onitsha and eastern Owerri Provinces. Besides there is abundant evidence to show that the primary form of rural settlement amongst the politically decentralized Ibo and Tiv was the nucleated village. The Tiv even surrounded their original nucleated settlement with clay walls and other fortifications!

Dispersed settlements have also been associated with areas which experience great pressure of population on the land. It is indeed significant that amongst all the groups mentioned above, the dispersed compounds are found in areas which are very densely populated. In the

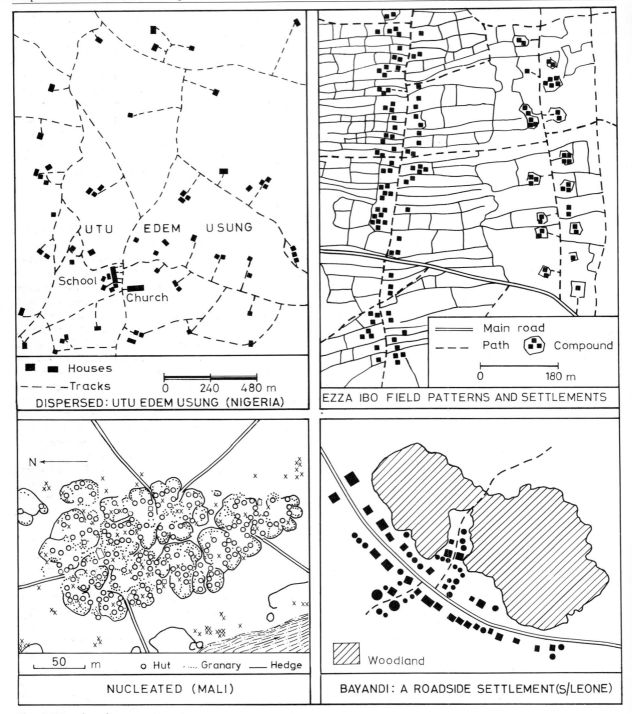

DISPERSED: UTU EDEM USUNG (NIGERIA)

UTU EDEM USUNG

School

Church

■ ■ Houses
--- Tracks
0   240   480 m

EZZA IBO FIELD PATTERNS AND SETTLEMENTS

Main road
Path   Compound
0   180 m

NUCLEATED (MALI)

N

50 m   o Hut   ..... Granary   ___ Hedge

BAYANDI: A ROADSIDE SETTLEMENT (S/LEONE)

Woodland

Fig. 4.4 Rural settlement patterns

Sudan, densely populated areas are also characterized by dispersed settlements. Available evidence suggests that in all of these areas, dispersal is a secondary form of settlement, resulting from the gradual disintegration of formerly nucleated village settlements. In these areas, the connecting link between high population density and dispersed settlements appears to be the emergence of individual land tenure. This hypothesis is supported by the fact that amongst such groups as the Ibo, the nucleated village has survived in very sparsely settled areas where land is still plentiful enough to permit the survival of the traditional communal land tenure systems. But in areas experiencing scarcity of farmland and where a measure of security is found in individual land ownership, the people have tended to move out to build on one of their farm plots (Udo, 1965). What has happened in such areas is that the inability of chiefs and elders to meet the demand for farmland has tended to weaken their authority over land and general social affairs. Amongst the Tiv, for example, it has been reported that a compound head who cannot provide adequate farmland will find himself 'sitting alone' because his dependants will desert him to establish their own compounds or migrate to other areas in search of farmland (Bohannan and Bohannan, 1962, p. 50).

The establishment of settled government all over tropical Africa during the colonial period contributed considerably to the dispersal of settlements. Among other things the need to live in large nucleated walled villages for defensive purposes no longer existed. In addition most defensive hill villages, which were usually nucleated, were relocated on more accessible sites on the nearby plains (Gleave, 1966). In many districts such as Afenmai (Nigeria), Mamfe Division (Cameroun) and Mashonaland, hill dwellers were forced to descend to the plains to facilitate the job of administering such areas. Often, the downhill migration of settlements was accompanied by an extreme dispersal of compounds as was the case in Shendam Division of Plateau State (Nigeria). Furthermore, the stabilization of village boundaries during the early colonial period and the creation of forest reserves sometimes resulted in land shortage in subsequent years and consequently accelerated the emergence of individual land tenure and the dispersal of settlements (Udo, 1966).

It is worth noting that the isolated farmstead is the typical form of rural settlement in countries with a highly developed agricultural sector such as Canada, the United States, New Zealand and Holland. The desire of people to live on or near to their farm holdings has contributed to the disintegration of village settlements in parts of tropical Africa. However, under the prevailing system in which a farmer cultivates several small, scattered holdings, the dispersal of compounds over a given village territory cannot be said to have brought the farmer nearer to his place of work. A man who has five plots, more than 1–2 km apart, and who has built his house on one of the plots, is still obliged to travel some distance to work on the remaining four plots. This undesirable situation exists because settlement dispersal in tropical Africa is largely haphazard and not part of an organized programme aimed at improving the rural economy. The economic advantages of the isolated farmstead are therefore not attainable in areas with dispersed compounds, which also suffer from the social disadvantages associated with isolation.

Village integration

During the first decade of the twentieth century, the German colonial administration of Cameroun is reported to have forced the Banyang people of Mamfe Division to abandon their former scattered bush settlements and to rebuild in large compact groups along the main roads built by the government (Ruel, 1962, p. 100). This was an example of settlement integration which in this case involved not only a forced assembly of dispersed compounds but also an order preventing future dispersal. In Zambia, government desire to keep the villages nucleated and prevent further dispersal, especially amongst the Tonga and in the Fort Rosebery district, was embodied in the 'hailing distance rule' of 1905. According to this rule, all buildings in a village were to be erected within hailing distance of the headman's hut or within an area of one square mile (Allan, et al., 1948; Kay, 1964).

A variant form of village integration which occurred during the colonial period featured the amalgamation of villages, the aim of which was to reduce the number of existing villages and to prevent further fission. In parts of Zambia, for example, the colonial administration in 1905 considered the number of villages and chiefs to be too numerous for administrative convenience. A regulation halting the fission of villages was made and Tonga villages with less than ten tax-payers were forced to move and amalgamate with neighbouring villages. In the Fort Rosebery district a new village could be formed only if a person 'suitable to be a headman collects fifteen able-bodied males whose removal from other villages will not deplete such villages unduly' (Kay, 1964). Village amalgamation was, however, more difficult to accomplish in comparison with the integration of dispersed compounds since the former involved a reduction in the number of chiefs.

The case against dispersed compounds and endless fission of villages during the early colonial period was that it made tax collection more difficult, particularly in areas poorly served by roads. Security became a major consideration in some areas during the 1950s and today, village integration is being encouraged in order to create favourable conditions for providing basic social services to rural populations. Village integration in Kenya during the Mau Mau emergency, which was declared in 1952, was aimed at protecting the rural people from Mau Mau terrorists and also at making it difficult for Mau Mau guerrillas to operate successfully in rural areas. In various parts of Zambia, Zaïre and Nigeria many small villages have been amalgamated to form larger settlements as part of programmes aimed at controlling and eradicating the incidence of sleeping sickness. The more recent cases of village integration, such as those in Abakaliki Division of Nigeria have been prompted by the desire to ensure greater social security and to provide a threshold population to support basic social services such as schools, rural electrification, rural water supplies, postal agencies and rural clinics.

References

Allan, W., Gluckman, Max, Peters, D. U. and Trapnell, C. G. (1948), *Land Holding and Land Usage among the Plateau Tonga of Mazabuka District (A Reconnaissance survey)*, The Rhodes-Livingstone Papers, no. 14, Lusaka.

Bailey, N. A. (1969), 'Native and Labour Policy', in D. M. Abshire and M. A. Samuels (eds.), *Portuguese Africa — A Handbook*, Pall Mall Press, London; Praeger, New York, p. 166.

Bohannan, L. and Bohannan, P. ... *Central Nigeria*, International African In...

Bridges, A. F. B. (1939), 'Report ... the Ibo, Ibibio and Cross River Areas', ...

Gleave, M. B. (1966), 'Hill S... Abandon-ment in Tropical Africa', *Tran... of British Geographers*, no. 40, pp. 39–...

Green, M. M. (1941), *Land ... e*, Mono-graphs on Social Anthrop... chool of Economics and Political Sci...

Jones, G. I. (1949), 'Ibo Lan... l of the International African Instit...

Kay, G. (1964), 'Aspects of Ushi Settlement History: Fort Rosebery District, Northern Rhodesia', in R. W. Steel and R. M. Prothero (eds.), *Geographers and the Tropics: Liverpool Essays*, Longman, London, pp. 235–60.

Ruel, M. J. (1962), 'Banyang Settlement: Part I, Pre-European Settlement', *Man*, 62, p. 100.

Thompson, V. and Adloff, R. (1958), *French West Africa*, George Allen & Unwin, London, p. 345.

Udo, R. K. (1965), 'Disintegration of Nucleated Settlement in Eastern Nigeria', *Geographical Review*, 55, pp. 53–67.

Udo, R. K. (1966), 'Transformation of Rural Settlements in British Tropical Africa', *Nigerian Geographical Journal*, 9, no. 2, pp. 129–44.

5 Population: Size, Distribution and Trends

Introduction

One of the major problems of development planning in tropical Africa today is the lack of reliable population data for most countries. At independence, most countries had not taken a complete count of their population and therefore had to depend on estimates, which were usually based on the number of tax-payers. Indeed as late as 1971 only sixteen countries out of the forty-one member states of the United Nations Economic Commission for Africa (ECA) had conducted at least one census enumeration. But even for these few countries the range of topics covered during the census was too limited to permit a meaningful analysis of the characteristics of their populations. The situation in the early 1980s is slightly better, following the setting up in 1971 of the African Census Programme (ACP) by the ECA Population Division which has since organized and supervised census enumerations in many countries. However, much of the data so far collected is still to be fully analysed and in a few countries, including Nigeria and the Central African Republic, political considerations have made it difficult to obtain any reliable population figures. Statements made about the characteristics of the population of tropical Africa are therefore based largely on estimates. The inability of some governments to plan effectively for such programmes as universal primary education or health services must also be understood against this background.

It is an established fact that Africa is the least populated continent, excepting Oceania. However, since the beginning of the twentieth century, the population of Africa has increased greatly, thanks to the widespread adoption of modern medicine, which has resulted in a marked decline in infant mortality and a significant increase in life expectancy. Furthermore, the destructive effects of famine have been largely eliminated through increased food production and the ready transportation of relief materials to victims of natural disasters and occasional civil wars. Slave raids and regular inter-group warfare, both of which occasioned considerable loss of life, have since stopped, while improved sanitation and preventive medicine have reduced the incidence of epidemics. The result is a marked drop in death rate which, together with the relatively high birth rate, has produced the current high average annual growth rate of about 2·7 per cent, a rate which is only exceeded by those of Latin America (2·9 per cent) and South Asia (2·8 per cent).

The size of the population

In 1970, the population of Africa was estimated to be 352 million as compared with 219 million in 1950. The 1970 figure represented 9·5 per cent of the world population while that of 1950 represented 8·7 per cent. The relative size of the population of Africa is therefore increasing to such an extent that, as shown in Table 5.1, Africa now has 10·5 per cent of the world population, while the estimated population of 614 millions for 1990 is more than the comparable figure for Europe (514 millions). Africa's share of the land surface of the earth is, however, much greater, its 30·2 million sq km constituting 22 per cent of the total. The two sets of figures suggest that Africa is comparatively sparsely populated. Its average density of 11·6 persons per sq km in 1970 was much less than the world average of 25. There are, however, great variations in the population densities of the various sub-regions of Africa, and indeed within different parts of each country (see Table 5.3, p. 61).

We are specifically concerned with tropical Africa which, according to Table 5.1, had a population of 338 millions in 1980, that is about 73·4 per cent of the population of Africa. Table 5.1 also shows that more than 70 per cent of the population of tropical Africa live in West and East Africa which together have about 53 per cent of the land area of tropical Africa. Notice also that about 51 per cent of the population of Africa lives in West and East Africa, that is, on 41 per cent of the land area of the continent. It is also significant that although Central Africa has a much larger area than West Africa, its population of 66 million is only half of the population of West Africa (see Table 5.2, p. 60).

The population of each country is presented in Table 5.3, which also shows the land area and the population

Table 5.1 Estimated population size (thousands) and rate of growth for tropical Africa and world regions (1950–90)

Sub-region	1950	1960	1970	1980	1985	1990	Growth rate 1975
Western Africa	64,533	79,884	101,496	132,483	152,994	177,323	2·75
Eastern Africa	48,206	60,801	78,988	105,139	121,999	141,778	2·84
Central Africa	33,355	40,643	51,770	66,228	75,834	87,071	2·44
Southern tropical Africa	16,228	20,069	26,217	34,595	40,125	46,726	2·89
TOTAL tropical Africa	162,322	201,397	258,471	338,445	390,952	452,904	11·12
Africa	218,803	272,795	351,727	460,915	531,701	614,085	2·77
Latin America	163,925	215,577	283,020	371,631	425,635	485,585	2·74
North America	166,073	198,662	226,389	248,833	262,344	275,136	0·99
East Asia	674,821	787,980	926,866	1,087,749	1,164,848	1,233,498	1·56
South Asia	692,916	855,711	1,101,199	1,426,843	1,624,722	1,836,258	2·65
Europe	391,968	425,154	459,085	486,541	499,972	513,605	0·56
Oceania	12,632	15,771	19,323	23,482	25,777	28,109	1·94
USSR	180,075	214,329	242,768	268,115	281,540	293,742	1·00
WORLD TOTAL	2,501,213	2,985,979	3,610,377	4,374,109	4,816,537	5,280,017	1·95

Note The sub-regions of Africa are as defined in the introduction of this volume.

Source United Nations (1977), *World Population Prospects as Assessed in 1973*, New York.

Table 5.2 Area and population of sub-regions of tropical Africa in 1980

Sub-region	Area ('000 sq km)	% of area of Africa	Population ('000)	% population of tropical Africa	% population of Africa
West Africa	6,142	20·32	132,483	39·1	28·7
East Africa	6,135·4	20·28	105,139	31·1	22·8
Central Africa	7,420	24·53	66,228	19·6	14·4
Southern tropical Africa	3,303	10·92	34,595	10·2	7·5
TOTAL tropical Africa	23,000·4	75·85	338,445	100·0	73·4
North Africa	6,026	19·87	91,635	—	19·9
South Africa	1,221	4·03	28,533	—	6·2
Other African countries	72·6	0·25	2,176	—	0·5
TOTAL Africa	30,320	100·00	460,915	—	100·0

Source United Nations (1977), *World Population Prospects as Assessed in 1973*, New York.

Table 5.3   Area, estimated population (1980), population densities and annual growth rates of tropical African countries

Sub-region and country	Area ('000 sq km)	Population ('000)	Density	Persons per sq km of arable land	Annual growth rate (1975–80)
WEST AFRICA	6,142	132,483	21·6	146	2·66
Benin	113	3,534	31·3	153	2·57
Cape Verde Is.	4	323	81·0	600	1·50
Gambia	11	563	51·2	172	1·77
Ghana	239	11,446	48·0	300	2·85
Guinea	246	5,014	20·4	—	2·42
Guinea-Bissau	36	573	16·0	202	1·56
Ivory Coast	322	5,579	17·3	46	2·54
Liberia	111	1,937	17·5	28	2·39
Mali	1,240	6,470	5·2	44	2·34
Mauritania	1,031	1,427	1·4	399	1·93
Niger	1,267	5,272	4·2	31	2·57
Nigeria	924	72,596	78·6	268	2·82
Senegal	196	4,989	25·5	71	2·20
Sierra Leone	72	3,392	47·1	64	2·45
Togo	56	2,596	46·4	176	2·78
Upper Volta	274	6,774	24·7	100	2·13
EAST AFRICA	6,135·4	105,139	17·1	183	2·74
Ethiopia	1,222	31,522	25·8	186	2·24
Kenya	583	15,688	26·9	561	3·29
Mauritius	2	969	484·5	820	1·13
Réunion	3	548	182·7	726	1·68
Seychelles	0·4	66	165·0	294	2·00
Somali Republic	638	3,652	5·7	261	2·79
Sudan	2,506	21,420	8·5	209	3·02
Tanzania	945	18,052	19·1	102	3·04
Uganda	236	13,222	56·0	163	2·92
CENTRAL AFRICA	7,420	66,228	8·9	46	2·40
Angola	1,247	7,181	5·8	573	2·41
Burundi	28	4,288	153·1	300	2·48
Cameroun	475	7,088	15·0	79	2·01
Central African Republic	623	2,004	3·2	25	2·08
Chad	1,284	4,473	3·5	51	2·05
Congo Republic	342	1,532	4·7	133	2·56
Equatorial Guinea	28	339	12·1	121	1·67
Gabon	265	546	2·0	365	0·69
Rwanda	26	4,865	187·1	509	2·83
Sao Tome & Principe	0·96	85	88·5	200	0·51
Zaïre	2,345	27,952	11·9	217	2·61
Zambia	753	5,875	7·8	77	3·10
SOUTHERN TROPICAL AFRICA	3,303	34,595	10·5	194	2·77
Botswana	600	795	1·3	150	2·67
Madagascar	587	9,329	15·9	236	2·99
Malawi	118	5,577	47·3	132	2·39
Mozambique	783	10,375	13·3	263	2·29
Namibia	824	1,024	1·2	89	2·88
Zimbabwe	391	7,495	19·2	232	3·47
TOTAL tropical Africa	23,000·4	338,445	14·7	—	2·64
TOTAL Africa	30,320	460,915	15·2	134	2·67

Note Figures based on calculations using population figures for the 1960 round of censuses.

Sources 1. United Nations (1977), *World Population Prospects as Assessed in 1973*, New York, pp. 90–1 (T. 28), 102–3 (T. 31).
2. United Nations: Economic Commission for Africa (1975), *Demographic Handbook for Africa*, Addis Ababa, pp. 17–19 (T. 4).

density for each country. Note the large size of the population of Nigeria. About 21 per cent of the people in tropical Africa live in Nigeria which has only 4 per cent of the land area of the region. The other large countries with populations of over 20 million are Ethiopia, Sudan and Zaïre. Medium-sized countries with populations of over 10 millions are Ghana, Tanzania, Kenya and Uganda. About ten countries have populations of less than one million each.

Spatial distribution of the population

We know from Table 5.3 that the average population density for East Africa is 17 persons per sq km as compared with only 9 for Central Africa; and that the average densities for Ghana, Kenya and Rwanda are respectively 48, 27 and 187 persons per sq km. But such figures do not tell us much about the great pressure of population on land in various parts of tropical Africa. We therefore propose to discuss the spatial distribution of population by examining the pattern presented in Fig. 5.1 which is based on the 1960 round of censuses. The map shows clearly that by far the greater part of tropical Africa has a population density of less than 10 persons per sq km, which is less than the average for the continent. Vast areas in the Middle Belt and far north of West Africa, Zaïre, Botswana and Tanzania are

Fig. 5.1 Population density

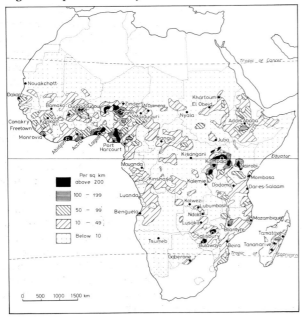

virtually uninhabited while pockets of very high population densities, often exceeding 200 persons per sq km, occur in parts of Nigeria, the Mossi district of Upper Volta, the shores of Lake Victoria, southern Malawi and in Rwanda and Burundi. In order to examine more closely the man–land relationship in the predominantly agricultural-based economies of tropical Africa, we propose to present a more detailed description of the population distribution by recognizing four rural population density zones. These are: 1. very densely settled (usually overfarmed) areas, 2. heavily farmed medium density areas, 3. low density areas, 4. very sparsely populated and virtually uninhabited areas.

Very densely settled areas

In a continent which is so sparsely populated, it is intriguing to find pockets of very high population density such as those already listed for West and East Africa. In the central Ibo districts of Awka, Onitsha and eastern Owerri, as well as in the Annang–Ibibio districts of Abak and Ikot Ekpene (all in Nigeria), the population densities exceed 400 persons per sq km (1,000 per sq mile). These districts are amongst the most densely populated rural areas in the world and are certainly overpopulated in view of the great pressure on available farmland. Other rural areas with very high population densities – exceeding 200 persons per sq km (500 per sq mile) – include the Kano close-settled district, the Sokoto home districts, the Bolgatanga district of north-eastern Ghana, parts of Rwanda and Burundi, and parts of the lake shores of Lake Victoria.

All areas with very high rural population densities experience acute shortage of farmland. Fallow periods rarely exceed three years and in some extreme cases permanent cultivation has become the rule. Farm sizes are very small, rarely exceeding two hectares, consisting of two to five plots which are scattered all over the village territory. Overcultivation in such areas has resulted in soil impoverishment, soil erosion and poor crop yields. It is not surprising therefore that these densely populated areas have become major food deficit areas as well as major source regions for migrant labour in tropical Africa. One curious fact about these areas is that they often exist in close proximity to very sparsely populated districts with abundant farmland.

Medium density areas

Rural areas having population densities of between 100 and 200 persons per sq km (250 and 500 per sq mile) constitute the medium density areas. In West Africa such areas occur along the coastal areas of industrial crop cultivation on peasant farms and in the mining districts. Examples of such areas include the groundnut belt of western Senegal, the Yoruba cocoa belt, southern

Tivland and southern Togo. In East Africa, western Buganda, central Malawi and the Kilimanjaro districts are amongst the heavily farmed medium density areas.

Large-scale deforestation is characteristic of medium density areas, all of which experience regular clearing and firing of bush for farming purposes. Farmland for food-crop production has become generally inadequate in such areas, largely as a result of the emphasis on industrial crop production, notably cocoa, rubber, coffee and cotton. However, the production of these crops has created considerable employment for migrant agricultural workers originating mostly from the very densely populated or congested rural districts.

Low density areas

A very large part of tropical Africa consists of sparsely populated areas with population densities of 10–100 persons per sq km (about 25–250 per sq mile). As a rule, lower population densities of less than 40 persons per sq km (100 per sq mile) are more typical of these low density districts. Farmland is abundant in such areas and fallow periods of over seven years are common. The coastal countries of Liberia, the Ivory Coast, Gabon and Mozambique are amongst the sparsely settled areas with abundant rainfall and fertile farmlands still awaiting development. In the drier savanna areas of West Africa, Central Africa and the East African plateau, the sparsely settled areas are usually infested by tsetse flies.

Although the people who live in these sparsely populated districts have abundant farmland, they are hardly better off materially than people living in the land-hungry congested rural areas. The development of such areas is usually less than that of the very densely populated districts, largely because most sparsely settled areas are isolated from the major centres of population and intensive economic activity. It is this relative stagnation that has tended to push the young and daring individuals to emigrate from some sparsely settled areas, including those with well-watered fertile farmland. However in recent years an increasing number of migrant farmers have been attracted to settle in some of the more accessible sparsely populated districts.

Very sparsely settled areas

The extreme unevenness in the distribution of population in tropical Africa is obvious from the fact that less than 5 per cent of the total population live in the very sparsely populated areas which cover more than two-thirds of the land area of the region. All districts having less than 10 persons per sq km (25 per sq mile) are considered to be very sparsely populated, but within such districts it is common to find virtually uninhabited areas with less than 4 persons per sq km.

Examples of such districts include the semi-arid regions of West Africa and the eastern Sudan, the dry Gonja district of northern Ghana, the Kalahari grasslands of Botswana and Namibia and the semi-arid areas of the Karamoja district of Uganda. Other extensive areas with sparse population include the dense forest region of Zaïre, the Niger Delta, the arid lands of the Somali Republic and the seasonally flooded Great Muri Plains of the Benue Valley.

Large parts of the very sparsely settled areas are in fact uninhabited. However, the lands officially recognized as uninhabited are the forests and game reserves as well as the desert lands of West Africa, the Sudan and the Somali Republic. By law, settlement and farming are prohibited in forests and game reserves except for forest guards and game reserve attendants. Cultivation and grazing are impossible in the deserts, hence the total absence of people, except in the few oases.

Factors influencing the distribution of population

Buchanan and Pugh (1955) described the pattern of population distribution in Nigeria in 1953 as immature, arguing that 'the close adjustment of densities to environmental conditions, which is typical of long settled areas' was lacking and that the process of land occupation and settlement was incomplete over much of the country. The point in referring to this statement is that it applies to all parts of tropical Africa. It will, however, be wrong to infer that the physical conditions of the environment are not important in influencing the distribution of population. The physical environment, along with historical, political and economic factors, is very important in explaining the contemporary spatial pattern of population distribution in tropical Africa.

Physical conditions

Aridity is the single most important environmental factor making vast areas of tropical Africa unsuitable for human settlement. Since irrigation is not yet common, cropping is usually restricted to areas with not less than 750 mm of rain per annum. All densely populated areas receive more than 750 mm of rain per annum although there are sparsely settled districts in areas such as central Zaïre, the Niger Delta and parts of Liberia which receive over 2,000 mm of rain per year. The influence of rainfall on the distribution of population is particularly noticeable in Kenya where the 750 mm isohyte provides a sudden divide between densely settled areas in the west and virtually uninhabited districts in the east.

Pl. 5.1 Soil erosion in Botswana

The influence of soil quality is less obvious. Indeed, one of the curious facts about the distribution of population in tropical Africa is the large concentration of people in the soil-impoverished districts of the eastern states of Nigeria. However, the high rural population densities in the Kikuyuland of Kenya and in Rwanda and Burundi are found in areas of deeply weathered fertile volcanic soils, which also receive adequate rainfall. Soil conditions have also contributed to the sparse population in the Accra Plains and the Niger Delta.

The menace of the tsetse fly, which spreads *trypano-somiasis* among cattle and human beings, is probably next to aridity in importance. Its effect is most noticeable in Tanzania where 60 per cent of the country is infested and where the worst affected areas of the western and southern provinces have population densities of less than 2 persons per sq km, even in areas where the rainfall is adequate for arable farming (Blacker, 1962). Vast areas of Zaïre, West Africa, Gabon and Zambia are also heavily infested by the tsetse fly which is thought to have contributed to the de-

population of some rural areas (Fitzgerald, 1957; Harrison Church, 1957). Indeed, government pro-grammes aimed at eradicating the tsetse fly in northern Nigeria and Zambia have resulted in further de-population of some districts through the destruction of infested villages, the inhabitants of which were re-quired to move to other settlements, usually located far away from the stream valleys which provide breeding grounds for the fly (Nash, 1948; Kay, 1964).

River blindness, although more localized compared with sleeping sickness, has been responsible for the depopulation of considerable areas in the savanna belt extending from Senegal to Uganda. In northern Ghana and Upper Volta, for example, the high incidence of river blindness has resulted in the complete de-population of the valleys of the Red and White Volta Rivers (Hunter, 1966). Rugged terrain in the region of the Cameroun–Adamawa Highlands, Ethiopia and East Africa have also proved an impediment to human settlement, thereby creating areas of low population density.

Historical factors

Decreasing population during the period of the slave trade and during inter-tribal warfare of the pre-colonial period has been an important factor in the depopulation of parts of Angola, Mozambique, Gabon and the Middle Belt of West Africa. On the whole, about 10 to 15 million Africans were landed as slaves in the New World, excluding the large number that died during the slave wars, during the long trek to the ports of export and in the slave ships. Eyewitness accounts of the destruction occasioned by Fulani raids in northern Yorubaland and in the Kontagora Province of Nigeria have been left behind in the journals of early European explorers such as Richard Lander and Hugh Clapperton (Clapperton, 1829). Mason's article on population density and slave raiding in the Middle Belt of Nigeria (Mason, 1969) also gives a comprehensive review of the evidence relating to the depopulation of this part of tropical Africa. Basil Davidson has suggested that the number of people exported from Angola to the New World as slaves was probably much larger than the 4·8 million people recorded as Angola's population in 1960 (Davidson, 1961).

The pre-colonial period of general insecurity and slave raids also resulted in the concentration of population in some areas, notably the Kano close-settled zone, the Jos Plateau and parts of Rwanda and Burundi. Indeed, wherever powerful rulers, such as the Emir of Kano or the paramount ruler of the Mossi of Upper Volta, were able to provide security and settled government, a large number of people usually flocked in to settle such areas, thereby giving rise to unusually high population densities which have survived to this day. Defensible hill sites in the West African Middle Belt, the Adamawa Highlands and the central highlands of Zimbabwe also provided important localized centres which attracted refugees from the nearby plains.

Political factors

Racial segregation in High Africa, notably in Zimbabwe and pre-independent Kenya, and the creation of forests and game reserves, are the two major political policy-decisions that have influenced the spatial distribution of population in tropical Africa. In Zimbabwe, where the minority European settler population pursued a racist policy of segregation similar to that in Apartheid South Africa, about 40 per cent of the land was set aside for the white minority population of only 240,000 people, or about 4·5 per cent of the total population of 5,310,000. The fact that about 70 per cent of the white settler population live in cities while most of the 5,050,000 Africans live in rural areas (mostly in the so-called Native Reserves) further goes to show that the White Settler Reserves are very sparsely populated in comparison with the rather crowded Native Reserves

Pl. 5.2 Demarcation of the Ovambo 'native reserve', Namibia

(Roder, 1964). It is significant that 28 per cent of white settler land is located in well-watered areas receiving not less than 700 mm of rain while only 11 per cent of the land allocated to Africans is found in such areas. The result is that the Native Reserves are not only congested but also suffer from acute shortage of good farmland. Many African adult males are therefore obliged to migrate to work for wages on white settler farms and in the mines.

Before the Mau Mau uprising of 1952–6, the position in Kenya was similar to that of Zimbabwe. The so-called White Highlands of Kenya, measuring about 31,000 sq km (12,000 sq miles) were occupied by only 12,000 Europeans and about 150,000 African squatters, and therefore had a population density of only 5·2 persons per sq km, compared with an overall average of over 230 persons per sq km in Kikuyuland. Indeed some localities in the African Reserves of Kikuyuland supported as many as 400 persons per sq km. It is not surprising therefore that most of the squatters in the

White Highlands were Kikuyu, who originally owned the land given to white settlers and who were forced to migrate from their Native Reserves because of acute shortage of farmland. The White Highlands have since been reallocated to African farmers following the establishment of African majority rule in Kenya in 1963. Grove (1970) has argued that the new situation in the former White Highlands may result in a marked decline in the quantity of surplus crops for export and that if the Africans who have replaced the white settlers adopt the same farming techniques as they do in the Native Reserves, the Highlands will support fewer Africans than was the case in the days when Africans worked as farm labourers on European-owned farms. We agree that total output of surplus crops may fall but reject as illogical the suggestion that the Highlands will support fewer Africans today than in the colonial period. Certainly if the former Kikuyu Reserves supported over 230 persons per sq km, how can the former White Highlands support less than 150,000 Africans for no other reason than that they are using the same farming methods as in the former Native Reserves?

As a political policy-decision, the creation of forest and game reserves in most countries resulted in restricting the area of land available to some ethnic groups in much the same way as the alienation of land to white settlers did in Kenya and Zimbabwe. Although the areas set aside as forest and game reserves were relatively small, varying from only 1·5 per cent of the land area in Nigeria to about 8·0 per cent in Tanzania and Mozambique, the reserves did deprive some ethnic groups of much of their farmland. In some countries the vast uninhabited reserve areas may exist side by side with a densely populated area in which the people are short of adequate farmland. Hence the repeated requests in parts of Nigeria that government should de-reserve parts of the forest to enable the expansion of tree-crop cultivation.

Economic factors

Since the end of the Second World War, economic factors have become increasingly dominant in influencing the distribution and redistribution of population in tropical Africa. Outside the main urban centres, the major areas of population concentration are the rural districts, which produce minerals for export, and the areas of intensive cultivation of industrial crops. Most of these 'economic islands' of development date from the early colonial period and since independence have tended to grow at the expense of other rural areas. They include the Zambian copper belt, the Jos Plateau tin fields, the Nigerian cocoa belt and the Senegal groundnut belt.

In West Africa, the major centres of economic growth are located within 200 km of the coast, with the exception of the Kano groundnut belt and the Jos tin fields. Opportunities for employment in industry and agriculture are therefore greater along the coast, where most of the capital cities and major sea ports are located, hence the continuing process of migration from the interior to the coastal belt. The situation in East, Central and southern Africa is slightly different since the major economic islands, such as the Kenya Highlands, the Katanga–Zambian copper belt, the Uganda cotton belt and the central highlands of Zimbabwe are all located at great distances from the coast.

Pressure of population on the land in the older densely settled districts has resulted in increasingly poor returns from traditional agriculture. Large-scale emigration from such areas, notably the Mossi district of Upper Volta, central Iboland in Nigeria, Rwanda–Burundi and southern Malawi, has brought about a considerable redistribution of population from these economically stagnant rural areas to the more rapidly growing economic islands. In addition, most migrants to the urban centres of tropical Africa originate from these land-hungry rural areas.

Population trends, policies and problems

Although Africa is the least populated continent, the rate of growth of its population at 2·7 per cent per annum is comparatively high being exceeded only by Latin America (2·9 per cent) and Asia (2·8 per cent). The comparative growth rates for Europe, Asia and North America are 0·8 per cent, 2·0 per cent and 1·4 per cent per annum respectively, while the world average rate of growth is 1·9 per cent per annum. At the present rate of growth, by AD 2000 the population of Africa will be about 813·7 million which is more than double the figure for 1975 (401·3 million). It will therefore be much greater than the estimated European population of 539·5 million (UN, 1973). This might appear at first sight to be a welcome development in view of the fact that vast areas of Africa are sparsely populated and also because it will help to offset the great loss of population which occurred during the slave trade. However, such a rapid rate of growth poses serious problems to governments which are struggling under difficult financial constraints to provide basic social services to their people. The growing demand for schools and hospital facilities and the increasing migration to the cities are causes of great concern to most governments in tropical Africa. How do government policies reflect the population situation? The population policy of any government will of course reflect a perception of the problem in its area of jurisdiction, and consequently there is a close relationship between population growth (or trends), perceived population problems and population policies.

The demographic transition theory

The demographic transition theory is an idealized sequence of changes over time in the birth and death rates, and therefore in the overall population trends of west European countries as they experienced the industrial revolution. The theory states that population changes occur as society moves from a predominantly agricultural to a predominantly industrial way of life. The demographic transition is divided into four main phases:

1. The high-stationary phase or the pre-industrial stage, which is characterized by a high and relatively stable birth rate and a high but fluctuating death rate. The greater variations in death rate are attributed to famines, epidemics and wars. The resultant total population is low and fluctuating.

2. The early-expanding phase or stage 2, which is characterized by a continuing high birth rate but a rapid fall in death rate. During this phase life expectancy increases and there is a marked increase in the population. This is the stage of early industrialization with the resultant improvements in nutrition, sanitation and medical services. It is also a stage of stable government (colonial period in tropical Africa) in which civil wars no longer occur.

3. The late-expanding phase or stage 3 when the rate of expansion of the population slows down as a result of the reduction in birth rate and the stabilization of death rate which is already low. This is the period of modernization associated with an urban-industrial society, characterized by the emergence of the nuclear family in place of the extended family and the wide adoption of birth control.

4. The low stationary phase or stage 4, representing a period in which the birth and death rate are stabilized at a low level, results in a stationary population. During this phase, the death rate is stable while the birth rate has a tendency to fluctuate (see Fig. 5.2).

According to the principles of the transition theory, the changes noted above will occur first in urban areas and amongst the upper socio-economic classes before being extended to rural areas and the lower social classes. Demographic transition is also characterized by rapid urbanization of the population.

Demographic transition in tropical Africa

How does the demographic situation in tropical Africa fit into this scheme? The vital rates for selected countries as presented in Table 5.3 suggest that contemporary population trends in tropical Africa fit into the second or early expanding phase. Although the level of industrialization is still low, tropical Africa has

Fig. 5.2 The demographic transition model

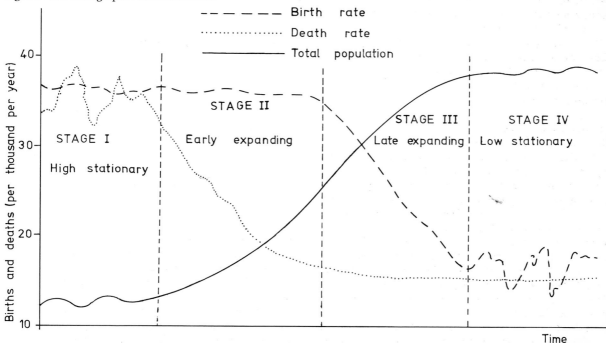

benefited considerably from medical technology developed in Europe and North America. In consequence, the death rate has fallen considerably especially as regards infant mortality, while the birth rate remains high, largely because of cultural considerations. The indications are that up to the end of this century, the death rate will continue to decline while the fall in birth rate will be relatively insignificant. At the same time, life expectation has continued to rise for all parts of tropical Africa.

The forces that brought about the late expanding phase and the low-stationary phase in west European countries – 1. the emergence of large urban centres, 2. the emergence of the nuclear family in place of the extended family of traditional societies, 3. the appearance of alternatives to early marriage and childbearing as a means of livelihood and prestige for women and 4. the weakening of community customs and taboos, moral codes and growing indifference towards religion – are already in operation all over tropical Africa. The proportion of the population affected by these forces is, however, still very small. A decline in the birth rate will only come about with a greater degree of urbanization and a rise in the number of educated people practising birth control methods. The current pace of economic development in tropical Africa suggests that it is unlikely to experience the last two stages of demographic transition in the foreseeable future.

Population problems as perceived by African governments

The main problem concerning world population is that it is increasing at a faster rate than food and other production. In developing countries as a whole, production is not increasing sufficiently fast to raise living standards. Today, there is a food problem in almost all countries of tropical Africa, most of which experience acute shortages of food at certain periods of the year. The food import bills for countries such as Senegal, the Ivory Coast, Zaïre and Nigeria are a major drain on the foreign exchange reserves of these countries. In most countries, traditional agriculture, characterized by low per capita output, still predominates. A near stagnant food production sector combined with a largely parasitic type of industrialization creates considerable economic and social problems in the face of a rapidly increasing population.

Yet most governments in tropical Africa do not consider the rapid rate of population growth to constitute a problem to economic development, apparently because of the sparse population of most rural areas. The argument of most state governments and academics in Nigeria, as in most other countries, is that the country possesses a large land area and vast natural resources which, when properly exploited, will create a viable economy capable of ensuring a steady rise in the standard of living. In consequence most governments are concerned with accelerating the rate of growth of their national economy rather than with measures to reduce the rate of population growth. Such governments appear to accept the view that social and economic growth will help to accentuate the forces that will lower the birth rate in the long run. Indeed some governments consider their total population to be too small and therefore wish to see an increase, even though they are currently facing serious food shortages. A rapidly growing population, it is argued, will provide the much needed manpower for such labour-deficit countries as the Ivory Coast, Gabon and Liberia, as well as the necessary market for sustaining large-scale industrialization. A few countries, such as Kenya, Ghana and Mauritius, however, consider the rapid rise in their population as a major obstacle to efforts aimed at raising living standards.

Although most governments in tropical Africa are not disturbed by the rapid increase in their total population, they are concerned about various aspects of the population problem. Specifically, most governments are disturbed about:

1. the rapid rate of urbanization and the related problems of increasing urban unemployment, urban housing congestion, and rural labour shortage;
2. the uneven distribution of population and resources over different parts of a given country;
3. the high dependency ratio created by rapid increase in population, and the resultant restriction on capital for investment;
4. inability of food production to keep pace with population growth and
5. the high incidence of poverty, malnutrition and illiteracy.

These problems have been referred to in various parts of this book and the reader is invited to give more thought to each set of problems with a view to examining why governments are concerned about them and how best these problems can be tackled.

Population policies and programmes

Government decisions and measures which deliberately seek to change the size, growth rate, composition and spatial distribution of the population of any country constitute a population policy. In tropical Africa only four countries, Ghana, Botswana, Kenya and Mauritius, have so far adopted policies and programmes explicitly intended to decrease the rate of population growth. Other countries have been rather cautious about making statements on population issues, especially that of human fertility which for political and religious reasons appears too delicate a matter amongst some groups. Indeed some of these countries have come to identify population policy with family planning which they erroneously associate with a reduction in fertility.

The development plans of tropical African countries, including those with no explicit national population policy, contain some policy statements on population. Most countries recognize very few or no problems in their development plans and a few, including Ethiopia and Gabon, declare directly or indirectly a desire for bigger populations for reasons of providing adequate labour and ready markets for industrial products. Many countries, including Nigeria, Sudan, Uganda and Gambia, support family planning activities for reasons of maternal health and family welfare. In a country like Tanzania, for example, where the influence of the Muslim faith and of the Catholic Church is still strong and where the government feels that there is adequate land for more people, family planning is unacceptable to the government who sees it as a measure for population control. Child spacing is considered acceptable and is implemented through the maternal and child health programme of the Ministry of Health. Other countries which do not support family planning are Sierra Leone, the Ivory Coast, Zambia, Cameroun and even the small and already very densely populated Rwanda.

References

Blacker, J. G. C. (1962), 'The Demography of East Africa', in E. W. Russell (ed.), *The Natural Resources of East Africa*, East African Literature Bureau, Nairobi, p. 23.

Brass, W. I. *et al.* (1968), *The Demography of Tropical Africa*, Princeton University Press, Princeton, p. 38.

Buchanan, K. M. and Pugh, J. C. (1955), *Land and People in Nigeria*, University of London Press, London.

Clapperton, H. (1829), *Journal of a Second Expedition into the Interior of Africa*, John Murray, London, p. 33.

Davidson, B. (1961), *The African Slave Trade*, Little, Brown and Co, Boston, p. 160.

Fitzgerald, W. (1957), *Africa: A Social, Economic and Political Geography of Its Major Regions*, Methuen & Co, London, p. 303.

Grove, A. T. (1970, 2nd ed.), *Africa South of the Sahara*, Oxford University Press, Oxford, p. 188.

Harrison Church, R. J. (1957, 1st ed.), *West Africa: A Study of the Environment and of Man's Use of It*, Longman, London, p. 164.

Hunter, J. M. (1966), 'River Blindness in Nangodi, Northern Ghana', *Geographical Review*, 56, pp. 398–416.

Kay, G. (1964), 'Aspects of Ushi Settlement History: Fort Rosebery District, Northern Rhodesia' in R. W. Steel and R. M. Prothero (eds.), *Geographers and the Tropics: Liverpool Essays*, Longman, London, pp. 235–60.

Mason, M. (1969), 'Population Density and "Slave Raiding" – the Case of the Middle Belt of Nigeria', *Journal of African History*, 10, pp. 551–64.

Nash, T. A. M. (1948), *Anchau Rural Development and Settlement Scheme*, HMSO, London.

Roder, W. (1964), 'The Division of Land Resources in Southern Rhodesia', *Annals of the Association of American Geographers*, 54, pp. 41–58.

UNESCO (1970), *Statistical Yearbook 1969*, Paris.

United Nations (1973), *World Population Prospects as Assessed in 1973*, New York.

6 Population: Characteristics

The characteristics of human population fall into two broad categories, biological and cultural. Biological characteristics, also sometimes described as 'assigned' because the individual has little or no choice in acquiring them, include race, ethnicity, the demographic characteristics of fertility and mortality, and sex and age. The cultural or achieved characteristics are those that are subject to individual choice and alteration. They include education, marital status, occupation and rural–urban residence.

Biological characteristics

Racial composition

The native and predominant peoples of tropical Africa belong to the negroid racial group. Negroes are characterized by black or dark-brown skins, black woolly hair, broad noses and thick lips. The peoples of

Fig. 6.1 The races of Africa

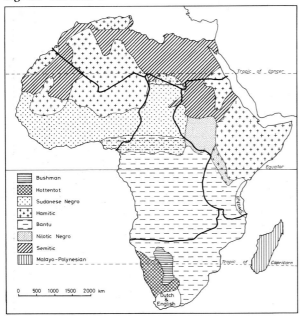

Ethiopia, the Somali Republic and some Arabs are also black although they are all classified as belonging to the Caucasoid racial group. The true or Sudanese Negroes, who live in West Africa, are usually distinguished from the Bantu Negroes of East, Central and southern Africa. The Yoruba of Nigeria, the Fanti of Ghana and the Wolof of Senegal are examples of Sudanese Negroes while the Kikuyu of Kenya, the Tswana of Botswana and the Bateke of Zaïre are Bantu Negroes. Amongst the Negroes, the Pygmies of the rain forests of Zaïre and the Tswana (Bushmen) of the Kalahari Plains of Botswana stand out as racially distinct aboriginal groups. Compared with the Sudanese Negro, who is about 1·7 m (5 ft 8 ins) in height, Pygmies have an average height of 1·4 m (4 ft 8 ins), while the height of the Bushmen averages 1·5 m (5 ft). Furthermore, both aboriginal groups lead a comparatively primitive life as hunters and gatherers of forest products. As a rule, Pygmies have a lighter complexion than Negroes while the complexion of the Bushmen is yellowish-brown.

Of the other two racial groups represented in tropical Africa, the Caucasoid and the Mongoloid, the former is more numerous. The northern Caucasoid peoples of the western Sudan and East Africa include the Arabs, the Tuareg, the Masai, the Cattle Fulani and the peoples of Ethiopia and the Somali Republic. Almost all these groups claim to have originated from the Middle East and are often classified as Hamitic (for example the Tuareg) and Semitic (for example the Arabs). Most of them profess the Muslim faith and have been settled in tropical Africa for a much longer period than the southern Caucasoid peoples of East Africa and southern tropical Africa. This latter group consists of Europeans of various nationalities, notably Dutch, English and Portuguese, who migrated to establish permanent settlements in the highlands of tropical Africa from the seventeenth century onwards. It is this southern Caucasoid people that until recently dominated the politics of Kenya, Zimbabwe, Angola and Mozambique, even though they constitute an ethnic minority in each of these countries.

Asiatics, consisting predominantly of Indians and Pakistanis, make up the Mongoloid racial group of tropical Africa. They are found mostly in Kenya, Tanzania and Mozambique. The Merina people of Malagasy are also classified as Mongoloid and are thought to have migrated there from south-east Asia.

Over the years, there has been considerable inter-breeding between the races, so that pure racial types are largely confined to relatively isolated areas such as those occupied by the Pygmies or to ultra-conservative groups such as the Masai and the Cattle Fulani. Examples of interracial breeding include the Hottentots, a cross between the Negroes and the Bushmen, and the mulatto groups of Angola and Mozambique – a cross between Negroes and the southern Caucasoid peoples.

Ethnic groups

Each racial group, but particularly the Negro, is divided into a large number of ethnic groups, often erroneously and derogatorily referred to as tribes. Each ethnic group has distinct customs, language and other cultural characteristics, and each occupies contiguous territory which its members consider to belong to them by right of occupation. The size of population and the territorial area of each ethnic group vary greatly. Indeed the vast majority of ethnic groups such as the Kofyar, Anga and Birom of the Middle Belt of Nigeria and the Tugen and Elgeyo of Kenya number less than 150,000 and occupy territories of less than 600 sq km. It is these smaller ethnic groups that some writers refer to as village states. There are, however, a few very large ethnic groups consisting of millions of people spread over hundreds of thousands of sq km. These larger groups, notably the Hausa (10 million), the Yoruba (12 million), the Ibo (8 million) and the Kikuyu (2·2 million), are basically a

Fig. 6.2 Principal concentrations of Fulani people (after Westermann and Bryan, 1952)

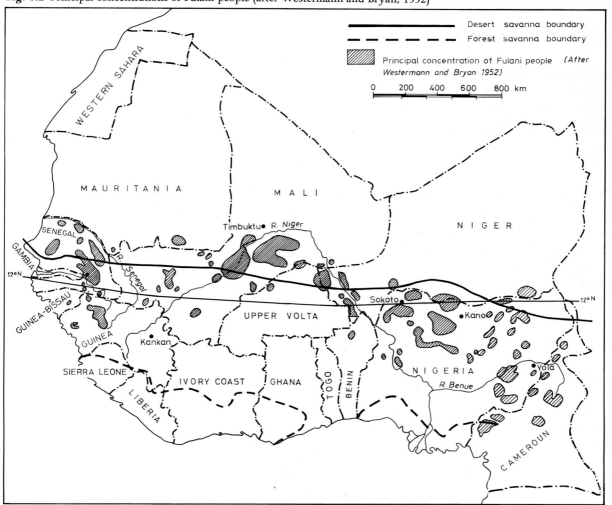

Pl. 6.1 A Pygmy man in the Ituri forest, Zaïre. Note the hunting net around his neck

confederation of peoples speaking the same language and having the same customs and taboos, rather than integrated political groups.

Every country consists of at least four ethnic groups, the number for Nigeria being as large as 200. Occasionally, especially before the colonial period and since independence, dissensions between different ethnic groups within the same country, such as the Ibo and Hausa in Nigeria, the Luo and Kikuyu in Kenya or the Hutu and Watutsi in Burundi and Rwanda, may be so deep-seated as to create tensions and conflicts of the same magnitude as exist between blacks and whites in South Africa. It is the increasing competition between the élites of the various ethnic groups and the fanatical ethnic loyalties shown by some of them that have created the greatest problem of national integration in most tropical African countries.

Demographic characteristics

The two biological characteristics of fertility and mortality, together with the rate of natural increase, which is determined by them, are usually distinguished as demographic characteristics. Both fertility and mortality vary considerably from one country to another and even between different social groups within the same country, since they are greatly influenced by the culture and the level of economic development attained by the society.

Fertility and birth rates
Fertility is the production of live births by a population and is usually assessed by relating the number of births

to the size of some section of the population such as the total number of women or the number of women of child-bearing age. It is measured by an index called the crude birth rate which is calculated by dividing the number of live births in a given year by the total population of that year, and multiplying by 1,000. A more realistic index of fertility is the rate which measures the births per year per thousand women between the reproductive ages 15–44.

Tropical Africa, like most developing regions of the world, is a region of high fertility, the highest crude birth rate being observed in West and East Africa where the rate per 1,000 population in 1975–80 exceeded 48 as compared with only 14·4 for western Europe and 25 for North America. This rather high fertility rate (see Table 6.1) reflects the early stage in the demographic transition (see p. 67), a stage which is characteristic of developing countries experiencing a gradual change from a subsistence to a more specialized economy. The high crude birth rate in tropical Africa is considered to be of recent origin and has been largely attributed to the rapid diffusion of modern health measures and medical technology developed in more advanced countries. Early, and a virtual universal, marriage has also contributed to the high birth rate which is considered to be higher than for pre-industrial Europe. The process of modernization has resulted in a decline in birth rate in parts of tropical Africa, especially in the larger cities where the birth rate is lower than in rural areas.

The persistently high fertility in most cultural areas has been associated with the fact that, traditionally, the single most important manner in which a woman can prove her value to her family and community has been through bearing many children. In addition children provide the necessary labour for farming and also serve as a form of insurance against old age. High infant mortality has also contributed towards the need for frequent reproduction to ensure that some children survive to reach adulthood. The relatively lower birth rate in some cities is caused partly by the higher cost of rearing children in urban areas, where it has become increasingly difficult for working mothers to find help from members of the extended family in looking after their children. In rural areas, children usually accompany their mothers to the farm or markets, but in urban centres baby sitters, who are usually young relatives, have to be employed, since nursery fees are too high for most working families.

Mortality and the death rate
Mortality is an important cause of change in population numbers in tropical Africa, particularly in areas and years in which great catastrophes occur such as droughts, floods and epidemics. As with fertility, the simplest measure of mortality is the crude death rate

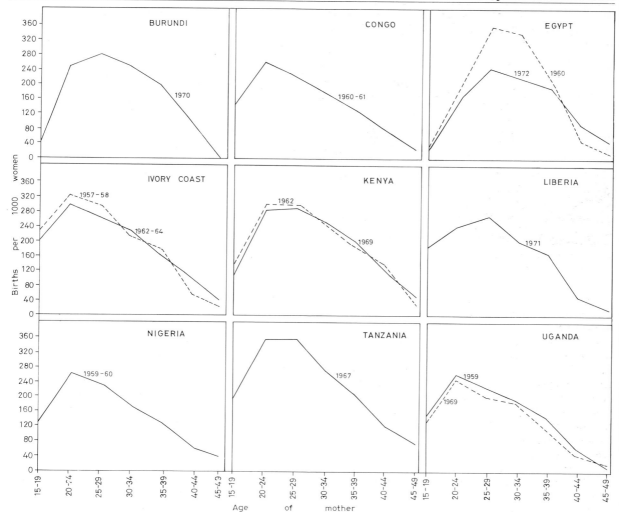

Fig. 6.3 Fertility patterns and age-specific birth rates, selected countries

which is calculated by dividing the total number of deaths (after live birth) in a given year by the total population of that year, and multiplying by 1,000. The crude death rate was very high in tropical Africa during the pre-colonial period. But although the death rate has fallen much more rapidly than the birth rate during the last eighty years, tropical Africa still has the highest mortality rate in the world. For the period 1975–80, for example, the crude death rate for West Africa was about 21 per 1,000 while that of Central Africa was 19·4 per 1,000. The corresponding figures for the developing regions of South Asia and Latin America were 15·2 and 8·3 per 1,000 respectively while the figure for Europe was 10·6 per 1,000.

All over tropical Africa the death rate is falling much more rapidly than was the case in Europe during the early part of the industrial revolution. This favourable situation has been helped by the steady improvements in medical facilities as well as in the quantity and quality of food. The greatest achievement has been a considerable decline in infant mortality although it is still relatively high. Improved economic conditions and better health facilities also account for the fact that the crude death rate is generally lower in urban areas than in rural areas.

Natural increase

The rate of natural increase in population is the balance of the birth rate over the death rate. The high and relatively steady birth rate and the high but rapidly

Table 6.1 1975–80 crude birth rates, crude death rates, infant mortality rates and expectation of life at birth for selected countries (rates per 1,000 population)

Sub-region and Country	Crude birth rate	Crude death rate	Infant mortality rate	Expectation of life at birth
WEST AFRICA	48·5	20·6	n.a.	43·2
Benin	49·2	20·5	150	43·5
Ghana	48·6	18·8	146	46·0
Ivory Coast	45·2	18·4	154	46·0
Mali	49·4	24·5	168	40·0
Niger	51·5	23·2	140	40·0
Nigeria	49·2	20·3	157	43·5
Sierra Leone	44·4	18·4	136	46·0
EAST AFRICA	47·3	18·3	n.a.	46·0
Ethiopia	48·3	23·0	162	39·0
Kenya	47·9	13·9	115	52·5
Sudan	48·5	15·9	121	51·1
Tanzania	49·2	17·7	165	47·0
CENTRAL AFRICA	44·2	19·4	n.a.	44·3
Angola	47·0	22·1	n.a.	41·0
Burundi	47·2	20·9	161	43·0
Cameroun	40·9	20·0	110	43·5
Gabon	27·9	22·2	184	43·5
Zaïre	44·9	18·1	115	46·0
Zambia	49·4	17·8	159	47·0
SOUTHERN TROPICAL AFRICA	43·8	14·3	n.a.	53·3
Botswana	47·9	19·7	175	46·0
Madagascar	49·2	18·7	102	46·0
Malawi	46·3	20·7	141	43·5
Mozambique	41·3	17·8	n.a.	46·0
Zimbabwe	48·3	12·6	115	54·0

Sources 1. United Nations (1977), *World Population Prospects as Assessed in 1973*, New York, pp. 116–17; 2. The infant mortality column is obtained from United Nations ECA (1975), *Demographic Handbook for Africa*, Addis Ababa, pp. 89–91 (Table 21).

declining death rate has resulted in a high rate of natural increase for all countries. The indication is that the rate of natural increase is likely to rise in the near future in those countries which continue to ignore and condemn measures aimed at birth control while at the same time investing more resources in efforts to lower the death rate.

Sex composition and sex ratio

The standard measure of the sex composition of human populations is the sex ratio which is defined as the number of males per 100 females in the population. Sex ratios of below 90 or over 110 are considered to be unbalanced. Most countries in tropical Africa have a sex ratio of less than 100 but over 90, that is, there are on the whole more women than men. The proportion of women in the population is highest in Gabon, Congo Republic, Rwanda and Malawi, each of which has a sex ratio of less than 90. There are, however, a few countries, such as Mauritania, Gambia, Angola and Equatorial Guinea, where the sex ratio is above 100. In some of these countries, the high proportion of men or women in the population is caused by the large number of emigrants or immigrants consisting mostly of males aged between 15 and 44. It is also as a result of sex selectivity in migration that, for most countries, the sex ratio in urban areas is much higher than for rural areas. The urban sex ratios for Liberia, Zaïre, Kenya and

Table 6.2   Estimates of percentage distribution of population by major age-groups for selected countries in 1970, 1985 and 2000

Sub-region and Country	1970			1985			2000		
	0–14	15–64	65+	0–14	15–64	65+	0–14	15–64	65+
WEST AFRICA	44·4	53·1	2·5	45·6	51·8	2·6	45·1	52·0	2·9
Benin	44·9	52·7	2·5	45·7	51·6	2·7	41·1	55·8	3·1
Ghana	47·0	49·4	3·6	46·6	51·0	2·4	44·8	52·4	2·7
Ivory Coast	42·5	54·8	2·7	44·2	52·7	3·1	42·8	53·8	3·4
Mali	43·4	53·9	2·7	45·2	52·0	2·8	45·3	51·8	2·9
Niger	45·0	52·7	2·3	46·7	50·9	2·4	46·7	50·7	2·6
Nigeria	44·8	52·9	2·3	46·1	51·4	2·5	46·3	50·9	2·8
Sierra Leone	42·4	54·5	3·1	43·4	53·3	3·3	41·7	54·8	3·5
EAST AFRICA	44·4	52·9	2·7	46·0	51·2	2·8	46·5	50·5	3·0
Ethiopia	43·0	54·2	2·7	45·0	52·2	2·8	46·1	51·0	2·9
Kenya	45·8	51·6	2·6	47·9	49·4	2·6	48·0	49·3	2·8
Sudan	45·3	52·1	2·7	46·4	50·8	2·7	44·5	52·5	2·9
Tanzania	46·4	51·1	2·4	47·3	50·2	2·5	47·3	50·1	2·6
CENTRAL AFRICA	43·0	54·3	2·8	43·4	53·5	3·1	45·0	51·7	3·3
Angola	42·0	55·7	2·3	44·1	53·2	2·7	45·9	51·0	3·1
Burundi	42·5	54·7	2·8	44·8	52·2	3·0	44·9	51·8	3·2
Cameroun	41·3	55·7	3·0	41·0	54·9	4·1	44·3	51·4	4·2
Gabon	28·9	66·9	4·3	31·3	63·0	5·7	32·6	57·6	9·8
Zaïre	44·4	52·8	2·8	44·4	52·7	2·9	45·6	51·3	3·1
Zambia	46·3	51·5	2·2	47·9	49·5	2·6	48·9	48·3	2·9
SOUTHERN TROPICAL AFRICA	41·0	54·9	4·1	44·8	51·5	3·7	43·7	52·5	3·8
Botswana	47·5	46·9	5·6	46·1	50·7	3·2	45·7	51·5	2·8
Madagascar	44·4	52·9	2·7	47·2	50·1	2·7	47·9	49·4	2·8
Malawi	43·9	52·1	4·0	44·8	52·3	2·9	45·0	51·7	3·3
Mozambique	42·0	55·5	2·5	42·4	54·5	3·1	45·0	50·8	4·2
Zimbabwe	48·2	49·7	2·1	48·3	49·5	2·2	48·2	49·0	2·8

Source United Nations (1977), *World Population Prospects as Assessed in 1973*, Dept. of Economics and Social Studies, Population Studies, No. 60, pp. 172–3.

Malawi, for example, are respectively 114, 136, 138 and 129, while the corresponding sex ratios for the rural areas are 92, 89, 97 and 89.

According to Brass, the sex ratio at birth in tropical Africa is below the world average, being less than 98 for most countries (Brass *et al.*, 1968). It is considered unusual for girls under one year of age to be more numerous than boys of the same age and this has been attributed partly to the under-reporting of boys and partly to mistakes in reporting since the registration of births is not widespread. Figures for many countries show, however, that the sex ratio begins to increase after the first year of birth when it exceeds 100 and continues to do so till the age of 14 or even 19 in some countries. Thereafter, there is a considerable fall which continues until the age of about 44, after which the sex

ratio rises again to over 100. What this means is that after the first year of birth more male children tend to survive until the age of 14. Thereafter, that is between the ages of 15 and 44, more men tend to die, but from the age of 45 the male population again becomes more numerous. Please note that the general trend presented here is not in line with trends in the more developed parts of the world.

Age structure and age pyramids

The age structure of a population is the proportion of people within various age-groups. It is one of the most basic characteristics of a population and one which distinguishes the population profiles of tropical Africa and other developing regions of the world from those of the more advanced countries. The age of a person

Pl. 6.2 Masai *moran* (warrior) with his cattle, East Africa

influences his needs, his occupation and the pattern of public expenditure on him. The large number of young people in tropical Africa, for example, is responsible for the relatively high expenditure on education in many of the countries, just as the increasing number of aged people has made big demands on public funds for old age pensions in the more developed countries.

Age structure is closely related to other population characteristics, notably the birth rate, marriage rate and the incidence of migration. In Kenya, for example, the age structure of the African population is basically different from those of the European and Asian populations. Since the rapid growth of population in tropical Africa is recent, dating back not more than fifty years, it is not surprising that children and young people still constitute a very high proportion of the total population. In most countries, at least two out of every five persons are children under 15 years of age. The proportion of children under 15 is highest in West and East Africa where over 44 per cent of the total population in 1970 belonged to this group (Table 6.2). The small proportion of only 29 per cent in Gabon is curious, although the figure is still higher than for the more developed countries where in 1975 25 per cent were children under 15.

The age structure of a population is best presented

graphically by constructing an age pyramid in which the various age-groups of 0–4, 5–9, 10–15 to 80–84 and over 85 are represented along the vertical axis with males on the left and females on the right of the vertical axis. As a result of the pattern of fertility and mortality,

Pl. 6.3 Hausa horseman, Nigeria

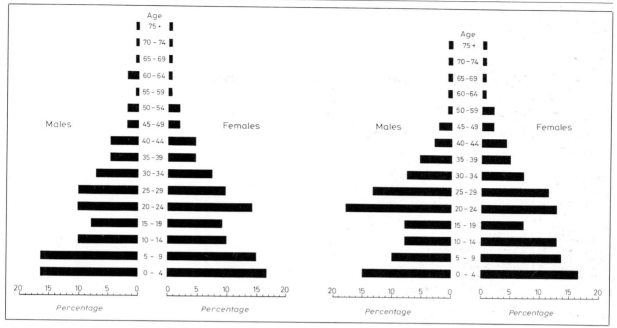

Fig. 6.4a Age and sex pyramids in Nigeria and Lagos

Fig. 6.4b Age and sex pyramids in Ghana

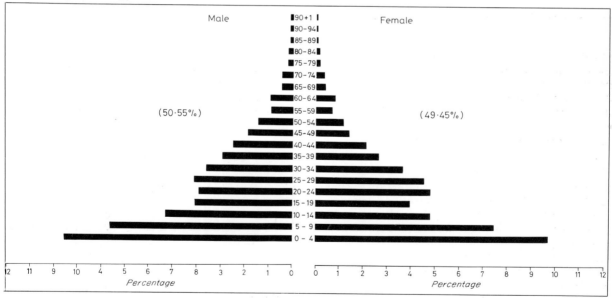

the age pyramid for tropical Africa, like those of other developing regions, has a characteristic broad base and a rather thin top, reflecting a predominantly young population with very few old people. In 1970, the proportion of old people of over 65 was less than 3 per cent for most countries. The age pyramids for two countries are shown in Fig. 6.4.

Dependency ratio

The dependency ratio is obtained by adding the total population of under 15 years of age to the total population of 65 years and over and dividing the result by the total population aged 15–65. In other words, the ratio gives an indication of the proportion of the unproductive groups in the population (children and

Pl. 6.4 Cattle Fulani herdsmen, Nigeria

aged people) and of the working population or the potential labour force (usually 15–64 years of age). A country with a high dependency ratio has a relatively small working population which is overburdened with many youths and aged people whose needs for food, health, education, etc. have to be provided for.

In tropical Africa, the high dependency ratio is caused by the very high proportion of children in the population. Mainly because of this, many governments have had to spend over 30 per cent of their annual budget on education since independence. Indeed most governments are currently embarrassed by the very rapid growth in school enrolment. Unfortunately the indication is that the dependency ratios for all countries will be much higher in 1985 and AD 2000 (see Table 6.2) largely because of the increase in birth rate and in the expectation of life at birth. The problem is that although huge investment in education will produce the much needed skilled manpower, it has also resulted in the allocation of relatively small sums for industrialization and basic social services.

Life expectancy

Life expectancy or the expectation of life at birth is a measure of the average number of years which a group of newborn infants is expected to live if they are subjected to risks of death on the basis of the mortality rates of a country observed at each level of age during the period to which the measure refers. In tropical Africa, life expectancy has increased considerably over the years. The West African sub-region, for example, had an estimated life expectancy of 35 in 1965, the lowest for all Africa, but by 1975 the figure had increased to 43. The figure for Central Africa increased during the same period from 42 to 44 while those for East and southern Africa increased respectively from 42 to 46 and from 47 to 53. As a rule, life expectancy values for females are higher than for males. The increase in the expectation of life has contributed to the rapid increase in total population which some countries have experienced and will eventually result in higher dependency ratios through an increase in the number of people aged 65 and above.

Cultural characteristics

Education and literacy

Literacy is the basic measurement of educational status, and is defined as the ability to write in one's native language. By this definition, most people in tropical Africa are still illiterate. In 1950, only about 5 per cent of children and young people below the age of 24 were enrolled in schools compared with the world average of 10 per cent. However, since then there has been a rapid growth in the total number and proportion enrolled. Between 1950 and 1967, for example, the total number of young people in all educational institutions in sub-Saharan Africa rose over three times from about 6.8 million to nearly 23 million (UNESCO, 1970, pp. 52–3). Yet in spite of this rapid expansion in education, the absolute number of illiterates has increased because of the equally rapid increase in population which has resulted in a more rapid increase in the number of school-age children compared with the number actually enrolled in schools.

During the colonial period, western-type formal education was restricted and greatly influenced by the political philosophy of the various colonial powers. Lack of funds, amongst other things, was a major factor inhibiting the expansion of educational facilities. In the English-speaking countries, the Christian missions played a major role as agents for educational development and although governments provided some funds in the form of grants, the schools were initially largely funded by grants from the home missions in Europe. Emphasis has always been placed on education of the grammar-school type, which seeks to produce white-collar workers. The result is that in spite of the great increase in secondary and university enrolments, especially since 1970, most countries still suffer from an acute shortage of technicians and technologists who form the bulwark of an industrial society, and this includes Nigeria, which has thirteen universities.

The great increase in school enrolment in recent years is largely a consequence of the increasing economic returns on skills obtained in schools, and the ever-widening disparity between the incomes of those with formal education and those who are illiterate. But although the demand for education is on the increase, further enrolment is handicapped by the high educational costs per child in terms of per capita incomes. In general, formal education has tended to create a dissatisfaction with traditional agriculture in rural areas where alternative employment opportunities hardly exist for those who have been educated beyond the primary level. A large number of school graduates therefore migrate to search for jobs in urban centres where wages are invariably higher.

The working force

The working force or the economically active section of the population consists of people above 15 years of age, but below 65. This potential working force is, as a rule, considerably higher in developed countries. Children and old people are a dependency burden and are excluded from the labour force. In the traditional African economic scene, however, children aged 9–15 make considerable contributions to farm labour and the marketing of farm produce, and are largely responsible, along with the women, for fetching water from streams, firewood and grass for livestock. But since an increasing number of children now go to school, and in order to be able to make meaningful comparisons with other parts of the world, we shall use the standard definition of the labour force.

With the exception of a few countries such as the Republic of Benin, Mauritania, Upper Volta, Zambia and Gabon, which have crude economic activity rates of over 50 per cent for the total population, the working force is below 50 per cent for tropical African countries. The comparable figure for developed countries is over 60 per cent – in the United States, for instance, it is 65 per cent. The lowest crude activity rates for the total population are recorded for Niger (29 per cent), Angola (29 per cent), Zambia (33 per cent), Nigeria (33 per cent) and Chad (34 per cent). However, almost every country has a male economic activity rate of over 50 per cent, the highest being recorded for Zambia (77 per cent) and Guinea-Bissau (60 per cent). There is a marked difference in the female economic activity rates which range from 63 per cent in Guinea Bissau, 52 per cent in the Republic of Benin to about 5 per cent in Niger and Mozambique (United Nations, 1975). As a rule the economic activity rates for females are lower than for males in almost every country. This situation is due

Pl. 6.5 Kalahari Bushmen hunting antelope with their dogs

largely to cultural practices and differences in the definition of some economic activities in relation to female workers. For instance, women in 'purdah', who are generally considered to be economically inactive, frequently 'engage in business and amass wealth for themselves when they are in the bondage of seclusion and wifehood' (Cohen, 1969, p. 64).

Available information on the occupational structure of the various countries confirms that the great majority of workers in tropical Africa still obtain a living from primary activities, namely agriculture, hunting, fishing and the collecting of forest products, with agriculture predominating. According to the United Nations (FAO) estimates for 1965 and figures published in the 1975 *Demographic Handbook for Africa* by the UN Economic Commission for Africa, the proportion of the active population engaged in agriculture was about 80 per cent in Nigeria, Liberia, Malawi, Togo and Zaïre. Higher proportions of about 90 per cent were recorded for Niger, Rwanda and Tanzania, while relatively low figures were recorded for Ghana (56 per cent) and Namibia (58 per cent).

The proportion of the working population engaged in primary activities decreases as the economy becomes more advanced and diversified. In some countries increasing government investment in manufacturing and expansion in commerce, transportation and other services have resulted in a considerable increase in the number of workers in secondary and tertiary activities. However, in countries like Nigeria and Ghana, the large number of people engaged in commerce and transportation does not necessarily reflect the developed stage of these sectors. It is rather the relative ease with which individuals and small groups can enter the transport business or establish themselves as petty traders and hawkers of goods, including cooked foods, that attract people to these occupations.

In view of the high proportion of workers in agriculture, it is not surprising that salaried workers form a very small percentage of the working population. The small number of wage-earners is also caused by the fact that in countries like Nigeria, Cameroun and Ghana, most of the people who earn a living from trading, crafts and even in transport services are either self-employed or are engaged in a family enterprise and therefore do not earn salaries. The proportion of wage-earners in Nigeria is therefore less than 10 per cent of the working population while those of Sierra Leone and Botswana are respectively 16 per cent and 13 per cent. The relatively high proportion of salaried employees and wage-earners in Zambia (64 per cent), Zimbabwe (45 per cent for African and 85 per cent for white settlers), Liberia (32 per cent) and Uganda (59 per cent) is worth noting. It is tempting to conclude that as in developed countries, those tropical African

Pl. 6.6 A Kikuyu (Bantu) girl

countries with a high proportion of salaried workers have a more modern or diversified economy. This need not be the case since the large number of wage-earners may reflect a lack of local entrepreneurship and the domination of the manufacturing, commercial and transport sectors by foreign investors.

Marital status

The proportions of a population that are single, married, widowed or divorced vary from one country to another and even within different parts of the same country, especially between urban and rural areas. These proportions also vary over time in a given country, and together they influence the size of the family and the rate of population growth. The high marital rate in tropical Africa, for example, has contributed to the current rapid growth in the population.

Most marriages are contracted under 'native laws and customs' and in most countries such marriages are rarely registered. Polygamy is common and amongst some cultural groups it is obligatory for traditional title holders to marry several wives. A considerable number of highly educated Africans who are legally married in the registry or the established churches are known to beat the law against bigamy by marrying other wives under 'native law and customs', while some have found it convenient to adopt Islam for the same purpose, since Islam permits a man to marry up to four wives. The proportion of unmarried women is therefore very low, especially in rural areas where many wives mean more farmhands. There is also a great tendency to marry at an early age, usually under 20 in the rural areas. In West Africa, for example, all countries record more than 50 per cent of women of 15–19 years of age as married, and nearly all women as married by the age of 50 (United Nations, 1975, p. 74.) An increasing number of urban residents, however, now marry fairly late, usually over the age of 28 for men; many of whom wish to earn enough money before assuming marital responsibilities.

In recent years, there has been a noticeable increase in the number of female professionals who marry relatively late (usually over 27 years of age). Most female professionals, especially graduates and nurses, do not complete their training before the ages of 23–25 and often many of them remain single for several years after graduating. The rising incidence of divorce amongst the educated urban élites has tended to encourage professional females to seek to maximize their security in society by delaying marriage until after completing professional training.

Religion

The three major groups of religions in tropical Africa are African traditional religions, Islam and Christianity. The number of people professing each religion varies considerably from one country to another. As a rule, Islam is the dominant religion in the northern parts as well as along the coast of East Africa, that is, in those areas which have had long-standing trade and cultural relationships with the Arab world, the cradle of Islam. In the northern parts of West Africa, for example, Islam has the largest following of the three types of religion. In Nigeria the proportion of those professing Islam is 47·2 per cent as compared with 34·5 per cent who profess Christianity. The small number of those who profess traditional religions in Nigeria (18·3) is, however, deceptive since, as in many other countries, many Christians and Moslems still believe in, and consult, the priests of traditional African religions.

With the possible exception of Ethiopia, where coptic Christianity has flourished for more than a thousand years, it was mainly European missionaries who introduced Christianity into the coastal areas of tropical Africa. In general, the adoption of Christianity was restricted to groups which had not come into direct contact with Islam, and up to about 1940 most Christians in tropical Africa were either Roman Catholics or members of the established European Protestant Churches – Presbyterian, Methodist, Anglican, Baptist and Lutheran. Today, the situation has changed so much that most Christians now belong to numerous spiritual churches founded by indigenous African Christians. In many countries, including Ghana, Nigeria and Zambia, these spiritual churches have become so dominant that the Roman Catholic and the established Protestant Churches have had to modify their style of worship by introducing drumming and dancing, features characteristic of the spiritual churches, to avoid losing more members.

African traditional religions consist of the worship of many gods such as the god of thunder, the forest god, the earth god and the river god, although some groups also believe in one supreme being which is the god of gods. Various calamities, such as droughts, epidemics, floods and motor accidents, are often attributed to the anger of gods or to evil spirits, which must be appeased. The great majority of Africans, including some who are highly educated, still believe in these gods even if a larger number claims to be Christian or Moslem.

Migration and rural–urban residence

If there is any universally acknowledged population problem in tropical Africa, it is associated with the ever-increasing rate of rural–urban population. The growing emphasis on manufacturing and the development of the retail trade has brought more and more people to the cities, especially the major port-towns, many of which are also the national capitals. The fact that most people still live in rural areas and an increasing number of educated people cannot obtain suitable jobs in rural areas suggests that the number of people who choose to live in urban areas will continue to increase during the next several decades.

Since the most important reason for migration is economic, and since some areas and ethnic territories are better endowed with resources than others, it is not surprising to find that groups, such as the Mossi of Upper Volta, the Ibo of Nigeria and the people of Malawi, are more migratory than other groups. In many cases, especially in West and southern Africa, these migrations involve the crossing of international boundaries. Often the labour deficit countries, such as the Ivory Coast and Equatorial Guinea, enter into labour agreements with the labour exporting countries to ensure a steady and regular supply of workers necessary to sustain their economy.

At present the urban population of tropical Africa is about 20 per cent of the total population. The most urbanized sub-region is southern Africa (45 per cent), followed by West Africa (15 per cent), the least urbanized sub-region being East Africa (10 per cent). In the developed countries of the world, the proportion of urban dwellers exceeds 65 per cent. A fuller discussion of the process, problems and future of urbanization is presented in Chapter 8.

References

Brass, W. I., et al. (1968), *The Demography of Tropical Africa*, Princeton University Press, Princeton, p. 38.

Cohen, A. (1969), *Custom and Politics in Urban Africa: A Study of Hausa Migrants in Yoruba Towns*, University of California Press, Berkeley, p. 64.

UNESCO (1970), *Statistical Yearbook, 1969*, Paris.

United Nations (1975), *Demographic Handbook for Africa*, Economic Commission for Africa, Addis Ababa, p. 107.

7 Migration and Rural Change

Migration defined

Migration is the permanent or semi-permanent change of residence from one administrative unit (district, county, province, state or country) to another. Movements may involve relatively short distances of under 10 km or may cover very long distances exceeding 1,000 km. Migration is an important component of population in some countries and especially in the growth of towns of tropical Africa. It is also an important determinant of the population profile, especially the age and sex composition of the population of those areas which receive large numbers of migrants. In this chapter we shall consider amongst other things the types, causes and magnitude of both internal and international migrations in tropical Africa. The effects of migration on rural areas are also considered.

Types of migrations

One method of classifying migrations is to describe their permanence. In the developed countries of the world migrations are mostly permanent since the migrants do not normally intend to return to their points of origin. In developing countries such as those of tropical Africa, migrations are basically semi-permanent, temporary or seasonal since most migrants intend to return home after spending some time at their destinations. The classification adopted in this chapter is based on the origin *vis-à-vis* the destination of the migrants. On this basis we recognize four important types of migration in tropical Africa. These are 1. rural–urban, 2. rural–rural, 3. urban–urban and 4. urban–rural migrations.

Rural–urban migration has attracted much attention in recent years largely because of the increasing number of people involved, but mainly because of the rapid growth of tropical African cities (see Chapter 8). Most migrants from rural areas to the growing urban centres consist of young educated people who are unable to obtain suitable employment in rural areas. In the Ivory Coast in 1968, for example, about 8 per cent of illiterate males and 11 per cent of illiterate females aged 15–29 years migrated from rural areas into the towns. The corresponding proportion of educated young people was 61 per cent males and 70 per cent females with primary-school education (Roussel, 1970). As a rule, the larger urban centres are growing much more rapidly but a

large number of migrants into the bigger cities originate from smaller towns and not directly from rural areas.

Although rural–urban migration has received so much attention in recent years, evidence from Ghana, Uganda and Nigeria shows that about 60 per cent of people who move from one rural area end up settling, at least for some time, in other rural areas. Rural–rural migration is therefore a very important type of migratory movement in tropical Africa. The vast majority of people who move from one rural area to another are illiterate and most of them originate from areas which are short of an adequate supply of suitable farmlands. Many of them work for wages as labourers in private farms, commercial plantations or mines while others are self-employed. Often this group of migrants takes up jobs which the local inhabitants regard as inferior (Addo, 1974; Udo, 1975).

Urban–urban migration usually involves movement from small or medium-size towns to larger cities which offer greater opportunities in terms of higher education and variety of jobs. It is more common in the larger countries such as Nigeria which have a large number of urban centres. Urban–rural migration, on the other hand, is relatively rare and consists largely of return migrants going back to their place of origin on attaining retirement age.

It is usual to distinguish labour migrations which involve the movements of single males to the mines, commercial farms and the cities for wage employment from commercial migration in which the migrants, both male and female, are largely self-employed. Commercial migration involves the transfer of capital and business acumen. Labour migration, on the other hand, involves the transfer of mostly adult males from labour surplus countries such as Upper Volta to labour deficit countries such as the Ivory Coast or Zimbabwe.

Finally there is a special type of migration consisting of refugees, of which there are over one million in tropical Africa. Refugees in Africa are usually international migrants and the movements are usually spectacular, being characterized by suddenness and considerable human suffering. According to a United Nations definition a refugee is an individual who, owing to well-founded fears of being persecuted for reasons of race, religion, nationality, membership of a particular social group or political opinion, is outside the country of his nationality and is unable, or owing to such fears, unwilling to avail himself of that country. Political refugees abound in Africa and so do other types of refugees such as those Nigerians who were expelled from Fernando Po in 1977 or from Ghana in 1969.

Causes of migration

Economic considerations constitute the most important cause of migration. This fact was recorded as far back as 1889 by Ravenstein in his study of migration in England which was based on the 1881 census of England. According to him,

Bad or oppressive laws, heavy taxation, an unattractive climate, uncongenial social surroundings and even compulsion (slave trade, deportation), all have produced and are still producing currents of migration; but none of these currents can compare in volume with that which arises from the desire inherent in most men to better themselves in material respects.

The rising expectations and changing values of the people have created new demands for goods and services which an increasing number cannot obtain in their districts of origin, and they are therefore obliged to migrate to areas where their expectations can be more adequately met.

Economic considerations in migration are sometimes analysed in terms of a push–pull model in which certain factors are said to exert a push effect in the areas where the migrants originate while other factors at the destinations (particularly the cities) exert a pull effect.

Since the beginning of the colonial period, when modern migrations started in tropical Africa, considerable developments in commercial agriculture, manufacturing and urbanization have resulted in a steady increase in the number of migrants. Increasing population resulting in extreme pressure on available farmland has proved to be a major push factor in some localities. Transport development, especially road transport, and the rapid expansion of education since the late 1950s, have also played a major role in the migration process. As a rule, it is the localities and regions where economic activity is expanding that attract net migration from other areas. But since migration is selective of age and sex, and since migration also involves the transfer of skill and capital, this movement by itself tends to favour the rapidly growing areas and to disfavour others. Thus, although migration is brought about by regional imbalance in growth, the process ends up widening rather than narrowing the gap between the growing areas and the relatively stagnant areas from where the migrants originate.

There are, however, many other reasons why people decide to migrate and these include the following:

1. The desire to escape from an inferior social status imposed by the community because of the social status of one's parents. In many villages in parts of Iboland, for example, some people are still culturally isolated as *Osu* because they are descendants of slaves who were dedicated to the earth god.
2. The desire to escape from domination or restrictions imposed on one's movements by parents or local customs.
3. Migration to attend higher educational institutions which are mostly located in the larger urban centres.
4. Migration to join one's husband.
5. The desire to escape punishment for crimes committed in the local community or to escape from local enemies and witchcraft.
6. The desire to move to an area with more varied recreational and cultural activities.

Characteristics of migrants

Some knowledge of the characteristics of migrants is helpful in making us understand some of the effects and consequences of large-scale migration on the population and economy of both the areas where the migrants originate and their various destinations. Usually migrant characteristics fall into three categories, namely demographic, social and economic. Various studies of migrations show clearly that it is these characteristics that distinguish migrants from non-migrants especially at their destinations.

Demographic characteristics

Starting with demographic characteristics, we note that some ethnic groups are more migratory than others. One reason for this has to do with their occupations; for instance the Cattle Fulani, the Tuareg and the Masai are nomadic cattle rearers and are therefore constantly on the move in search of water and grazing for their cattle. The large-scale migration of Hausa, Ibo, Mossi and Tonga is, however, associated with limited opportunities in their ancestral homes. The most important demographic characteristics of migrants in tropical Africa are concerned with the age and sex of the migrant population. Usually young adult males predominate, their ages ranging between 15–25. Normally young men of this age-group have no families or firm job commitments and therefore have nothing to prevent them from travelling. Indeed one reason why people in this age category migrate is to earn money to pay for their wives, although a large number migrate because going to work in a big city gives them some prestige amongst local youths. It is important to remember too that it is young men of this age category who are in secondary schools, technical colleges and universities which are in most cases located outside their districts of origin.

Pl. 7.1 Migrant farmer's house on stilts in the Ogun flood plain, Nigeria

Migrations in tropical Africa, both rural–urban and rural–rural, are also selective of sex since there is a much greater proportion of male migrants. In Ghana and Nigeria, but especially in Malawi, Zimbabwe and Botswana, male migrants predominate. Often even young married men migrate without taking their wives, thereby creating a predominance of males in some cities and a predominance of females in certain rural areas. The uncertainty of securing employment in the cities is partly responsible for this situation, but the extreme shortage of urban accommodation and the resulting high rents is another important factor. In southern Africa migrants are not permitted to travel with their families to work in the mines, farms or industrial areas located in non-African Reserves. In Nigeria it is largely the seasonal rural–rural migrants such as Hausa migrants into the cocoa belt of south-western Nigeria that do not travel with their wives. The Urhobo, Isoko and the Igbira, mostly self-employed farmers, normally take their wives with them.

Male predominance in migration is not universal and in any case there is now an increasing number of female migrants into the cities. In the Cameroun, for example, Podlewski (1975) has reported that female mobility is everywhere more important than male mobility. And in the Ivory Coast, Roussel (1970) has found that in the villages he studied 8 per cent of illiterate males and 11 per cent of illiterate females migrated, the corresponding figure for literate villagers being 42 per cent males and 55 per cent females.

Social and economic characteristics
The most important social and economic characteristics of migrants are associated with their educational levels, skills and occupations. As a rule it is the better educated young people who migrate since they are generally unable to obtain suitable employment in their home districts. The migrant population is also largely made up of the more daring and more highly motivated members of the community. Migrants going to the cities are usually better educated than those who go to settle in rural areas. Indeed illiterate migrants rarely go to the cities today since government departments and firms require such unskilled employees as gatemen, cleaners and messengers to be able to express themselves in English or French.

In considering the occupations of rural–rural migrants it is important to recognize that in southern Africa most migrants work in the mines and on farms belonging to European settlers. They are therefore basically wage-earners who have no opportunity to settle down permanently as tenant farmers or to purchase land outright for establishing their own farms. On the other hand, a large and increasing number of rural–rural migrants into Uganda and in various parts of West Africa are self-employed. Indeed many migrants who originally worked for wages in these areas have since acquired farmland to cultivate on their own. As a result, some indigenous farmers continue to face problems of labour shortage in spite of increasing migration into their areas.

Origins and patterns of migratory flows

Migratory movements have featured in tropical Africa for many centuries, but pre-colonial migration was associated with trade, drought, ethnic conflict and land colonization. During the colonial period, the character and extent of migration changed in response to the new colonial economy. Today colonization-type migration has given way to modern migration featuring temporary (seasonal) and permanent migration from the countryside to the city or from one rural area to another, both within and across national boundaries. In most cases the migrants intend to return to their district of origin to die and are basically strangers (or aliens) at their destinations.

The colonial economy, in which Africa was to serve as a primary producer for the factories of Europe as well as a market for European manufactures, created a great demand for labour to work in the mines, the commercial plantations and the timber concessions of tropical Africa. In many parts of the continent indigenous people also adopted the cultivation of such industrial crops as cocoa, rubber, cotton and groundnuts. The demand for labour was therefore considerable, and constituted the major pull factor in colonial-period migration in Africa. But there were also some push factors which 'forced' potential migrants to move, and these included shortage of farmland and the desire to earn money to pay taxes and school fees.

During the first twenty years of the twentieth century, the demand for labour exceeded the supply in all parts of tropical Africa. This was caused partly by the reluctance of most people to migrate to work in distant places and partly by the adoption of industrial crop production by African farmers. The introduction of cotton into Uganda in 1904, for example, brought about acute shortages of labour for the construction and maintenance of essential government buildings and services from 1908. Before cotton was introduced, the Ganda people were found all over East Africa, working to earn cash to pay for imported goods. But from about 1908, Buganda became a net importer of migrant labour to work on the cotton fields (Powesland, 1954).

Efforts made to solve the labour problem of early colonial Africa included the importation of labourers from Mexico, China, India and Ceylon. Direct forced labour through the imposition of a poll tax, payable in cash, was used to construct roads, railways and sea ports. In Upper Volta, men who were unwilling or unable to pay taxes in cash had their properties seized and sold by French colonial officers and those who had neither taxes nor goods were compelled to migrate to work in Ghana or face punishment by the administration (Skinner, 1965).

Forced labour was associated with many abuses and was abolished by 1950 in all French and British territories. The system, however, continued into the early 1960s in Mozambique and Angola where it attracted much publicity (Bailey, 1969). The vast majority who migrated to work during the colonial period were, however, not forced, at least not directly, but did so for economic reasons. They were attracted to the growing port-towns which had become the political and commercial capitals of the various territories. At the time of independence most countries had mounting unemployment of school-leavers in all the capitals and other large cities. In some countries, such as the Ivory Coast, Ghana and Liberia, the steady increase in the urban unemployment rate has tended to mask the continued shortage of labour in the mines and on commercial plantations.

The direction of movements of people or the flow pattern of modern migrations is presented in Fig. 7.1. In West Africa, most migrants go to the more accessible and better developed coastal areas which include the mines, commercial plantations, peasant tree-crop farms and timber concessions, as well as the major industrial and commercial centres. The most important migration streams in terms of the numbers involved include Mossi

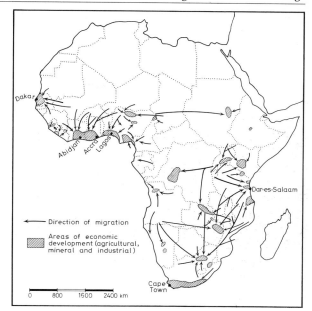

Fig. 7.1 Pattern of migrations

migration into Ghana and Urhobo/Isoko migration into south-western Nigeria. A few developing regions in the interior, such as the Jos tin fields and the Kano groundnut belt, also attract a considerable number of migrants.

By contrast, most migrants in southern, Central and East Africa go to interior locations, the only coastal areas attracting migrant labour being the sisal-growing districts of Tanzania and the sugar belt of Natal in South Africa. Important components of the migration streams in these regions include rural–rural migrations from Rwanda and Burundi into the cotton belt of Uganda, and migrant labour from Malawi into Zimbabwe and South Africa.

The magnitude of internal and international migrations

The data available for internal migrations within each country is scanty because no directly relevant questions are asked when national censuses are taken. The position with data on international migration is, however, much better owing to immigration checks at the borders and ports of entry. Data on international migration is also available from government and private labour recruitment agencies which handle the recruitment, transportation and placement of migrant labour from countries such as Mozambique, Malawi, Upper Volta, Zambia and, until 1978, from Nigeria. However, such agencies do not operate in most countries and besides, even in countries where they exist, only a small fraction of migrants take advantage of the services that they provide. Large-scale smuggling of agricultural workers across international borders has been reported in Upper Volta (Cornelisse, 1972) and in Mozambique (Bailey, 1969). The figures that follow are therefore based on estimates made at different times for different countries.

One example of large-scale movements of people in tropical Africa is the long-distance migration of West Africans to the Republic of the Sudan. In 1956 there were about 600,000 West Africans in that country, increasing to about 750,000 in 1963 (Davis, 1964). Most of these migrants were from Nigeria, Chad and Niger Republic, who had settled permanently or temporarily in the Sudan while on their way to or returning from the pilgrimage to Mecca. The migrants are therefore predominantly Moslems and it follows that this migration started long before the colonial period. However, the economic factor is very important today and according to Davies these West Africans constitute an important force in the economic growth of the Sudan, particularly in the Gezira district.

It has also been estimated that about 75,000 *navetanes* or 'strange farmers' take part in the annual seasonal migration of farmers into the groundnut growing districts of Senegal and Gambia (Berg, 1965). Most of these migrants originate from Mali and Guinea. Some of them work for wages on groundnut farms, but the vast majority are employed on terms which provide time for them to cultivate farmland allocated to them in lieu of cash payment for work done on the farms of their employers. About 90,000 Hausa take part in the seasonal migration to south-west Nigeria and southern Ghana while another 150,000 Igbira, Urhobo and Ibo settle as labourers or self-employed migrant tenant farmers in the cocoa- and rubber-growing areas of Nigeria.

In West Africa, the two countries that depend mostly on migrant labour for the development of export agriculture and mining are the Ivory Coast and Ghana. About one-half of the total labour force of the Ivory Coast in 1965 was made up of foreigners consisting of 670,000 Africans and 30,000 non-Africans. Seventy per cent of the unskilled labour force working in the coffee and cocoa plantations originated from the neighbouring countries of Mali (220,000 workers), Upper Volta (200,000) and Guinea (150,000). In Ghana, the mines and cocoa farms always depended on foreign migrant labour from about 1910 to 1969, when the Ghana government of Kofie Busia ordered a massive expulsion of aliens. According to the 1960 census, over 850,000 persons or 12 per cent of the 6·7 million population of Ghana were of foreign origin, most of them having been born outside the country. The vast majority of these migrants came from the neighbouring countries of Togo

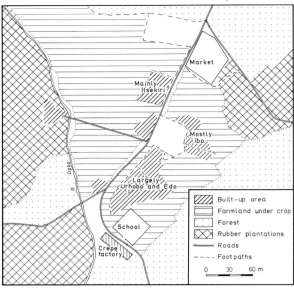

Fig. 7.2 A predominantly migrant village near Benin, Nigeria (based on a survey by E. Allison, July 1962)

(280,670), Upper Volta (194,570) and Nigeria (190,780).

Like other sub-regions of tropical Africa, East Africa is currently experiencing large-scale migration of people into the cities. The main stream of rural–rural migration, however, consists of about 150,000 farm-workers originating from Rwanda and Burundi. The distance covered by migrants as well as the number of people involved in labour migrations is much greater in Central Africa, where the main centres of attraction of wage labour are the copper mines of Katanga and Zambia, and the growing agricultural and industrial areas of the highlands of Zimbabwe. Migrants to Zimbabwe originate predominantly from Malawi, Mozambique and Zambia, with Malawi supplying over 40 per cent of the 280,000 non-indigenous males employed there in 1956 (Barber, 1961). Katanga attracts about 56,000 migrants from Burundi, Rwanda and Angola while the Zambian copper belt employs 45,000 people from Malawi, Angola, Tanzania and Mozambique.

Although South Africa is outside tropical Africa, a large number of African migrants working in the gold and coal mines of the Transvaal, Orange Free State and Natal originate from tropical African countries. In 1958, for example, these mines employed about 341,000 African workers, about 235,700 of whom were recruited from tropical African countries, a large number travelling by lorries, trains and steamers, some of them covering a distance of well over 3,000 km.

Finally, we come to the class of migrants made up of refugees, of which there are about one million in

Pl. 7.2 Basotho men signing on to work in the South African mines

tropical Africa. Obviously, the total number of refugees varies from time to time depending upon the political climate of the continent. The largest number recorded in any country is 400,000 Angolans in Zaïre which has also received refugees from Sudan, Rwanda and Burundi. Landlocked Uganda was also a haven for refugees originating from Rwanda, Sudan and Zaïre and totalling about 180,000 in 1972. Recently, the situation has been reversed, refugees emanating from Uganda. Tanzania also attracted a large number of Rwandan refugees in 1972 while Senegal was the main destination of refugees from Guinea-Bissau before that country became independent in 1978.

Major source regions of migrants

As a general rule, the rural areas which export large numbers of workers are very densely populated. The pressure on available farmland is great, often resulting in soil impoverishment, declining crop yields and even soil erosion. Indeed, in almost all cases, shortage of farmland is the main push factor in these migrations. In southern Ghana, for example, Krobo and Shai migrant cocoa farmers came from the dry and infertile Accra Plains, whose unproductive soils had compelled the people to move to establish foodcrop farms and later

cocoa farms in the more productive humid forest areas of the south-west (Field, 1943). Other major source regions for migrant cocoa farmers in Ghana include the Akwapim Ridge district whose steep-sided slopes do not provide adequate farmland for the local population, and the densely settled north-eastern district where the ravages of river blindness have forced the indigenous population to abandon up to 40 per cent of their territory (Hunter, 1967).

Pressure of population on land also accounts for the high incidence of emigration from the Kikuyu areas of Kenya, the African Reserves of Zimbabwe and South Africa, the Mossi district of Upper Volta, southern Malawi, parts of south-eastern Nigeria, and the small but very densely populated East African countries of Rwanda and Burundi. In the most densely populated parts of these areas, the density exceeds 300 persons per sq km (750 per sq mile) and family holdings rarely exceed one hectare. Continuous cropping is now common and in south-eastern Nigeria, the compound land has almost replaced the main farmland, just as grazing land has been replaced by continuous cropping in southern Malawi. In both areas, crop yields are poor and therefore it is not surprising that over 300,000 persons from Malawi and more than 600,000 from the congested districts of south-eastern Nigeria migrate to work outside their districts of origin.

Often, as is the case in the Mossi district of Upper Volta, the African Reserves of South Africa and Zimbabwe, the Fouta Djallon Highlands of Guinea and parts of south-eastern Nigeria, land shortages have been aggravated by sheet and gully erosion. In the drier grassland areas of Sokoto Province of Nigeria, Mali, Niger Republic and parts of Zimbabwe, poor harvests and famines, caused by unreliable rainfall, have resulted in the seasonal and permanent migration of young adults.

There are, however, many sparsely settled areas which also export population. Often such areas have no source of earning cash income except through the cultivation of food crops, and thus labour migration offers the easiest method of obtaining money for meeting various expenses. Examples of such areas include the Okoro Highlands district of Uganda, the Shaki district of Nigeria and the Bamako district of Mali.

The major source regions for migrants, therefore, are characterized by a relative lack of wage-earning opportunities. Often the head of the family in such a region does not earn enough money to pay his tax and feed his family for the whole year. It is the mounting poverty of these regions that has induced the more enterprising able-bodied men to migrate to work in the mines, plantations, timber concessions and industrial centres.

Migration and rural change

The consequences of large-scale movements of population are usually considered in terms of the problems posed by the depopulation of rural areas and the problems created by a large influx of people into the cities. The problems of rapid urbanization are considered in Chapter 8. Our concern in this section is with the consequences of migration for rural areas, and we will consider the changes which migration has brought about in them.

Changes in the receiving areas
As might be expected, the changes occasioned by large-scale migration are most obvious in the areas that attract migrants. The increased tempo of activities and the resultant changes in the economy and society are not difficult to identify. The benefits, if any, to the areas exporting labour are not so obvious. Many writers argue that migration is often detrimental to the economy and disruptive to the social organization of the source areas. It appears, however, that the migration process continues today because it is mutually beneficial to both the exporting and the receiving districts.

Starting first with rural destinations, the most obvious change appears to be increasing economic activity shown by rising production figures in mineral and agricultural exports from such areas. The complete replacement of extensive areas of impenetrable forests by man-made forests of cocoa, rubber, oil palms and even forest plantations of teak in some districts has been accomplished largely through the use of migrant labour. Plantation villages and camps have been built in areas that were formerly uninhabited or that supported only a small number of hunting groups and shifting cultivators. In areas where self-employed migrant farmers are found, the traditional settlement patterns have been radically modified by the establishment of numerous camps and farming villages that are basically different from the larger and more compact villages and towns occupied by the indigenous population. This is the case in the Nigerian cocoa belt and the Uganda cotton belt where migrant tenant farmers tend to squat throughout the territory.

In the Akwapim region of the Ghana cocoa belt, Krobo migrants have left a lasting imprint on the local cultural landscape. Krobo migrants usually form a 'company' with a headman who negotiates and acquires a large block of farmland which is then laid out in strips and shared out to each member in proportion to the amount of money he contributed. This sytem of land acquisition has given rise to the 'huza' system of land-holding with its typical street villages (Fig. 7.3) which are basically different from the small compact villages occupied by the indigenous people.

As a general rule, the migrant population in a given district has a much larger population of active adults (15–45 years) compared with the indigenous population. Indeed, in districts such as Ahoada in the Rivers State of Nigeria or parts of Uganda, where migrants outnumber the indigenes, the demographic characteristics of the population have changed. Most self-employed migrants who depend heavily on family labour are married and usually live with their wives. Wage-earning migrants, on the other hand, tend to leave their wives behind in their village of origin. This is particularly so in Central and South Africa where African workers are not allowed to settle permanently in the farms and mines located in 'European Reserves'.

Several examples exist to demonstrate the fact that returning migrants may bring lasting change to their district of origin. One such example is the Ijebu-Remo district of Ogun State in Nigeria, where kolanut production has brought about marked changes in the economy, the agricultural landscape and the growth of settlements. Although a wild variety of kola (*Cola acuminata*) called *Abata* grows locally, it was not until the commercial variety (*Cola nitida*) called *Gbanja* or *Goro* was introduced by returning migrants from Ghana

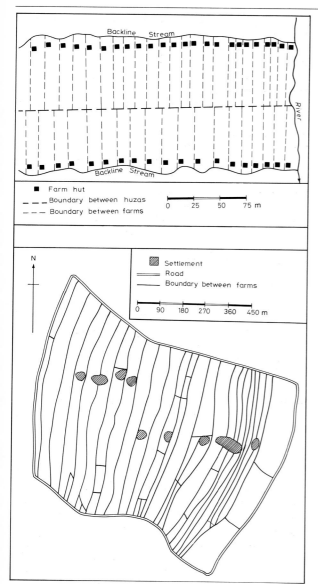

Fig. 7.3 Huza field system of Krobo migrants, Ghana

Farm hut
Boundary between huzas
Boundary between farms
0 25 50 75 m

N

Settlement
Road
Boundary between farms
0 90 180 270 360 450 m

Backline Stream
River
Backline Stream

change on the rural landscapes of tropical Africa. The complete transformations that have taken place in the Katanga and Zambian copper belts, and similar but less pronounced changes that have occurred in the Jos tin fields, the Udi coal mines, the Liberian iron-ore fields and the Sierra Leone diamond fields, have been caused exclusively by mining and auxiliary activities which have attracted large numbers of migrants. At the beginning of this century, most of these mining districts consisted of uninhabited or sparsely settled land occupied by pastoralists or hoe cultivators. Today, these same areas support large towns with many manufacturing and service industries. In addition, some of the villages dating from before the mines have been completely transformed into dormitory settlements for those workers who do not live in the camps. Most of these settlements now receive electricity, piped water and medical facilities provided by the mining syndicates.

Loss or gain in the district of origin

The effects the loss of manpower has on the economy and society of the districts from where the migrants originate feature prominently in the literature on migrant labour. Many writers maintain that although these migrations are induced by economic conditions at the source regions, the loss in population suffered by such regions has often adversely affected the local economy as well as family life and civil authority in traditional societies. Some writers, however, argue that for seasonal migration, the benefits far outweigh the cost (Berg, 1965) and that, on the whole, permanent emigration is still beneficial to the economy of the source regions. We now examine the evidence for these two viewpoints.

Economic disadvantages

Age-selectivity of the migrant population is considered to be the cause not only of some of the economic problems, but also of the social problems prevalent in districts that export population. Starting first with the economic situation, we accept that since most migrants are able-bodied adults of 15–40 years of age, it is reasonable to expect a fall in local food production if the proportion of emigrants is high. It has also been observed that the absence of many young men has created a serious labour shortage for certain jobs such as making yam mounds, roofing houses, or pounding oil palm fruits, all of which are traditionally considered to be male activities. In the Alur ethnic territory of Uganda and in parts of Botswana, it is reported that some families are no longer able to produce enough food because of the absence of men (Southall, 1954; Schapera, 1956).

Detailed studies of the labour situation in several

that large-scale production began. Today, *Cola nitida* has displaced cocoa as the major cash crop in the Ijebu-Remo district and has attracted thousands of migrant Hausa kola traders, many of whom can be found settling in the larger villages. A large number of the indigenous Yoruba population also earn their living from the kolanut trade which is now the most important economic activity in the growing city of Shagamu.

It is in connection with the development of mineral resources, the products of which have influenced the types and location of manufacturing industries, that migration has created a most impressive and lasting

Pl. 7.3 Refugees from Burundi encamped in Zaïre

source regions suggest, however, that the assumption of labour shortage resulting from emigration cannot be sustained. Among the Esu people of Cameroun, for example, Ardener and Ardener (1960) report that although about 40 per cent of the active adult population were absent during the period of their investigation, there was no noticeable drop in food production. A similar observation has been made for the Tonga of Mozambique. At any given time, over 50 per cent of the economically active Tonga males are reported to be absent from their home area, going mostly to the mines of South Africa, but, according to Harris, such a loss has never seriously threatened the 'ability of the population to survive or reproduce' (Harris, 1959, p. 57). The effect of migration on labour in the districts exporting population is even more insignificant in areas such as the Sokoto Home Districts where the timing of seasonal migration coincides with the slack period in the local farming calendar, and does not, therefore, interfere with local demand for farm labour. In many rural areas, there appears to be considerable underemployment, and it is reasonable to argue that in such a situation, the loss of some of the population should lead to a fuller use of available manpower.

Social disadvantages

Many writers consider the social disadvantages of migrant labour to be more serious than the economic disadvantages. Amongst other things, labour migration is said to have contributed to a weakening of 'tribal cohesion' and an undermining of the authority of chiefs in the villages. It is also argued that labour migration has brought about a greater incidence of broken homes and has had the effect of reducing the birth rate in the villages that export population. Indeed, one of the main reasons why the British colonial government rejected the plantation system in Nigeria was the belief that the system would set in motion large-scale movements of people which would result in the disruption of local tribal life by labourers brought into the plantation districts from other parts of the country.

Critics who have written at length about the 'evils' of the migrant labour system appear to ignore the fact that in districts that export population broken homes, lack of respect for elders, sexual immorality, the drop in food production and other associated 'evils' are not necessarily caused by migration. They are essentially part of the much broader processes of social and economic change, in which traditional values and authority are being replaced by those emanating from the urban–industrial way of life. It follows that these changes will continue whether or not labour migration is halted.

The future of migrant labour (rural–rural)

The greater demand for labour to develop the mineral deposits, commercial plantations, private farms and timber concessions has been responsible in large measure for the movement of people from one rural area to another. Today, the demand for labour in many rural areas remains high in spite of mounting unemployment in the cities. In Liberia, labour shortage has been the main factor limiting the expansion programme of the Firestone Rubber Company. The rapid development of the mining sector has aggravated the labour shortage in this country so that in 1957 the Liberian government had to close down some new diamond mines to stop a diamond rush that threatened to worsen the labour situation in the rubber plantations and the iron-ore mines (Jurgen, Tracey, and Mitchell, 1966). In countries like the Ivory Coast, Ghana and Equatorial Guinea, which depend heavily on migrant labour from internal and external sources, production would be drastically curtailed if the migrant labour system were disrupted. Thus, although the authorities of some of the labour-deficit countries are very concerned about their heavy dependence on foreign labour, it is quite clear that the free flow of labour is indispensable for continued economic growth. Stricter immigration controls in West Africa since independence, culminating in the expulsion of about 500,000 aliens from Ghana in 1969–70, have only worsened the labour situation in that country. It appears, therefore, that whether or not the advantages outweigh the disadvantages, labour migration is likely to continue for many decades.

Labour migration has persisted for over eighty years in most parts of Africa. Since the system is rooted in the essentially open colonial economy of the continent, only a complete transformation of that economy can result in any drastic reduction in the volume of rural–rural migrations. There are indications that in Central, East and West Africa, structural changes in the economy are likely to result in a decrease in rural–rural migration and a corresponding increase in rural–urban migration.

References

Addo, N. O. (1974), 'Population Movements in West Africa', *West Africa Regional Seminar on Population Studies*, University of Ghana, Legon, Accra, pp. 47–8.

Ardener, E. and Ardener, S. (1960), *Plantation and Village in the Cameroons*, Oxford University Press, Oxford, p. 227.

Bailey, N. A. (1969), 'Native and Labour Policy', in D. M. Abshire and M. A. Samuels (eds.), *Portuguese Africa – A Handbook*, Pall Mall Press, London, ch. 8, pp. 165–74.

Barber, W. J. (1961), *The Economy of British Central Africa*, Oxford University Press, Oxford, pp. 208–10.

Berg, E. J. (1965), 'The Economics of the Migrant Labour System', in H. Kuper (ed.), *Urbanization and Migration in West Africa*, University of California Press, Berkeley, pp. 160–81.

Cornelisse, P. A. (1972), 'An Economic View of Migration in West Africa: A Two Country Study', unpublished MS. presented at the International African Seminar on Modern Migrations in Western Africa at Dakar, Senegal, April 1972.

Davis, H. R. J. (1964), 'The West African in the Economic Geography of the Sudan', *Geography*, 49, pp. 222–35.

Field, M. J. (1943), 'The Agricultural System of the Manya-Krobo of the Gold Coast', *Africa*, 14, pp. 54–65.

Harris, M. (1959), 'Labour Emigration among the Mozambique Tonga: Cultural and Political Factors', *Africa*, 29.

Hunter, J. M. (1967), 'Population Pressure in a Part of the West African Savanna: A Study of Nangodi, Northeast Ghana', *Annals of the Association of American Geographers*.

Jurgen, H. W., Tracey, K. A. and Mitchell, P. K. (1966), 'Internal Migration in Liberia', *Bulletin, Sierra Leone Geographical Association*, 10, pp. 39–59.

Podlewski, A. (1975), 'Cameroon', in J. C. Caldwell (ed.), *Population Growth and Socio-Economic Change in West Africa*, Columbia University Press, New York, p. 559.

Powesland, P. G. (1954) 'History of the Migration in Uganda', ch. 2 of A. I. Richards (ed.), *Economic Development and Tribal Change*, Cambridge University Press, Cambridge, p. 18.

Roussel, L. (1970), 'Measuring Rural–Urban Drift in Developing Countries: A Suggested Method', *International Labour Review*, 101, no. 3.

Schapera, I. (1956), 'Migrant Labour and Tribal Life in Bechuanaland', in D. Forde (ed.), *Social Implications of Industrialization and Urbanization in Africa South of the Sahara*, UNESCO, p. 208.

Skinner, E. P. (1965), *Labour Migration among the Mossi of the Upper Volta*, University of California Press, Berkeley.

Southall, A. W. (1954), 'Alur Migrants', ch. 6 of A. I. Richards (ed.), *Economic Development and Tribal Change*, Cambridge University Press, Cambridge, p. 158.

Udo, R. K. (1975), *Migrant Tenant Farmers of Nigeria*, African Universities Press, Lagos.

8 The Process and Consequences of Urbanization

Introduction

Africa has the distinction of being both the most sparsely populated and the least urbanized continent. It also has the distinction of recording one of the highest population growth rates (about 2·5 per cent per annum) and the fastest rate of urban growth (about 5·4 per cent per annum from 1950–60). Today the main source of concern to most governments is not the rate of growth of the total population, but the very rapid rate of growth of urban centres. The remarkable political, economic and social changes that have taken place since the end of the Second World War have brought about a phenomenal increase in the total urban populations and in the number of urban centres. Concern over this growth is because it is caused mainly by large-scale migration from rural areas and also because of the intractable problems that the urban explosion is posing for the efficient administration of the cities.

A clear testimony of this concern is the near neurotic reaction of administrators, politicians and traditional rulers, who have continued to denounce the massive influx into the cities. Often, daily newspapers and these public functionaries have urged governments to do something to arrest 'the mass exodus of youths to the cities'. In Nigeria, for example, one main reason why local politicians changed the anti-plantation policy of the British colonial government in 1951 was the belief

Pl. 8.1 The ruins of ancient Zimbabwe

that the plantations would provide employment in rural areas and thereby help to arrest the drift to the cities. The same reason was given in support of the establishment of farm settlements in various parts of the southern states shortly after independence in 1960. Yet the percentage of the population living in areas classified as urban is only 18 per cent for all Africa and 12 per cent for tropical Africa! (The comparative figure for North America is 70 per cent and that of Europe 60 per cent.) The increasing emphasis by most governments on industrialization and the rapid expansion of school enrolments, amongst other factors, suggest that more and more people will continue to migrate to the cities. In the circumstances, the strategy should be one of preparing the urban centres to receive more migrants rather than the current ineffective periodic exhortations for people to stay on the land or for the urban unemployed to return to the land.

The precise definition of the term 'urban centre' varies enormously throughout the world as well as within tropical Africa. Its definition is a part of the procedural decisions of national census authorities and varies even from time to time within the same country. In Nigeria, for example, an urban centre was defined in 1953 as a compact settlement of not less than 5,000 inhabitants, but in 1963 the base population of settlements considered to be urban was raised to 20,000. Settlements with 2,500 inhabitants or more are considered to be urban in Mexico while in Europe the minimum figure recommended in 1964 by the conference of European statisticians was 10,000. The corresponding figure for the United States of America is 2,500 and for Argentina 1,500. For the purpose of international comparisons, the United Nations has adopted a definition of an urban area as a settlement with at least 20,000 inhabitants. The urban population of most countries as nationally defined is therefore generally different from the figure given in United Nations statistics. This point should be borne in mind when making comparisons as well as in interpreting conflicting figures for the urban population for the same country at a particular point in time.

The history of urbanization

The process of urbanization in Africa dates back many centuries. The main area of concentration of pre-colonial urban centres was the West African sub-region which still has the largest number of urban centres in the continent. Apart from the ancient city of Zimbabwe, now in ruins, and the port city of Sofala, the southern African sub-region had no urban centres. Existing urban centres in southern Africa, Central Africa and the non-coastal areas of East Africa are all a creation of

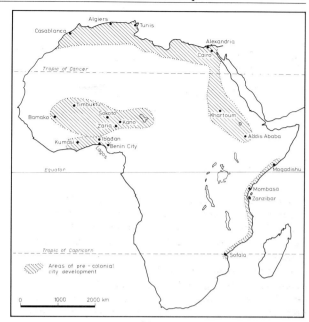

Fig. 8.1 Areas of pre-colonial urbanization

the colonial or post-colonial period. We shall therefore discuss urban development in tropical Africa under three historical periods, namely 1. the pre-colonial period, 2. the colonial period and 3. the post-colonial (independence) period.

Pre-colonial urban centres

All the pre-colonial urban centres were originally basically pre-industrial cities which owed their importance to long-distance trade, administration or religion. Indeed almost all of them were the political capitals of city states. In the West African sub-region, where about 75 per cent of all pre-colonial urban centres are located, the main areas of city growth were in the far northern area lying between latitudes 12°N and 17°N and in the Yoruba ethnic areas of south-west Nigeria. The most prominent of the surviving pre-colonial urban centres of the West African Sudan include Timbuktu, Segou, Bamako, Gao, Ouagadougou, Agades, Katsina and Kano. In Yorubaland, the largest of these urban centres are Ibadan, Ile-Ife, Ogbomosho, Oshogbo, Ilorin, Oyo and Ilesha. There were also a few prominent urban centres in the forest belt, notably Benin City and Kumasi. All these urban centres were associated with both state formation and long-distance trade with the Mediterranean cities of North Africa and southern Europe. Craft industries were also an important economic base of these cities although their populations were predominantly engaged in farming.

93

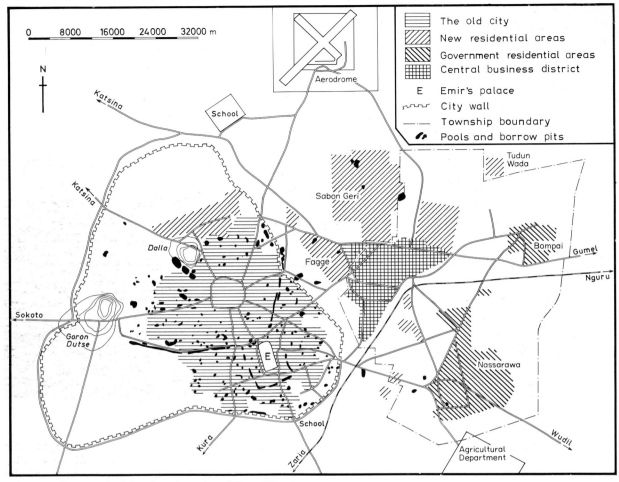

Fig. 8.2 The pre-colonial and modern city of Kano, Nigeria

Along the coast of West Africa, there was another set of traditional urban centres which grew up in response to the trade in slaves and later in palm oil between the coastal people and European traders. Most of these towns were no more than fishing and salt-making villages before the development of the transatlantic trade with Europe. Examples of such coastal urban centres include the city states of Duke Town, Creek Town and Henshaw Town in the Cross River Estuary, the Niger Delta city states of Bonny, Opobo Town, Okrika, Buguma, Abonnema, Warri and Brass and the Yoruba Lagoon port-towns of Epe, Lagos and Badagry, all in Nigeria. Outside Nigeria, the more prominent pre-colonial coastal towns were Whydah, Porto Novo, Keta, Accra, Winneba, Cape Coast, Elmina, Sekondi and Axum. Compared with the pre-colonial urban centres

of the interior, the coastal port-towns had a more cosmopolitan population and were generally much smaller in size. Many of them have since declined in size or ceased to exist following the loss of their middleman position in the trade with Europe which was re-organized during the early colonial period.

In East Africa, where trade contacts with the Mediterranean date back to the Greek period, most of the pre-colonial urban centres are located along the coast. Arab influence is strong in all the cities and indeed the Arabs are credited with introducing an urban way of life into the coastal areas of the sub-region. Like the coastal cities of pre-colonial West Africa, those of East Africa also consisted of very mixed communities reflecting trade contacts with Persia and India, in addition to Arabia. It is the languages of these

Pl. 8.2 The seafront at Lamu – the mangrove poles are awaiting shipment to the Arabian Gulf

various communities that have eventually fused to create Swahili which is now adopted by the predominantly Bantu African peoples of the sub-region. The most prominent of these coastal trading cities are Zanzibar, Mombasa, Lamu, Malindi, Kilwa and Mogadishu. The only pre-colonial cities of the interior in the sub-region are the Ethiopian cities of Harar, Gondar and Axum, associated with state formation dating back to the fifth century AD.

Central and southern Africa are unique in their history of urbanization since almost all the existing cities are associated with European colonization and settlement. A few states and kingdoms existed in these sub-regions before colonization but none of them appears to have been associated with urban development as was the case in West Africa. The ancient city of Zimbabwe which is now in ruins is perhaps the only exception.

Urbanization in the colonial period

During the colonial period a large number of new towns were established to serve the colonial administrative structure and the new economic order. The colonial territories were to produce raw material for the factories of metropolitan Europe, which in turn supplied the territories with manufactured goods. Political stability and trade were the major considerations of the European officers and both preoccupations demanded the concentration of certain activities at centres, some of which eventually grew up to become large towns. Mining, transportation and administrative convenience became important factors in the development of new towns during the period. Important new towns associated with mining activities include Enugu, Jos, Lumumbashi (Elizabethville), Likasi (Jadotville), Kitwe, Ndola and Gwelo. Many new port-towns were also built to handle the export of both minerals and agricultural produce, among which are Conakry, Takoradi, Tema, Port Harcourt, Lobito, Beira and Lourenço Marques (Maputo). Some new towns grew up at important road and railway junctions to serve as administrative headquarters for their districts, for example, Tabora, Kafanchan, Bulawayo and Dodoma.

Outside West Africa, almost all the national capitals of tropical African countries were established as administrative new towns during the colonial period, for example, Nairobi, Kampala, Salisbury and Lusaka. Even in West Africa there is the classic example of

Kaduna which was established by Lord Lugard after he had made several attempts to use existing settlements as the nucleus for the capital of the then Northern Nigeria Protectorate. However in areas like Yorubaland and Hausaland existing cities were selected to serve as administrative headquarters for the various administrative units – district, division or province.

In the eastern states of Nigeria where the village form of settlement was predominant, it was the practice to select a centrally located village to serve as the local administrative headquarters. Usually the name of the village so chosen was also given to the administrative district, division or province for which it served as the capital. The rapid transformation of erstwhile villages into administrative urban centres was an important innovation in the cultural landscape of such areas. Usually the transformation started with the establishment of a district office, police station, prisons, customary and magistrate courts and a post office. These were followed by schools and churches and the construction of special residential quarters for civil servants. The increase in the number of the non-farm population, which included an increasing number of wage-earning labourers as well as those providing basic services to the wage-earners, created an adequate threshold to support daily markets in such centres as Onitsha, Umuahia, Ikot Ekpene and Afikpo.

Fig. 8.3 The colonial district town of Fort Portal, Uganda

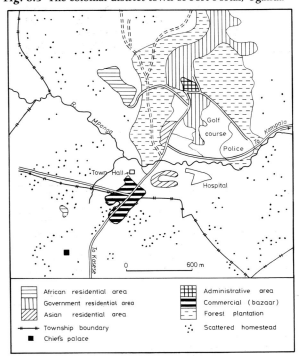

☰ African residential area	⊞ Administrative area
∥∥ Government residential area	▬ Commercial (bazaar)
⧄ Asian residential area	- ‒ - Forest plantation
＋―＋ Township boundary	∴ Scattered homestead
■ Chief's palace	

0   600 m

Post-colonial urban development

Urban development since independence has featured 1. the establishment of new towns, 2. the upgrading in status of many small urban centres which have in consequence experienced a remarkably rapid growth and 3. the rapid growth of the major cities in each country. These new developments have taken place largely in response to political decisions aimed at decentralization in order to further the process of national integration. They are also the result of a deliberate policy of active industrialization aimed at reducing the dependence on foreign goods, thereby conserving foreign exchange and providing employment opportunities for the increasing number of job seekers.

The capital cities of colonial Africa were mostly along the coast serving as the most important ports for the various countries. Apart from extreme congestion in the residential areas of these capital cities, their locations have been found to be unsuitable for effective administration. Some countries have therefore built new capital cities at more central locations. Landlocked Malawi was the first to move its capital from the colonial primate city of Blantyre (104,461 in 1970) to the more centrally located small town of Lilongwe (19,000 in 1970). Tanzania has also moved its capital from Dar-es-Salaam to Dodoma (in 1978) while work is progressing on the new Nigerian Federal capital near Abuja.

Separatist tendencies resulting in attempted secession in Nigeria, Zaïre, the Sudan and Ethiopia have featured prominently since independence. In order to encourage greater involvement and a feeling of belonging, a number of new states, administrative divisions and districts have been created in many countries. The creation of nineteen states in Nigeria, as compared with the four states of 1966, has meant the upgrading of many small urban centres into the status of state capitals. The establishment of government ministries and state offices of federal statutory bodies in these new state capitals has brought about a rapid growth in population and economic activity in such erstwhile dormant urban centres as Akure, Calabar, Owerri, Yola, Maiduguri and Makurdi. Furthermore, the desire of each state government to develop manufacturing in the state capital has considerably broadened the economic base of these urban centres. On a much smaller scale, decentralization has brought about considerable growth in population and diversification of the economy in settlements which have been upgraded to divisional and district headquarters.

The larger cities of the colonial period, such as Dar-es-Salaam, Lagos, Kano, Accra, Blantyre and Abidjan, however, continue to grow rapidly in spite of decentralization. Most new industries continue to be attracted to these larger older cities which already have a relatively highly developed infrastructure and port facilities. In addition, the larger older cities have the advantage of being the leading educational, cultural and commercial centres with better communication links with the outside world.

Characteristics of urbanization

The spatial distribution and size of urban centres

In 1960, only 18 per cent of the population of tropical Africa lived in urban centres as nationally defined, compared with about 47 per cent for South Africa and 30 per cent for North Africa. Within tropical Africa, the largest concentration of urban centres is found in West Africa, especially in the Yoruba ethnic area of south-west Nigeria and in the Hausa Emirates of the Nigerian Sudan. West Africa also has the largest number of cities with over 100,000 people, and most of these were

founded long before the colonial period. East Africa has a few pre-colonial cities but is the least urbanized sub-region (Table 8.1). The spatial distribution and size of the cities are shown in Fig. 8.4.

The three categories of urban size recommended by the United Nations Economic Commission for Africa (ECA) are: urban localities (20,000–100,000), cities (100,001–500,000) and big cities (over 500,000 inhabitants). Using this classification for sub-Saharan Africa in 1970, 32·5 per cent of the urban population lived in urban localities, 42·3 per cent in cities and 25·2 per cent in big cities. West Africa had the largest number of urban centres in each of the three categories (Table 8.1).

It is significant that for any sub-region of tropical Africa, the highest proportion of urban dwellers lives in cities (100,001–500,000 inhabitants). In 1970 there were 69 cities in this size category, 30 of which were located in the West African sub-region. The smaller urban centres, as might be expected, are much more numerous in each sub-region, as shown in Table 8.2. For

Table 8.1 Projections and rates of growth of urban population of tropical Africa 1965–80

Sub-region	1965		1970		1975		1980	
	A	B	A	B	A	B	A	B
West Africa	12,425,000	12·8	15,710,000	14·2	21,075,000	16·5	27,575,000	18·8
Central Africa	2,855,000	9·8	3,695,000	11·1	4,690,000	12·7	5,950,000	18·3
East Africa	5,455,000	6·2	7,010,000	7·3	8,990,000	8·4	11,540,000	9·7
Southern Africa	7,815,000	21·3	9,490,000	23·1	11,445,000	24·7	13,750,000	26·0

Note A – Total population in towns of 20,000 or more.
B – Urban population as percentage of total population.
Source ECA Demography and Social Statistics Section.

Table 8.2 Urbanization in tropical Africa by size of cities in 1970

Sub-region	20,000–50,000			50,001–100,000			100,001–500,000			over 500,000		
	A	B	C	A	B	C	A	B	C	A	B	C
West Africa	79	2·32	17·29	33	2·37	18·05	30	5·81	43·61	4	2·77	21·05
Central Africa	34	0·99	16·13	16	0·97	16·13	14	2·65	45·70	1	1·32	22·04
East Africa (including Ethiopia)	36	1·16	20·00	14	0·83	16·00	13	2·68	42·33	2	1·31	21·67
Southern Africa	35	1·14	15·71	8	0·65	8·80	12	2·63	37·15	3	2·64	38·34
Africa south of the Sahara	184	5·61	17·50	71	4·81	15·00	69	13·77	42·30	10	8·04	25·20

Note A – No. of urban centres.
B – Urban population in millions.
C – Urban population in size category as percentage of total urban population.
Source H. I. Ajaegbu's calculations from Table II of ECA Demographic Handbook for Africa, April 1975.

Table 8.3   Distribution of urban growth rates in tropical Africa

Rate of growth (per cent per annum)	Sub-region			
	West Africa	Central Africa	East Africa	Southern Africa
20–25	Dahomey Mali	—	Rwanda	Botswana
15–20	Liberia Nigeria Upper Volta	—	—	—
10–15	Ghana Ivory Coast Niger Senegal Sierra Leone Togo	Chad Gabon	Uganda Tanzania Zambia	—
5–10	Gambia Guinea	Burundi Central African Republic Congo (Republic) Zaïre	Ethiopia Kenya Madagascar Mauritius	Angola Namibia
2–5	—	—	—	Zimbabwe
0–1	—	Cameroun	—	Mozambique

Source United Nations, *Demographic Handbook for Africa*, Addis Ababa, April 1975, p. 61.

Table 8.4   Rates of increase of urban population in selected countries

Country	Centres with over 20,000		Centres with over 100,000	
	Period	Annual growth rate	Period	Annual growth rate
Ghana	1948–60	11·5	1948–60	9·1
Ivory Coast	1955–61	12·2	1955–61	6·9
Nigeria	1953–63	16·5	1953–63	13·8
Senegal	1955–60	10·8	1955–60	15·1
Congo Republic	1956–62	7·9	1962–65	8·7
Kenya	1948–62	6·6	1948–62	9·7
Tanzania	1957–67	10·9	1957–67	7·8
Rhodesia (Zimbabwe)	1951–65	2·0	1951–56	9·3
Sierra Leone	1955–63	10·4	1959–63	6·3
Zambia	1963–69	12·1	1963–69	18·8
Angola	1950–60	7·0	1950–60	4·7
Uganda	1959–69	10·7	1959–69	10·4

Source United Nations, *Demographic Handbook for Africa*, Addis Ababa, April 1975, pp. 50–2.

example in 1970 there were 184 urban centres with 20,000–50,000 people and 71 with 50,001–100,000. The total number of people living in these smaller urban settlements was however much less, being 17·5 per cent and 15·0 per cent respectively.

Large cities with 500,000 or more people are still very few in tropical Africa, and by 1963 consisted only of Ibadan. In 1970 the number of large cities increased to include Lagos, Kinshasa, Accra–Tema and Addis Ababa, and given the current rate of growth, the large cities of the 1980s in Nigeria alone will consist of Lagos, Ibadan, Kano, Abeokuta, Port Harcourt, Zaria, Onitsha and Kaduna. Outside Nigeria the large cities of the 1980s will include Addis Ababa, Accra, Khartoum, Nairobi, Abidjan, Dakar, Kinshasa, Kananga (Luluabourg), Salisbury, Kampala and Antonanariva (Tananarive).

Although there are few large cities in tropical Africa, there are also few incidences of city primacy, in which a large gap exists between the population of the dominant or primate city and the second-ranking city. A good example of a primate city is Dakar which has a population of about 500,000 compared with 70,000 for the second largest city of Kaolack. Primate cities also exist in the Ivory Coast and Malawi where the populations of the dominant cities of Abidjan and Blantyre are 500,000 and 104,000 respectively as compared with 100,000 for Bouake and 20,000 for Zomba.

Rate of urbanization
The rate of growth of urban populations is currently of greater significance than the actual level of urbanization in the countries of tropical Africa. The rate of increase for the sub-regions, selected countries and selected towns are shown in Tables 8.3 and 8.4. Considering the continent as a whole, the rate of increase of the urban population from 1950–60 was 5·4 per cent per annum, which is about twice the rate of increase of the total population. In most countries of tropical Africa, however, the rate of increase of the urban population is as much as four or five times the rate of increase of the total population. Since the total population is increasing at the rate of 2·5–3·0 per cent per annum, urban growth rates in excess of these figures can be ascribed to migration.

Lagos is considered to be the fastest growing city since 1970, when the Nigerian civil war ended. Others include Kumasi (20 per cent from 1955–60), Yaoundé (14 per cent), N'Djamena (16 per cent) and Monrovia (12 per cent). Some of the new state capitals in Nigeria have also recorded phenomenal increases in population since 1970. The growth of the larger cities of more than 100,000 was about 8·5 per cent from 1950–60 but many capital cities with over 500,000 grew at a much higher rate.

Although the rapid growth of cities in tropical Africa is certainly due to migration, it appears that a large number of migrants to the largest cities originate from smaller urban centres, and not directly from rural areas. The importance of this should not be underrated by those who are engaged in schemes aimed at reducing migration to the larger cities. To achieve this, greater emphasis should be placed on improving living and working conditions in these smaller and medium-sized urban centres.

Internal structure of tropical African cities
The functional zones of traditional urban centres were few during the pre-colonial period and consisted mostly of the residential area of the king or paramount chief, in front of which was located the king's market (amongst the Yoruba), and various other residential districts. The coastal cities had a port zone and beach markets. There was no special industrial zone since local manufacturing was carried out in cottages. Most pre-colonial cities were surrounded by walls and like all pre-industrial cities were characterized by low and crowded buildings, poor sanitation and narrow winding streets or passage-ways for pedestrians and for animal transport. Growth was slow except in times of civil war when rural people flocked into the city for protection; at all times the non-farm population within the city rarely exceeded 10 per cent. Many pre-colonial cities, however, attained populations of over 100,000, especially in Yorubaland; but even for such large cities, there was no dominant business district comparable to what exists today.

It was during the colonial period, when many new cities were founded, that the spatial structure of the older cities changed considerably as a result of the more diversified functions which these cities were made to perform under the new political and economic order. In those British territories were the policy of indirect rule applied, the chief preoccupation of the colonial administrative office was political stability and expansion of trade with Britain, and not social change. Therefore in areas like Yorubaland and the Nigerian Sudan there was a deliberate effort to prevent any disruption of local administration in those large traditional towns which were selected as headquarters for administrative districts, divisions or provinces. New residential areas were created outside the city walls to house the non-indigenous migrant population, hence the growth of *Tudun Wadas* for northern Nigerian strangers and *Sabon Garis* for southern Nigerian strangers in Hausa cities such as Kano and Zaria. Further residential segregation in these old cities was occasioned by the creation of special government residential areas (GRA) which were reserved exclusively for British colonial administrative staff. The

European managers and senior officials of commercial firms also lived in these all-white segregated zones. Usually the GRA was separated from the African residential areas by a green belt or zone of open space or *cordons sanitaires*, much of which has been built up since independence. The central business district (CBD) in all the old towns is located outside the city walls, usually close to the railway station, if it exists. However, the busiest centre of activity in the daytime is not the colonial-period central business district but the main marketplace which in the older cities is also usually outside the ancient city walls.

The internal structure of the colonial-period new town is basically different, being much better planned and generally much healthier. The grid pattern streets with wide pavements in such cities as Accra, Dar-es-Salaam, Nairobi, Dakar, Abidjan and Salisbury provide a great contrast to the narrow winding unpaved streets of the traditional African cities of Ibadan, Kano, Katsina and Zaria. The central business district stands out clearly in each new town and is usually characterized by high-rise buildings as is the case in European cities. Indeed the business area of Dakar is more like a French Mediterranean town while the central parts of Nairobi or Salisbury are typically British. Specialization by area is more obvious, so that there are distinct industrial, military, administrative, business and residential districts. Government residential areas are also typical of the colonial-period new towns of Enugu, Port Harcourt, Kaduna, Kampala and Lusaka.

Recreational facilities such as bars and sporting grounds in the older pre-colonial cities are located outside the city walls, usually in the predominantly migrant residential areas. In the colonial-period new towns, such facilities are located near to the city centre or close to port facilities in the case of the coastal port-towns. In all cases the needs of Europeans were provided for in private social clubs which remained segregated in British territories until the eve of independence.

City growth has been particularly rapid since independence, and has resulted in a serious shortage of suitable residential accommodation, and consequently high house rents. A large number of low-class residential areas, peopled by a predominantly migrant population, has grown up in the peripheral districts of all large cities. These are the so-called shanty towns, or *bidonvilles*, that is 'towns built of tin-cans', a few of which are quite close to the city core. In the major cities, such as Lagos, Lusaka and Dakar, the shanty towns house up to one-third of the city population. In Lusaka, for example, the number of shanty towns increased from nine to thirty-two during the period 1967–70 and housed as many as 100,000 of the total city population of 270,000 (Simmance, 1973). A few permanent

Pl. 8.3 The ex-colonial port of Maputo

buildings exist in these shanty towns but the typical building consists of a tin roof supported on planks or wooden poles and with walls of planks or tin sheets. There is no planning whatsoever since the buildings are not usually authorized. Shanty towns have few or no amenities and are characterized by narrow winding lanes and large heaps of household refuse which often block the streets. They are extremely congested and filthy, especially during the rainy season, and usually provide hide-outs for thieves, prostitutes, smugglers and drug-peddlers.

Socio-economic characteristics

African cities, like those in other parts of the world, are the centres of modernization and change. As seats of governments and the main educational, financial and industrial centres, cities are also the foci of political activity. The great diversity and size of the population have tended to create a rather impersonal atmosphere, making it possible for people to live in isolation in the midst of crowds! Yet the city is not quite a melting-pot of cultures; some form of kinship, even if voluntary, exists. Voluntary associations such as clan, district, provincial and ethnic unions abound in all African cities. Such associations usually meet once every month and aim to protect the interests of its members, including new arrivals, by helping to find them jobs and residential accommodation. The emergence of urban residential areas in which members of particular ethnic groups are dominant is often the result of the co-operation existing between members of ethnic associations.

Even the extended family system, which some writers claim to be incompatible with city life, has survived in many African cities, although there are indications of its continuing disintegration. Studies of the family system in both the older pre-colonial cities such as Lagos, Ibadan, Timbuktu, and the newer colonial-period cities of Dakar, Kinshasa, Brazzaville and Accra, confirm its continuing existence. Indeed most migrants to the cities are usually housed by members of the extended family before they are able to find their feet and can afford to rent their own accommodation. The security provided by the system has certainly encouraged large-scale migration of unemployable persons into many cities. An increasing number of urban residents are however rebelling against the system that tends to create excessive demands on their meagre income.

Class or caste differentiation was common in the older pre-colonial cities, especially in relation to the production of crafts as well as in the performance of religious rites. The breakdown of the guild system in the crafts industry and the influence of Christianity and Islam on people's beliefs have tended to reduce social barriers wherever they existed. During the early colonial period there were instances in which the sons of freed slaves readily accepted a western education and subsequently became bosses to less-educated sons of the so-called free men. Unrestricted social mobility is an important characteristic of contemporary African cities.

Since independence, the expansion of educational facilities and deliberate government policy have combined to eliminate the dominant role of Europeans, Asians and Arabs in the commercial sector of the urban economy, as well as in the professions. This is particularly so in countries formerly under British rule. Furthermore, the larger cities have become important industrial centres.

Demographic characteristics

The largest cities are characterized by high population densities especially in the core areas and in the shanty towns. The core area of Lagos, for example, had about 13,000 persons per sq km in 1963 compared with only 3,110 persons per sq km for the colonial town of Port Harcourt. In all cities there is a great variation in the population density of the low-income residential area compared with the areas occupied by the middle class and the high-income groups.

Ethnic heterogeneity is another important demographic feature of African cities, including such pre-colonial cities as Zaria, Kano, Mombasa and Kumasi. Some of the newer cities, such as Jos, Abidjan, Dakar, Nairobi, Lusaka and Dar-es-Salaam, however, have a much more cosmopolitan population. Urban centres with substantial populations of Europeans and Asians are largely restricted to the sub-regions of East Africa, southern Africa and to some extent Central Africa. In West Africa the largest concentrations of European peoples are in the capital cities of former French West

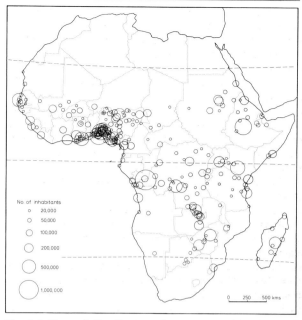

Fig. 8.4 Size and distribution of major cities

Africa, notably Dakar, Abidjan and Cotonou.

The age and sex composition of African urban populations reflects the fact that migration is the main component of urban population growth. Migration, as is well known, is selective of age and sex, hence the relatively large proportion of people in the age cohorts of 15–39 and also the predominance of males in African urban populations. In Lagos, for example, the 1963 census showed that those aged below 15 years made up 31 per cent of the male population and 43 per cent of the female population, compared with 47 per cent under 15 years of age in the total population of the country. The age pyramid for Lagos, as indeed for other African cities, however, has approximately the same shape as for the national population. The small number of those aged 60 years and above (only 2 per cent for males and 3 per cent for females) is partly a reflection of the still relatively short life expectancy and also of the fact that most retired migrants usually return to their place of origin.

Male predominance in the urban population is caused largely by the fact that most young migrants consist of unmarried males and partly by the fact that some married migrants tend to leave their wives in the villages until they are able to secure accommodation in the city. This phenomenon is more pronounced amongst such ethnic groups as the Hausa who are predominantly Muslims and whose religion frowns on the free movement of unmarried women. In Lagos, for example, the 1963 census showed that 58 per cent of the population consisted of males while 42 per cent were females. The sex ratio of the Lagos Hausa population was 2,076 males to 1,000 females as compared with a sex ratio of 1,685 among the Ibo and 1,198 among the Yoruba. In Kinshasa, the overall sex ratio in 1957 was 1,720 males to 1,000 females.

As a rule, urban fertility levels are lower than for rural areas, except in Zaïre where the fertility rate is higher in urban areas (Ohadike, 1968; Knoop, 1966). Unlike other rural parts of Africa, low fertility levels are a feature of rural Central Africa including Zaïre, and the higher fertility level in Kinshasa appears to be the result of improvements in health services and living standards in the city as compared with rural areas. On the other hand modernization in other cities, notably in the sub-regions of West Africa and East Africa, has resulted in the increasing desire for fewer children. The fact that birth control clinics and modern contraceptives are more readily available in the cities than in rural areas is another factor influencing the decline of fertility levels. And furthermore most professional women in the cities, especially trained teachers, nurses and university graduates, marry much later than women in rural areas.

Mortality levels are also lower in urban areas than in rural areas, in spite of the low standard of environmental sanitation in the shanty towns and other areas occupied by low-income urban workers. The concentration of city medical and health facilities, which receive clean piped water, have been largely responsible for the great reduction in infant mortality, death at birth and from infectious diseases.

Consequences of rapid urbanization

Political events in African countries since independence have confirmed that a rapidly urbanizing society is socially and politically very volatile. People flocking into the cities are generally highly motivated individuals with high expectations and governments have to endeavour to satisfy them. Their demands on governments for improved social services appear to be insatiable and yet a large number of the migrants are not in a position to contribute financially towards the cost of the services which they demand as a right. In this concluding section we present a brief review of the problems posed by rapid urbanization.

Mounting unemployment in the cities is one of the main consequences of rapid urbanization. Job opportunities are not growing as fast as the number of migrants and, in addition, a large number of migrants are not qualified for available jobs. The result is that many migrants are obliged to live as parasites on relatives and fellow clansmen so that in the big cities it is common to find as many as seven people sleeping in a room meant for one or two persons. Many others roam the streets by day selling goods such as handkerchiefs, radio cassettes, watches and toys, and sleep at petrol stations in the night; while a considerable number take to pilfering

Table 8.5   Growth of selected cities in tropical Africa

City	Year	Population	Year	Population	Annual growth rate
Accra	1948	136,000	1960	491,000	11·3
Abidjan	1955	127,000	1960	180,000	7·2
Bulawayo	1946	53,000	1964	214,000	8·1
Calabar	1952	46,700	1963	76,400	4·5
Conakry	1945	26,000	1960	113,000	10·3
Dakar	1945	132,000	1960	383,000	7·4
Dar-es-Salaam	1948	69,000	1957	129,000	7·2
Douala	1954	118,000	1964	187,000	4·7
Fort Lamy (N'Djamena)	1955	29,000	1963	92,000	15·5
Kaduna	1952	38,800	1963	149,900	13·1
Kinshasa	1946	110,000	1961	420,000	9·3
Kumasi	1955	75,000	1960	190,000	20·4
Lagos, greater	1952	328,900	1963	1,089,900	11·5
Nairobi	1948	119,000	1962	315,000	7·2
Lourenço-Marques (Maputo)	1950	94,000	1961	184,000	6·3
Luanda	1950	150,000	1960	220,000	3·9
Lusaka	1950	26,000	1964	122,000	11·7
Yaounde	1955	38,000	1962	93,000	13·8

Source Ajaegbu, H. I., 'Urbanization in Africa', in Udo, R. K. *et al.* (eds.) *Population Education Source Book for Sub-Saharan Africa*, Heinemann, London, 1979, Table 7, p. 87.

Pl. 8.4 Mathare Valley slum area in Nairobi

in public places by day and to robbery at night. Begging for alms by able-bodied men is also a common feature of life in African cities, especially in West Africa.

The demand for housing far exceeds the supply so that even those who can pay for a room are obliged to lodge with friends or relatives. The result is extreme congestion and excessive use of household facilities such as toilets and baths which readily break down. Overcrowding has also resulted in the generation of large quantities of waste water and household rubbish which constitute a source of environmental pollution as there are no adequate drainage or refuse disposal facilities. The situation is particularly bad in cities such as Lagos, where in 1975 only 17 per cent of houses in the Lagos metropolitan area had flush toilets, while 50 per cent had bucket latrines and 26 per cent pit latrines (Morgan, 1979). Often, in the outlying districts and shanty towns, the pit latrines fill up and overflow while the large piles of uncleared rubbish block the streets and drainage channels. Bathrooms in most low-income residential areas usually consist of small enclosures fenced with planks or iron sheets and are also used as urinals. The waste emanating from these enclosures flows directly into the streets, most of which have no drainage channels, often making them muddy and impassable and at the same time generating a most unpleasant odour! It is at its worst during the rainy season when the surroundings are extremely messy. The pollution of well water by seepages from pit latrines is quite common.

Small-scale industries in the larger cities are also a major source of environmental pollution. In the absence of drainage channels, industrial wastes, including those of toxic cyanide, are allowed to flow into the streets. And yet most of these small-scale industries are located within or near to the already congested and filthy low-class residential districts.

Given the situation presented above, it is not surprising that all but 15 per cent of schoolchildren in Lagos have either hookworm or round-worm, and that 10 per cent of all deaths in that city are attributed to diarrhoea and dysentery. The great demand for medical facilities is caused partly by the increasing population but also by the unhygienic surroundings in which most people live. The large influx of people into Lagos is responsible for the fact that the doctor–population ratio in 1975 was 1:5,000 as compared with 1:2,000 in 1955. Yet the number of doctors has increased about five times since 1955 – an example of expanding facilities failing to keep pace with the rapidly growing population.

The chaotic traffic situation in the largest cities is largely caused by rapid urbanization and the mushrooming of residential areas in which houses are built without regard to planning regulations. Most streets are very narrow and unsurfaced and in some cases it is impossible to gain access by car to houses in the peripheral but rapidly growing suburbs. Public transport is even more poorly developed so that in some of the largest cities workers have to queue for hours to wait for a bus.

The demands which the larger African cities make on governments are therefore considerable. It is not surprising that most governments react by making ineffective requests that people should return to the land, particularly in view of increasing labour shortages in the rural sector. On the positive side, governments have sought to tackle the problems of the city by establishing more manufacturing industries with a view to creating more jobs. Some governments have also embarked on building houses for low-income workers although it must be realized that this strategy cannot hope to resolve the problem of the increasing growth of shanty towns, the inhabitants of which are mostly self-employed. Considerable urban redevelopment is also taking place in the form of the widening of roads and slum-clearance schemes. Much still remains to be done to make African cities habitable for the vast majority of the population.

References

Knoop, H. (1966), 'Some Demographic Characteristics of a Suburban Squatting Community of Leopoldville: A Preliminary Analysis', *Cahiers Economiques et Sociaux*, VI, no. 2. Kinshasa, pp. 119–46.

Morgan, R. W. (1979), 'Migration into Lagos, Nigeria', in R. K. Udo *et al.* (eds.), *Population Education Source Book for Sub-Saharan Africa*, Heinemann, London.

Ohadike, P. O. (1968), 'Marriage, family and Family Growth in Lagos (Nigeria)', in J. C. Caldwell and C. Okonjo (eds.), *The Population of Tropical Africa*, Longman, London, pp. 379–92.

Simmance, A. J. F. (1973), *Urbanization in Zambia*, Ford Foundation International Urbanization Survey, New York.

Section C
Primary Economic Activities

9 Agriculture of the Traditional and Colonial Periods

Throughout tropical Africa, agriculture is still the most important sector of the economy in terms of the large number of people who earn a living from it and also because it is the main source of food and raw materials for manufacturing. This applies even to those countries such as Nigeria, Zaïre, Guinea, Mauritania and Zambia where the main source of foreign exchange earnings and government revenue is derived from minerals. The fact that mining is a wasting asset has been recognized by the governments of these mineral-rich countries, and so has the need to develop the agricultural sector from funds derived from mining. Currently, agriculture employs more than 60 per cent of the total economically active population. Indeed in some countries the proportion is much greater, the figure for Niger being as high as 97 per cent, while that of Botswana is 91 per cent. Zaïre, Sudan and the Ivory Coast each have about 86 per cent of their active population engaged in agriculture (United Nations, 1975). It is against this background that the role of agriculture in the future development of tropical Africa must be assessed. Here we shall consider aspects of traditional agricultural practices and the efforts and progress made during the colonial period to develop modern agriculture with a view to raising living standards.

Basic features of traditional agriculture

Traditional agriculture in Africa is characterized by low-level technology and extreme dependence on nature. Farm implements consist of a great variety of hoes, machetes, sickles and the digging stick. Much human labour is required for all farm operations and in consequence, output per man is very low. The rainfall regime determines the farming calendar and the size of the harvest is greatly influenced by its variability. Prolonged droughts often result in disastrous crop failures, loss of livestock and severe famines such as the one which occurred in the Sahelian region from 1972–4. Rudimentary irrigated agriculture is practised along the seasonal floodplains (*fadamas* in Hausaland and *dambos* in Zambia and Zimbabwe). Such floodland irrigation, however, depends on the natural flow of the rivers and flood heights, both of which vary with the amount and regime of the rainfall.

The farming system is extensive and is characterized by long fallows, except in areas of extreme population pressure on the land. Shifting cultivation, characterized by the rotation of cultivated fields, accompanied by the movement of settlements, thrives wherever farmland is abundant, and is the predominant system of cultivation in much of East and Central Africa as well as in parts of West Africa. In the more densely settled areas, a modified system of the rotation of bush fallows around a fixed settlement has emerged and in the congested districts this system has been further modified to create pockets of permanent cultivation. Permanent cultivation, where it exists, has been made possible by the generous application of household manure, the use of which is very restricted in areas of shifting cultivation and rotation of bush fallows.

Field shapes are irregular and although field sizes are small by any standards, they vary enormously from one ecological area to another and also with the size of the family. In the forest belt of West Africa only a few farms exceed 0·8 hectares (2 acres) although farm sizes of 2–4 hectares (5–10 acres) are common in the open grassland areas. Smaller fields of about 0·2 hectares are more usual in the very densely populated areas of the eastern states of Nigeria. Indeed in the whole of the three eastern states of Nigeria about 58 per cent of all fields under cultivation in 1963–4 were under one hectare in size (Federal Office of Statistics, 1966). In East Africa the farms are relatively larger in size, the upper limit being about 3 hectares. It is therefore not surprising that African farms are generally referred to as gardens, by some European and American writers. However, in any given year one farming family may cultivate three or more separate fields which are usually located anything between 2 and 11 km from one another.

Variations in field size between the forest and savanna regions is caused partly by the greater difficulty in clearing a forest of trees when preparing farmland compared with grassland areas where the bush is set on fire without having to fell trees or chop branches. The amount of labour which the farmer can muster for weeding also helps to determine the size of the farm that he can cope with. In the densely settled areas of Iboland, Mossi territory and Kikuyuland, the small size of farm plots is caused by shortage of farmland. Dry-season farms located along river flood-plains (*fadama* or *dambo*) are also generally very small in size because of the limited area of seasonally flooded land in any given locality. The amount of seed yam available for cultivation is also a major factor influencing the size of farmland in the yam-growing areas, the cost of seed yam for a hectare of land being about forty times as much as that of rice seeds.

Mixed cropping is the rule in traditional African farming. A typical Kikuyu field, for example, contains maize, beans and sweet potatoes grown together, while a typical Ibo farm plot contains yams, maize, okra, pepper, pumpkin, fluted pumpkin and melon, grown together. About the middle of the farming season, that is before the first crops are harvested, the appearance of the farm plot is usually chaotic, as plants compete with one another for light, while the creeping vegetables provide a near complete cover for the ground. Mixed cropping may result in a net decrease in yield per hectare per crop, but its great advantage is that it serves as an insurance against the failure of any one crop. In addition mixed cropping ensures a continuous harvest throughout the farming year. It also provides a greater variety of diet and protects the ground against erosion and the growth of exotic weeds. Most farmers in tropical Africa keep some domestic livestock, notably, goats, sheep and the hardy indigenous poultry. In addition many farmers in the grassland areas also own cattle. However, livestock are rarely integrated with arable farming. The cattle population is under the care of specialist nomadic herders such as the Masai, the Cattle Fulani and the Tuareg, many of whom own large herds and also take charge of cattle owned by some sedentary farmers. A rudimentary form of mixed farming is, however, practised in some areas.

Classification of farmland

Two classes of farmland are recognized by most settled agricultural groups. These are the distant or main farmland which the Yoruba refer to as *oko egan* (that is farms in the forest or bush) and home plot or compound land referred to as *oko etile* in Yoruba. The compound land is an area of intensive and permanent cultivation which is located within and in the immediate surroundings of the compound or homestead which houses the farming family. Cultivation includes vegetables for making soup or stew such as okra, pepper, fluted pumpkins, tomatoes and spinach, and also maize, yams and fruit trees. Compound lands rarely exceed 0·2 hectares and are generally much smaller than plots located in the distant farmland. The variety of crops grown on the compound land is greater and the crops from it are usually meant for home consumption.

Although the distinction between the compound land and the distant farmland exists all over tropical Africa, farmlands in the drier savanna are usually classified as upland or wet-season farms and *fadama* (*dambo*) or dry-season farms. In effect the upland farms which are cropped during the rainy season consist of compound lands and distant farms. *Fadama* farms are located on river floodplains which are usually so small in extent that the size of plots is also very small. Indeed many villagers do not possess *fadama* farms and are obliged to concentrate on making local crafts during the dry season or to migrate to work in distant areas to obtain cash to supplement their farm income. Crops of the *fadama* in West Africa include tobacco, rice and sugarcane which are planted soon after the annual flood subsides. In south Central Africa, the main crops of these dry-season farms are maize, beans and pumpkins. It is in the *fadamas* that some rudimentary form of irrigation is practised such as in the Gungawa district of the Kainji Lake Basin of Nigeria.

Farming systems and farming regions

The farming system adopted in a particular area is a reflection of the stage of technological development of the people and their adjustment to the physical environment. For any given area, the traditional system of farming may change as a result of increasing pressure of population on the land or because of the introduction

Fig. 9.1 Systems of cultivation

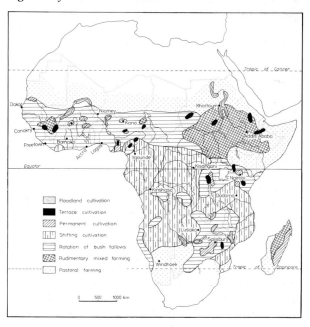

of new crops, especially perennial tree crops. In tropical Africa the systems of farming associated with traditional agriculture are (see Fig. 9.1, p. 107):

1. Nomadic herding
2. Rudimentary mixed farming
3. Shifting cultivation
4. Rotational bush fallow
5. Permanent cultivation
6. Terrace cultivation
7. Floodland cultivation
8. Market gardening

Nomadic herding

In tropical Africa, nomadic herding is based on cattle, sheep, goats and to some extent camels. Owing to the widespread occurrence of the tsetse fly, most of the cattle population in western, north-central and eastern tropical Africa is concentrated in areas which are too dry for cropping and where water and natural forage are available for only a few months in the year. Herders therefore have to move from one place to another in search of water and grazing and the length of stay at a particular place depends on the availability of these resources. Of course the annual migrations follow defined routes and there are fixed points of settlement in the process, a situation which makes it possible for the nomads to carry out some cultivation of grains. Indeed amongst some groups, such as the Tswanas of Botswana, the herding of cattle in distant cattle posts is carried out by young men while other members of the family concentrate on food-crop farming. The purely nomadic herder who obtains all his needs from animals does not exist in tropical Africa since the Masai and the Cattle Fulani, for example, exchange milk and meat for grains and pulses with the Kikuyu and the Hausa respectively. The settlements of nomadic herders consist of temporary tents or wooden structures with grass thatch. Overgrazing is a common feature of this primitive form of pastoralism and so is the destruction of vegetation caused by the annual burning of coarse grass to enhance the rapid growth of fresh grass. Both practices result in environmental deterioration, soil erosion and further reduction of available grazing land.

Rudimentary mixed farming

Mixed farming, which involves the integration of livestock and crop farming, as practised in countries like New Zealand, England and parts of the United States of America, is absent in tropical African traditional agriculture. Some ethnic groups, such as the Shuwa Arabs of Nigeria, the Chagga of Tanzania and the Tonga of Zimbabwe, do practise some rudimentary form of mixed farming in which cattle are stall-fed. The cultivation of fodder crops for feeding cattle is, however, absent and, given the seasonality of natural grazing, it has not been possible to keep more than a few

head of cattle around the homestead. Most cultivators keep a few livestock, mostly goats and sheep, which are stall-fed in the forest belt, as well as hens which are let loose to forage for themselves, as are goats and sheep in the grassland areas. Large mixed farms owned by European settlers are common in Kenya and Zimbabwe.

Shifting cultivation

This is the most primitive and most extensive system of cultivation and was very widespread in the past. It is a system which is adapted to the relatively poor skeletal soils of the forest and savanna regions which become readily impoverished in the absence of manure. Cultivated fields are therefore moved every two or three years and when the fields become very remote from the village, the settlement is also moved. Shifting cultivators in tropical Africa keep such domestic animals as poultry, goats, sheep, pigs and, in some areas, cattle. Today this system of farming is restricted to very sparsely settled and relatively isolated areas such as the Ekoi ethnic territory of Nigeria, the southwest of Ivory Coast and parts of central Zaïre. The building of more permanent houses has tended to restrict the regular movement of settlements.

Fig. 9.2 Land use near Ibadan, Nigeria (after J. O. Oyolese)

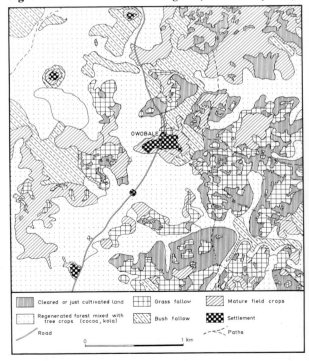

Cleared or just cultivated land	Grass fallow	Mature field crops
Regenerated forest mixed with tree crops (cocoa, kola)	Bush fallow	Settlement
Road	0 1 km	Paths

Rotational bush fallow

Several factors, including increasing population, the need to settle permanently in an accessible village or hamlet with basic social services and the building of more permanent houses, have combined to bring about the predominance of the rotational bush fallow system which is basically a modification of shifting cultivation. Cultivated fields rotate around a fixed settlement and the length of the fallow period varies from four to over seven years depending on the amount of land available to the local population. In parts of the eastern states of Nigeria shrubs are planted in fallow bush to help generate more leaf fall and to provide yam poles. Under this system increasing demand for farmland and the adoption of commercial tree-crop farming have resulted in the cultivation of fields located at distances of up to 10 km from the village. Many farmers, especially in the cocoa belt of Nigeria and in Botswana, have therefore had to build temporary huts in the distant farms where they spend about five days of the week and in some cases the whole of the farming season (Goddard, 1965).

Permanent cultivation

Cultivation without fallow is permanent cultivation, generally associated with compound land and floodland cultivation. Permanent cultivation is also found in areas of great population pressure on available farmland. It is a labour intensive form of cultivation in which the output per hectare is very high, and is the only practicable alternative to large-scale emigration from such areas. Prominent districts where permanent cultivation is practised include the Kano 'close-settled zone', the Sokoto Home Districts, parts of the Ibo and Ibibio districts of south-eastern Nigeria, the Mossi district of Upper Volta, parts of Kikuyuland and much of Rwanda and Burundi. In almost all of these overcrowded areas, the population density is over 200 per sq km (500 per sq mile). Soil impoverishment and soil erosion are common and as a rule such areas are characterized by fragmented holdings, low per capita income and a shortage of food.

Terrace cultivation

Indigenous terrace cultivation in tropical Africa is associated with defensive settlements established during the pre-colonial period of civil unrest in many parts of the region. Remnants of abandoned terraces are common in areas such as the Nsukka district of Nigeria, parts of the Jos Plateau as well as parts of Kenya, Ethiopia and Zimbabwe where people have since deserted their hill settlements to build on more accessible sites on the nearby plains (Floyd, 1964).

Pl. 9.1 Strip fields at the foot of the Panyam Crater, Nigeria

Indigenous terrace cultivation continues in some densely settled upland areas such as the Maku district near Awgu in Nigeria where the terraced slopes of the Awgu escarpment are cultivated every year. In this district the terrace walls, which vary from a few cm to over 1·5 m, are constructed with irregular-shaped lateritic stones. Modern bench terraces constructed by soil conservationists during the colonial period are also common in Zimbabwe, Zaïre and Kenya where the terraced fields are planted with tree crops such as tea, coffee and citrus fruits. Terracing requires skill and capital. Terraced farming is therefore not only intensive but permanent, a situation made possible by the generous application of household manure.

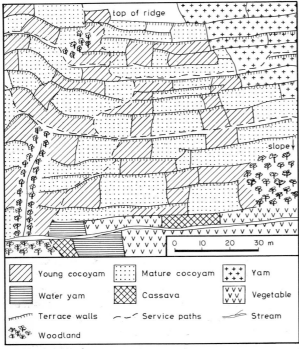

Fig. 9.3 Terrace cultivation at Maku, near Enugu, Nigeria (after B. Floyd)

Floodland cultivation
Although large-scale irrigated agriculture has become very important since the end of the Second World War in developing the dry savanna and semi-arid areas of tropical Africa, traditional irrigated agriculture is rare. In most cases irrigated cultivation occurs in seasonally flooded river plains, in grassland areas where the water is provided naturally by floodwaters. Artificial or man-controlled irrigation involving the use of calabashes to lift water from the riverbed for valuable crops such as onions is practised in a few areas like Oyo Province and the Gungawa district of the Kainji Lake Basin while

shaduf irrigation is common in the northern Nigerian districts of Kano and Zaria. A relatively well-developed floodland cultivation involving the use of canals and channels is practised in the Barotse Plain of western Zambia. Irrigated plots are very intensively cultivated and the field sizes are generally very small. Important crops of floodland farms in grassland areas include onions, carrots, sugarcane, guinea corn, sweet potatoes and rice. Along the coast of Guinea and Sierra Leone rice is produced in locally prepared polders involving the clearance of mangrove swamps and the construction of enclosed rice fields in which drainage is skilfully controlled in order to reduce salinity.

Market gardening
The development of market gardening in the suburbs of large urban centres is a relatively new feature of traditional African agriculture. It is an intensive form of cultivation featuring the production of special crops such as lettuce, cabbages, carrots, tomatoes and potatoes, all of which were formerly imported from Europe to parts of tropical Africa, especially West Africa. The adoption of these crops and the rapid expansion of market gardening around the cities show that, like farmers all over the world, the African farmer responds readily to local market conditions.

Crops

Staple food crops and regions of dominant crops

Although food habits are difficult to change, the peoples of tropical Africa have adopted a number of staple food crops introduced from other parts of the world, notably cassava, cocoyams, the hybrid corn, swamp rice and certain varieties of yams. In general, however, the rate of adoption of new food crops in most areas has been much slower than for such industrial crops as cocoa, cotton, wattle and tobacco. This appears to be related to the great emphasis which the colonial powers placed on the expansion of industrial crop production for export and the ready market which existed for such crops. Staple food crops in comparison had a very limited market in the largely subsistent food economy of the early colonial period. In most countries, rapid urbanization, which started in the 1950s, and the consequent upsurge in the non-farm population have since created a great demand for local staples. In consequence, the yam- and guinea-corn-eating Nupe people and the yam-eating Ezza Ibo of Abakaliki, both in Nigeria, now produce large quantities of swamp rice for sale to other parts of the country. A considerable internal trade in staple food crops exists between different ecological regions, especially the forest and

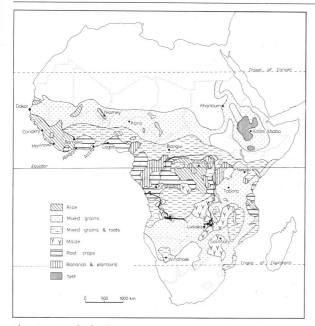

Fig. 9.4 Staple food crops – regions of dominance

Pl. 9.2 A rice field in Casamance Province, Senegal

the savanna, and the variety of staple food commonly eaten in most cultural areas has increased. Regions of dominant staple food crops determined by ecological factors as well as by food habits still stand out distinctively (Fig. 9.4) and are discussed below.

Grains

There are three major groups of food crops cultivated in tropical Africa. These are grains, roots and fruits. The most widespread grains are guinea corn (sorghum), millet and maize, the first two being restricted to the grassland areas while maize is also cultivated in the forest belt. Both guinea corn and millet are indigenous to tropical Africa, but maize was introduced from tropical America by the Portuguese. In general, guinea corn and millet are the staple foods of the grassland areas north of the Equator, that is in the Guinea, Sudanese and Sahelian grasslands extending from Senegal through Nigeria to Ethiopia and the Horn of Africa. Both guinea corn and millet are often inter-cropped, especially in West Africa where guinea corn is much more widespread, and where the more hardy millet is cultivated largely on the poorer, light sandy soils of the drier Sudan and Sahel regions. Maize is also important in the Guinea savanna of West Africa but assumes the role of a dominant staple food crop in Angola, Zimbabwe, Malawi and parts of Zaïre, that is, in the cooler upland grassland areas south of the Equator.

Wheat, barley and teff are dominant only in Ethiopia, although wheat and barley, which originated from

south-west Asia, are now widely cultivated in the Kenya Highlands, northern Tanzania and central Zimbabwe. Wheat is also cultivated under irrigation in the Lake Chad Basin of Nigeria. Teff (*Eragrostis abyssinica*) is indigenous to Ethiopia and is still the main staple food crop of the Ethiopian plateau area.

Unlike the other grains, rice thrives well in areas of heavy rainfall and high humidity, where root crops are also cultivated. In West Africa, which is by far the largest producer of rice in tropical Africa, the coastal belt is divided by the Bandama River in the Ivory Coast into a western rice zone and an eastern yam zone. Varieties of swamp rice introduced from India and Indo-China are widely cultivated along the mangrove swamps of Guinea and Sierra Leone as well as in inland freshwater swamps such as the bolilands of Sierra Leone. Since about 1950, swamp rice cultivation has extended into the yam zone of West Africa, notably in the Bida area of the Niger Valley and the rain-fed swamps of Afikpo and Abakaliki. Swamp rice is also the staple crop in parts of eastern and central Zaïre, Madagascar and parts of the coastal areas of East Africa. An upland variety of rice which, like some varieties of swamp rice, is indigenous to tropical Africa and which is often intercropped with maize, cotton, guinea corn and beniseed is widely cultivated in various parts of West Africa. Upland rice is a much hardier crop than swamp rice and has a much shorter life cycle, although the yields are much lower.

Root crops

Root crops, especially yams, cassava, cocoyams and sweet potatoes, are the second most important staple food crops of tropical Africa. The yam is by far the most

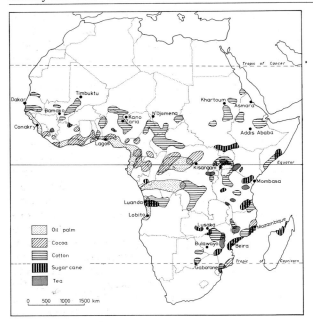

Fig. 9.5 Industrial crops, 1

important root crop in the West African root crop zone, especially in southern Nigeria. It is a 'prestige' crop in much of south-eastern Nigeria, but in recent years an increasing number of farmers have preferred to cultivate cassava which is a hardier crop, and therefore more suited to the increasingly impoverished soils of the very densely populated districts. The very low cost of cassava cuttings for planting, compared with yam seedlings, is also a major factor responsible for the rapid displacement of yams by cassava in parts of West Africa. Also, unlike yam, cassava can be left in the ground unharvested for several months and therefore provides a good security against famine. It is now the most important staple root crop in Zaïre and the Republic of Congo where it has displaced yams in most districts. As a rule cassava is the final crop planted before the farmland is allowed to revert to fallow. It is cultivated both in the forest belt and in grassland areas.

Cocoyams are particularly important as the staple crop in the coastal areas of Cameroun and in parts of south-eastern Nigeria. The crop is also widely cultivated in southern Ghana and parts of the Nigerian Middle Belt. The cultivation of sweet potatoes is much more widespread in comparison with yams or cocoyams, although there is no part of tropical Africa in which the sweet potato is a basic staple food crop. It is an important root crop both in Uganda, where it is grown amongst plantains, and in the highland areas of Rwanda and Burundi. In all these countries as well as in Sierra Leone, Gabon and parts of Guinea, the sweet

potato is a low status crop that people fall back on when more preferred foods like yams and rice are in short supply.

Fruit

The last group of dominant staple food crops is fruit, the most important of which are the banana and plantain, both originating from south-east Asia. These two fruits are the staple food of Uganda, especially in Buganda province, as well as of parts of southern Ghana and parts of equatorial Africa. Elsewhere in the forest belt, bananas and plantains are secondary or even very minor crops, although large commercial farms owned by European companies produce bananas for export in several countries, such as Cameroun, the Ivory Coast, Zaïre and Guinea (see Fig. 9.6).

Industrial and other commercial crops

The main industrial crops of tropical Africa consist of such perennial tree crops as the oil palm, cocoa, coffee and rubber, and annual crops, such as cotton and groundnuts. Kolanut, beniseed, wattle and ginger are also important commercial crops in various parts of tropical Africa. It is significant that in tropical Africa all these crops are produced mostly by small-scale peasant farmers, whereas in other parts of the tropical world many of them are produced in large commercial plantations. This is particularly so in Low Africa where there were little or no permanent white settlements during the colonial period. In High Africa, on the other

Fig. 9.6 Industrial crops, 2

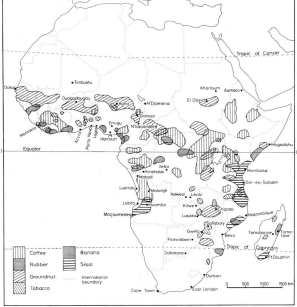

Pl. 9.3 Young oil palm trees

hand, European settlers dominated the commercial production of such crops as coffee in Kenya, while African farmers were prevented from cultivating them. Large concessions were also given to private European planters in some countries of Low Africa, notably Zaïre, Ivory Coast and Cameroun for the production of tree crops. In Nigeria, the most populous country in tropical Africa, the colonial government policy was against the plantation system, hence the fact that Nigerian peasant farmers have always dominated the agricultural export sector.

The oil palm is one of the few indigenous commercial crops of tropical Africa and is produced almost exclusively in western Africa and parts of central Africa. Most of the oil palms in Africa grow wild in the bush and are normally protected from fires when the land is prepared for farming. As a rule the density of oil palms per hectare is greatest in areas of great population concentration such as the Abak, Ikot Ekpene, Aba and Owerri Divisions of south-eastern Nigeria. An increasing number of farmers now cultivate small farms of oil palms, using improved seedlings supplied by ministries of agriculture. There are also a large number of government-owned and private oil palm plantations in Nigeria, Sierra Leone and Ghana but the largest oil palm plantations owned by foreign private companies are

found in Zaïre and Ivory Coast. The crop thrives best in areas with little or no dry season and a rainfall of not less than 1,520 mm (60 ins). Oil palms grow on low altitudes of under 700 m although plantings occur at altitudes of over 1,000 m in Bamenda (Cameroun). Cultivated palms are low in height and begin to yield after five years, reaching their peak at about thirty years after which the yield begins to decline.

Like the oil palm, cocoa production is restricted to West Africa and parts of equatorial Africa. The Ivory Coast is now the leading world producer of the crop and together with Nigeria, Ghana and Cameroun, produced about three-quarters of the world output in the 1970s. The cocoa tree, introduced from tropical America, thrives best on well-drained deep loamy or clay soils and requires an annual rainfall of 1,270–2,000 mm and high relative humidity. Young trees have to be protected by banana plants from direct sun rays and strong winds. Also like the oil palm, the cocoa tree begins to yield after five years and continues to produce for thirty-five years. Swollen shoot and black pod are the two most serious diseases which affect it and have resulted in the destruction of extensive farms, especially in Ghana and Nigeria where cocoa production is in the hands of small cultivators. By contrast, much of the cocoa produced in the Ivory Coast, Cameroun, Gabon, Zaïre and the Congo Republic comes from European-owned plantations.

The kolanut tree thrives under the same ecological conditions as the cocoa tree and has largely displaced the latter in districts that have suffered severe black pod and swollen shoot epidemics. There are two main species of kola, *Cola acuminata* (*Abata*) and *Cola nitida* (*Gbanja* or *Goro*), both of which are native to the forests of West Africa. *Gbanja* is the kola of commerce and is produced mainly in south-western Nigeria (100,000 tons), Ghana (14,000 tons) and the Ivory Coast (14,500 tons). The bulk of the kola is traded within West Africa where it is consumed as a stimulant by people living in the savanna and desert areas. Less than 10 per cent of the crop is exported to Europe and North America.

Coffee is indigenous to Africa and is probably the most widespread commercial crop produced in tropical Africa. There are three main varieties, the *Arabica* which is native to Ethiopia, the *Robusta* which is native to the Zaïre Basin and the *Liberica* which is native to the forests of West Africa. *Liberica* coffee is comparatively poor in quality and has largely been displaced in West Africa by the *Robusta* variety which is also the most widely cultivated variety in East Africa. In general the *Robusta* does best at lower elevations while the *Arabica*, which is grown in Cameroun, Ethiopia and around Mounts Kilimanjaro, Elgon and Kenya, does best in upland locations. On the whole, coffee is an upland crop which requires an annual rainfall of 1,140–1,520 mm

(45–60 ins) and an average daily temperature of 21°C (70°F). The largest producers in tropical Africa are the Ivory Coast, Uganda and Angola. Commercial production of coffee in Angola, the Ivory Coast, Cameroun, Zaïre and Kenya was formerly confined to European planters but local African farmers now produce most of the coffee in these countries. In Ethiopia, where the crop grows wild in some localities, and in Uganda, production has always been dominated by small-scale farmers. Although coffee is native to Africa, most of the coffee traded in the world market comes from South America.

Rubber is another forest crop and like cocoa and the oil palm is restricted to West Africa and the Zaïre Basin. The three indigenous rubber-bearing plants, the *Funtumia elastica* and the *Landolphia* of Nigeria and the *Kickxia elastica* of southern Cameroun have since been displaced by the para-rubber tree (*Hevea brasiliensis*) which was introduced from South America. Para-rubber grows best on gently sloping land with fertile deep soils, located in regions having 1,770–2,030 mm (70–120 ins) of evenly distributed rainfall, and a uniformly high temperature of about 27°C (80°F). Nigeria is currently the largest producer and exporter of rubber in Africa and much of the production comes from small peasant farms. In Liberia, Cameroun and Zaïre, on the other hand, production is mainly by commercial plantations owned by foreigners although an increasing quantity is now being produced by small-scale African farmers.

Cotton is native to Africa and has been cultivated in the grassland areas for several centuries. It is cultivated in all the major regions of tropical Africa, the largest producers and exporters being the Sudan, Uganda and Tanzania. Ideal conditions for production include rich

Pl. 9.5 Groundnuts as they are harvested

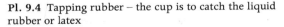

Pl. 9.4 Tapping rubber – the cup is to catch the liquid rubber or latex

and well-drained soils and a rainfall of 760–1,400 mm (30–55 ins) most of which falls during the growing season. The crop also requires abundant sunshine and a marked dry season when the bolls dry and are harvested. In the Gezira and the Sahelian areas of West Africa, cotton is produced under irrigation. Small-scale farmers dominate the production of cotton all over tropical Africa. An increasing proportion of the crop is now used in local textile factories and in Nigeria, which has over twelve, local production is inadequate to meet the demands of the textile mills. The total production of tropical Africa is put at less than 10 per cent of the world output.

Like cotton, the groundnut is an annual crop of grassland areas and was originally grown as a food crop in the drier savanna lands of West Africa. It has since become the most valuable export of Senegal (90 per cent of the total value in the 1970s), Gambia (95 per cent of the total value) and Niger (60 per cent of the total value). Until the early 1960s, groundnut was also one of Nigeria's major exports, but now almost all the crop produced in Nigeria is consumed locally. Other important producers include Upper Volta, northern Ghana, Cameroun and Zambia. On the whole tropical Africa accounts for 21 per cent of the total world output of groundnuts; and almost all the crop comes from small peasant holdings. The best conditions for commercial production are found in areas with light, sandy soils, which have a rainfall of 640–1,000 mm (25–40 ins) and a marked dry season.

Sisal is an important commercial crop in Kenya, Tanzania, Mozambique and Angola. It was first introduced into Tanzania from Mexico in 1893 by the German colonial government and it spread to Kenya in 1908. Ideal conditions for the crop include a fertile soil and a rainfall of 1,000–1,250 mm (40–50 ins). Sisal also thrives on relatively poor sandy soils in areas with less than 750 mm of rain which has therefore made it possible to cultivate sisal commercially in extensive areas of marginal lands with little alternative use. Sisal is rather a bulky crop and demands low-cost transport by rail, hence the concentration of production along railway lines and near the major exporting ports of Tanga, Lindi, Dar-es-Salaam and Mombasa. Production is mainly from large estates owned by European and Asian firms, although the number of small-scale African cultivators has increased considerably since the early 1970s. Sisal leaves are the source of a coarse fibre used for making ropes, strings and sacks.

Other important commercial crops cultivated in tropical Africa include sugarcane, tea and tobacco. Sugarcane is widely cultivated by peasant farmers in West and East Africa along stream beds for local consumption as a sweet to chew or for making brown sugar. There are, however, a number of large commercial sugar plantations such as the Bacita Estate in Nigeria, the Lugazi Estate, west of Jinja in Uganda, the Kisumu and Ramisi (near Mombasa) Estates in Kenya and several other large estates along the coast of Mozambique and in the Luanda district of Angola. These estates form the basis of local sugar factories for the domestic markets of the various countries as well as for export in a few cases.

Tea is basically a highland crop which requires a deep, light well-drained soil and a fairly heavy rainfall of up to 1,800 mm, well distributed over the growing season. Tea production is prominent in the Kericho district and the Limuru area (near Nairobi) in Kenya, the Ankole and Toro regions of Uganda and the Usambara Highlands and the slopes of Mount Kilimanjaro in Tanzania. Eastern Zimbabwe and southern Malawi are also important producers.

Tobacco is widely grown in West and East Africa, Zambia and Zimbabwe for local consumption in the form of snuff or for making rough cigarettes called 'bookies' in Nigeria. Peasant commercial production organized through co-operatives sponsored by major tobacco companies is important in western and north-central Nigeria as well as in Uganda and Zambia and is the main source of tobacco leaves for local cigarette factories. Large tobacco plantations also exist in Tanzania and Zimbabwe, which is a major exporter of the crop in tropical Africa.

Farming practices

Peasant cultivators or commercial plantations

Peasant farmers cultivating rarely more than three hectares of land dominate the production of industrial crops especially in West Africa and Uganda. During the colonial period, in Sierra Leone, Ghana, Nigeria and Uganda the British were against the alienation of native land for the purpose of establishing plantations, which they considered to be economically, socially and politically unsuited to these countries. Instead local farmers were encouraged to cultivate improved seedlings and to adopt better methods of processing their crops for export. From 1907–25, for example, the firm of Lever Brothers made several unsuccessful attempts to obtain concessions for cultivating oil palms in southern Nigeria and were subsequently obliged to approach the then Belgian Congo administration which granted them rights to establish the first large oil palm estates in Zaïre (Udo, 1965). In Kenya and Zimbabwe, however, where the climate favoured European settlement, the British alienated large areas of African land for European settler farmers. Large tree-crop plantations were also established by private foreign firms in the Ivory Coast, Liberia, Cameroun, Angola and Congo Republic, amongst others.

It is significant that in Nigeria, the anti-plantation policy of the colonial administration was reversed in 1951 when Nigerian politicians took over responsibility for agricultural policy during the period of internal self-government which preceded independence in 1960. It is also significant that the industrial crops produced in tropical Africa by peasant farmers are produced primarily in large plantations in other parts of the tropics. Furthermore, Nigeria now imports palm oil from the plantations of Malaysia whereas until 1933 Nigeria was both the world's largest producer and exporter of palm oil and remained a major exporter up to the early 1960s. It is this type of situation that advocates of the plantation system are apt to cite, and since an increasing number of plantations have been established in many countries in recent years, it is worth considering more closely the arguments in support as well as those against the plantation system in Africa.

The arguments in support of the plantation system are as follows:

1. The plantation is a highly efficient system of farming in which land, labour and the produce for marketing are

organized on the same lines as in a modern factory. Because of its size and organization, it is in a position to produce a steady and regular supply of good quality produce. In Nigeria, for example, peasant farmers are able to extract only about 55 per cent of the oil content of oil palm fruits by traditional methods, compared with about 90 per cent by the factory mills used in large plantations.

2. Commercial plantations bring about large-scale development of remote rural areas through the provision of houses for workers, and a balanced infrastructure of roads, water, electricity, medical services and schools.

3. Plantations provide a chance for local people to learn new skills on the job. Such skills often spread to other rural people since plantation workers eventually return to their villages.

4. The plantation creates opportunities for earning wages in rural areas and therefore helps to reduce the influx of rural people into the cities.

The arguments against the plantation system, some of which contributed to the decision of the British to reject the system in West Africa, are:

1. The plantation is a relatively inflexible system of farming which, unlike the peasant system, cannot easily adjust to extreme price fluctuation and economic depression. In times of economic depression large foreign-owned plantations are usually abandoned by their bankrupt planters and in consequence the local plantation workers become economically worse off than self-employed small-scale farmers.

2. The plantation, which traditionally thrives on cheap labour, is often plagued by labour disputes between workers and management. That with increasing agitation for wage increases and the fixing of national minimum wages for workers in many countries, a large number of plantations have become less profitable. In Nigeria, for example, almost all government-owned plantations operate at a loss.

3. The plantation requires a large area of land, usually measured in thousands of hectares, as well as a large supply of cheap unskilled labour. Since these two basic requirements cannot be obtained at one and the same locality, the plantation has either resulted in the displacement of indigenous farmers in the process of acquiring the land or has become the main cause of labour migration, including the forced migrations in the past of Africans as slaves to the Americas.

4. Plantations are capital-intensive and generally the enviable infrastructural facilities provided are not available to other citizens living in the same areas.

Today tropical Africa is still very sparsely populated and there are still vast areas of unsettled land

Pl. 9.6 Giant yam mounds in Abakaliki, Nigeria

which are suitable for the development of large-scale plantation agriculture. Many governments have taken various steps to encourage local farmers to cultivate more industrial crops, while at the same time encouraging the development of large commercial plantations. An increasing number of governments now opt for state participation in the ownership of large plantations operated by foreign commercial firms. The proportion of produce from plantations remains far below 10 per cent of the total output of most crops. Hence the growing emphasis on the strategy of encouraging local farmers to establish larger industrial crop farms around nucleus plantations such as the Lobe oil palm estate of Cameroun Republic.

Farming practices in the forest belt

The tropical rain forest is a comparatively difficult environment for the peasant farmer who still operates with such primitive tools as the machete and the hoe. In this section we consider farming activities for one year in the southern Nigerian rain-forest district of Eket in the Cross River State. Preparation of farmland starts in December and continues to early March. During this period the bush is cleared and non-economic trees are felled so that the bush can be burnt before the onset of the first rains. Unburnt branches are then collected into heaps for use as firewood while the men proceed to dig yam holes or prepare yam mounds in areas that are waterlogged. Yams are planted in January or February, as soon as the fields have been prepared, while maize is cultivated after the first heavy rainstorm in March. Delay in the onset of the rains may prove disastrous to cultivated seed yams while maize and vegetables planted after the first rains may be scorched and destroyed if no more rain falls for another week or two.

Yam is a man's crop and after it has been planted by the combined labour of the man, his wives and children, the farm is divided into smaller units and allocated to the wives who plant maize, okra, melon and other vegetables. During the months of April and May, when the plants are fully grown, it is difficult to penetrate the farm. The thick vegetative growth resulting from mixed cropping helps to protect the soil from erosion by rainwater. Mixed cropping makes for a higher output per hectare and provides an insurance against the failure of a particular crop.

Weeding the farm is done by women and children. The peak periods of demand for farm labour are during the planting season up to the first weeding when yam vines are staked and trained (February–April) and during the main yam harvest (October–November). Maize is harvested in May and June while early yam is harvested in late July and August. Cocoyams are planted by women after the maize harvest and cassava is planted after the first yam harvest. During the second year of farming, cassava is the only crop on the plot. Many farmers, however, plant cassava as a first crop in areas with short fallows and where yams do not normally give good yields.

Farming practices in grassland areas

Compared with the rain forest belt, less effort is required in preparing farmland in grassland districts, especially in the drier savanna areas such as the Kano Emirate in Nigeria. In this particular district bush clearing consists of cleaning the previous year's farm by removing millet and guinea-corn stalks which are used for fencing and the construction of huts. This is done in January and February, which is the season of the cold and dry harmattan winds. We recall here that the Kano district is a zone of permanent cultivation, a fact made possible by the intensive application of manure which is distributed to the farms in the months of March and April. The donkeys that carry the manure from Kano City and other settlements to the farms return home with loads of firewood and harvest from tree crops like tamarind, locust beans and the silk cotton tree.

The first rains come in May which is a very busy month in the farming calendar. Guinea corn and millet are planted immediately after the first rains, after which ridges are made for the planting of groundnuts in June. Cowpeas are intercropped in July and August when the harvesting of millet begins. Severe floods caused by heavy rainfall may result in extensive damage to crops in July and August. As soon as the harvesting of millet is completed in September, cassava is planted on the same fields. Groundnuts and guinea-corn harvests take place in September and October while cowpeas are harvested in November. Kano farmers usually plant cotton and groundnuts on separate fields without

mixing them with other crops. Swamp rice, tobacco and onions are important dry-season crops grown on *fadama* land. In December, domestic animals, which have been stall-fed since May, are let out to graze on farmlands in which cassava has not been planted.

Farming practices in the Gezira (Sudan)

The Gezira Irrigation Scheme which started in 1925 has been described as the largest successful capital-intensive farm in the world and is certainly the most successful irrigation and land development scheme in tropical Africa. Through this scheme, which covers an area of about 420,000 hectares (1 million *feddans*), the pastoral semi-nomads who inhabited this area before 1925 have become a settled agricultural population of tenant farmers and wage-earners earning a living from the cultivation of cotton and a few subsidiary crops. The land belongs to the Sudan Gezira Board, an agent of the government, and all farmers are tenants of the Board which allocates to them holdings which are held for one year. In the 1950s each tenant was allocated about four hectares made up of several plots in different blocks, but with the increase in population the allocation to each farmer in the 1970s was about two hectares. The tenant cultivates cotton, which is handed over to the Board for sale, and also guinea corn and other foodstuffs for home consumption, the surplus of which is sold for additional income. Proceeds from the sale of cotton are shared between the three partners, the tenant (48 per cent), the government (36 per cent), and the Gezira Board (10 per cent). The remaining 6 per cent is shared equally between the Tenants' Reserve Fund, the Social Development Fund and the local government councils.

The great success of the Gezira derives largely from

Fig. 9.7 The Gezira irrigation scheme, Sudan

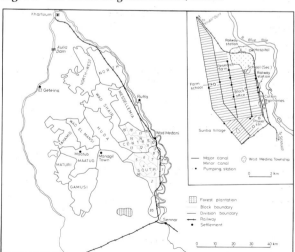

efficient management. Inspectors who manage the blocks into which the scheme is divided are responsible for controlling the distribution of irrigation water and farm inputs such as fertilizers and seeds. They even decide the plots on which tenants have to cultivate particular crops and may refuse to allocate any land to a tenant who proves unsatisfactory. Inspectors also see to the strict adherence to the farming calendar. This begins in May with the uprooting and burning of the previous year's cotton stalks followed by the ridging of farmland in June and early July. The rains start in July when guinea corn (sorghum) is planted. Other crops, including wheat, groundnuts and luba (a leguminous fodder crop), are planted shortly after the sowing of guinea corn. August is a very busy month since the sowing of cotton starts on the first day. The men spend all day in the fields, lunch being sent out to them on donkeys. Work slackens off in September which is the period for thinning cotton, watering, weeding and ridging. The grain harvest starts in November while cotton watering at intervals of 12–15 days continues till December. Cotton-picking starts from the middle of January and continues till the end of April, which is also the end of the farming calendar, when the Gezira landscape is dry and bare. Many farmers who can afford it employ wage labour to help on their farms (Culwick, 1951).

European settler farming in High Africa

Owing to the dominance of small-scale peasant farming, discussions of agricultural practices in Africa have tended to make only passing reference to large-scale farming except as practised on commercial plantations. There are, however, many large commercial farms notably in Kenya, Tanzania, Zambia and Zimbabwe in which Europeans carry out mechanized mixed farming on the same lines as in Europe or North America.

Kenya

In Kenya, these farms vary in size from 100–400 hectares (250–1,000 acres) and in 1964 in the Kenya Highlands, there were as many as 2,000 such mixed farms covering over 800,000 hectares (O'Connor, 1966, p. 21). Many of these farms have since been expropriated by the government and subdivided for Africans. An increasing number of African farmers have bought farms with public loans, thereby maintaining the scale of operation.

The European farmers still in the Kenya Highlands grow a wide range of crops and keep more than one type of livestock. There is a close integration of arable and livestock farming, some crops being grown for fodder for cattle which in turn produce the manure for the farm. A typical large European settler farm consists of about 100 hectares under crops, 55 hectares under planted grass and about 240 hectares under natural pasture. The cattle population on such a farm is about 200 head and the total investment would be of the order of ₦40,000. The average annual cash income of such large farms is about ₦24,000 of which ₦4,500 would be profit (O'Connor, 1966). Although the number of large-scale farmers remained small throughout the colonial period, they were mainly responsible for much of the commercial supply of such food items as milk, meat, wheat, fruit and vegetables sold in the urban markets. Their products are still handled by well-organized and established marketing organizations such as the Kenya Farmers Association and the Kenya Planters Co-operative Union. Efficient large-scale farming was responsible for the fact that although the total farmland in the Kenya Highlands amounts to about 30,000 sq km or just over 5 per cent of the land area of Kenya, the Highlands accounted for most of the agricultural exports, especially coffee, tea, sisal and pyrethrum (Morgan, 1963).

Zimbabwe

Most large European-owned mixed farms in High Africa are to be found in Zimbabwe, where the 240,000 European settler population occupied about 18 million hectares in 1979 and the 5 million indigenous African population occupied about the same area. European farms in Zimbabwe are much bigger, varying between 800 and 2,000 hectares (2,000–5,000 acres) in the wetter parts as compared with about 20,000 hectares (50,000 acres) in the dry cattle-ranching areas of the south-west. These large commercial farms are concentrated near the main urban centres and along the railway lines.

European agriculture in Zimbabwe is so highly developed that land preparation, ploughing, sowing and transportation are all mechanized. The harvesting of most crops is done by hand, using African wage labour which forms a high proportion of the farm costs. Unlike on African farms, virtually all the crops on European farms are produced for sale, except for a small quantity reserved for feeding the labour force employed on the farm. The European farm family, like the urban family, purchases all food items and other provisions, except vegetables, eggs, chicken and milk, from grocery shops.

In 1965 when the minority European settler population made a unilateral declaration of independence (UDI) from Great Britain, there were about 7,800 large European-owned farms in the country. Total output from these farms was valued at about R$130 million and accounted for one-third of the total exports by value in 1965. By comparison the total sales from African farms amounted to only R$7 million or about 5 per cent of the gross sales from European farms (Curtin, 1971).

The economic sanctions imposed on the country following the illegal declaration of independence contributed greatly towards agricultural diversification. The predominantly tobacco, maize and livestock farms started to diversify into cotton and wheat cultivation. Formal independence came in 1980 and there are indications that, as in Kenya, many of the large European-owned farms will be expropriated by the government and subdivided for re-allocation to African farmers.

Zambia

In Zambia the number of large commercial mixed farms exceeds 1,000; and although the country has been independent since 1964, many of these large farms are still owned by Europeans. Maize is the dominant crop on the large farms which are concentrated along the railway line between Lusaka and Livingstone (see Fig. 9.4). There are also many large commercial farms in the Copper Belt which supply the local mining towns with vegetables, fresh milk and other foods. In Angola and Mozambique where the European settler population consists of Portuguese peasants, there are fewer commercial farms and they are much smaller in size.

Commercial African farming in High Africa

Except in Uganda and Ethiopia, African farmers in High Africa played an insignificant role in commercial farming during the colonial period. In Kenya, for example, African farmers were for many decades prevented from growing and selling cash crops, especially coffee; and when later the restriction was relaxed, they were still required to fulfil stringent conditions to qualify for a licence to grow coffee. The position in Zimbabwe was even more restrictive, because African farmers were not only refused permission to grow flue-cured tobacco, but were also discouraged from selling their maize crop to the statutory Grain Marketing Board. The Grain Marketing Board deducted a special levy from the price paid to African maize farmers but not from European maize growers, because the levy, it was argued, was meant to be used for financing public works in African areas. By contrast, African farmers in such West African countries as Ghana, Nigeria, Sierra Leone, Togo and Ivory Coast have always been encouraged to produce for the export market. Hence the fact that in most West African countries, not less than 90 per cent of all industrial crops came from small-scale African farmers during the colonial period.

Kenya

The situation in Kenya started to change during the last decade of the colonial period, when the government embarked upon a scheme of rehabilitation of Kikuyuland following the declaration of the Mau Mau emergency which lasted from 1952 to 1960. Under the Swynnerton scheme of 1954 many fragmented holdings were consolidated and re-allocated to enable the people to farm on a commercial scale. About a million hectares of land in Central, Rift Valley and Nyanza provinces were laid out into 300,000 farms of varying sizes. The smallest farm size allowed was about 1·5 hectares. The smallest fenced mixed farms averaged about 3 hectares and the larger farms were usually more than 4·5 hectares. Compared with the European-owned commercial farms, these African rehabilitated farms were very small. They were, however, much larger than most farms in the crowded Kikuyu homelands and in most of West Africa. The land consolidation scheme was accompanied by some new schemes, such as the introduction of improved cattle breeds and cash crop cultivation.

There were fewer planned commercial farms for African farmers in colonial Uganda. These were, however, larger in Uganda, where there is no shortage of land.

In the process of land consolidation many landless tenants-at-will were displaced, so that the number of landless people increased considerably. Fortunately the end of the Mau Mau emergency in 1960 was followed by the enactment of the Kenya (Land) Order in Council of November 1960, which brought to an end the practice of reserving land in the Kenya Highlands for European settlers. The government was therefore in a position to purchase, through the Land Development and Settlement Board established in January 1961, some European farms which were subdivided and transferred to African farmers. Many European farmers who were scared of living in Kenya administered by Africans readily sold their farms and left the country, thereby releasing the much needed land for the effective implementation of the African Settlement Programme.

The African Settlement Programme consisted of three distinct schemes. These were as follows.

1. The Assisted Owner Scheme. This was restricted to experienced farmers who could produce up to a third of the required capital. The size of farms under this scheme varied between 20 and 80 hectares. Each farmer was expected to make an income of about £259 per annum after paying his annual loan charges. Since the number of qualified Africans was expected to be small, the scheme initially provided for 1,800 families.
2. The Low-Density Small-Holder Scheme. This consisted of farms of about 12 hectares on high-potential land. It was intended for people with some farming experience and a reasonable amount of capital. The net income of farmers settled on low-density schemes was expected to be about £100 per annum after paying loan charges. This scheme provided for about 6,000 families.
3. The High-Density Small-Holder Scheme. This consisted of farms of about 6 hectares on relatively poor

land. Settlers for this scheme were not required to have capital or any farming experience. It provided for about 12,000 families each of which was expected to make a net income of £40 per annum. This scheme has been criticized for placing emphasis on the number of people to be settled rather than on the economic viability of the farms.

Tanzania (Tanganyika)
The Tanganyika Agricultural Corporation of the colonial period in Tanganyika (now Tanzania) established a large number of small farms (8–16 hectares) and large planned farms (about 25 hectares) on land originally used for the ill-fated East African Groundnut Scheme of 1945.

The farms were leased to tenant farmers who were all encouraged to practise mixed farming. The Corporation undertook to plough and ridge mechanically each farmland at the expense of the tenant farmer who was expected to carry out all other farming operations on his own. A high level of supervision helped to ensure that tenant farmers built up healthy small herds of cattle and took good care of their holdings.

Zambia
As in other African countries, most African farmers in Zambia still practise the primitive bush fallow system of agriculture. A comparatively small but increasing new class of commercial farmers which has emerged since about 1945 now plays an important role in the production of maize and tobacco in the country. The earliest of these were successful Tonga maize farmers who had acquired experience and some capital after working on European farms. These progressive farmers are eligible for loans from the African Improved Farming Scheme which started in the Tonga area in 1946–7 season. Most of the successful independent commercial African farmers are found near the railway line especially near Monzo and Kalomo, both in the Southern Province. The size of holdings varies from a few hectares to over 20 hectares, and there are between two and about one hundred cattle on each farm. Marketing of farm crops is well organized through co-operative societies, and farmers are paid promptly as soon as their grain and other crops have been weighed and graded.

The Zambian Peasant Farming Scheme which started in 1948 represents a more direct government involvement in promoting African commerical farming. Under this scheme many farmers have been settled on planned settlements such as the Chiwefwe Peasant Scheme in Central Province. The land on this scheme was cleared by the government which also undertook to stump 1·5 hectares for each farmer. The standard size of holding was about 6·5 hectares. In addition, the government provided each farmer with an ordinary plough, a ridging plough and harrow, four oxen and two cows.

Each farmer was required to follow a recommended four-year rotation of a legume, Kaffir corn, sunnhemp and maize, and to practise good husbandry (Cole, 1962). Each farmer could borrow up to £150 repayable within ten years. Other Peasant Farming Schemes include those of the Fort Jameson and Katete areas of Eastern Province.

Zimbabwe
In Zimbabwe, which as Rhodesia was dominated by a minority white settler group until 1980, the first major move to transform African agriculture was made in 1951. Under the Native Land Husbandry Act of that year, efforts were made to replace traditional communal land tenure with individual title to land throughout the African reserves. Provisions were made for the enforcement of good farming practices by regulation, granting grazing rights for limited numbers of livestock and farming rights over limited areas to eligible persons. Subsequent fragmentation of land was prohibited while amalgamation of small holdings was encouraged. The amount of arable land granted to each family varied from bout 3·5 hectares to about 5·5 hectares. Those granted land rights were required to apply improved farming methods on about one hectare of land for four years under the supervision of government agricultural officers. The farmer who had successfully extended the improved methods to the rest of his holding was deemed to have qualified as a 'master farmer', and was therefore eligible to apply for a freehold farm of 20–400 hectares in the so-called Purchase Areas set aside for African settlement.

The Master Farmer Scheme was not very successful partly because land available in the reserves was inadequate to create enough economically viable farms. The programme was also unacceptable to African political leaders who undertook to discourage participation by African farmers. In any case most farmers in the Purchase Areas continued to apply traditional farming methods except that the crop areas were larger. The use of fertilizers, however, resulted in higher yields and greater income per farm family.

Farming in the Firestone Harbel rubber plantation in Liberia

The Firestone rubber plantation at Harbel in Liberia covers a total area of 56,000 hectares. It is the largest and most modern rubber plantation in the world. The plantation in its present form started in 1924 with the acquisition by Firestone of an abandoned 800 hectare rubber estate established in 1908 by a British Company on Mount Barclay (Harrison Church, 1969). Two years later Firestone obtained the right to acquire up to 400,000 hectares (1 million acres) of land for 99 years, but the concession was later restricted to 64,000

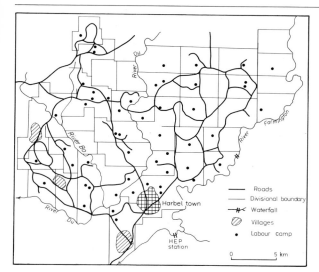

Fig. 9.8 The Firestone rubber plantation at Harbel, Liberia

hectares of which 56,000 hectares are at Harbel and 8,000 hectares at the smaller Cavalla rubber plantation near Harper in south-east Liberia. Planting started at Harbel in 1927 and by the mid 1970s there were about nine million trees on 36,000 hectares of land.

Like most large plantations, the Harbel rubber plantation is located in a very sparsely populated region and from the start, the management has always had problems in recruiting labour. In the early 1950s, for example, the Firestone Rubber Company had a labour force of only 22,000 out of a required total of 300,000 (Jurgens *et al.*, 1966). The result was that expansion was slowed down and mature trees in some of the 45 divisions into which the plantation is divided went unharvested. In recent years, the labour situation has been aggravated in particular by competition from the iron-ore and diamond mines. The labour force has continued to decline from 27,000 in 1948, through 21,300 in 1964 to 15,000 in 1973.

The Harbel rubber plantation is more than an agricultural enterprise in that it performs a number of subsidary activities in addition to providing the normal plantation facilities like a hospital, divisional clinics, schools and housing for the workers. These activities include factories for manufacturing latex cups, soap, rubber sandals and a brick and tile factory. The plan-

tation sawmill provides the timber needs of the estate while the Harbel Coca-cola factory services the entire country. There is also a large poultry farm and a 400 hectare oil-palm plantation to supply cooking oil as well as oil for manufacturing soap in the plantation's soap factory. In addition the management of Harbel plantation provides farm advisory services to thousands of independent small-scale Liberian rubber farmers who produced about one-third of the 85,000 tons of rubber exported from the country in 1972. The plantation also purchases rubber produced by these local farmers and since about 1970 almost 30 per cent of the rubber processed at the giant modern processing plant at Harbel is purchased from these farmers. The Firestone plantation at Harbel is the largest private employer of labour in Liberia.

References

Cole, M. M. (1962), 'The Rhodesian Economy in Transition and the Role of Kariba', *Geography*, 47, pp. 15–40.

Culwick, G. M. (1951), *Diet in the Gezira Irrigated Area, Sudan*, Government Printing Press, Khartoum, pp. 4–21.

Curtin, Timothy (1971), 'The Economy of Rhodesia', in *Africa South of the Sahara*, Europa Publications, London, pp. 595–602.

Federal Office of Statistics, Lagos (1966), *Rural Economic Survey of Nigeria, Farm Survey 1963–4*.

Floyd, B. N. (1964), 'Terrace Agriculture in Eastern Nigeria: The Case of Maku', *Nigerian Geographical Journal*, 7, pp. 33–44.

Goddard, S. (1965), 'Town–Farm Relationships in Yoruba-land', *Africa*, 35, pp. 21–9.

Harrison Church, R. J. (1969), 'The Firestone Rubber Plantations in Liberia', *Geography*, 54, pp. 430–7.

Jurgen, H. W., Tracey, K. A. and Mitchell, P. K. (1966), 'Internal Migration in Liberia', *Bulletin, Sierra Leone Geographical Association*, 10, pp. 39–59.

Morgan, W. T. W. (1963), 'The "White Highlands" of Kenya', *Geographical Journal*, 129, pp. 140–55.

O'Connor, A. M. (1966), *An Economic Geography of East Africa*, G. Bell & Sons, London, p. 21.

Udo, R. K. (1965), 'Sixty Years of Plantation Agriculture in Southern Nigeria 1902–1962', *Economic Geography*, 41, pp. 356–68.

United Nations (1975), *Demographic Handbook for Africa*, Economic Commission for Africa, Addis Ababa, pp. 116–17.

10 Agricultural Development since Independence

The overall economic situation in most countries in tropical Africa has shown considerable improvement since independence in the early 1960s. Economic growth has invariably been largely due to expansion in the mining and industrial sectors. The vast majority of the population who live in rural areas and obtain their living from agriculture have yet to benefit from the wealth of their countries. This is mostly because the agricultural sector has remained relatively stagnant in many countries, resulting in a precarious food situation. Apart from Zambia, Zimbabwe and Madagascar, the food import bill since independence has continued to increase in all countries. In Nigeria the food import bill at independence in 1960 was ₦47·8 million, rising to ₦60·4 million in 1977 and to a disturbingly high figure of ₦1·5 billion in 1980.

In the past the high expenditure on food imports was generally attributed to the elitist food habits of a minority of well-to-do citizens. The truth of course is that most countries are importing basic food crops which are also produced locally, but in insufficient quantities. The leading rice importers such as Nigeria, Sierra Leone, Liberia and Senegal are at the same time important rice producers. Nigeria also imports large quantities of maize every year from the Americas for making poultry feed even though maize is grown all over the country. Hence the indefensibly high price of ₦6 payable for a chicken in 1981. Currently the countries which suffer most from food deficits are the Sahelian countries which are still trying to recover from the disastrous droughts of 1972–4.

The poor performance of the agricultural sector is not confined to the food crop sub-sector but also extends to the industrial crop sub-sector. Nigeria, formerly the largest producer and exporter of palm oil in the world, has become a net importer of it since 1972; similarly with cotton and groundnuts. Ghana has been displaced by the Ivory Coast as the leading world producer of cocoa. A rapid increase in population, the high rate of urbanization, the diversion of labour to industry and mining, and loss of labour due to increased registration in primary and secondary schools, are often given as reasons for the food deficit. An additional reason for the importation of industrial crops is the rising demand by local manufacturing industries. A careful consideration of each of these reasons will show that they are not peculiar to the African scene. What is peculiar is the continued dominance of primitive technology in agricultural production.

All the governments of tropical African countries are fully aware of the precariousness of the food supply and of the need for a prosperous agricultural sector. This is why these governments have invested large sums of money in agricultural research, extension work, large-scale irrigation and plantation agriculture, among other programmes. Unfortunately, and this is rather disturbing, the investments of the last twenty years do not appear to have paid off yet in many countries. Some of the strategies adopted by various governments since independence are considered in this chapter, which also focuses on some of the achievements and mistakes made so far.

Many of the programmes, including some large-scale irrigation and land settlement schemes and plantations, have been inherited from the colonial period, but many more of these highly capitalized schemes have been initiated since independence. The Tanzanian experiment in rural transformation, the *ujamaa* village co-operatives scheme, is unique but has not yet produced the revolutionary changes which its sponsors envisaged. Programmes aimed at stimulating agricultural production with the view to increasing rural incomes and living standards have not been co-ordinated till recently. Often programmes such as rural electrification, agricultural credit schemes, land consolidation, rural co-operatives and rural water supply schemes, are carried out by governments or private agencies, including the Church, as isolated projects in different parts of a country. In most cases the results of the programmes fall far short of expectations, hence the new trend towards integrated rural development (discussed on pp. 128–9).

The extent and limit of direct government involvement in agricultural production and marketing remain a thorny problem. Some governments have reacted to the rather embarrassing food deficit by sponsoring campaigns such as the Operation Feed the Nation (OFN) of Nigeria or the 'grow more food' campaign of Ghana. As part of these campaigns some governments have gone into direct food production, by forming food production corporations, as well as the direct purchase and distribution of imported staple foods. In all cases the unit costs of food produced in a government farm has been very much higher than that of food produced by even the most inefficient small-scale farmer. The food marketing companies have also failed to supply basic consumer goods at controlled prices, because they have been hindered by the poor state of development of consumer co-operatives and transportation as well as the endemic corruption. There is indeed no future for these companies, which are competing with peasant-type farmers and petty traders. It appears that much more can be achieved by making direct subsidies to farmers than by attempting to compete with them.

Expansion of industrial and tree crop production

Throughout tropical Africa the production of industrial crops generally and of tree crops in particular has always been dominated by small-scale peasant-type farmers. New plantings by these farmers as well as on large commercial plantations have been undertaken since independence. Tree crop improvement programmes featuring the rehabilitation of existing oil palm groves, cocoa and rubber farms have also been undertaken in many countries. The expansion of tree crop farming can therefore be considered under the heading of commercial plantation schemes and small-holder improvement schemes.

Commercial plantation schemes

The largest number of commercial tree crop plantations in West Africa is found in Nigeria where over 90 per cent of the estates were established and run by government corporations. Most of the plantations were established between 1952 and 1962, that is just before and during the early years of independence. By 1972 it had become clear that almost all the government-owned plantations had failed to pay their way. At the same time all the privately owned plantations continued to make a profit. Unfortunately, although all the State governments recognize that the attitudes of the people to what they call 'government work' and administrative red tape have been responsible for the economic failure of these highly capitalized projects, they have been reluctant for political reasons to sell these farms to private entrepreneurs. The early enthusiasm for large-scale plantations has, however, waned; the current strategy is to encourage private individuals to establish small plantations and to rehabilitate existing plantations as well as small-holder farms.

In Sierra Leone the Industrial Plantation Development Programme announced by the government in 1964, that is three years after independence, was politically motivated. The government's plan to establish commercial plantations in all the provinces was aimed at creating job opportunities in rural areas so as to reduce the rate of rural–urban migration. When fully implemented the plantations programme was expected to provide jobs for 60,000 labourers and artisans, 200 junior office staff and 60 senior office staff (Spencer, 1977). The programme turned out to be a disastrous failure for several reasons: frequent political interference; the wrong siting of oil palm plantations in the north, for example, for political reasons; and lack of funds. The experience of Sierra Leone suggests that there is little future for government-owned plantations in tropical Africa.

In Liberia, Cameroun, Ivory Coast and Zaïre plantations were mostly established by foreign private entrepreneurs and have always made substantial profits. Since African governments are increasingly seeking to reduce foreign domination of the economy, and since the performance of government-owned plantations is poor, the options open appear to be state encouragement of indigenous private plantation companies and further investments in some small-holder improvement schemes.

Small-holder improvement schemes

Small-holder improvement schemes have featured the rehabilitation of wild palm groves and old and diseased cocoa and rubber farms. The palm grove rehabilitation scheme requires farmers to cut down existing wild palms and replant the land with improved seedlings supplied by the Ministry of Agriculture. Replanting schemes also exist for cocoa, rubber and coffee. New planting programmes form an important part of the small-holder scheme and have been largely responsible for increased production of industrial crops in many countries since independence. Government financial aid is usually available to farmers or farm co-operatives, but in many countries the customary land tenure systems constitute formidable obstacles to small-holder improvement schemes.

Farm settlements in southern Nigeria

The farm settlement scheme of the former Western Nigeria was launched in 1959 on the eve of independence, and that of the former Eastern Nigeria took off in 1961, a year after independence. The architects of both schemes were greatly influenced by the great success in promoting agricultural development through land settlement in Israel. Indeed the original designs of the farm settlements were based on the Israeli Moshav and were actually under the direct supervision of Israeli consultants. One of the main objectives of the farm settlement scheme was to bring about rural progress through increased output of food and industrial crops. By making farming efficient and lucrative the scheme hoped to attract hundreds of primary school-leavers and thereby reduce the influx of these young people into the cities. It was also hoped that each farm settlement would act as a model for people in neighbouring villages to copy.

At the end of the second year of independence (1962) there were six large farm settlements, averaging about 4,000 hectares each in the eastern states and twenty-four smaller settlements (usually less than 450 hectares) in the western states of Nigeria. Settlers were recruited from within a radius of about 50 km of each farm settlement and were required to undergo two years of training at farm institutes. In a tree crop farm settlement such as at Ibiade in Ogun State, each settler was allocated 8 hectares made up of about 5 hectares of oil palm and 3 hectares of rubber. In addition, the settler was allocated another 1–hectare plot for cultivating food crops. The original cost for establishing such a settler was estimated to be ₦6,000, but by 1965 this had increased to about ₦10,000. Each settler was expected to make a net income of about ₦1,200 per annum and to pay back the capital invested on his farm over a period of fifteen years.

As in many other highly capitalized schemes, such as the Mokwa Settlement Scheme and East African Groundnut Scheme both of which failed, there was considerable regimentation in the hope of ensuring the success of the scheme and so facilitating the recovery of the money invested. Thus the farmland was cleared and ploughed for the settler who also had his house built for him. The seeds given to him had to be planted in prescribed rotations and other operations including application of fertilizers had to be as recommended. The processing and marketing of the crops were done for him but all the costs were charged to him. Sometimes the movements of settlers had to be restricted to ensure that they spent adequate time on the settlement. In the Western Nigerian farm settlements even the farm labourers required by individual settlers were hired and paid for by the government (Olatunbosun, 1971).

By the end of the first ten years of independence (1970) it had become obvious that the farm settlements could not achieve much either in terms of increased productivity or in helping to reduce the influx of school-leavers into the cities. The expected 'demonstration effect' of the scheme turned out to be a farce. This is not surprising because demonstration plots owned by the Extension Division of the Ministry of Agriculture are not new features in rural areas. It has therefore been difficult to justify the high cost of settling each farmer. Today neither the State governments nor the public appear to be enthusiastic about farm settlements as they were in the early 1960s when the settlements were seen as agents of social change and modernizing traditional agriculture.

One of the operational weaknesses of the Nigerian farm settlements appears to be too much direct involvement by the government. For instance, this involvement is said to have resulted in reducing the status of the settler from that of an owner/operator who takes his own decisions to that of a farm labourer acting under orders (Olatunbosun, 1971). This may be a valid point, although the degree of control of farmers under the farm settlement scheme has never been greater than in the very successful Gezira Scheme of Sudan Republic. The main problem with the Nigerian farm settlements appears to have been that the wrong settlers were chosen. Unlike the so-called 'master' farmers of Zimbabwe or the Assisted Owner Scheme farmers of Kenya, the young settlers of the Nigerian farm settlements had neither previous farming experience nor any working capital. Indeed, many of the school-leavers who had no intention of taking up farming as a career gladly accepted places at the farm institutes where they were paid a monthly allowance in addition to free food and lodgings. It is not surprising that many of them left the institutes as soon as alternative employment had been obtained for them in the cities by their friends and relatives.

In the eastern states of Nigeria, the farm settlements were also expected to help relieve congestion in the very densely populated areas. This objective could not be achieved because of the desire to prevent political disturbances arising from settling non-indigenes on the land. Accordingly as many as 40 per cent of settlers were chosen from the villages on whose land the settlement was located, 20 per cent came from other villages in the division and another 20 per cent came from the same province. Only 20 per cent of settlers were recruited from the rest of the eastern states (then known as Eastern Nigeria). However, since the farm settlements were necessarily sited in districts with relatively abundant farmland, citizens from the congested districts were unable to benefit much from the scheme.

Farm settlements and resettlement schemes in East and Central Africa

The programme of settling Africans on farms purchased from European settlers, which started during the last two years of the colonial period, has continued in Kenya and to a smaller extent in Tanzania and Zambia. A number of new farm settlements and resettlement schemes have also been started since independence in Uganda, Kenya and Tanzania.

Kenya

In Kenya the resettlement of African farmers on the Highlands was primarily a political move, but right from the beginning the programme was expected to result in increased productivity through the intensification of the use of the land. On the whole, production of dairy produce and crops has been maintained while pyrethrum has been overproduced (Odingo, 1971). The Kenya resettlement scheme, however, suffers from the general criticism applicable to other land settlement schemes, which is that the small number of families benefiting from the scheme does not justify the large sums of public funds expended. African settlement on the Kenya Highlands also resulted in a considerable decrease in the number of Africans employed on white farms from 269,000 in 1960 to 194,000 in 1967, during which period the number of large farms had declined from 3,609 to 2,745 (Odingo, 1971). There is clear evidence, however, that the Kenya Highlands resettlement scheme has resulted in the extension of commercial farming to thousands of African farm families and in improved rural development yet to be achieved in most parts of tropical Africa. The resettlement programme has been largely responsible for the fact that the contribution of small farmers to the gross value of agricultural produce marketed in the country increased from about 35 per cent in 1962 to over 50 per cent in 1971 (Morgan, 1973, p. 337).

Uganda

The objectives for establishing farm settlements in Uganda since independence include the introduction of modern agricultural techniques to a new generation of farmers, providing jobs in rural areas for young school-leavers and thus checking the increasing migration from rural to urban areas, and demonstrating to young people that farming can be a profitable and satisfying occupation. The Nyakashaka farm settlement, for example, was established by missionaries for the express purpose of settling young school-leavers. Compared with the farm settlements in Nigeria, it is a much less elaborate scheme in terms of capital investment, the cost per settler being only about ₦600. The more elaborate Mubuku settlement scheme which started in 1966 is based on irrigated agriculture. It supports 132 settlers at a cost of about ₦3,400 per settler family.

Resettlement schemes

A number of resettlement schemes in Eastern and Central Africa have been associated not with the desire to modernize agriculture *per se*, but with government efforts to eradicate sleeping sickness and to reclaim areas infested with tsetse flies. In Uganda about 40,000 sq. km of land has been reclaimed through resettlement of population between 1947 and 1973. An increasing number of resettlement villages since about 1965 have been mainly associated with population displaced from major irrigation or multi-purpose river development projects such as the Volta River Project, the Kainji dam or the Kariba Dam Projects. Unfortunately many of such settlement villages have not been planned with the view to stimulating agricultural productivity.

Ujamaa, the Tanzanian experiment in rural development

The transformation of rural life has been the main objective of the Tanzanian government since independence in 1961. It is the wish of the government to change fundamentally the nature of rural society through village integration, as well as to raise the level of agricultural production. At independence most Tanzanians lived in scattered settlements made up of clusters of a few family huts. The strategy has been to establish large nucleated villages, so as to make it economical to provide for rural people basic services such as improved water supplies, schools, dispensaries, cattle dips and electricity. In this way it is hoped that the benefits of development will get to the vast majority of the people, while the gap between urban and rural incomes will be reduced.

Ujamaa is the name given to this villagization policy. It is a Swahili word which means 'family-hood'. According to President Julius Nyerere, *ujamaa* is a reactivation of the well-established principles of African traditional social life featuring mutual respect, the universal obligation to work and the sharing of joint production. Each *ujamaa* village is expected to function like a typical African 'extended family' which in the past was basically a social and economic unit. The degree of co-operation expected in an *ujamaa* village is, however, greater than in a typical African village, since land is supposed to be farmed collectively and not individually.

There are over 5,000 *ujamaa* villages with an average population of 300 each. The general procedure in the village is that land is cleared and cultivated collectively, after which individual plots are planted, weeded and harvested by their owners in collaboration with their neighbours. In practice, the level of *ujamaa*, by which is meant the level of communal production and sharing, varies considerably from village to village. All crops, both staple food crops and cash crops, are cultivated and owned communally in the few villages with a very high level of *ujamaa*, such as Horohoro. At Ndiva all crops are also farmed and owned communally, but the

Pl. 10.1 Constructing a house in a new *ujamaa* village

livestock belongs to individual families, though it is herded together. Yet in another village called Upper Kitete, both cash crops and livestock are owned by the community, but each family is allowed a private plot of about one hectare for cultivating food crops (Mushi, 1971).

The level of *ujamaa* at Kwamkono is low but very similar to what obtains in traditional communal farming in most of tropical Africa. Communal activity is restricted to clearing the farmland which is then divided into individual holdings and allocated to members to cultivate. In all cases, the farmland and village sites are selected and surveyed with the help of government agencies. The government also provides supervision and control over water supplies, conservation and land-use to ensure proper and efficient practices.

Self-reliance is the overriding principle of the Arusha Declaration of 1967, of which the *ujamaa* concept forms a part. Unlike the other highly capitalized settlement schemes discussed in this chapter, the *ujamaa* villages depend largely on the energy, self-help and initiative of the settlers. Only volunteers may join the villages, and

so far it is the poorer rural people who have been attracted by the scheme. The more well-to-do coffee farmers of Kilimanjaro district, who already enjoy most of the basic amenities promised by the *ujamaa* villagization scheme, do not support it. The future of the *ujamaa* village experiment therefore appears to depend very much on the state of the rural economy of the country. The level of *ujamaa* appears certain to become lower with improvement in living standards, although the integrated village associated with the *ujamaa* concept is likely to survive.

Irrigation schemes

Outside the Nile Valley traditional irrigation farming was restricted to a few localities in tropical Africa, notably north-western and south-eastern Kenya, the middle Niger Valley and parts of the drier savannaland of West Africa. Yet apart from the rainforest climatic zone all tropical Africa exhibits a climatic water deficit of varying duration during the year. It is this water deficit within a system of rain-fed agriculture that has contributed to the precarious food supply all over tropical Africa. This deficit can be made good through irrigation which is now recognized to be necessary, not only to permit double-cropping but also to ensure a good wet-season harvest in the grassland and Sahel zones. Irrigation is also necessary for practising double-cropping in the forest zone. The increasing number of small- and large-scale irrigation projects which have been established since independence are designed not only to ensure an adequate supply of water to plants during the dry season, but also to help effective flood control during the wet season.

Many of the large irrigation schemes have benefited from the experience of the very successful Gezira Scheme, although a few of these can claim to be as successful. In other parts of tropical Africa large-scale modern irrigation schemes such as the inland delta scheme in Mali, the Richard Toll Scheme in Senegal and the Kariba Scheme in Zimbabwe and Zambia, established during the colonial period, were few and far between. There were, however, many small irrigation schemes covering a few hundred hectares in countries like Nigeria, Kenya and Zimbabwe. Most of the existing large schemes, especially in Nigeria, have been established since independence.

West Africa

In West Africa, the natural conditions of the environment favour the production on a large scale of rice under irrigation. Yet each year large sums of money are spent on imported rice by Nigeria, Sierra Leone and Liberia, for instance. Currently the 5,600–hectare Richard Toll Scheme in Senegal, which was established as far back as 1948, is devoted to rice production. The older and more ambitious inland delta scheme, which started in 1932 on the lines of the Gezira Scheme, has been less successful. Rice, cotton, tea and sugar cane are grown, but in 1980, that is almost fifty years after the scheme started, less than 10 per cent of the projected 900,000 hectares had been irrigated. Since independence the government of Mali has, however, undertaken other major integrated river basin development schemes in which irrigation features prominently. The Selingue barrage on the Sankarani River which was commissioned in 1980 provides for the irrigation of 60,000 hectares, and the Manantali dam on the Bafing River is expected to irrigate 400,000 hectares.

Nigeria

At independence in 1960 there were only eight operational irrigation projects in Nigeria with a total area of about 3,000 hectares. The projects which were constructed and managed by the Irrigation Division of the then Northern Region Ministry of Agriculture were rather small in size, the largest having an area of about 1,100 hectares. All the projects were located in the northern states. The first decade of independence witnessed the rapid expansion of irrigated agriculture following the establishment in 1960 of the 1,600 hectare River Yobe Scheme near Lake Chad, closely followed by the 4,050 hectare Bacita sugar estate near Jebba in 1962.

Pl. 10.2 Irrigated cultivation by River Niger, Bamako, Mali

Other major irrigation projects of the 1960s were the Ebeji River Scheme near Lake Chad which started with the development of 4,000 hectares in 1963, the Kainji Scheme and the Sokoto–Rima Basin Scheme. Modern irrigated agriculture was introduced into the southern states in the early 1960s at the Uzo–Uwani farm settlement scheme and in the Niger Delta where the emphasis was on flood control.

The greatest concentration of large-scale modern irrigation in tropical Africa since the 1970s is in Nigeria, thanks to the availability of funds from crude petroleum. The Sahelian drought of 1972–4 also drove home to the government the urgency of developing irrigated agriculture. The major schemes of the 1970s include the 16,200–hectare Tiga Dam Scheme near Kano, commissioned in 1974; the 66,000–hectare South Chad Irrigation Project for wheat, rice, cotton and vegetables, the first 22,000 hectares of which was commissioned in 1978; and the 40,000–hectare Bokolori Dam Project in Sokoto State which was commissioned in 1980. Feasibility studies have been completed for the 40,000–hectare Birnin Kebbi Polders Project in Sokoto State and the 80,000–hectare Gongola Dam Project. Pre-feasibility studies have been completed for more than twenty other large-scale irrigation projects. Unfortunately there is no proper management of the land and water resources in the areas served by such completed schemes as the Tiga Dam near Kano. The large sums of money invested in these schemes can yield adequate dividends only if the land and water resources are efficiently utilized by allocating to each farm family as much irrigated land as it can effectively cultivate without resort to hired labour.

Kenya

Kenya is one of the few countries of tropical Africa where traditional irrigation farming was practised in many districts in pre-colonial times. Some of the ethnic groups who irrigated their fields were the Kamba, the Turkana, the Suk and the Marakwet. In some areas irrigation is still practised in much the same way as in the past, but in a few other areas the Agricultural Office has tried to modernize the traditional irrigation system. In the Endo Irrigation Scheme and the Koitirial Irrigation Scheme, which are located along the Kerio River, modernized traditional irrigation farming is practised over areas measuring only 600 and 150 hectares respectively (Hecklau, 1974). The only large modern irrigation scheme in Kenya is the 5,000–hectare Mwea Tebere on the Upper Tana River Basin (Stein and Schulze, 1978). The irrigated area here is divided into holdings of 1·5 hectares which are allocated to tenant farmers from Kikuyu and Embu ethnic territories. The potential irrigable area under this scheme is 100,000 hectares. There are also extensive irrigable areas in the Kano plains (12,400 hectares), the Yala Swamp (9,200 hectares) and the Miwani district, all in Nyanza Province in the Lake Victoria region.

Central Africa

The most extensive potential irrigable area in Central Africa is in the Kariba Lake Basin which contains Africa's third largest man-made lake (after Lakes Volta and Nasser). The largest areas currently under irrigated agriculture are however, in the Sabi–Lundi Basin in Zimbabwe and the Kafue Flats of Zambia. The Sabi–Lundi potential irrigable area is estimated to be about 136,000 hectares, but the irrigated land in 1980 was less than 3,500 hectares, mostly in the Mkwasini and the Hippo Valley – Chiredzi – Triangle districts where sugar cane is the dominant crop. The dams which supply water to these areas were all built before independence, the largest being the Kyle Dam built in 1960. About 3,000 small dams have also been built, mostly in European farms throughout Zimbabwe.

Zambia also has vast areas of permanent swamps such as the Bangwelu and Lukanga Swamps, as well as extensive seasonal swamps such as the Kafue and Luena Flats which could be drained for irrigated agriculture. In the Kafue Flats where pilot schemes have been established, the total area subject to annual flooding is about 520,000 hectares. Much of the land is reported to be suitable for large-scale cultivation of wheat, barley, groundnuts, cotton and potatoes. Plans to develop the Kafue Flats include the construction of polders over an area of about 8,000 hectares which will be settled by tenant farmers operating under conditions similar to those of the Gezira Scheme in Sudan Republic.

Integrated rural development

The numerous development programmes undertaken by the governments of tropical African countries since the end of the Second World War, but especially after independence, have been directed largely at increased agricultural production, and also at overall rural development. Both the farm settlement schemes and the plantations established by governments have, for example, sought to provide jobs in rural areas in the hope of reducing rural–urban migration. On the whole there has been an increase in agricultural production, although the food supply remains precarious. Rural development achievements are less certain since the various programmes and capital investments cannot be said to have reduced substantially the incidence of poverty, under-employment in rural areas, or the gap between the incomes of rural people and urban dwellers.

Considering the basically agricultural schemes like

commercial plantations and farm settlements, we find that these capital–intensive schemes do not involve a large proportion of the rural population. The 'demonstration effect' which the schemes were expected to have on people living in the districts where they were located has not materialized. The plantations and farm settlements have rather emerged as islands of modern farming in a vast sea of relatively stagnant traditional agricultural systems. The result is persistent rural underdevelopment and, in consequence, the continuing unattractiveness of rural areas for young school-leavers. The integrated approach to rural development seeks to remedy this. It is based on the premise that the complicated nature of the process of rural development and the magnitude of the problems involved demand that action be taken simultaneously on several fronts. This unified approach views a rural development project as a total planning process which provides for increased rural incomes, adequate roads, marketing and credit facilities and training people.

Many of the agricultural development schemes already discussed qualify as integrated agricultural projects. The farm settlement schemes in particular and such planned irrigation schemes as the Mwea Tebere Scheme on the Upper Tana Valley in Kenya or the Sabi–Lundi irrigation scheme in Zimbabwe are basically integrated rural development schemes. Other integrated rural development projects include the Bangem Integrated Agricultural Project in the Cameroun, which is a land settlement scheme, and the pilot integrated rural development project established in the Mampong Valley by the Ghana Rural Reconstruction Movement (Gyasi, 1978). The Mampong Valley Social Laboratory, as the Ghana project is called, covers an area of 65 sq. km and involves a rural population of 3,370. The project consists of a four-fold integrated programme which aims at improving simultaneously livelihoods, health, education and civic responsibility in the area.

Multi-purpose or integrated river basin development

In recent years more and more rivers in tropical Africa have been harnessed to produce hydro-electric power. In many cases the provision of power is just one of the several reasons for undertaking these schemes. Others usually include flood control, irrigation, conservation, regulation of the flow of rivers for navigation and the provision of recreational facilities. As far as agriculture is concerned, the importance of river basin development lies in the provision of water for irrigation and watering stock, the fishing facilities provided by the lakes and to a lesser extent the transport facilities that the lakes also provide. The major river basin develop-

ment schemes in tropical Africa are therefore basically multi-purpose.

The construction of a dam for irrigation or hydro-electric power creates a man-made lake behind the dam while the fish life of the valley below the dam as well as the flood plain agriculture may be adversely affected. Often the lake extends into another administrative unit or even another country and in almost every case a resettlement programme for the displaced population is called for. This is one reason why many governments have come to accept the drainage basin as a suitable planning unit. In Nigeria, great emphasis has been placed since about 1975 on development planning based on river basins. Some of the statutory quasi-government corporations already established include the Niger Basin Development Authority, the Cross River Basin Development Authority and river basin development authorities for the Benue, Imo, Ogun, Sokoto–Rima and Kaduna Rivers.

Currently the various river basin planning authorities in Nigeria are concerned primarily with increased food production and conservation. Existing and proposed irrigation dams have been placed under the control of the relevant river basin. The much publicized green revolution programme of the Shagari administration, which has since replaced the Operation 'Feed the Nation' campaign of the last three years of military rule, is being executed in close collaboration with the various river basin development authorities.

References

Gyasi, E. A. (1978), 'Rural Development Through Autonomous Indigenous Organisations: Example of the Ghana Rural Reconstruction Movement', in J. S. Oguntoyinbo et al. (eds.), Resources and Development in Africa, II, IGU Regional Conference Papers, University of Ibadan, Nigeria.

Hecklau, H. (1974), 'Irrigation Farming in Kenya', Applied Sciences and Development, 4, pp. 75–88.

Morgan, W. T. W. (1973), East Africa, Longman, Harlow.

Mushi, S. S. (1971), 'Modernization by Traditionalization: Ujamaa Principles Revisited', Taamuli (University of Dar-es-Salaam), 1, no. 2, pp. 13–29.

Odingo, R. S. (1971), 'Settlement and Rural Development in Kenya', in S. H. Ominde (ed.), Studies in East African Geography and Development, Heinemann, London, pp. 162–76.

Olatunbosun, D. (1971), 'Western Nigeria Farm Settlement: An Appraisal', Journal of Developing Areas, 5, pp. 417–28.

Spencer, C. R. (1977), 'Politics, Public Administration and Agricultural Development: A Case Study of the Sierra Leone Industrial Plantation Development Program, 1964–7', Journal of Developing Areas, 12, pp. 69–86.

Stein, C. and Schulze, C. (1978), 'Land Use and Development Potential in the Arid Regions of Kenya', Applied Sciences and Development, 12, pp. 47–64.

11 Livestock Rearing and Fishing

A brief discussion of cattle rearing appears in the section on traditional farming systems in tropical Africa (see p. 108). This chapter gives a more comprehensive account of livestock production, including cattle, various domestic animals and poultry. The fisheries and the state of the fishing industry in tropical Africa are also discussed. As with arable farming, livestock production and fishing are still handicapped by conservative and primitive methods, which have combined with environmental handicaps to restrict output. The result is that the demand far exceeds the supply. The countries of tropical Africa have therefore been obliged to expend a considerable proportion of their scarce foreign exchange earnings on imports of meat, milk, butter, cheese, poultry and fish from Europe, South America and North America. Nigeria, for example, imports milk to the value of over ₦7 million every year and in 1966, that is before restrictions on the import of certain food items, the country paid almost ₦14 million for stockfish imported from Norway! Yet the country has vast fishery resources along the sea coast and in inland waters, including large man-made lakes.

Currently, the acute protein deficiency in the diet of the people of tropical Africa, especially of those in the forest belt, is a great source of concern amongst health administrators. Unfortunately, the position is worsening because of the increasing cost of meat, other livestock products and fish. There is therefore a pressing need to develop the livestock and fishery resources to satisfy the rising demand for animal protein. Furthermore, live animals and animal products constitute the most important export of countries such as the Somali Republic, Upper Volta and Botswana. The development of the livestock industry in such countries will not only increase the national income, but will also help to reduce the growing incidence of unemployment.

Livestock populations and distribution

Reliable livestock censuses are rare in tropical Africa since many owners of livestock are unwilling to supply the necessary information for fear of taxation. The figures presented in Table 11.1 therefore represent the latest available estimates for each country, and in a few cases actual censuses. Since some countries are much larger in area and size of population than others, the mere size of the livestock population as presented in Table 11.1 is not very helpful in assessing the importance of livestock to the economy of the various countries. More meaningful yardsticks are the distribution of livestock per sq km and the ratio of cattle to the human population particularly when the unit of calculation is the administrative district or province.

The cattle population of tropical Africa is estimated to be over 90 million out of which 22 million are found in East Africa and about 31 million in West Africa. The East African concentration is mainly around the Lake Victoria district and the Kenya Highlands which are free from tsetse flies and where the cattle density exceeds 15 per sq km. In West Africa the cattle population is concentrated in the Sahel and drier savanna zones. The other areas with large cattle populations include Ethiopia, western and southwestern Sudan and central Malagasy. As a rule, the

Fig. 11.1 Main livestock and freshwater fishing areas

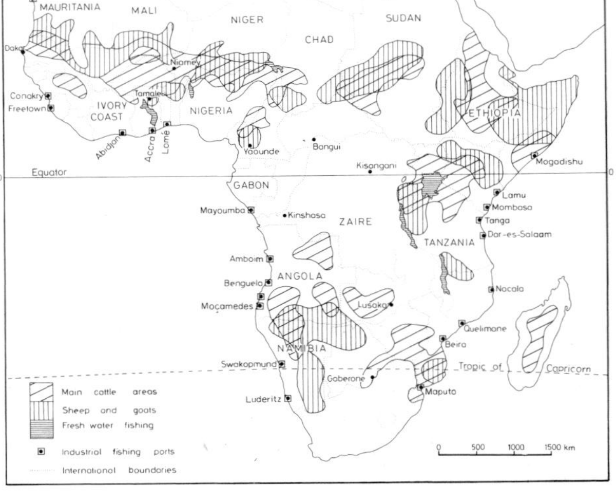

Table 11.1   Livestock population of major producing countries in 1978 ('000)

Country	Cattle	Goats	Sheep	Pigs	Poultry	Horses	Donkeys	Camels
Angola	3070	925	215	370	5,200	6·2	5	—
Benin	730	850	850	370	3,400	3	1	—
Botswana	3,000	1,150	440	21	600	12	36	—
Cameroun	2,972	1,636	2,155	789	9,620	50	73	—
Chad	4,012	2,250	2,254	6	2,900	154	300	350
Ethiopia	27,500	17,120	23,150	17	52,100	1,500	4,000	964
Gambia	275	108	90	9	250	—	4	—
Ghana	900	1,900	1,600	390	11,000	4	25	—
Guinea	1,600	385	420	37	5,200	1	3	—
Guinea-Bissau	262	182	72	174	380	—	3	—
Ivory Coast	680	1,150	1,100	250	10,000	1	1	—
Kenya	9,100	4,415	3,980	65	17,100	2	—	574
Malagasy	10,000	1,500	607	560	13,900	2	1	—
Malawi	760	818	88	274	8,242	—	—	—
Mali	4,263	5,629	5,849	29	10,592	170	470	198
Mauritania	1,500	3,200	5,000	—	2,980	17	300	718
Mozambique	1,370	325	100	105	17,000	—	20	—
Namibia	2,950	2,100	5,130	35	445	44	65	—
Niger	2,990	6,700	2,600	29	7,638	227	437	370
Nigeria	11,600	24,188	8,254	973	97,210	300	750	18
Rwanda	685	682	248	71	809	—	—	—
Senegal	2,671	1,000	1,950	178	7,062	230	215	6
Somalia	4,000	16,400	9,900	9	2,700	1	22	5,400
Sudan	16,567	11,974	15,670	8	25,072	20	679	2,904
Tanzania	15,272	4,700	3,000	25	21,054	—	162	—
Togo	245	650	880	270	3,300	3	2	—
Uganda	5,321	2,144	1,068	220	13,000	—	16	—
Upper Volta	2,000	23,000	1,450	150	9,000	90	170	5
Zambia	1,800	300	51	180	14,000	—	1	—
Zimbabwe	6,600	2,050	650	202	8,600	10	96	—

Source FAO, *FAO Production Yearbook*, Rome, 1978, Vol. 32, pp. 199–207.

areas of cattle concentration are either open grassland or highland areas with elevations of over 1,000 m above sea level, since these are the areas which are free from tsetse fly infestation. The forest areas of West Africa and the Zaïre Basin are generally unsuitable for cattle rearing although some localities support small herds of the dwarf Muturu cattle. The heavily forested areas of the Zaïre Basin have a ratio of only 5 cattle per 100 people as compared with over 110 cattle per 100 people in the Lake Victoria coastal districts of Kenya and Tanzania.

Since most cattle rearers also keep goats and sheep, and since the largest flocks of goats and sheep are kept by pastoral nomads, the broad pattern of the distribution of these two animals is similar to that of cattle. However, goats and sheep are much more numerous than cattle. The greatest concentration of goats and sheep are in Ethiopia, Somalia and the drier parts of northern Nigeria. The pig population of Nigeria is

however concentrated in the forested southern zone which contains over 70 per cent of the 900,000 pigs while the predominantly Muslim areas of the far north of Nigeria contain less than 10 per cent. Other major producers of pigs include Angola, Malagasy, and the southern parts of Cameroun and Togo.

Cattle rearing

Economically and socially, cattle are by far the most important livestock to the people of tropical Africa. Traditionally, the religious and ceremonial value of cattle is far more important than the economic value. Accordingly, it is the size of the herd that confers great social prestige to the cattle rearers, although the quality is also important. Indeed most cattle rearing groups such as the Fulani and the Masai regard cattle as a trust to the present generation from the past generation – a medium between the living and the dead. Their attitude to cattle is therefore similar to that of settled cultivators who traditionally consider the land to belong to the dead, the living and generations as yet unborn. In consequence, cattle are rarely slaughtered for meat except during festivals and on important social occasions, hence the tendency to overstock, resulting in overgrazing in many parts of tropical Africa. Fortunately, an increasing number of cattle rearers now sell their animals to raise money to pay tax and defray other family expenses.

Cattle rearing in tropical Africa is carried out under any of the following four production systems. These are 1. nomadic pastoralism, 2. combined livestock rearing and arable farming but without integrating the two, 3. integrated mixed farming and 4. cattle ranching.

Nomadic pastoralism

Nomadic pastoralism entails cattle men and their cattle moving every year during the dry-season months from their home base to distant grazing lands and back again in the rainy season. In tropical Africa pastoralists are found predominantly in areas with an annual rainfall of less than 1,000 mm (40 ins), that is in the drier savanna and Sahel regions as well as in the wetter highland grasslands of Ethiopia and East Africa. Nomadic pastoralism in the region, as in other parts of the world, including the Barbary states of north-west Africa, is largely a response to climate. But unlike north-west Africa where Fitzgerald (1957) attributes pastoralism solely to the rainfall characteristics rather than to cultural heritage and race, we find that in tropical Africa, nomadic pastoralism is largely confined to people from specific ethnic groups such as the Cattle Fulani, the Masai, the Nuer and the Baggara.

The Cattle Fulani of the western Sudan and the Masai of the East African plateau are amongst the best-known pastoralists in the world. The Cattle Fulani are found all over the Sudan and Sahel zones of West Africa from Senegal in the west to Chad and Cameroun in the east. They are by far the largest group of cattle rearers in tropical Africa. During the rainy season, the pastoral Fulani settle with their cattle in the far north of West Africa as well as in the highlands free from the tsetse fly, such as the Fouta Djallon, the Jos Plateau, the Bamenda and the Cameroun Highlands. As the dry season sets in, the tsetse fly retreats and the Cattle Fulani spread into pastureland in the Middle Belt while those in the highlands descend to graze in the neighbouring lowlands. As a rule the Cattle Fulani have no permanent settlements, not even in their wet-season homes. They live in temporary huts of grass thatch supported on a wooden framework.

As a group of pastoralists, the Cattle Fulani travel considerable distances every year in search of pasture and water. The straight-line distance or the 'trans-humance orbit' between the wet-season camp and the dry-season camp of most of them is about 100 km, giving an annual orbital distance of about 200 km from the wet-season camp to the dry-season camp and back (Stenning, 1965). Of course, these distances do not include the daily trek to the grazing fields and water points. The Cattle Fulani live a rather simple life and hardly ever intermarry with other groups. They live on milk and butter as well as from grains purchased from local markets with cash derived from the sale of surplus milk and butter. Many Cattle Fulani families also cultivate guinea corn, millet, maize and beans in their wet-season camps. Most of them also keep some goats and sheep, both of which provide the main source of meat, since cattle are rarely slaughtered for food.

Cattle are kept by almost all the ethnic groups in East Africa, both pastoralists and settled cultivators. Amongst the pastoral groups, it is only the Masai and the Turkana that concern themselves almost exclusively with livestock, whereas the Jie, the Galla and the Karamojong combine cattle rearing with arable farming. Masai pastoralists concentrate mostly on cattle, unlike the Turkana who attach as much importance to goats and sheep as they do to cattle. The Masai are therefore the East African brethren of the Cattle Fulani and we will make a closer comparison of the two modes of life.

The Masai are of Hamito–Negroid origin while the Cattle Fulani are classified as pure Hamitic. In physical appearance, both the Masai and the Cattle Fulani are tall and slender. The other distinguishing features of both groups include a relatively fair complexion, a straight narrow nose and straight or wavy hair. The Masai inhabit the central part of the East African plateau lying between Lake Victoria and the coast and are found mostly in Kenya and northern Tanzania. Like the Cattle Fulani, they live and rear their cattle in areas occupied by sedentary cultivators, but have totally rejected hunting and arable farming as unworthy occupations. The Masai, like the Cattle Fulani, are always on the move with their cattle, and live in temporary huts which, as with the Fulani, are usually constructed and maintained by the women. The Masai traditional diet consists of milk, blood and meat, although they also eat a considerable amount of purchased millet and maize and the women and children eat root crops and bananas, which are scorned by the men. Masai cattle are never ridden or made to carry loads, since each household has a few donkeys which are used as beasts of burden. Goats are herded along with sheep, and their milk, meat and blood provide the main source of food.

Other major pastoralist groups in tropical Africa include the Nuer people of southern Sudan, the Baggara Arabs of central and western Sudan, and the Turkana of

Pl. 11.1 Dinka man – Dinka are pastoralists like the Nuer

northern Kenya. The seasonal migrations of the Nuer are controlled by the flood level of the River Nile system. During the Nile floods, the Nuer graze their cattle around their compounds which are located on high ground in the Nile Valley, but as the flood recedes, they migrate with their cattle to the grassy plains uncovered by the receding floodwaters. Nuer pastoralists live in temporary camps scattered over a very wide area and are known to cover transhumance orbits of over 250 km. Nuer women and children usually remain in their flood-season compounds where they cultivate maize, millet and tobacco.

The Baggara Arabs live in a relatively wet area in an otherwise dry and sandy environment. During the rainy season, Baggara territory, which is underlain by red clays, is characterized by deep pools of water similar to those found in the rain-fed swamps of Abakaliki in Anambra State of Nigeria. This is the season when swarms of mosquitoes and other biting flies constitute a serious nuisance, forcing the Baggara men to migrate with their cattle to the better drained sandy Qoz district where the rainfall is also lighter. At the end of the rainy season the men return to the clay district called *Muglad* to graze their cattle on crop residues on the farms cultivated by their wives while they were away. The local pools dry up completely as the dry season advances and water shortage becomes a serious problem. The Baggara are forced to migrate again, this time to river valleys in the south of the Sudan. When the first rains start again, the Baggara return to the *Muglad* for a short while, only to migrate again to the Qoz district when the pools of water begin to form in the *Muglad*.

In the case of the Turkana, the pattern of migration is influenced more by the poverty of grazing than by shortage of water. Although the Turkana live in a sub-desert country with less than 400 mm of rainfall, the region has a number of watercourses which provide water from pools and shallow wells along their beds during the dry season. The Turkana therefore migrate from one watercourse to another except during the driest period of the year when they migrate to the massive granite hills which receive a higher rainfall and where there is always some grazing. The Turkana are therefore partly nomadic and partly transhumant. In addition to cattle, Turkana pastoralists keep camels, sheep and donkeys, and in general the cattle population is kept on the hills for most of the year while the goats, sheep and camels are mainly confined to the drier plain.

There has been a tendency to consider nomadic pastoralism as a primitive form of animal rearing in much the same way as shifting cultivation is often considered to be both a primitive and wasteful use of arable land. However, while pressure of population and the extensive use of fertilizers have helped to reduce the incidence of shifting cultivation, die-hard pastoralist groups continue despite the constraints of overstocking and overgrazing. In modern cattle farms, the beasts are slaughtered for meat at the age of 20 months to 3 years. So far, various attempts have been made by governments to settle some pastoral groups, but it appears that the Cattle Fulani, for example, are not interested in such schemes and in Kenya, those who have so far embraced the schemes are not 'pure' Masai (Morgan, 1973, p. 225).

Combined livestock rearing and arable farming

Settled cultivators in East Africa and southern Africa keep cattle, mostly of the Zebu type, as an adjunct to peasant agriculture. In West Africa, some settled cultivators also keep cattle, such as the Hausa, the Toucouleur, the Mossi, the Bambara and the Songhay, all of whom live in grassland environments, and in the Ivory Coast, the Dioula of the forest belt now raise cattle for meat and milk. In most cases the cattle owned by settled cultivators in West Africa are placed under the care of the nomadic Cattle Fulani, although some animals are kept permanently close to the homesteads for the purpose of providing milk for domestic use. Most settled cultivators all over tropical Africa also keep goats, sheep and poultry around the homesteads. Like the pastoralists, the settled cultivators also regard cattle, sheep and goats as a social asset. Cattle are rarely sold although the smaller livestock are readily disposed of whenever the family is in need of cash to buy clothing and food or to pay school fees.

There is, however, no integration between cattle rearing and arable farming. In general, except for dry-season pasturing on farmland, stock rearing and cultivation are carried out as separate occupations by the same people. Some farmers amongst the Serer people of Senegal, however, practise mixed farming in which the use of pastureland is integrated with cropland. Other groups that practise some form of mixed farming, in which the cattle are stall-fed, include the Shuwa Arabs of Nigeria, the sedentary Fulani of the Fouta Djallon in Guinea, the Tonga of Zambia and the Chagga of Tanzania. However, the cultivation of fodder crops for feeding cattle is absent amongst these peoples.

The Tswana people of Botswana are a typical group who combine livestock rearing with arable farming but with no integration between the two. The traditional Tswana family keeps three homes: the main or permanent one in the village, a crude one in the distant farmland and another crude one at the cattle post or grazing area. As a rule the Tswana live together in large villages so that the distance from the village to the farms often exceeds 12 km. In the village of Gabane (2,000),

for example, only 9 per cent of the farms are located within a radius of 5 km from the village centre. About 50 per cent are more than 11 km from the village while 44 per cent are over 15 km from the village (Silistshena, 1977). During the farming season, therefore, a large proportion of the village population of only 2,000 settle in temporary homes in distant farms. Moreover, in keeping with a long-established tradition, cattle posts are located at considerable distances, often exceeding 80 km from the villages and under the care of adolescent sons of the owner or his servants. In recent years the cattle posts have become more widespread following the establishment of many bore holes. A few herds are kept on arable farms during the ploughing season after which they are returned to the cattle post.

Amongst the settled cultivators of West Africa, who also keep small herds of cattle, the practice is to keep the animals within or near the homestead at night. In the day the cattle are taken out for grazing by young male children or servants. Some settled cultivators also take care of cattle owned by well-to-do city dwellers such as businessmen and senior civil servants who invest in cattle for prestige in society. Under such an arrangement, the caretaker retains all income from sales of milk, while the owner retains the animals and their offspring. Some very rich businessmen employ herdsmen who each receive, in addition to cash payment, at least one young animal a year as well as some milk and foodstuffs. The use of paid herdsmen or settled cultivators as caretakers is preferred since the city cattle owners are often suspicious of the returns made on cattle placed under the care of the nomadic Cattle Fulani (Van Raay, 1970).

Pl. 11.2 Fulani watering their cattle and goats

Integrated mixed farming

Mixed farmers keep livestock and also cultivate a variety of crops in rotation. These include grass and fodder crops which are fed to the animals, which in turn provide milk, meat, hides and wool as well as manure for the farm. All farms are fenced and mechanization is the rule in areas with flat or gently undulating land.

The advantages of mixed farming compared with pastoral nomadism on the one hand and peasant hoe cultivation on the other appear to be obvious. Fortunately with the spread of education in areas where cattle can be kept an increasing number of farmers are showing interest in mixed farming. In some areas, notably in East Africa and Zimbabwe, improved European livestock, such as the pedigree British cattle, have been introduced to replace or to be crossed with African breeds. Indian bulls, which are used to hotter climates, have also been introduced into East Africa to improve the breeding of commercial herds. In addition, governments have encouraged co-operative marketing organizations to handle milk and meat marketing.

Integrated mixed farming by African farmers has now been firmly established in the former White Highlands of Kenya where there are many African farms with good quality cattle and well-tended crops. This has been made possible by purchasing farmland from European settlers who decided to leave the country on the eve of independence. Such farmlands have been subdivided and sold to African farmers under the Assisted Owner (or Tenant) Project and Smallholder Schemes of the Kenyan Government. Most of the mixed farmers are Kikuyu, but many Europeans and Indians have also been allocated farmland under these schemes. Small farmers who had no land before and no capital are settled in high density schemes where each plot is less than 20 hectares, some being as small as 6 hectares. Richer Africans with some experience in farming and some capital of their own settle in the low density schemes where the plot size varies from 20–100 hectares. The successful operation of these schemes has been assisted by the commercial banks who now readily grant loans to African mixed farmers (Morgan, 1963).

In Zambia, thousands of small-scale mixed farmers have emerged thanks to the introduction in 1946 of the African Farming Improvement Scheme in Tongaland and the development in the 1950s of the Peasant Farming Scheme in the Eastern Province. Most of these modern farmers are educated people who have gained considerable knowledge and experience while working on European farms, where some of them also saved a part of their working capital. Under the government Peasant Farming Scheme, selected farmers are eligible for loans to cover the cost of stumping, equipment, trained oxen and breeding stock (Allan, 1965). The farmers adopt a simple rotation of two cereal crops with a leguminous and a green manure crop, applying cattle manure to at least one of the cereal plots.

Mixed farming in Zimbabwe is still dominated by European settlers who occupy the richest farming area of the eastern high veld. Beef cattle are important all over the region while dairy cattle and pigs provide an additional and substantial income. Each European farmer owns a large area of land, often exceeding 1,000 hectares, of which up to 300 hectares are cultivated in rotation with maize, beans, tobacco and sown pasture, while the remaining land consists of permanent pasture for up to 500 herds, and wasteland. African mixed farmers are relatively few and their farms are generally much smaller, rarely exceeding 300 hectares in the Native Purchase Areas which cover about 3 million hectares of territory in which Africans may buy land. It is very likely that the current exodus of European settlers from Zimbabwe will, as in Kenya, result in a considerable increase in the number of African mixed farmers now that it is independent.

Various attempts have also been made by the Department of Agriculture in West African countries, notably Nigeria and Ghana, to establish mixed farming in areas where cattle can exist. So far, the results have not been impressive partly because of the existing land tenure systems, but largely because the cattle population is owned by nomadic pastoralists who are still to be persuaded to settle down to practise mixed farming. Current land reforms in Nigeria and the ongoing high investments on irrigation dams are likely to yield substantial results in this direction during the 1980s.

Cattle ranching

Livestock ranching is the large-scale commercial rearing of animals such as cattle, sheep and goats and is usually practised in semi-arid and arid lands. It is similar in some ways to nomadic herding because although the movements of stock are normally confined to the ranch, it is sometimes necessary to take the cattle to graze in distant pastures located outside the ranch. Livestock ranching, like nomadic herding, is characterized by a low ratio of animals per unit area of land and cropping on the ranch is often restricted to providing fodder for periods when natural grazing is inadequate or not available.

As a form of agriculture, livestock ranching is not usually associated with tropical Africa. There are, however, an increasing number of privately owned and government operated ranches in tropical Africa, particularly in the highland areas of East and south-Central Africa. Most of the private ranches were established by European settlers, many of whom still continue to manage them. In Angola, for example, cattle ranching is dominated by Portuguese settlers who own large ranches in the Huambo and Huila Plateau districts.

The Companhia Agro-Pecuaria de Angola ranch, which is located near the mouth of the Cuanza River, is one of the largest. It covers a total area of 100,000 hectares and supports a herd of 15,000 cattle. The smaller 30,000 hectare ranch, supporting 3,000 cattle, raised mainly for meat supply to the diamond mining company DIAMMANG, is located in the north-eastern district of Lunda while the much larger 300,000 hectare ranch of the Uniao Commercial de Automovies, which caters for 18,000 cattle, is located in the Huila Plateau district. Local European farmers also maintain modern cattle ranches in the Maputo district of Mozambique.

Many private ranches have been established since 1964 in the Ankole-Masaka Ranching Scheme area of Uganda where each rancher is allocated about 1,200 hectares. The scheme is under strict government supervision and amongst other regulations imposed is the limit of 500 head of cattle per ranch and compulsory pest control through regular spraying and dipping of cattle. The commercial ranches in the high plateau area of Tanzania, such as the beef cattle ranch near Dodoma, are owned by the government. In Zambia, government sponsored cattle ranches concentrate on improving breeding stock and now supply good quality young cattle to local farmers for fattening. Many co-operative ranches have also been set up by the Zambian Government for the purpose of encouraging traditional cattle owners to keep their breeding stock. In addition to close supervision by agricultural extension workers, cattle owners on the co-operative ranches are also shown better ways of rearing cattle.

Large cattle ranches abound in the Matabeleland plateau of south-west Zimbabwe. In the 7,190 hectare ranch at Balla Balla near Bulawayo, for example, about 24 hectares of land are cultivated with silage crops such as beans, green maize and cow peas, which are used for feeding the stock during the dry season. The rest of the ranch is grazing land for the 1,260 cattle which consist largely of cross-breeds of imported British Herefords with local stock.

Cattle ranching is much less developed in West Africa and with a few exceptions, the ranches are owned by government agencies. One of the oldest and best developed ranches is the Moka cattle ranch in the Equatorial Guinea island of Fernando Po. In Nigeria, which has an estimated cattle population of over 10 million, cattle ranching by foreign private investors was prevented by the British colonial government who refused to permit European investors to acquire land on a large scale. However, in 1914, a 6,400 hectare ranch was established at Allagarno in Bornu by African Ranches Ltd of Liverpool. Unfortunately the ranch had to disband in 1923, five years after the government had come to the conclusion that there was no justification in granting the management more land. Its results were considered by government to be not much better than a Fulani cattle owner could have achieved under similar conditions (Dunbar, 1970). Government attitudes towards cattle ranching changed dramatically after independence in 1960 and most of the existing ranches, which are mainly under public ownership, were established after 1960. The more important of these ranches include the 8,000 hectare Borno ranch at Gombole near Maiduguri, the 5,500 hectare ranch at Mokwa, the Upper Ogun ranch in Oyo State and the Obudu cattle ranch in the Cross River State.

Goats, sheep and pigs

Goats and sheep are found all over tropical Africa whereas pigs are largely concentrated in non-Muslim areas. We have seen that most cattle rearers, including nomadic pastoralists and settled cultivators, also keep goats and sheep. In addition goats and, to a lesser extent, sheep are reared in most rural settlements in the forest belt. Fortunately goats and sheep are regarded as a more economic asset than cattle since the religious and ceremonial value attached to cattle does not apply to them. They therefore make a greater contribution to local meat supplies, especially during festivals when large numbers are usually slaughtered. Milking is not common except in grassland areas, where goat's milk and skins form an important item of local trade.

In the grassland areas, goats and sheep are usually kept together and generally left to browse around the homesteads, except at night and during the rainy season when they are penned to keep them away from food-crop farms. Homestead flocks are generally small compared with those of nomadic stock rearers. Goats tend to be undiscriminating about food and have proved a great asset in the very dry districts such as the West African Sahel and northern Kenya, where grazing is often too poor for cattle. As a rule, grassland goats are larger in size and are long-legged, compared with the dwarf breeds of the forest belt. Mixed flocks of goats and sheep are rare in the forest belt since the goat is usually tethered to a pole in the backyard and fed with forage. In most forest communities goats belong to the women, and, unlike in grassland areas, the animals are not skinned when slaughtered. By contrast, the Sokoto Red and Kano Brown goats, the source of the famous Moroccan leather, still provide highly valued skins for making footwear, containers, knife sheaths and bellows.

Sheep command a high value in Muslim areas where the long-legged breeds predominate. In the forest belt, the sheep population consists of dwarf breeds which are more resistant to high humidity and to *trypanosomiasis*. Dwarf sheep are kept in small numbers by settled

Pl. 11.3 Goats for sale at Ibadan market, Nigeria

cultivators while the long-legged savanna breeds, reared by pastoralists, are kept in large herds usually exceeding 50 animals. Wool is not an important product of West African sheep except in the region of the inland Niger Delta where the Macina wool sheep, which are considered to be of Syrian origin, are highly valued for their fleece. Both the Macina and the Coundoun sheep, found in the middle Niger Valley between Timbuktu and Niamey, produce wool used in making local cloth and blankets. Wool sheep, notably the Merino and Corriedale breed, are common on European farms in Kenya.

Pigs are kept all over East Africa by Africans and European settlers, the greatest concentration being in the Kenya Highlands. African stocks in Tanzania and Uganda are widely scattered as in West Africa where pig rearing is largely confined to the non-Muslim areas of the Guinea savanna and the forest belt. Most pigs live on food scraps and are allowed to wander about the villages and towns. The number kept is usually so small that pigs do not contribute much to the output of animal protein in tropical Africa. An increasing number of modern pig farms have been established in many countries since about 1965 but the high cost of pig-feed constitutes a major problem in sustaining existing pig farms.

Poultry

Chickens are by far the most numerous and widespread livestock in tropical Africa and are to be found in almost every rural homestead. Guinea-fowl, turkeys, ducks and geese are also kept but are less numerous and often restricted to grassland areas. All the birds are allowed to wander about the homestead to fend for themselves and are rarely fed. The birds therefore take a longer period to mature compared with modern exotic breeds. They are also rather stunted and although the meat is relatively tough, the people consider it to be tastier than meat from exotic breeds. Eggs from local chickens are also much smaller in size.

Poultry provides the most common source of meat protein in tropical Africa. A large number of farmers in peri-urban areas have since adopted modern poultry farming with the result that eggs are now a common feature of the diet of many households. The great advantage which poultry has over the larger livestock is that it yields quick results since broiler birds mature within four to five months. In addition, the initial cost of establishing a poultry farm is comparatively small and the local manufacture of poultry cages has made small-scale operation possible for numerous households in the cities. Inadequate supply of day-old chicks and the high cost as well as irregular supply of feed, however, constitute major constraints to the expansion of modern poultry farming. In Nigeria, for example, a large proportion of the maize used in manufacturing poultry feed is still imported from the Americas and so are the ingredients. Chickens are still therefore a relatively expensive form of protein.

Pl. 11.4 Freshwater fishing in Lake Chilwa, Malawi

Fishing and fish farming

Fish is an important source of animal protein. It is currently much cheaper than meat and fortunately parts of tropical Africa are rich in freshwater fisheries as well as in marine fisheries. As an occupation fishing is widespread along the coastal areas as well as in large rivers and lakes, but the total catch is far less than the demand, hence the large sum of money still expended on fish imports by most countries. Efforts to develop the fish resources to satisfy the demands of a rapidly increasing population have largely been concerned with the expansion of fishing grounds and the adoption of improved technology in marine and lake fishing. Fish farming has also received increasing attention and investment by many governments, although the performance of commercial fish farms in some countries such as Nigeria has so far not been particularly impressive.

Freshwater or inland fishing

Freshwater fishing is much more important than marine fishing throughout tropical Africa, both in terms of the size and value of the catch and also in terms of the number of people who obtain a living from it. In the East African countries of Kenya, Uganda and Tanzania, for example, the catch in 1969 from freshwater sources was 272,000 tons, worth ₦20 million, compared with only 24,000 tons, worth ₦4 million, from the sea (Morgan, 1973, p. 125). The great lakes of East Africa are amongst the most important fresh water in tropical Africa. The importance of Lake Victoria lies partly in its great size and partly in the fact that its shallow depth provides excellent breeding conditions

for a wide range of naturally occurring species of fish. Also, unlike Lakes Turkana and Tanganyika, Lake Victoria is bordered by very densely populated districts which provide a large market for a flourishing fish industry.

In West Africa the most important freshwater fisheries are the inland Niger Delta, the middle Niger Valley and Lake Chad. The inland Niger Delta when under flood covers an area of about 40,000 sq km which is much larger than Guinea-Bissau or about the size of Oyo State of Nigeria. Unfortunately fish production in the inland Niger Delta has declined greatly in recent years because of prolonged drought in the Sahel region and the consequent reduction in the flooded area, which has in turn resulted in the overfishing of the truncated fishing grounds. In 1960, for example, the inland Niger Delta produced 20 per cent of the freshwater fish of 530,000 tons for tropical Africa but ten years later the proportion of inland water fish originating from the region had declined to only 4 per cent. The total catch in 1970 was 110,000 tons, declining to only 52,000 tons in 1973 when Mali also suffered severe losses in its cattle population because of the Sahelian drought. About 200,000 people in the area obtain a living from fishing and the fish trade (Barth, 1976).

Lake Chad is a rather shallow and extensive expanse of water which covers an area of about 26,000 sq km. It is very rich in fish, the dominant varieties of which include *Heterotis*, Nile Perch (*Lates niloticus*) and *Tilapia*. Production in the Nigerian section of the Lake is about 70,000 tonnes per year and about 4,000 full-time and another 600 seasonal migrant fishermen are involved. The output of fish in the Cameroun and Chad sections of the lake are estimated to be much greater owing to easier fishing conditions. The bulk of the catch from the lake is however marketed in Nigeria.

Although most fishermen in the Lake Chad Basin are full-time, the vast majority of freshwater fishing in tropical Africa is carried out by part-time fishermen who operate mostly during the dry-season months, which is also the slack season in the farming calendar. In the inland Niger Delta, for example, the main fishing groups are the Sorko, the Samono, the Bambara, the Babo and the Bozo. Of these, the Bambara, Sorko and Somono combine fishing with hoe cultivation and cattle rearing while the Bozo are full-time fishermen. Bozo commitment to fishing is in some ways comparable to the Cattle Fulani attachment to cattle rearing and like the Cattle Fulani, the Bozo fishermen are wholly nomadic, their movement up and down the middle Niger being dictated by the flood periods of various sections of the river. These migrant fishermen live in temporary huts built on the levees or sandbanks along the riverbeds.

The methods used in catching freshwater fish vary considerably from one region to another. The most widespread methods are the use of fish traps, which are usually conical in shape, fixed nets and dragging nets from canoes. Hand nets are more popular in the smaller rivers where spears, lines and poisons are also used. The use of fish poisons has been banned in many districts since the poison destroys the eggs and young fish along with the mature ones, resulting in the impoverishment of the resources of the affected fishing grounds.

Sea fishing

Sea fishing is still largely undeveloped in tropical Africa since the equipment used by the local coastal peoples is still primitive. Since about 1970 an increasing number

Pl. 11.5 Unloading kingfish from an ocean-going dhow, Zanzibar

of African businessmen, notably in Nigeria and Ghana, have invested in trawler fishing, while many governments have established some fishing terminals and ancillary facilities to aid the expansion of marine fishing. However, most of the industrial fishing fleets, including those operating off the coast of Nigeria, are owned and operated by foreign companies registered in Japan, France, Britain, Portugal and the Soviet Union. In Nigeria about 100 of these foreign trawlers operate under charter arrangements with Nigerian companies. The Nigerian Federal Government-owned National Fish Company and the National Shrimp Company also carry out large-scale modern distant-water fishing along the Nigerian coast.

Most professional local African sea fishermen, such as the Ijaw and Ilaye Yoruba of Nigeria, the people of Zanzibar and the Wolof of Senegal, do not go far out to sea, because of the problems of navigating away from land in their small fishing craft. They are largely confined to coastal waters, river estuaries and the lagoons. The Wovea of west Cameroun are, however, known to practise distant-water fishing in the hunting of whales with harpoons. Distant-water fishing for most of the other coastal people is essentially long-distance migration to fish in the coastal waters of other countries. For instance, Kru fishermen from the Ivory Coast are to be found camping along the coast of West Africa from Sierra Leone to Nigeria.

The richest marine fishing grounds are found off the coast of Mauritania, where the vast fish resources have for a long time attracted fishing trawlers from Portugal, France, Britain and the Canary Islands, amongst others. The main fishing season in these waters extends from April to November and the catch consists mostly of sardines, shad, mackerel and tuna. Other important fishing grounds along the West African coast are the region of the *Rivières du Sud* or drowned estuaries extending from southern Senegal to south-eastern Sierra Leone and the Gulf of Guinea, where the catch consists mostly of sardines and shad or bongo fish.

A fairly large area of continental shelf and the presence of a zone of upwelling coastal waters associated with the south-Atlantic trades and the convergence of the cool and saline Benguela current with the warm and less saline Guinea current combine to create favourable conditions for the abundance of fish off the coast of Angola. The main species caught here are horse mackerel (carapau), sardine and tuna. Shrimps, molluscs and spiny lobster are taken in large quantities along the northern parts of the Angola coast. Portuguese manpower has been the main source of labour for developing both the Angolan and the Mozambique sea fisheries since many of the indigenous coastal peoples have no liking for the sea (Dongen, 1969). The fishing resources of the Mozambique coast are however much less developed than those of Angola even though Mozambique has a longer coastline. This is partly because the East African coast, stretching north from Mozambique to Kenya, is not as rich in fish as the Angolan coast. The main fishing ports along this coast include Mombasa, Dar-es-Salaam and Zanzibar while the dominant fish species are tuna, bonito and sardines.

Fish farming or aqua-culture

Our discussion has so far been concerned with catching fish rather than raising fish. The art of raising fish is akin to that of raising livestock or even crops, hence the use of such graphic words as aqua-culture and aqua-husbandry to describe the practice. Aqua-husbandry, as the Chinese call the art of raising fish, has been practised in China for over 3,000 years. The Chinese concept of fish farming is obvious from the ancient Chinese saying: 'If you give a man a fish he will have

Pl. 11.6 Panyam fish farm, Nigeria

food for a day, if you teach him to raise fish he will have food for a lifetime.'

Aqua-culture offers vast opportunities for producing large quantities of fish to help meet the rapidly expanding demand for animal protein. Fortunately the technology is relatively simple and inexpensive although more research is necessary to adapt the methods and some fish species to the tropical African environment. Apart from the extensive coastal lagoons in West Africa and along the Indian Ocean coast, there are many other ecological areas which are suitable for aqua-culture. These include the extensive swamps and marshlands which border the major lakes, extensive areas of seasonally rain-fed swamps such as the Cross River Plains in Anambra State of Nigeria and the bolilands or grassland swamps of Sierra Leone. The large man-made lakes resulting from hydro-electric schemes, as well as the more numerous irrigation lakes and canals, provide further opportunities for fish farming. Indeed in Nigeria official government policy is to make maximum use of these multi-purpose man-made lakes rather than expend scarce resources in establishing fish farms through excavation such as the Panyam fish farm in the Jos Plateau.

References

Allan, W. (1965), *The African Husbandman*, Oliver & Boyd, Edinburgh.

Barth, H. K. (1976), 'Fishing in the Interior Delta of the Niger in Mali', *Applied Science and Development*, 8, pp. 26–43.

Dunbar, G. S. (1970), 'Africa Ranches Ltd. 1914–31: An Illfated Stock Raising Enterprise in Northern Nigeria', *Annals of the Association of American Geographers*, pp. 102–23.

Fitzgerald, W. (1957), *Africa: A Social, Economic and Political Geography of Its Major Regions*, Methuen & Co, London, p. 389.

Morgan, W. T. W. (1963), 'The "White Highlands" of Kenya', *Geographical Journal*, 129, pp. 140–55.

Morgan, W. T. W. (1973), *East Africa*, Longman, London.

Silistshena, R. M. K. (1977), 'A Framework for the Study of Rural–Rural Migration in Botswana', unpublished MS, Workshop on Issues in Rural Transformation in Africa, Arusha.

Stenning, D. J. (1965), 'Transhumance, Migratory Drift, Migration: Patterns of Pastoral Fulani Nomadism', in S. Ottenberg and P. Ottenberg (eds.), *Cultures and Societies of Africa*, Random House, New York, pp. 139–58.

Van Dongen, I. S. (1969), 'Agriculture and other Primary Production', in D. M. Abshire and M. A. Samuels (eds.), *Portuguese Africa – A Handbook*, Pall Mall Press, London, pp. 253–93.

Van Raay, J. G. T. (1970), 'Animal Husbandry', in M. J. Mortimore (ed.), *Zaria and Its Region*, Department of Geography, Ahmadu Bello University, Occasional Paper no. 4, Zaria, pp. 149–56.

12 Minerals, Mining and Power Resources

Introduction

The continent of Africa has extensive deposits of a large variety of minerals. In 1978, for example, Africa produced almost all the world's diamonds, about 80 per cent of the gold and 25 per cent of the phosphate and manganese. Other important minerals produced included crude oil (10 per cent), chromite (30 per cent), iron ore (10 per cent) and bauxite (6 per cent). In addition, Africa produces almost all the key strategic minerals traded in the world market, notably chromium, lithium, cobalt and radium. Today vast reserves of iron ore, bauxite, phosphate and other minerals are still to be tapped while the search for more minerals continues. However, a considerable amount of these mineral deposits are found in South Africa and North Africa, both of which are outside tropical Africa.

Within tropical Africa minerals play a dominant role in the economy of many countries as the chief source of government revenue and the major earner of foreign exchange. Indeed in many countries mining provided the first incentives for the building of railways, sea ports and hydro-electric power stations. Today minerals top the list of exports by value in Mauritania and Liberia (iron ore), Zambia and Togo (copper), Congo Republic, Gabon and Nigeria (crude petroleum), and Guinea (bauxite). The countries exporting crude oil, in particular, have recorded the most dramatic growth in the contribution of the mining sector to the total Gross Domestic Product (GDP) and to foreign exchange earnings. In Nigeria, for example, crude petroleum mining rose from 1·1 per cent of GDP in 1962 to 16 per cent in 1972 and 35 per cent in 1973. In terms of the total revenue of the Federal Government, oil revenue accounted for 28 per cent in 1970, but increased dramatically to 81 per cent in 1975.

The dominant position of the mining sector in the economy of several other countries of tropical Africa is similar to the situation in Nigeria. In Zambia, where the three most important exports by value are copper, zinc and lead, minerals accounted for over 38 per cent of GDP in 1973, copper alone being responsible for 30 per cent. About 56 per cent of the total government revenue and 95 per cent of the foreign exchange earnings in the same year were derived from mining. In Zaïre, Africa's second largest producer of copper and the world's largest producer of both cobalt and industrial diamonds, about 80 per cent of its exports by value come from minerals, with copper accounting for 60 per cent. In Liberia iron-ore exports account for 74 per cent of foreign exchange earnings and 30 per cent of GDP while the comparative figures for crude-oil exports from Gabon are 77 per cent and 30 per cent respectively.

Nevertheless, the contribution of the mining sector to total paid employment is generally very low, in relation to the large amount of revenue generated by it. In Nigeria, petroleum mining has made little impact in terms of employment opportunities available to the inhabitants of the Niger Delta where the oil is mined, and in Zambia mining accounts for no more than 14 per cent of paid employment. This is so partly because of the high level of mechanization in modern mining and partly because of the shortage of locally skilled personnel in mining technology, marketing and management. However, the labour employed in mining is much higher in some West African countries where small-scale self-employed citizens take part in working diamond and tin, using primitive methods.

Mining and the development of the infrastructure

In addition to making a direct contribution to government revenue, foreign exchange earnings and paid employment, the mining sector has played a major part in the provision and extension of infrastructure which has served other sectors of the economy. Railways, roads and ports built by mining syndicates or by the government for the primary purpose of servicing mines are amongst the most important examples. Power generated specifically for mining districts by private mining companies, as well as piped water, has been extended in later years to serve other sections of the population and the economy.

The poor state of transportation during the colonial period made it necessary for special roads and railways to be built to connect mines to the ports of export. Today the situation is slightly better since in most cases new mines can be connected by feeder roads or railways to existing transportation lines. Sometimes the transportation route was built by the government but in many other cases, the mining company had to build its own road or railway as well as the port of export. In Nigeria, for example, Port Harcourt and its railway link with Enugu were built by the government specifically to facilitate the export of coal from the Enugu coalfields to other parts of Nigeria and the then British West Africa. In 1898 mining also stimulated the building by the government of the first railway in Ghana from Secondi to the Tarkwa goldfields and when later the line was extended to Obuasi, this was because the mining company guaranteed the revenue. Still in Ghana, the branch line from Dunkwa to Awaso, opened in 1944, was specifically built to carry bauxite to the port of export.

In Liberia, the first railway was built in 1950 by the Liberian Mining Company to evacuate iron ore from the Bomi Hills to Monrovia (75 km). Later, the line was extended by another 72 km, to tap the iron-ore deposits at Mano River, near the border with Sierra Leone, and once again the cost of construction was borne by another mining company, this time the National Iron Ore Company. Mining companies in Liberia are also responsible for building and operating the other two railways from Bong Range to Monrovia (80 km) and from Mt Nimba to Buchanan (270 km). There is also a mineral line from the Fria bauxite mines of Guinea to the port of Conakry. And in Sierra Leone, where the government decided in 1972 to close down the government-owned 500 km main railway line, it is significant that the 90 km mineral line from the Marampa iron-ore fields to the port of Pepel, which is

owned by a private mining company, has continued to operate.

Copper mining in Katanga provided the incentive for constructing the Bas Congo–Katanga (BCK) [railway?] Kukama to Ilebo (Port Franqui) in 1928. [...] mining was restricted to the vicinity of [...] (Elizabethville) and most of the copper [...] transported along the Zambia–Zimbabwe [...] Mozambique port of Beira for export to Eu[...] of the great cost and delays involved in u[...] River route. The opening of the BCK ra[...] resulted in the extension of copper m[...] Bukama. The decision to link up the Ka[...] mines with the Benguela Railway in [...] essentially a political decision taken by [...] government of Zaïre in return for securing some land from Angola to enable the widening of the Matadi strip. The deal in effect resulted in considerable loss of traffic from the BCK rail route of Zaïre to the more direct shorter route of the Angolan-owned Benguela railway. Today the main source of revenue for the Benguela route is mineral cargo from Katanga. It is not difficult to see that it was the thriving copper-mining industry of Katanga that encouraged the Angolan colonial administration to extend the Benguela railway to the Zaïre border in 1928 and to insist that Zaïre provide a link between the Katanga line and the Benguela railway as reported above. This was done in 1931.

Many new ports and roads have been built to facilitate mineral exploitation, while some existing ports have been expanded for the same purpose. New ports built originally to handle mineral exports include Port Harcourt in Nigeria (coal), Buchanan in Liberia (iron ore), the new oil terminal at Bonny in Nigeria (crude petroleum) and a number of piers including those at Kpeme in Togo (phosphate) and at Pepel in Sierra Leone (iron ore). Special mineral berths have also been built in such general cargo ports as Dakar (phosphate), Monrovia (iron), Beira (copper and chrome ore) and Lobito (copper and coal).

Mining has also been instrumental in the development of power installations in various parts of tropical Africa. In Nigeria, for example, the Jos Plateau tin-mining area had the largest power installations in 1952. The towns of Jos and Bukuru, as well as most of the larger mining centres, were all supplied with electricity generated locally from four hydro-electric stations, three of which were located on the Kurra River. These installations were eventually taken over by the Electricity Corporation of Nigeria, now the National Electric Power Authority. In Katanga and northern Zambia, the early power stations were also built by the mining syndicates. Recently, mining companies have been responsible for generating power to supply mines in Liberia, Guinea and several other countries.

Fig. 12.1 Transport links between the Copper Belt and the coast

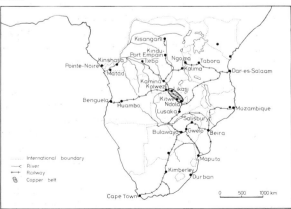

Important minerals and mining methods

Some minerals, such as tin and columbite or copper and cobalt, occur together in the same mines, and in some highly mineralized districts such as southern Ghana, Katanga and central Zimbabwe, many different minerals usually occur in close proximity. The distribution of the major minerals, as presented in Figs 12.2 and 12.3, is therefore highly generalized. In this section we consider some of the more important minerals with special reference to their physical distribution, mining methods and their uses in industry.

of iron ore from tropical Africa and the third largest exporter in the world, the average annual export tonnage since 1965 being about 20 million. Liberian ore was first mined in 1951 when the Bomi Hills mines were opened, followed by the Mano River mines (1961) and the Bong Hill mines (1965). The Bomi Hills concession has reserves of 50 million tonnes of rich ore with an iron content of 66 per cent and is surrounded by a more extensive reserve of 150 million tonnes of poorer ore with an iron content of 44 per cent. The Mano River and Bong Hill reserves are even more extensive, being estimated to be 165 million tonnes (54 per cent iron content) and 230 million tonnes (37 per cent iron

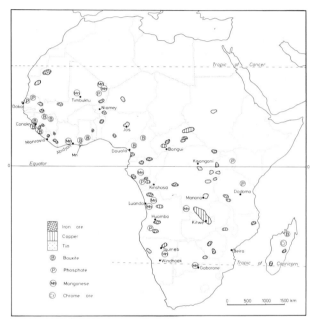

Fig. 12.2 Distribution of minerals, 1

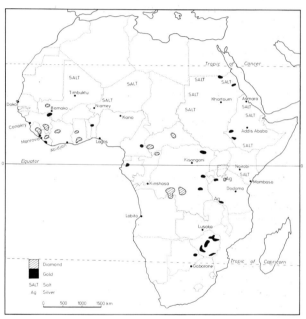

Fig. 12.3 Distribution of minerals, 2

Iron ore

Iron ore is the basic raw material of the iron and steel industry. It is by far the most widespread mineral in tropical Africa and is to be found in one form or another in every country, although mining is restricted to localities with extensive deposits of rich ore. Iron ore has been smelted in parts of tropical Africa for several centuries but the indigenous charcoal iron industry has since died out and today, almost all the iron ore mined is exported to Europe, North America and Japan. The leading producers include Mauritania, Liberia, Sierra Leone, Guinea and Zimbabwe. The total output from tropical Africa is small compared with the major producers of the world, but production is increasing rapidly.

Liberia is currently the largest producer and exporter

content) respectively. The largest mining district is however the Mt Nimba mines, near the Guinean border, which produces about 10 million tonnes of ore each year. Mining is by the open-cast method and is highly mechanized, and in all the mines the lower grades of ore are concentrated before being railed to the ports of export.

Of the other major iron-ore mines, those of Sierra Leone were opened much earlier than the Liberian mines while the vast iron-ore deposits of the Fort Derik district of Mauritania have only been worked since 1963. Production started in the Marampa mines of Sierra Leone in 1933 and five years later mechanical shovels replaced manual labour. The ore, which contains about 47 per cent iron, is obtained by open-cast mining and is concentrated to 65 per cent at

Pl. 12.1 Earth-moving equipment at Marampa iron ore mine, Sierra Leone

Marampa before being exported through Pepel. The rather extensive Fort Derik district field in Mauritania has an estimated reserve of 250 million tonnes of rich iron ore (63 per cent iron content) plus 8,000 million tonnes of poorer deposits (40–45 per cent iron content).

Commercially, the most important ores of iron are haematite (Fe_2O_3), magnetite (Fe_3O_4), limonite (hydrated iron oxide) and the carbonate siderite ($FeCo_3$). In West Africa the largest and richest ore deposits mined are haemitite (with red streaks), the major mines of which include Mount Nimba (Liberia), Marampa, Tonkoli River and the Sula Mountains in Sierra Leone and Fort Derik in Mauritania. The Bomi Hills iron-ore deposits in Liberia are the richest known source of magnetite ore (65 per cent iron content) in tropical Africa while the main locations of limonite are Mount Patti, near Lokoja in Nigeria, and in the vicinity of Conakry in Guinea. The 50 million tonnes of iron-ore deposits at Redcliff, near Que Que in Zimbabwe, consist of haematite and limonite. As in other parts of tropical Africa, the Redcliff ores are near the surface and are extracted by open-cast mining.

Iron is the most used metal in industry and the manufacture and use of iron implements dates from the dawn of civilization. In tropical Africa, the demand for iron and steel products has increased tremendously since independence and, with the exception of Zimbabwe, almost all the iron and steel used in local manufacturing is imported from Europe and North America which in return buy most of the iron ore produced in tropical Africa.

Copper

Next to iron, copper is the most widely used industrial metal although it may soon lose this position to aluminium. Copper is a good conductor of heat and electricity and is very resistant to atmospheric corrosion. In addition, it is highly ductile, that is, it can be readily pressed, beaten or drawn into shape while cold. It is therefore widely used in making electronics, electrical and telecommunications appliances as well as in the manufacture of pipes and cisterns in hot-water systems and for roofing. Brass is an alloy of copper and zinc while bronze is an alloy of copper and tin.

Zambia and Zaïre are the most important producers and exporters of copper in tropical Africa. Indeed, the Zambian copper belt is the second largest producer of copper in the world (after USA), and the largest supplier of copper to the world market. The economy of Zambia is heavily dependent on copper which accounts for over 90 per cent of its exports by value. Production since 1973 averages about 600,000 tonnes per annum and about 50,000 persons are employed in the mines, the oldest of which consist of Roan Antelope, Rhokana, Nchanga, Chibuluma, Baucroft and Mufulira. The Zambian copper reserves are estimated to be in excess of 700 million tonnes with a copper content of 3·7 per cent. In mines such as Nchanga and Chambishi, where the ore occurs near the surface, mining is by open-cast or quarry method. Shaft or underground mining, which is more expensive, is practised in areas like Roan Antelope where the ore occurs deep below the surface. Almost all the ore mined in Zambia is refined at the three electrolytic copper refineries at Nkana, Ndola and Mufulira and cast into copper anodes, which are 99·97 per cent pure.

The Katanga copper fields of Zaïre are an extension of the Zambian copper-mining district although the local ore oxides are much richer (15 per cent copper content) than those of Zambia. With the exception of the Kipushi underground mine, Katanga copper is worked by open-cast methods. Unlike in Zambia, where several copper-mining companies operate, Katanga mines are under the management of a single corporation, the Union Minière du Haut-Katanga. Local hydro-electric plants supply the power required for processing the ore before export.

Copper has been worked by the people of the Central African copper belt for about 1,000 years and it was the large number of copper bracelets, necklets and anklets worn by local women that prompted the search leading to the discovery of extensive deposits of copper ore in the region. Commercial mining started in Zambia in 1909.

Outside Central Africa, copper is also mined in the Kilembe Valley of Uganda, where production started in 1957. Other minor producers of copper are Tanzania, Angola and Zimbabwe. Copper deposits have also been discovered in Mozambique, Congo Republic, the Central African Republic and the Sudan.

Pl. 12.2 Copper nickel converter at the Empress Mine, Zimbabwe

Bauxite

Bauxite, the principal ore of aluminium, is a mixture of hydrous aluminium oxides formed through the weathering of different types of rocks. It is therefore one of the most common minerals in the earth's surface although production is limited to a few areas. In tropical Africa the production of bauxite is limited to the West African sub-region where Guinea and Ghana are the leaders. Proven reserves in Guinea show that the country possesses the world's third largest bauxite deposits after Jamaica and Guyana. Mining started in 1951 on Kassa Island but has since shifted to Tamara Island following the closure in 1967 of the almost exhausted Kassa Island mines. On the mainland, bauxite is mined at Boke, Dabola and Kindia. Some of the ore is now processed into alumina (aluminium oxide) at the Fria alumina plants, before being exported.

Ghana also has large reserves of bauxite (about 240 million tonnes) at Awaso, Mpreaso and Yenahin.

Existing mines are located at Mpreaso and Kibi. Until 1980 there was no alumina processing plant in Ghana; all the bauxite was exported while the huge VALCO alumina smelter complex at Tema depended on imported alumina from Guinea. Bauxite is also mined at the Mokanji Hills in Sierra Leone where production started in 1964. The Mokanji Hills bauxite deposits, like those of Guinea and Ghana, lie in thick beds near the surface and are mined by open-cast methods involving the use of mechanical shovels. Extensive bauxite deposits estimated at one billion tonnes have been discovered in Cameroun at the town of Minim-Martap near N'Gaoundéré. Exploitation of the deposits has been held up by lack of funds, even though a mining company was set up in 1969. Cameroun, however, has an alumina smelting plant at Edea (near Douala) which depends on imported alumina from Guinea.

Aluminium, like copper, is a good conductor of electricity, easy to work (ductile) and resistant to corrosion. In addition it is very strong but light in weight and is therefore specially suited to the aircraft industry. Also like copper, it combines readily with other metals to form alloys such as duralumin (aluminium and magnesium), which is much tougher than the pure metal. It is these qualities that make aluminium particularly suitable for making water pipes, pistons for motors, household utensils and of course aircraft.

Tin

Zaïre is the largest producer of tin in tropical Africa and ranks as the ninth world producer. Together with Nigeria, Rwanda and Burundi, it accounts for about 95 per cent of the total tonnage export from tropical Africa. The Zaïre tin fields are located in north-eastern Katanga and in parts of the Oriental and Kivu provinces. Although there are now two major mining companies, the Symetain Company in Kivu and Geomines in Katanga, a considerable proportion of Zaïre tin is still produced by many small-scale operators. The average output per year is about 14,000 tonnes.

In West Africa tin occurs as gravel deposits along the beds of ancient river valleys in the Jos Plateau area of Nigeria and in the Air Massif region of Niger. As with copper in Central Africa, local mining by African metal workers started in the Jos Plateau many centuries before large-scale mining was undertaken in 1903. Open-cast methods are used in the Nigerian tin fields where tin-panning or hand-working by Africans has largely been replaced by large hydro-turbine gravel pumps. A tin-smelting plant was built in 1962 and since then the bulk of the metal has been exported in its pure form (tin ingots). Production since 1968 has averaged less than 12,000 tonnes valued at ₦13 million.

The Air Massif deposits in Niger Republic were discovered in 1947 and mining started two years later. In recent years mining has become uneconomical because of the high cost of transporting the ore to the coast for export and the prohibitive expenditure on maintaining access roads and providing water in an arid environment. The tin deposits in Cameroun and the Central African Republic are yet to be developed while the ore bodies of Uganda and Tanzania, which have been mined for several decades, have never been of much importance in the economy of either country. The distance of these mining areas from the port of export has generated excessive transport costs.

Tin is used in the manufacture of tin plates which are thin sheets of mild steel or wrought iron covered with a thin coating of tin to prevent rusting. Tin plates are in turn used for manufacturing containers for canned foods such as milk, fruits and beer as well as for other numerous items including tobacco and polishes. Tin is also used for making important alloys such as bronze, gun-metal and bell-metal.

Manganese

Until 1962, when the exploitation of the vast manganese deposits at Moanda in Gabon started, about 90 per cent of the total output of manganese in tropical Africa came from Ghana and Zaïre. Today Gabon is the third largest world producer of manganese (after USSR and India), a position which Ghana held for almost sixty years. The other producers in tropical Africa are the Ivory Coast, Angola and Zambia. Mining started at Nsuta (near Tarkwa) in Ghana as early as 1917 and during the First World War, Ghana was the largest supplier to Britain, Canada and the United States of America. Production since 1970 has averaged 250,000 tonnes per annum. The Ghanaian ore lies in thick deposits (about 30 m thick) on the crests of low hills and is mined by open-cast methods. In the Ivory Coast, manganese is quarried near Grand Lahoe, where production started in 1960. The annual export from the Ivory Coast is about 100,000 tonnes.

The discovery of the vast manganese deposits at Moanda and the consequent sudden rise of Gabon to become the third largest world producer confirm that our knowledge of the mineral resources of tropical Africa is still incomplete. The Moanda reserves are estimated to be over 200 million tonnes and in 1973 about 1·9 million tonnes were produced, about eight times the annual output from Ghana. Production in Zaïre and Zambia is localized in the copper belt and is by open-cast methods. The annual output from Zaïre is over 250,000 tonnes per annum while the only mine in Zambia, at Kampumba (near Kabwe), produces about 10,000 tonnes per annum. The output from the Malange district mines of Angola is about 30,000 tonnes per annum.

Manganese is used primarily in the iron and steel industries to harden steel, and is therefore an important strategic mineral. It is also used in the manufacture of electric batteries, bleaching powder used in the textiles industry, and for colouring tiles and pottery.

Chrome ore

Chrome ore deposits have been reported in many countries including Tanzania, Mozambique, Ethiopia and Togo, but at present mining is confined to Zimbabwe following the closure in 1964 of the Sierra Leone mines. Zimbabwe produces about 645,000 tonnes per annum or about 20 per cent of the total world output and is currently the third largest producer in the world after the Philippines and Turkey. The chief deposit is at Selukwe in the region of the Great Dyke and the ores occur either as seams in the dyke or as large ore masses near it. The ore, exported mainly to the United States and Great Britain, is the source of chromium, used in manufacturing chrome or stainless steel. Car bumpers, bicycle handle-bars, cutlery and furniture fittings are some of the varied articles made from chrome steel, which is harder than ordinary steel and is also rustless and stainless.

Cobalt

Tropical Africa is the largest producer of cobalt, which is found in association with copper ore bodies. The Zaïran copper belt of Katanga and the Zambian copper belt together produce 60 per cent of the world total ouput, Zaïre being the leading world producer and Zambia ranking fifth. In Katanga, which has estimated reserves of over 225,000 tonnes, production is centred around Kolwezi, while the two main mines in Zambia are at Nkana and Chibuluma. Extensive deposits have been discovered in the Kilembe copper mines of Uganda and mining is by adits, horizontal or near-horizontal tunnels dug into the hillsides.

Cobalt is used chiefly as an alloy because of its hardness, high melting-point and magnetic properties. The magnets in telephones are usually cobalt alloys, which are also used in jet engines and in the production of atomic energy.

Gold

Gold is widely distributed all over tropical Africa and has been mined at one time or another in at least twenty countries. The total production represents only about 6 per cent of the world output. The chief producers in order of importance are Ghana, Zaïre and Zimbabwe. In Ghana (formerly called the Gold Coast) gold has been mined since the tenth century AD, although modern mining started in 1880. Today, Ghana is the largest exporter of gold in tropical Africa and ranks as the fifth world producer after South Africa, Canada, USSR and USA. The mineral is found in many parts of Ghana, but the main workings are in Dunkwa district, where Obuasi, the world's richest gold mine, is located. Ghanaian gold occurs in blankets or load deposits similar to those of South Africa as well as in alluvial deposits along river valleys. The lode deposits are obtained mostly by deep mining and to some extent by open-cast methods while the alluvial or placer deposits are mined by dredging or panning river gravels along the beds of the Offin, Tana and Ankobra Rivers. Most of the gold produced in Zaïre comes from Kivu and Oriental Provinces, where the mineral is obtained from alluvial and other surface workings (open-cast methods) as well as by deep mining. In Zimbabwe, gold occurs in small scattered deposits in the form of lode (or reef) especially around Bulawayo, Salisbury, Umtali and Gwelo. Mining here is now highly mechanized and most of the smaller firms have been forced out of business. In other parts of tropical Africa gold is still obtained largely by the use of traditional methods of panning river gravels.

Gold is highly treasured because of its high metallic lustre and attractiveness when polished. It is used extensively in making jewellery and coins, but the bulk of the gold produced is accumulated in the form of bars or bullion used to back up paper currency in circulation.

Diamonds

Diamond is a crystalline form of pure carbon and as the hardest naturally-occurring known mineral, it has been put to a variety of uses in industry. It is used for the manufacturing of grinding wheels for sharpening metal-cutting tools, in polishing operations and for making drills such as dental and oil-well drills. As a precious stone of great beauty, diamonds are used extensively in making jewellery. Tropical Africa produces about 80 per cent of the world's output of both industrial and gem diamonds, the two largest producers in the world being Zaïre and Ghana. The other important producers in tropical Africa are Sierra Leone, Angola, Central African Republic and Botswana. Minor producers include the Ivory Coast, Guinea, Congo Republic and Tanzania.

About 90 per cent of the diamonds produced in Zaïre are of the industrial type. Mining is concentrated in two areas: the Bakwanga deposits of Mbuji-Mayi district, which is located south-east of Kananga (Luluabourg) and which produces 95 per cent of Zaïre's total output; and the middle Kassai valley area, which is an extension of the Angola diamond field. The deposits are all alluvial and are worked by open-cast methods using modern earth-moving machinery. Annual output increased steadily from 0·2 million carats to a peak of 14 million carats in the 1950s, but has averaged about 12 million carats since 1968.

Pl. 12.3 The Eureka diamond

Although Ghana is the second world producer of industrial diamonds, the total annual output of about 3 million carats is far below that of Zaïre, but much closer to that of Sierra Leone which is another important producer (2 million carats per annum). Other diamond producers in West Africa are Liberia (1 million carats), the Ivory Coast (500,000 carats) and Guinea (70,000 carats). In Ghana the mines are located in the Birim River Valley and as in other West African countries, the stones are produced by large mining companies as well as by individual African diamond diggers, who produce about 35 per cent and 40 per cent of the total annual output in Ghana and the Ivory Coast respectively. Industrial grade diamonds constitute 70 per cent of the diamonds mined in Ghana, 55 per cent in Sierra Leone and 66 per cent in Guinea. Illegal mining and sales are widespread in Ghana and Sierra Leone, and have resulted in great financial losses to the governments.

Angola produces about one million carats from alluvial deposits along the valleys of the tributaries of the Kassai River. About 60 per cent of the total output are gem diamonds. In Tanzania, 50 per cent of the annual output of 500,000 carats are industrial diamonds and 65 per cent of the 80,000 carats produced in the Central African Republic are also of industrial quality.

Phosphate

Phosphate is used primarily for the production of fertilizers and is bound to play a major part in the development of tropical African agriculture in the near future. So far, the largest worked deposit in tropical Africa is the Tororo district field in Uganda which was discovered in 1950. It has estimated reserves of 200 million tonnes of about 13 per cent phosphate content which is readily beneficiated to 42 per cent at Tororo. The other major deposit in East Africa is located near Lake Manyara (south-west of Arusha) in Tanzania. The reserves here are estimated to be only 10 million tonnes, but the quality of the ore is much higher. Phosphate is also mined in the Thies area of Senegal which produces about 700,000 tonnes per annum. The largest and richest known deposit of phosphate in West Africa is, however, located near Anecho in Togo where mining started in 1961. The Togo reserve is estimated to be over 50 million tonnes and the annual production figure has averaged more than 1·75 million tonnes since 1971.

The mining companies

Large sums of money and high-level manpower, both of which are still lacking in tropical African countries, are required for prospecting for minerals and in the actual process of mining. Foreign mining companies, usually the subsidiaries of multinational corporations, have therefore dominated mining activities in tropical Africa since the early colonial period. Most of the mining companies (excluding oil companies) are in southern Africa where mining development started. The Anglo-American Corporation of South Africa, which is basically a South African owned company, manages the Wankie coalfield in Zimbabwe, the lead and zinc mines, and some copper mines in Zambia. The de Beers diamond-monopoly of South Africa, which markets most of the world's diamonds, operates in Tanzania and Botswana. The Union Minière du Haut-Katanga, organized in 1906, was a foreign company until 1967 when it was nationalized by the government of Zaïre. Another major foreign mining company is the Consolidated African Selected Trust which owns and works the diamond mines in Ghana and Sierra Leone while the American company, Union Carbide, operates the manganese mines in Ghana and the chrome mines in Zimbabwe.

Other important foreign mining companies include Kaiser and Reynolds of America, which own the VALCO aluminium smelter at Tema, the French Compagnie de Mokta, which owns the Grand Lahou mining company of the Ivory Coast and holds shares in the uranium mines of Gabon and Niger Republic. Most of these companies have been taken over, at least in part, by the various governments since independence. Nationalization or part-nationalization of mining interests has been carried out largely for political as well as economic reasons. In most cases, the so-called take-over has proved ineffective since skilled manpower is still imported.

Power resources

Apart from the fact that mining has been largely responsible for the development of power installations in various parts of tropical Africa, there is yet another link between minerals and power resources. Three of the primary sources of power in industry, coal, crude petroleum and natural gas, are minerals. The other major source of power is from water (hydro-electricity). Some countries in tropical Africa also produce the mineral, uranium, which is the source of nuclear power, although there are as yet no nuclear power installations in the region. In this section we consider the power resources of tropical Africa, beginning with mineral fuels.

Coal

Coal is a fossil and an irreplaceable source of energy. During the days of steam it became the dominant source of power and most manufacturing industries were

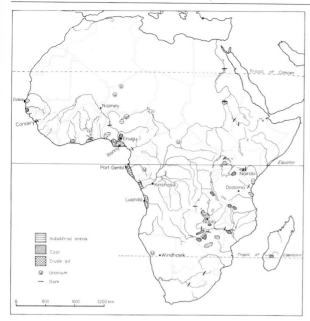

Fig. 12.4 Power resources

located on coalfields. Today coal is more often used in an indirect way to generate electricity. The coal-mining industry is currently ailing in most countries partly because of competition from petroleum and hydro-electricity both of which are much cleaner and more readily transportable sources of energy.

Compared with other parts of the world, tropical Africa is relatively poor in coal resources, and this is particularly so in West and East Africa. The most extensive known reserves occur in Zimbabwe which is also the largest producer. Zimbabwe has several coalfields but production is restricted to the Wankie coalfield where mining started in 1903. The Wankie field has estimated reserves of over 800 million tonnes and is considered to be one of the largest in the continent. It produces about 3·5 million tonnes each year, most of it high quality coking coal, out of which about 1 million tonnes are exported to Botswana, Zambia, Malawi, Mozambique and Zaïre. Mining is mostly by open-cast methods, since the 10 m thick main seam is close to the surface.

Nigeria is the second largest producer of coal in tropical Africa and the only producer in West Africa. Mining started in 1915 at the Enugu coalfield which has reserves of only 72 million tonnes consisting of low quality sub-bituminous coal. The much more extensive reserves of over 170 million tonnes in the Middle Belt states of Kwara, Benue and Plateau are still largely untapped except for a small mine opened in 1968 when the Enugu field was temporarily closed down as a result

of the civil war. Mining is by the adit method and production since 1960 has averaged only 600,000 tonnes per annum. The main problem of the Nigerian coal industry is that it has lost its market since the Nigerian Railways, formerly its main customer, now uses diesel rather than steam engines.

The two other countries currently producing coal are Zaïre and Mozambique. In Zaïre, production is carried out in eastern Katanga where the coal is of sub-bituminous grade. Most of the 500,000 tonnes produced each year are used in the copper mines and the railways. Compared with Zaïre, which has estimated coal reserves of only 50 million tonnes, Mozambique is relatively rich in coal resources, the estimated reserves for the Moatize coalfield (near Tete) being over 700 million tonnes. Production rarely exceeds 250,000 tonnes per annum and is unlikely to increase significantly until the establishment of an iron furnace complex in the Tete area. The Caboraso Dam, the main source of power for the country, is also located there.

Petroleum and natural gas

Crude petroleum and natural gas are fossils, like coal, and are therefore irreplaceable sources of energy. Natural gas, which is made up largely of methane associated with other hydro-carbon gases, is generally found in the same wells as crude petroleum although it may occur by itself. Like coal, both sources of energy are used for generating electricity and in most countries have largely displaced coal as the main source of power. Petroleum is in high demand all over the world and has come to be regarded as liquid gold. The search for this source of power continues in many tropical African countries but by 1980 commercial production was restricted to Nigeria, Gabon and Angola, although commercial finds have been reported in Senegal and Ghana. Petroleum products are such a key component of modern economic activity that almost all other countries now have at least one oil refinery which depends on imported crude oil.

Nigeria is currently the largest producer and exporter of crude oil in tropical Africa and indeed in all Africa, producing in 1976 a monthly average of 8·5 million tonnes. Oil prospecting in Nigeria started in 1937, but it was not until 1956 that oil was found in commercial quantities in the Niger Delta. Export started two years later with only 9,000 tonnes of crude oil, rising to over 20·7 million tonnes in 1966, the year before the civil war which disrupted production for three years. The total earnings from the 96·4 million tonnes of crude oil exported in 1974 was ₦5·5 billion or 90 per cent of the export earnings for that year as compared with 33 per cent in 1966 and 0·8 per cent in 1958. In recent years offshore production has become increasingly important. Most of the crude oil is exported from the two oil terminals of Bonny and Warri. 1979 saw the completion of the first crude oil pipeline from Warri to the Kaduna refinery which started operating in October 1980. The other two refineries at Port Harcourt and Warri are located in the oilfields. At the end of the Third National Development Plan period in 1979, the multi-million naira liquefied natural gas project had still not gone into operation. The result is that almost all the annual output of 300,000 million cu ft of natural gas and all the crude oil has had to be burnt off since the gas consumption at the only gas fired thermal electric plant at Afam is very small. The proven reserves of the Nigerian oilfields in 1978 were put at 2,700 million tonnes.

Crude petroleum production in Gabon started with only 450,000 tonnes in 1957 and by 1969 the production figure had reached 5 million tonnes, increasing to 11·3 million tonnes in 1975. Production comes from both inland and offshore locations and prospecting for further supplies is continuing. The extended Port Gentil refinery with an annual capacity of 2 million tonnes provides motor fuel, oil, paraffin and jet fuel for the country and the other UDEAC (The Central African Economics and Customs Union, see Chapter 20, p. 228) countries. In Gabon, unlike in Nigeria, most of the natural gas produced (30·5 million cu m in 1971), is used locally for generating electricity.

Oil was first discovered in Angola in 1955 and the following year the export of crude oil started. Production remained modest until 1966 when the Gulf Oil Company struck oil offshore at Cabinda where the estimated reserve is put at over 300 million tonnes. By 1971 the total crude output had risen to over 5·7 million tonnes. Since 1973, oil has become the most important export by value. There is as yet only one oil refinery, at Luanda, with a capacity of one million tonnes per year.

Hydro-electric power

The use of water power in manufacturing dates from ancient times when it was used for grinding corn and for working iron bellows and looms for spinning and weaving. The machinery had to be sited by the river bank. With the discovery and use of the steam engine and steam turbine, the old-fashioned water-wheel disappeared. The opening in 1882 of the first hydro-electric power plant in the United States brought water power back again. Some people regard hydro-electricity as the source of power of the future, petroleum as the power source of the present and coal as the power source of the past. The great advantage that hydro-electricity has over coal, petroleum and natural gas is that it is inexhaustible since rivers are permanent features of the landscape. Furthermore, in areas where the volume of water in rivers fluctuates seasonally or is insufficient, it is possible to store it in reservoirs by building dams to contain the flow. Dams are also built to ensure an adequate 'head' or vertical height to generate the required power.

Recent estimates of the world potential in hydro-electric power suggest that Africa has about 200 million kW or 40 per cent of the world total, the total for tropical Africa being put at 37 per cent. However, owing to the high cost of harnessing water power, the installed capacity of hydro-electric plants in the

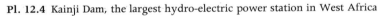

Pl. 12.4 Kainji Dam, the largest hydro-electric power station in West Africa

continent before 1960 was about 1·5 million kW, which was less than 1 per cent of the world total. The situation has changed considerably since independence, largely because most countries in tropical Africa have neither coal nor crude petroleum but now have at least one small hydro-electric power station. Because of the large number of installations in existence, we intend to undertake a brief review of the hydro-electric potential and the major hydro-electric schemes in the sub-regions of Central, East and West Africa.

Central Africa has by far the greatest hydro-electric potential in tropical Africa. Zaïre alone has a potential of 500 billion kW-hr (see notes at end of chapter) annually, or about 12 per cent of the estimated world potential, leaving the rest of tropical Africa with about 25 per cent of the world total potential or an annual output of over 1,040 billion kW-hr. The heavy and steady rainfall in the Zaïre Basin and the fact that the Zaïre River descends more than 240 m (800 ft) in a series of thirty-two falls and cataracts within a distance of 352 km (220 miles) are responsible for this high potential water power. The installed capacity of HEP in Zaïre in 1971 was however only 3·4 billion kW-hr, most of the power being consumed by the Katanga copper industry. The larger HEP stations in the Katanga district include the Cornet Falls stations on the Lufira River (40 miles from Jadotville) and the Nzilo Gorge station on the Lualaba River (16 miles north of Kolwezi). There are over thirty HEP plants in Zaïre, but the largest is the massive Inga Dam near the mouth of the Zaïre River, at a site which has a potential capacity of over 30 million kW. The Inga Dam, which was completed in 1974, is located between Matadi and Kinshasa, and has an installed capacity of only 300 MW (i.e. 300,000 kW), which is rather small in relation to its potential.

The other large hydro-electric power stations in Central Africa include the 276 MW Le Marinel Dam at the Nzilo gorge on the upper Lualaba (New Kolwezi), the 270 MW Edea Dam on the Sanaga River near Douala in Cameroun, and the 260 MW Cambambe Dam in Angola. The Cambambe power station, which is located along the lower Cuanza Valley, was commissioned in 1962, that is, thirteen years before Angola became inde-

pendent in 1975. The 750 MW Kafue Dam station near Lusaka (Zambia) and the much larger 1600 MW Kariba Dam power stations also belong to the Central African sub-region.

Both in West Africa, which has the main concentration of population in tropical Africa, and in East Africa, the water-power potential is relatively low partly because of the extreme seasonal fluctuation in the water level of most rivers, and partly because of the nature of the terrain. A large number of small power stations established by mining syndicates exist all over West Africa dating from the colonial period. The major HEP stations, however, belong to the post-colonial period. The 960 MW station at Kainji in Nigeria is currently the largest, followed by the 883 MW Volta Dam at Akosombo in Ghana. In East Africa the oldest major HEP station is the 150 MW Owen Falls Dam in Uganda while the largest is the 2200 MW Cabora Bassa in Mozambique. The Cabora Bassa station, on the lower Zambezi, is currently the largest hydro-electric power station in the African continent.

Notes

1 kilowatt hour = 1000 watt × 1 hour
The capacity of 200 million kilowatt will produce 200 × 365 × 24 kW-hr per year or 1,752 billion Kw-hr. The billion in this context means 1,000,000,000 i.e. one thousand million.

Watt. The basic unit of electric power, expressing the rate at which electric energy is being expended.

Kilowatt: 1000 watts (kW).

Kilowatt-hour: The unit in which electric consumption is billed. Two 60 watt electric bulbs kept switched on for 24 hours will produce a total consumption unit of 20 × 60 × 24 or 2,880 watt-hours which is the same as 2·88 kilowatt-hours (kW-hr).

Megawatt: A system of units for measuring power. 1 megawatt (MW) = 1,000 kilowatts (kW) or 1,000,000 watts.

1 horsepower (HP) = 746 watts.

13 Forestry and Forest Products

Tropical Africa has an extensive but rapidly declining forest area of which the tropical rain forest of the equatorial region is economically the most important. In addition to timber, the principal forest product, there are many other vital products, such as gum arabic, shea butter, raffia palm wine, tannin, charcoal and firewood, which still play an important role in the economy of the rural areas where they are available. A wide range of food items, including special vegetables, snails (or congo meat) and different types of edible fruits, are still obtained from the forests especially during the slack season in the farming calendar. For example, today many migrant tenant farmers in the Benin forest region of Nigeria obtain considerable income from gathering these products, particularly snails. Forest products other than timber are therefore an important source of income to a large number of rural families in the forest areas of tropical Africa.

In many countries, the forest sector of the economy has experienced a gradual decline, partly because of the over-exploitation of the best timber species and also because of the rapid growth of other sectors of the economy. In Nigeria, for example, the exploitation of indigenous wild rubber-bearing plants, notably the *Funtumia elastica* (a tree) and the vines *Landolphia* and *Clitandra*, produced rubber exports valued at almost ₦ 5 million in 1895. Reckless tapping resulted in the collapse of this wild rubber industry before the beginning of the First World War. The colonial administrations of many countries granted licences and concessions in forests to private companies of foreign origin to exploit timber, raffia, ivory, palm kernels and palm oil from the oil palm tree which at that time was hardly cultivated.

The importance of the forest to the economy and people of tropical Africa and indeed to all parts of the world, however, extends beyond timber and the other forest products. The value of forest cover in preventing soil erosion and in protecting water catchment areas is well known. Furthermore, forests serve as reserves for wildlife and are widely utilized as national parks for recreational purposes in the more developed countries of the world. It is also a well-established fact that forests play an important part in influencing and stabilizing climates. It is against this background that we present below an account of the forest resources of tropical Africa and the way they have been exploited.

The forest areas and types of forests

There are three major timber-producing natural forest types in tropical Africa: the tropical rain forest, savanna woodlands and montane forests. The tropical rain forest covers an area of about 5 million sq km and is confined to the Guinea coastlands of West Africa, the Zaïre Basin, south Cameroun and Gabon. It is the main source of hard-wood timber, although the commercially recognized economic species are generally few and widely scattered. The best-known timber species include mahogany, obeche, wawa, sapele and baku, most of which are exported as logs to Great Britain and Europe.

Savanna woodlands yield very little valuable timber. The major products consist of poles and firewood, which is the most common source of domestic fuel. Forest plantations established for producing electric transmission and telegraph poles are also concentrated in the savanna woodland zone. Poles from such plantations are always preferred to bush poles from natural forests because of their superior shape. Savanna woodlands also produce a wide range of other forest products including gum arabic, shea butter and beeswax.

Montane forests are largely restricted to the highlands of East and southern Africa. In Kenya the productive natural forests occur between 1,500 m and 2,700 m above sea level, beyond which timber species give way to bamboos. The most common tree species are coniferous, such as *Juniperus procera* (East African cedar), *Podocarpus gracilior* and *Podocarpus milanjiana* as well as some indigenous hardwoods, including *Ocotea usambarensis* (East African camphor-wood) *Vitex keniensis* (meru oak) and *Maesopsis eminii*. Much of the highlands of Ethiopia are covered with montane forest although extensive deforestation has largely restricted dense forest to hillsides. The most prominent trees in the highlands consist of varieties of juniper, notably ted (*Juniperus procera*) and zegba (*Podocarpus gracilior*). Broad-leafed rain forests occur in the south-west plateau areas where the temperatures and the annual rainfall are much higher. The common tree species here include karraro (*Pouteria ferruginea*), dogma (*Syzygium guineense*) and sissa (*Albizzia Schimperiana*). The imported eucalyptus (*Eucalyptus globulus*) which is referred to locally as *bahr zaf*, that is, tree from over the sea, is now widespread all over the Ethiopian plateaus, especially around all Amhara villages and towns.

Other areas in which montane forest occurs include the Great Escarpment of the eastern border of Zimbabwe where yellow-wood (*Podocarpus milaajiana*) and cedar (*Widdringtonia Whytei*) are the most common species, and the highlands of northern Malawi. Closed moist forest also occurs along the western mountain massifs of the Zambesia district of Mozambique as well as along the Cameroun Highlands.

Forest reserves

Forest resources are renewable if properly managed, but thoughtless and reckless exploitation may result in serious depletion and even complete destruction of extensive forest areas. The forests of tropical Africa have already suffered widespread destruction because of centuries of shifting cultivation. A good example of this is the extensive derived savanna belt of West Africa which testifies to the state of depletion of the tropical rain forest. In order to ensure the supply in perpetuity of forest products as well as to preserve water supplies and prevent erosion, the governments of tropical Africa have set aside vast areas of forests as reserves in which farming, grazing and sometimes hunting are prohibited. The four reasons given for the establishment of forest reserves in Ghana in 1927 applies to almost all the countries. These were:

1. to improve the growth of existing forests and to establish new forest growth where necessary; 2. to safeguard water supplies. Forests prevent rapid run-off from watersheds and therefore ensure a steady and longer supply of water through springs to the rivers; 3. to ensure a permanent supply of timber for the domestic and export markets and 4. to maintain climatic conditions suitable for the growth and survival of forest crops.

The extent of forest reserves varies considerably from one country to another. In Nigeria the total area is 92,740 sq km, while the reserves of Tanzania, Kenya and Uganda cover 118,300 sq km, 17,250 sq km and 16,120 sq km respectively. In each country, the state government manages most of the forest reserves while a relatively small fraction is controlled by local authorities who receive advice from the State Department of Forestry.

With the exception of a few isolated cases, such as the River Lewa Game Reserve of Zambia, where the colonial government was obliged to evacuate villages from the area, forest reserves have generally been established in uninhabited tracts of country. Nevertheless, the creation of forest reserves has often generated much local opposition in various countries. In Ghana, for

example, such opposition was responsible for the fact that the forestry laws, proposed in 1909, were not passed until 1927, by which time much damage had been done to the country's forest estate (Batten, 1956, p. 76). There have also been repeated requests in parts of Nigeria for the governments to de-reserve parts of the forest estate to enable the local people to extend their farmlands.

In the much more sparsely settled French colonial territories, official concern over the severe depletion of the forest resources came much later. Before 1935, when the forest domain was declared to be state property, permission to cut timber was readily granted by governments to individuals, including Africans, over small areas not exceeding 1,000 hectares as well as to large companies for areas not exceeding 10,000 hectares in Cameroun or 40,000 hectares in French Equatorial Africa. In all cases those granted permits were directed not to interfere with the rights of the local people to cut wood, farm and graze on the land. Between 1935 and 1950 large areas of land were converted to forest reserves and the customary rights to fell trees and to collect firewood and other plant products were taken away. Many villagers were fined or imprisoned for breaking the forest laws. This caused much resentment since people felt aggrieved at being deprived of their traditional rights over their forest resources.

It is tempting to dismiss lightly the complaints made by villagers whose lands have been converted to forest reserves, on the grounds that the total area involved in any one country is relatively very small. In the Ivory Coast the total area under forest reserves at the end of the colonial period was only 28,860 sq km. The corresponding figures for Senegal and Guinea were 13,440 sq km and 5,410 sq km respectively. For most countries the area set aside as forest reserves varied from only 1·5 per cent of the land area (as in Nigeria) to about 8·0 per cent in Mozambique, Tanzania and Uganda. The loss of land to particular groups should be considered against the background of traditional African land ownership laws. There is no doubt that some villages and clans lost considerable land to the forest reserves and today members of such groups are obliged to subsist on land which is no longer adequate for their needs.

In some countries, such as Nigeria and Ghana, where the timber resources of the free forest areas have already been seriously depleted, the bulk of the timber for export and for the domestic market now comes from the forest reserves. The Nigerian Government Department of Forestry supervises the exploitation of all reserves in each state, and usually only large firms may obtain and work timber concessions. Currently a timber concession is granted for twenty-five years at a time. The forestry law demands that timber in the leased

Pl. 13.1 Forest shelter belt, Sokoto state, Nigeria

concessions be treated as a crop, in order to preserve the forest resources for posterity. Lease-holders are therefore required to plant a certain number of trees to replace each of the species that has been felled, or to help natural regeneration of seedlings by weeding, thinning and freeing young seedlings from excessive shade and from climbing plants. In the licensed forest areas of Benin Division of Nigeria, for example, as many as 45,520 seedlings of mahogany have been planted by various licensees since 1908, and a large number of suppressed naturally regenerated seedlings were also freed (Adeyoju, 1975, p. 89).

Forest plantations

In many countries, the great demand for timber, poles and firewood has necessitated the planting by governments, private companies and individuals of forest plantations to supplement the primary forest estate. Extensive forest plantations have been established in various parts of Zimbabwe to supply wood and fuel for mining and for flue-cured virginia tobacco. The extensive destruction of natural forest timber in that country has been largely attributed to overcutting of trees to supply the mining sector, which up till 1939 consumed about 200,000 cords[1] a year for steam generation and 16,000 cords for laggings and pit props (Wellington, 1955, p. 89). Zimbabwe's tobacco industry also consumes so much wood that about 4,800 hectares of forest plantations are required to sustain it every year. The largest state-owned plantations include the Stapleford plantation along the eastern border and the *brachystegia* forest plantation in the Mafungabissi Plateau. Many tobacco farmers have also established small forest plantations on their farms.

The great demand for mine timber, sawn timber for railway sleepers and wood fuel has also led to the establishment of forest plantations of tropical pines in the Zambian copper belt. In Angola, there are many soft-wood plantations of eucalyptus and cypress along the Benguela railway and near the city itself. Cuttings from the plantations near Benguela supply the pulp and papermills of the city, while wood harvests from distant plantations are used mainly for fuel.

In Ethiopia the forest plantations consist mostly of the highly valued eucalyptus tree which was introduced into the country from Tasmania. Groves of eucalyptus occur around most settlements and provide the main source of wood for fuel and for building. Timber plantations also abound in the East African countries of Uganda, Kenya and Tanzania. Cypress and pines are the dominant species in the five major forest plantations of Uganda, all of which are in the grassland areas of the higher and more temperate northern and western districts. Smaller plantations of eucalyptus and some cassia have also been established close to the main centres of population to supply wood and building poles for local use. In Kenya the most successful forest plantation species are *Cupressus lusitanica*, *Pinus radiata* and *Pinus patula*. Eucalyptus is highly valued as an exotic source of general utility poles and as firewood. In Tanzania the government and some local authorities have forest plantation programmes featuring the cultivation of exotic pines, cypress and some hardwood species, notably teak in estates owned or supervised by the Forestry Department.

Forest plantations of the indigenous wild ire rubber tree, *Funtumia elastica*, started in Nigeria as early as 1906 when the then newly established Forestry

Department started planting rubber seedlings in the Gambari, Ilaro and Oshun River forest reserves. In 1912 mixed fuel plantations of *Casuarina, Anogeissus leiocarpa* and *Delonix regia* were established at Ibadan, Ijebu-Ode and Lagos and the following year work started in the firewood plantations of Sokoto and Zaria. There are currently three categories of forest plantation in the country. These are: 1. Forestry Department timber and fuel plantations, 2. communal and small private plantations of teak, mahogany and rubber trees and 3. mahogany plantings by timber licensees. Forest plantations of exotic species, notably teak (*Tectona grandis*) and *Gmelina arborea*, are now a common feature along major access roads into the cities. Eucalyptus and neem are preferred in the drier northern states.

Most of the peri-urban forest plantations in Nigeria are basically for firewood and the emphasis is on fast-growing species with a short felling cycle. The need for shade from intense sun as well as the desire to protect the soil from accelerated erosion has been largely responsible for the greater number of plantations in the grassland areas of Nigeria. In the tobacco growing districts of Oyo State, many private individuals and communities have also established small forest plantations varying in size from 0·5–10 hectares for the purpose of providing firewood for the production of flue-cured tobacco. Since 1975 the Federal and some state governments have also established plantations to provide suitable wood for the manufacture of toothpicks and matches and for the indigenous pulp and paper industry.

Forest products

Although timber is now the major forest product of tropical Africa, and indeed of all regions of the world, it is the so-called minor forest products that are more important to the economy of various groups in traditional African societies. The right to exploit forest produce remains unrestricted to members of the village or clan which owns the forest and it is still unusual for any one individual or family to claim exclusive rights to any forest. Traditionally, any member of the community has a right to collect a wide range of naturally occurring produce, such as edible vegetables, fruits, medicinal herbs, chewing-sticks, yam sticks, firewood and various fibres and canes for crafts. In this section, we consider the importance and development of forest products in tropical Africa.

Timber
The forests of tropical Africa are famous for the supply of tropical hard-wood for the international market. The felling and extraction of timber from these forests for export dates from the early years of European colonization and today timber remains one of the major exports by value from Ghana, the Ivory Coast, Cameroun, Zaïre and Gabon. Currently, Ghana is the principal world producer of hard-woods, the main source of supply being in the area west of the Pra River. In both Ghana and the Ivory Coast timber is the third most important export by value, the average annual value of timber exports since 1970 being about ₦15 million for Ghana and ₦60 million for the Ivory Coast. Nigeria exports timber worth only ₦2·5 million annually while exports from the East African countries of Kenya, Uganda and Tanzania are valued at only ₦1·5 million per annum. Timber exports from Mozambique and Angola are also considerably higher than from the East African countries.

In most countries a much greater proportion of the felled timber is now consumed locally and the industry offers employment to thousands of people in the major timber-producing districts. Timber from West Africa, except Ghana, as well as from Gabon, Angola and Mozambique, is exported mostly as logs, although there are hundreds of hand-sawyers and many sawmills in every country. In East Africa, where there are over 200 sawmills employing over 11,000 people, as well as numerous hand-sawyers, the timber exports consist mostly of sawn timber. East African timber forests, unlike those in West Africa, are located far inland and cannot therefore afford the high transport costs of exporting logs as is done in West Africa where the forests lie close to the coast.

Transport remains one of the major problems facing the timber industry in most countries. There are no forest roads and timber lorry drivers encounter great difficulties, especially during the rainy season in the course of evacuating logs through forest paths. The poor state of transportation is responsible for the fact that in some areas, notably in the Benin Division forests of Nigeria, logs are still carried by wheeled tractors to the nearest waterside to be floated to the port of export at Sapele. Since some logs float while others sink, the practice is to secure the sinker between two floaters before floating all three to Sapele. Rafting was also common in Ghana until 1920, when the use of the Pra and Ankobra river systems for floating logs to the coast was discontinued. Another problem facing the timber industry is the high cost of extraction caused by the small number of marketable species per hectare of forest. Often the number of marketable trees which are mature for felling is less than eight in each hectare of dense tropical rain forest.

Firewood and charcoal
The annual consumption of wood fuel in the form of firewood and charcoal is very high throughout tropical

Africa, far greater than the consumption of timber or poles and posts. In Kenya, for example, the annual consumption of firewood and charcoal in the 1970s was estimated to be over 205 million cu ft, compared with 3·3 million cu ft for sawn timber and 10·5 million cu ft for poles and posts. Firewood is used for cooking in most households as well as for heating in the highlands of Ethiopia, East Africa and southern Africa. It is also used for curing tobacco and drying fish, and in the past was even used as fuel for the railways of East and Central Africa. Charcoal is a more expensive form of domestic wood fuel and is usually preferred to firewood by the urban low-income group who cannot afford to cook with kerosene, gas or electricity.

Wood for fuel is usually obtained from the newly prepared farmland or fallow bush rather than from distant forests. However, in many countries the total depletion of woodland in closely settled areas has brought about a thriving trade in firewood and charcoal. In some densely populated rural areas of the drier savanna region of West Africa, the shortage of firewood has been largely responsible for the use of dry cattle dung as fuel, rather than as manure. Local government councils and some individuals have therefore established forest plantations of exotic species to provide firewood for such areas.

Poles and posts

In tropical Africa building poles are indispensable in the construction of all types of huts even of the most temporary kind such as the shelters used by the pastoral nomads or huts with mud walls. Building poles and firewood constitute the major forest produce of the grassland areas. Wooden posts, consisting of branches of trees, are also important in the farming operations of many ethnic groups. Crops like yams, fluted pumpkins, tomatoes and beans have to be staked by using wooden posts to raise them from the ground in order to obtain good harvests. Yams in particular require high poles which are strong enough to withstand attack by white ants as well as the unusually violent winds of the rainy season; and in the very densely populated forest region it is now difficult to obtain suitable yam sticks within reasonable distance of the settlements. Wooden posts are also in great demand in some areas for storing yams and maize in barns.

Wooden poles are also widely used as telephone, telegraph and electric transmission poles. Often poles from local trees are unsuitable because they are bent, and governments have had to establish special forest plantations of imported tree species such as *Eucalyptus saligna*, pine and teak for the purpose of producing suitable general utility poles. In many countries there is a tendency to emphasize the production of poles and firewood in forest plantations while seeking to meet the future requirements of timber by restocking the forest reserves through replanting and tending the more valuable naturally regenerated seedlings.

Minor forest products

The list of what constitutes minor forest products varies from one country to another and also within different parts of the same country. In colonial Nigeria yam sticks, chewing sticks, wrapping leaves, bamboo, camwood, shea nuts and tie-tie (ropes) were considered in the eastern provinces to be minor forest products which the local people could gather from any forests including the forest reserves. However none of these items appeared in the list of minor forest products of the western provinces, and in the northern provinces, the local people were allowed to freely collect gum arabic, shea nuts and tannin.

Minor forest products which feature prominently in the local economy of some rural areas include a wide range of foodstuffs, medicinal herbs and raw materials for local crafts. In some countries, these products, notably gum arabic, beeswax, piassava and shea nuts, play an important part as foreign exchange earners especially in Nigeria, where wild rubber also contributed to the foreign exchange earnings. Indeed until 1925 exported palm produce from Nigeria was considered to be a minor forest product rather than an agricultural product, while wild rubber was separated from plantation rubber in the presentation of the annual export returns between 1930 and 1936.

A considerable variety of foodstuffs is still obtained by gathering minor forest products. The foodstuffs include the leaves of some trees and creeping plants used in preparing soups, wild grains such as wild rice (*Oryza barthii*) and *founi kouli* (*Brachiaria deflea*), wild yams which are often survivors of a former crop, and seeds such as those of the baobab tree and the oil bean tree. Many edible fruits and several small animals, notably snails from the forest belt and locusts from the savanna areas, are also gathered for food in various parts of tropical Africa. According to Pierre Gourou, in Ghana there are about 114 kinds of edible fruits, 46 kinds of leguminous seeds and 47 kinds of green leaves cooked like spinach (Gourou, 1955). A considerable proportion of these food items are still collected from the bush as minor forest products.

Gathering forest products is an all-season occupation in some parts of tropical Africa since products such as snails, seeds and leaves are in demand throughout the year as food or for medicinal purposes. However, in most areas some food items from the forests are gathered only in times of scarcity. In those parts of tropical Africa, such as the eastern states of Nigeria, where goats and sheep are always confined to the backyard sheds in the homesteads, the gathering of fodder for the animals is an all-season occupation. Fodder for livestock is also sold all the year round in the larger urban livestock markets such as Timbuktu, Kano, Zaria and Ibadan, where large herds of goats and sheep are assembled every day for sale. The more important forest products which are also collected all through the year, even if on a part-time basis, include oil palm fruits and palm kernels, piassava, palm wine and shea nuts. With the exception of palm wine, all these forest products are collected for local consumption as well as for export while gum arabic, obtained by tapping various species of acacia trees, is mainly for export. The economic importance of these trees has made it necessary for an increasing number of people to cultivate them in order to supplement the harvest from wild trees.

Minor forest products are an important source of fibres used in the local textile and craft industries. Important crafts which still rely on forest fibres include the making of ropes, twines and fishing nets and the weaving of mats, baskets and hats. Piassava from the raffia palm provides tie-tie, used in house building and in staking field crops. One of the very highly valued fibres in the forests of West Africa is the *anaphe* silk which is called *sanyan* by the Yoruba and *tsamia* by the Hausa. It is produced by wild silkworms and is used in embroidering high quality hand-woven textiles. Traditional cloth-dyeing in Yorubaland as well as in Kano City still depends partly on indigo and other plant-derived dyes. A variety of canes from the high forest and waterside woodlands of the savanna regions also provide valuable raw materials for making cane chairs and baskets.

Beeswax is another important minor forest product which is produced for export in various parts of tropical Africa including Tanzania and northern Nigeria. Tanzania also exports a considerable quantity of honey although the bulk of the output is consumed locally. The forests of tropical Africa are also very rich in herbs and trees, whose barks and leaves, and sometimes the fruits and roots, are used for making traditional medicines or fish poisons. Trees whose barks are used for medicines include the baobab (*Adansonia digitata*), Indian tamarind (*Tamarindus indica*) and mahogany (*Khaya senegalensis*). The roots of the Indian tamarind, the copaiba balsam (*Daniella oliveri*) and the sabara (*Guiera senegalensis*) are also used for medicine (Morgan & Pugh, 1973).

Hunting

The forests and grasslands of tropical Africa are very rich in big and small game, and hunting is practised in most rural areas. As a rule, hunters are accorded considerable respect as brave men and legends abound amongst most ethnic groups concerning the role of brave hunters in founding settlements. In the early

days of settlement, hunters performed the dual role of providing bush meat for sale as well as keeping at bay the wild animals which constituted a threat to life and a menace to farmland. The destruction of farmland by elephants, for example, is still common in some countries including Nigeria, Tanzania and Cameroun, and the police are often called upon to track down and shoot the offending beasts.

Hunting is practised by many more people in the grassland areas where the bigger animals are concentrated although the demand for bush meat is greatest in the forest areas which support relatively few livestock. Some animals, such as the lion, bush-buck, roan antelope, wild cat and the grass cutter are found all over the grassland areas although some of them, notably the bush-buck and the duiker, shelter and breed in the high forest areas. Extensive destruction of high forest for farming purposes has tended to encourage the penetration of grassland animals into the forest belt. Elephants, for example, are generally found in high forest areas that have been cleared for cultivation.

Although there are many full-time hunters, the vast majority of hunters in tropical Africa are part time who take to hunting in the dry season when the field crops have been harvested. The dry season also favours hunting in the savanna areas because of the drying up of most small streams and rivers, and the consequent restriction of drinking water sources for wild animals. Tswana hunters of Botswana are known to employ various devices to kill animals along their routes to watering points. One such device is to construct large pitfalls of considerable depth with a veiled thin cover of brush; another common device is to prepare a mud basin near the water point and fill it with water poisoned with branches of euphorbia (Forde, 1957, p. 29). It is also during the dry season that grassland hunters effectively employ bush burning as a hunting technique to drive animals to suitable locations where they can be easily trapped. Many hunters use dogs during hunting expeditions. A great variety of traps are used while the commonest traditional weapons consist of spears, bows and arrows and dane guns which are fabricated locally in many parts of tropical Africa. An increasing number of the élite who hunt for sport use more sophisticated weapons.

Group hunting involving two or more hunters is common all over tropical Africa. Every year several accidents involving the shooting of a member of the hunting group are reported in the daily newspapers. Most part-time hunters, however, hunt individually and amongst the Tswana, for example, every man hunts for his own immediate family. Animal skins and hides are a valuable by-product of hunting and are used mostly in local crafts such as making water bottles, sandals, waist belts and knife sheaths. Specialist

Pl. 13.2 Sapele sawmill, Nigeria

hunters also supply a considerable quantity of smoked bush meat to the village and nearby urban markets. Hunting is, however, on the decline all over tropical Africa and the indications are that this trend will continue.

Forest industries

The development of forest or wood-based industries is restricted in most countries to sawmilling, the manufacture of furniture and boat-building. Many countries have, however, recognized the need to establish modern wood-based industries to substitute for imports not only because such industries will help to conserve foreign exchange and provide employment to school-leavers, but also because it is more economical to export processed wood products than timberlogs. The existing and planned wood-based industries of the early 1980s include sawmilling, plywood and veneer, pulp and paper, cellulose, boat-building, furniture and matches.

In some countries, such as Ghana and Kenya, most of

the timber exported is now in the form of sawn wood. Some of the sawn wood is the product of pit-sawing, a rather wasteful and primitive method which is still common in tropical Africa. However the thousands of African hand-sawyers make only a small contribution to the total output of sawn wood which is becoming increasingly dominated by modern sawmills. Most of the sawmills are small family-owned concerns, and in East Africa the small sawmills are owned mostly by Asians. There is, however, an increasing number of very large sawmills in the forest regions of southern Nigeria, southern Cameroun, Gabon, Zaïre, Congo Republic and Angola. In some countries, notably Nigeria, Kenya and Ghana, there has been a marked shift of sawmilling from forest locations to the outskirts of the major towns and cities.

The manufacture of plywood and veneer is the most economical way of converting logs to usable wood, but so far there are only a few plywood factories in tropical Africa. Compared with sawn timber, plywood is virtually a stable and homogenous material which does not shrink or warp. It can be manufactured in panels of a size rarely attained in solid wood and has a wide variety of uses including the manufacture of tea chests and furniture. The few large plywood factories include the Sapele plant of the African Timber and Plywood Company of Nigeria, the Takoradi plywood mill and the three East African plywood factories at Jinja in Uganda and at Moshi and Tanga in Tanzania. The largest plywood factory in tropical Africa is located at Port Gentil in Gabon which also has two other smaller plants at Libreville and Ndjole.

Another important basic wood industry which is still restricted to a few countries is the manufacture of pulp and paper. This is a rather capital intensive industry with a high consumption of wood. The pulp can be used to make a great variety of papers used for wrapping goods, as newsprint, for cartons and for writing and printing. The rapid rise in school enrolment all over tropical Africa has created a great demand for paper with the result that several countries have now established or are planning to establish pulp and paper factories. One of the largest pulp and paper factories is located at Catumbela in Angola. The factory, which went into production in 1961, is owned by the Companhia de Celulose do Ultramar Portugues which also owns an extensive plantation of eucalyptus trees for pulp making. Pulp and paper factories have also been established at Maputo in Mozambique and Umtali in eastern Zimbabwe while the ₦200 million pulp and newsprint factory at Oku Iboku in Nigeria is expected to start production in 1981. In addition there are smaller papermills in many countries including Nigeria (Jebba), Uganda (Jinja) and Kenya (Mombasa). The largest pulp factory in production is the new giant multi-million Naira cellulose plant with an annual capacity of 245,000 tonnes of bleached pulp from local timber. This ultra-modern factory is located at Port Gentil which is the most important industrial centre for wood-based products in Gabon.

The other important wood industries are boat-building, match-making, furniture and floor tiles. Boat-building is confined largely to sea ports and river ports with rich forest hinterlands while the other industries are urban based. Both match-making and floor tiles are associated with plywood and veneer factories especially in Nigeria, Kenya and Tanzania. Plywood is also widely used in the manufacture of furniture which is by far the most widespread wood-based industry in tropical Africa.

Forests and recreation

In the developed countries of the world, the forests play an important role in recreation and tourism. City dwellers in the United States and Europe take delight in

Pl. 13.3 View looking down into Ngorogoro Crater National Park, Tanzania

driving out to spend public holidays in neighbouring forest locations where camping facilities for picnickers are provided by local government authorities. In tropical Africa, the impenetrable character of the rain forest offers no possibilities for camping. The extensive savanna woodlands with their great wealth of wildlife and beautiful scenery are, however, very suitable for recreational purposes. Indeed, wildlife is currently a major natural resource in the East African countries and in Kenya, tourism has for many years been the second largest source of revenue, estimated to be over ₦14 million per annum. The famous safari parks of East and Central Africa are well known in Europe and America and thousands of visitors flock to Africa every year.

It is a well-known fact that the demand for holidays and travel expands with increase in population and a rise in living standards. It follows that the current marked increase in the standard of living of Africans is likely to generate a larger domestic tourist traffic which, when added to the traffic from Europe and North America, is bound to prove problematic unless tourist facilities are expanded and existing ones are improved. Currently, the main sources of revenue accruing from holiday travels include money paid to hotels, for transport, photography and souvenirs. Money is also collected in the form of entrance fees and other expenditure in the national parks and the manufacture of special safari clothing has become an important industry employing several hundred people.

Some countries, such as Kenya, Tanzania, Zambia and Zaïre, possess national parks where fauna and flora are conserved and facilities are provided to enable tourists to visit and enjoy the country and the animals that live there. These are distinct from game reserves which serve as reservoirs from which game spreads into the surrounding country. National parks cover some of the most beautiful parts of Kenya and Tanzania, the most famous of which include the 30,170 hectare Lake Nakuru National Park of Kenya and the 264 sq km Ngorongoro National Park of Tanzania. In East and Central Africa the game reserves serve as potential national parks of the future but in Nigeria, where there are no national parks, the famous 3,300 sq km Yankari Game Reserve serves the dual purpose of a game reserve and a national park for visitors.

Note

1. A cord is a pile of wood 2·4 m long, 1·2 m high and 1·2 m wide. Its weight varies according to the type and dryness of the wood, averaging about one tonne.

References

Adeyoju, S. K. (1975), *Forestry and the Nigerian Economy*, Ibadan University Press, Ibadan.

Batten, T. R. (1956), *Problems of African Development: Part I Land and Labour*, Oxford University Press, Oxford.

Forde, C. D. (1957), *Habitat, Economy and Society*, Methuen & Co, London.

Gourou, P. (1955, 5th ed. 1980), *The Tropical World*, Longman, London, pp. 65–6.

Morgan, W. B. and Pugh, J. C. (1973), *West Africa*, Methuen & Co, London, pp. 153–5.

Wellington, J. H. (1955), *Southern Africa: A Geographical Study*, vol. II, Cambridge University Press, Cambridge, p. 89.

Section D
Manufacturing and Service Industries

14 Development of Manufacturing and Craft Industries

Introduction

Although capital investment in manufacturing and the range of locally manufactured goods have increased substantially since independence, Africa is still far behind the other continents in the development of the manufacturing sector of the economy. Unfortunately, the indications are that this position is likely to remain unchanged for several decades. Indeed, apart from South Africa and Egypt, both of which are outside tropical Africa, the contribution of manufacturing to the economy of each country in 1980 was still far below 20 per cent of the Gross Domestic Product (GDP). A few countries, such as Nigeria, Zimbabwe, Kenya, Ghana and Senegal have, however, made remarkable progress in developing the manufacturing sector, while other countries are struggling against severe handicaps to establish more industries.

There are many reasons why developing countries, including those of tropical Africa, have become seriously committed to ensuring rapid industrial development. The most plausible is that the most developed countries of the world are also the most industrialized. The newly independent countries of Africa have therefore come to regard the development of manufacturing industries as a sure step towards modernizing their economies and improving the standard of living of their people. Other reasons are as follows:

1. The need to raise the quality of local primary exports – mostly industrial crops and minerals – by semi-processing and exporting them in a form that will earn more money per unit weight. Nigeria, for example, now exports its tin ore in the form of semi-processed tin ingots.
2. The desire to diversify the economy by reducing the heavy dependence on primary exports which in comparison with manufactured goods are more vulnerable to price fluctuations in the world market and which are continuously being threatened by competition from synthetic products.
3. The desire to provide employment for a rapidly growing urban population, most of whom are migrants who have graduated from primary or secondary school and who have completely rejected the traditional ways of life in the village.
4. The need to conserve foreign exchange by substituting locally manufactured goods for foreign goods.
5. The desire to transfer skill and technology from the developed to the underdeveloped countries. Attempts to transfer technology in agriculture have often proved disastrous in many African countries, but not so in the manufacturing sector.

The countries of tropical Africa have therefore devoted an increasing amount of their capital resources towards developing the manufacturing sector, to the extent that in some countries the agricultural sector is now stagnant or even declining. Each country has placed more emphasis on the manufacturing of consumer goods rather than capital goods, and this has resulted in the absence of large-scale industrialization which is characteristic of the major industrial powers of Europe, Asia and North America. Indeed the performance of the manufacturing sector has been largely disappointing for the following reasons:

1. Most of the manufacturing industries already established, predominantly of a valorization type and import-substitution type, are capital intensive rather than labour intensive. In consequence the net creation of additional direct employment has been modest considering the amount of money committed by the state to this sector. Hence the fact that urban unemployment continues to rise in spite of the establishment of many more manufacturing industries in cities like Nairobi, Lagos, Accra, Tema and Abidjan.
2. A large number of the import-substitution industries such as breweries, mineral waters, flour mills, plastics and medical drugs still import some or all of their raw materials, except water, as well as all the machinery, some industrial skill and even containers. The result is that the saving on foreign exchange is minimal in some cases, while the cost of production is generally so high that the finished products often cost more than imported products. Governments have therefore had to protect these industries by banning imported goods or by imposing high tariffs.
3. The quality of locally produced goods has generally been much inferior to that of imported goods, hence the

increasing incidence of smuggling which has had adverse effects on the sales of locally made goods.

4. The absence of heavy industries such as iron and steel, petro-chemical industries and car manufacturing has militated against effective transfer of technology.

5. Emphasis on and a disproportionately high investment in manufacturing have led to a relative neglect of the agricultural sector. Increasing migration from rural to urban areas has resulted in a stagnant agricultural sector since those left in the rural areas continue to use traditional farming methods and farm implements. Most countries have therefore had to spend their meagre foreign exchange on importing large quantities of food which could be produced locally (see p. 122).

6. The tropical African countries have so far failed to utilize the by-products of existing industries, notably in oil-refining, sawmilling and sugar-refining.

The growth of manufacturing and crafts

Although manufacturing is now used to describe the production of goods on a large scale by machinery housed in factories, the root meaning of the word manufacture is to make a thing by hand. Manufacturing is therefore nothing new in tropical Africa since the people have had a long tradition of producing such goods as iron farm implements, cotton cloth, salt and fishing gear. Essentially, manufacturing involves:

1. changing one or more raw materials into more useful commodities;

2. the use of special equipment or machinery which may be operated by hand but usually by inanimate power;

3. the provision of a special work place which is the factory but may also be the veranda or the backyard of a dwelling house;

4. the turning out of uniform finished products. In a modern factory, workers are usually assigned to distinct specialized activities.

The pre-colonial period

Relics from archaeological sites in Zimbabwe, at Igbo-Ukwu and the Nok terra cotta heads of the Jos tinfields in Nigeria, and finds in various other parts of tropical Africa confirm that the manufacture of items such as pottery, iron tools and weapons, copper wire ornaments and bronze figurines was an important economic activity as far back as the ninth century AD. At a time when contact with the outside world was very restricted, farm tools and weapons were manufactured from locally smelted pig iron. A number of these small iron furnaces were still common in the grassland areas

of West Africa during the early years of the colonial period. It was the products of these local charcoal-fired iron foundries that provided the raw materials for the celebrated brass and bronze figurines of Ife, Benin and Igbo-Ukwu (all in Nigeria) and of various parts of Central Africa.

Other important manufactures of pre-colonial Africa include wood and ivory carvings of religious and artistic objects, beadwork, pottery and a wide range of fibre crafts including the well-known raffia crafts of Ikot Ekpene in Nigeria. By far the most widespread and best-developed traditional manufacture was the spinning and weaving of cotton and silk cloth, and the associated activity of cloth-dyeing. The raw materials for all these manufactures came from local sources and in each town, the professional craftsmen were usually organized into guilds similar to those of medieval Europe.

Some of these traditional industries have survived until today. The cloth industry in particular has received a new lease of life since independence,

Pl. 14.1 Adire cloth manufacture – dyeing the cloth in indigo

Pl. 14.2 The finished cloth displayed by its manufacturer

although the celebrated *kente* cloth of Ghana and the Akwete cloth of Nigeria now depend on yarns from modern textile factories. Similarly the cloth-dyeing industry, particularly of Kano City and Yorubaland, now rely on baft and shirting produced in modern textile factories, while the *adire* dyeing industry of Yorubaland relies more on imported synthetic dyes rather than locally produced indigo. Small-scale traditional manufactures are therefore of more than historical interest, since they still provide employment for a considerable number of people. Indeed during the early 1960s these small-scale industries provided employment for many more people in comparison with factory manufactures which we have already observed to be capital intensive rather than labour intensive. These small-scale or cottage industries are still carried out as family businesses in which the workers are trained on the job. In the ancient city of Kano, traditional cloth-making, leather works and perfume-making continue side-by-side with large-scale factory production.

The colonial period

Indigenous African technology suffered a major setback during the colonial period partly because of lack of support from the governments and partly because its products could not compete with cheaper and better-quality factory products from Europe. The colonial economic policy or the colonial pact, as the French preferred to call it, was that each colony should be self-supporting, and that the funds necessary for administration and development should be raised from the sale of primary products (industrial crops and minerals) to the imperial country, which in turn would

supply manufactured goods to the colonies (Webster & Boahen, 1970). Japanese and German goods were prohibited in British colonial territories while people in French colonial territories were forced to buy and sell in French markets. Manufacturing of any sort was discouraged so as to prevent any competition with industrial products from the metropolitan countries. In 1938, for example, the export of groundnut oil from Senegal to France had to be restricted because of protests from French oil-millers.

A considerable number of primary processing industries were, however, developed during the 1930s and early 1940s. Raw cotton was ginned before being baled for export, and rubber and timber were also semi-processed before they were exported. In Nigeria, for example, tin ore came to be exported in the form of processed tin ingots as from 1962. Valorization-type industries were understandably located at or near the source of the raw materials. Such industries remain dominant and are often the only type of manufacturing in some countries; but in other countries, such as Ghana and Nigeria, the contribution of semi-processing of raw materials to the manufacturing sector has declined substantially since independence.

The outbreak of the Second World War in 1939 provided a great stimulus to industrialization in tropical Africa. There were restrictions on shipping space for general cargo, resulting in an irregular supply of some industrial raw materials to Europe and of manufactured consumer goods to tropical Africa. In consequence, the quota system of 1938, restricting groundnut oil import into France to only 5,800 tons, was abolished in 1939 with the result that the processing of groundnut oil in French West Africa rose rapidly to 70,000 tons (Thompson & Adloff, 1958, p. 384). The quota was, however, reimposed after the war, but the quantity was increased to 36,320 tons in 1946. Widespread shortages of consumer goods in the colonial territories at this time were largely responsible for the establishment of several factories producing such goods as beer, soft drinks, cotton textiles, cigarettes and soap. Again, the rate of growth of these manufactures slowed down after the war because of a deliberate policy of encouraging the colonial territories to buy from the revitalized industries of the metropolitan countries of Europe. It was not until the first few years of independence that greater emphasis was again given to manufacturing for reasons given on p. 162.

The period after independence

The first decade after independence witnessed determined efforts by most countries to increase the size and range of manufacturing. In Nigeria, for example, the share of manufacturing in the GPD rose from 0·6 per cent in 1950 to 5·6 per cent in 1963 and 8·4 per cent in

1967. The principle of import substitution pursued by the newly independent countries contributed greatly to the rapid growth and diversification of manufacturing. In Kenya, which is still the most industrially advanced of the East African countries, the diversification of manufacturing since 1963 has been remarkable. Here, as in many other countries, manufacturing is no longer concerned with agricultural processing and mining as was the case during the colonial period. A wide range of industries including cement, steel rolling mills, tyres, radios, textiles and paints is common.

Import-substitution manufacturing established after independence discriminated against imports from abroad as well as from neighbouring African countries. In East Africa, for example, Tanzania and Uganda served as markets for many manufactured goods produced in Kenya during the colonial period. After independence, Uganda and Tanzania established many more industries in order to diversify their economies and to provide more job opportunities, in addition to conserving foreign exchange. This resulted in considerable loss of market for some consumer goods manufactured in Kenya, even though Kenya, Uganda and Tanzania were members of the East African Community, which eventually collapsed in 1978. Manufacturers from the Dakar industrial district of Senegal suffered the same fate following the break-up at independence of the colonial period Federation of French West Africa, when countries like the Ivory Coast, Togo and Guinea established their own import-substitution industries. This development is significant because it resulted in the further fragmentation of African markets and the establishment of expensive industrial plants, many of which were obliged to operate below capacity because of the small size of the national markets.

The period after independence witnessed the creation of industrial estates in many large towns, especially the national capitals, where industrialists could readily obtain land for their factories at a reasonable cost. Foreign investors were attracted by various incentives including tax relief, pioneer industry status and profit repatriation laws. High tariffs on foreign goods also created a guaranteed local market for the products of local industries. In some countries, local manufacturers who have been foremost in lobbying for government protection of local goods, have often proved incapable of making the best use of opportunities offered through such protection. Periodic and sustained shortages of goods like sugar, beer, flour, cement and soft drinks have become common with the result that the consumer is made to pay exorbitant prices. Furthermore, some manufacturers have tended to take undue advantage of this protection by producing low-quality goods, and thereby indirectly encouraging large-scale smuggling of imported goods which people prefer to buy even at higher prices, although most smuggled goods are usually cheaper.

In many countries, capital for industrial development is still largely provided by the subsidiaries of foreign multinational corporations, but in a few countries the situation has changed considerably since independence. At independence, almost all the factories in existence were owned and financed by private foreign companies such as UAC (United Africa Company), SCOA (Société Commerciale de l'Ouest Africain), PZ (Patterson Zechonis) and John Holts, which had been trading in tropical Africa since the early days of the colonial period. The decision of most of these companies to withdraw from the commodities trade and to invest in manufacturing followed the establishment in some territories of produce marketing boards which compelled all produce buyers to sell to the boards and not in the open world market. Governments also provided capital to state development corporations to establish manufacturing industries, in addition to encouraging foreign firms to expand their investments. The restriction in some countries of retail trade to citizens of the relevant country a few years after independence also induced Asians, Lebanese and other foreign traders to divert their capital into manufacturing. The latest development in this trend is the Enterprises Promotion or Indigenization Law in Nigeria which came into effect in January 1979, and which requires that all businesses, including manufacturing companies, must have 60 per cent Nigerian participation. These companies have therefore sold 60 per cent of their share capital to various state governments as well as to private citizens. The source of capital for manufacturing in Nigeria is therefore now largely indigenous.

The structure of manufacturing

The structure of the manufacturing sector is defined as the relative share of the various industrial groups in total value. Two main groups are often recognized, light industry and heavy industry; in this section we find it more appropriate to recognize three groups, capital, intermediate and final manufactures. Capital manufactures are basically heavy industries featuring the production of iron, steel, machinery and permanent equipment for producing other goods; intermediate and final manufactures are essentially light industries producing such goods as textiles, rubber products, chemicals, food and drink, footwear, furniture and transport equipment.

Almost every country in tropical Africa has a weak industrial structure in the sense that the sector is dominated by low-technology light industry featuring the production of final manufactures and, to a lesser extent, of intermediate goods. Countries which have the weakest industrial structure include Gabon, the Central African Republic, the Somali Republic, Mali, Malawi and Ghana. On the other hand, Nigeria and Ethiopia, the two most populous countries in tropical Africa, have a relatively more balanced industrial structure.

The first important feature of the structure of manufacturing in the region is the virtual nonexistence of factories producing capital goods. Yet capital manufactures constitute the basic generative factor of industrialization. Iron and steel is yet to be developed even in Nigeria and so is real engineering involving the manufacture of agricultural and industrial machinery. In Nigeria in 1973 industries producing capital goods accounted for less than 10 per cent of the value added in manufacturing as compared with over 75 per cent from industries producing consumer goods.

The second important feature of the manufacturing sector is the relative weakness of intermediate manufactures, which produce goods serving as raw materials for final manufactures. This is particularly true of intermediate manufactures which require a high level of technology, especially basic industrial chemicals, paper and fertilizers. In a few countries, however, there is a high concentration of capital and labour in low-technology intermediate manufactures, notably textiles and basic metal.

The marked concentration on final manufactures in most countries is the third important characteristic of industrialization in tropical Africa. In the 1970s Ghana had almost 80 per cent of its fixed capital in final manufactures. The corresponding figures for Malawi, Zambia and Uganda were 78 per cent, 70 per cent and 61 per cent respectively.

We end this section by calling attention to the observations made in the following two short quotations from *False Start in Africa* by René Dumont (1968). The passages are:

In the Soviet Union and China an absolute priority was granted to heavy industry on every level. This enabled them to develop rapidly, but at the price of enormous efforts and the sacrifice of a generation. Africa does not seem disposed to accept such a sacrifice at present . . . (p. 87)
Latin America has heavily emphasized the manufacture of consumer goods, and in so doing slowed down industrial development. (p. 88)

It is clear that tropical Africa, which is industrially far behind the Soviet Union, China and Latin America, has chosen the Latin American path. It is also true that Africa does not seem disposed to accept the sacrifice of giving priority to heavy industry at present. As recently as March 1979, for example, the Nigerian Head of State is reported to have stated that the government could not with unnecessary haste mortgage the future of the country on one project, that is the Ajaokuta blast furnace complex (*Sunday Times*, Lagos, 25 March 1979). As in Latin America, industrialists in Nigeria and other countries of tropical Africa have been concerned with manufactures that guarantee short-term quick profits in the rapidly expanding market for consumer goods.

Types of manufacturing industries

Our discussion of the structure of manufacturing in tropical Africa has dealt with the three broad groups of industries, namely capital, intermediate and final manufactures. In this section we discuss seven main types of manufacturing with special reference to their sources of raw materials, their location and other characteristics. The seven types are: 1. semi-processing of primary raw materials, 2. food and drink, 3. textiles and footwear, 4. the chemical and pharmaceutical industries, 5. building and construction materials, 6. metals and light engineering and 7. heavy industries.

Pl. 14.3 The Volkswagen plant in Nigeria

Semi-processing of primary raw materials
Industries in this category are amongst the oldest and the most widespread. They include the extraction of vegetable oils by peasants as well as in factories, the manufacture of rubber sheets, cotton ginning and the beneficiation of mineral ores. In the smaller and mono-cultural countries of Gambia, Mali and Niger these valorization-type industries are still the dominant forms of manufacture. In most of the larger countries, especially in Nigeria, Ethiopia, Kenya, the Ivory Coast and Ghana, since independence, the share of semi-processing of primary raw materials in the total contribution of the manufacturing sector has declined considerably. In Nigeria, for example, the share de-

clined from 50 per cent in 1958 to 25 per cent in 1967.

Semi-processing factories are usually located at or near the source of the raw materials to save transport costs. Another important feature of semi-processing factories is that they are mostly privately owned, especially in English-speaking countries. Some of them, such as cotton ginneries, leather tanning and sheet rubber processing, are small enterprises costing less than ₦5,000. Other examples of industries in this group are the manufacture of tin ingots, giant oil mills for extracting groundnut oil or palm oil and palm kernels, fruit canning and the production of sawn timber, plywood and veneers.

Food and drink

Although this industry dates from the Second World War it was during the post-independence period of large-scale investment in import-substitution manufactures that it became prominent all over tropical Africa. In Kenya, which has a predominantly agricultural economy, and a cool highland tropical climate which permits the cultivation of temperate crops, the food and drink industry produces a wide range of high-quality items including dairy products, flour, canned fruits and vegetables, tea, coffee and beer. Unlike most of the other countries the Kenyan food and drink industry depends almost entirely on locally produced raw materials.

With the possible exception of the huge modern sugar refineries such as those at Bacita in the Niger Valley (Nigeria), the Niara Valley in Zaïre and the Sena sugar estate of the lower Zambesi (Mozambique), as well as the few modern large fish canning factories which are located at the source of raw materials, the food and drink industry is market oriented. Like other import-substitution industries most of them are located in the port cities, many of which are also capitals with large urban populations. Many food industries have also been established in large inland cities such as Kano, Kumasi, Kaduna, Enugu, Bulawayo and Jinja which are not national capitals, but which have a large market provided by regular wage-earners.

The major food industries include meat and dairy products, biscuits, bread and chocolate while the main types of drinks produced include lager beer, stout and a variety of mineral waters. Spirits, including gin, whisky and brandy, are now bottled in almost all the capital cities and local gin is manufactured in some of them. Although the value added in the manufacture of beers and spirits is very high, there is also cause for concern. The insatiable demand for beer, in particular, has resulted in making beer brewing the most profitable industry in countries like Nigeria, Ghana, Zaïre and Guinea, but there is already a high incidence of alcoholism in the population.

Textiles and footwear

The demand for cotton goods is high and continues to increase so that in most countries cotton goods are amongst the largest items imported. In the larger countries such as Nigeria, Ghana, Ethiopia and the Sudan where many large modern textile mills have been established, governments have since imposed severe restrictions on the importation of cotton goods, including second-hand clothes.

Textile manufacture is a very old and probably the most widespread traditional industry in tropical Africa. Cotton and silk cloths woven from locally produced fibres have featured prominently for many centuries in the inter-group trade in West Africa, Sudan and East Africa. The dyeing of cotton cloth using indigo dyes dates back to the founding of Kano City in about AD 1080 and is even more widespread today because of the ready supply of large quantities of synthetic dyes and factory-made white shirting and bafts. Furthermore the locally woven heavy and high-quality textiles such as the Kente cloth of Ghana as well as the Akwete, Okene and Iseyin cloths of Nigeria are still in great demand. As in the past, the production of these traditional cloths is still carried out in cottages or on the verandas of the entrepreneurs' houses.

The Ivory Coast, closely followed by Senegal, is the leading manufacturer of textiles in French-speaking Africa. The total annual output of cloth from Nigeria or Zimbabwe is however much greater than for Senegal or the Ivory Coast. The fact that the modern textile mill is relatively inexpensive compared with many other factories has made it possible for almost every country to build at least one textile factory. Cotton textile factories are also widespread because the industry is not tied to the source of raw materials, since cotton is neither perishable nor weight-losing. Another important factor in favour of the textile factory is that it is labour intensive and therefore well-adapted to providing employment for the increasing number of unemployed immigrants into the cities, where the factories are all located.

Like cotton cloth, leather goods, including sandals, sheaths for daggers and swords, and pouffes, have been manufactured in the grassland areas of tropical Africa for many centuries. Today, hand-made sandals still provide full-time employment for many people in the ancient cities of Timbuktu, Kano, Zaria and Omdurman. Most of the footwear now made in tropical Africa, however, comes from large modern shoe factories located in the major cities of Lagos, Dakar, Abidjan, Kano, Accra, Nairobi, Salisbury and Dar-es-Salaam. Leather for the shoes and rubber, including crepe rubber, for the soles are all produced and processed locally. The raw materials for plastic shoes, which are much cheaper, are however imported.

Pl. 14.4 Tyre factory in Tanzania

The chemical and pharmaceutical industries

The chemical industry is not one but many industries which produce three major groups of products, namely: 1. basic chemicals such as acids, alkalis and organic chemicals, 2. chemical products such as synthetic fibres and plastic materials which serve as raw materials for other manufactures and 3. finished chemical products such as soaps, drugs (aspirin, etc) for immediate consumption and such products as explosives, paints and fertilizers which are used as supplies for other industries. The chemical industry uses such common raw materials as salt, coal, crude oil, air and water, but is a heavily capitalized industry which demands advanced technology and a large market. Integrated chemical industrial plants are therefore very few in tropical Africa although there is an increasing number of import-substitution chemical manufactures, notably paints, insecticides, dyes, pharmaceuticals and storage battery factories which rely on imported raw materials. These factories are all located in the major urban centres as are those which manufacture a wide range of plastic goods such as household utensils, combs, toys and pipes made from imported polythene and polystyrene.

The few large chemical plants producing fertilizers are those at Matola in Mozambique, Thies in Senegal and the nitrogenous fertilizer plant at Que Que in Zimbabwe. The petro-chemical complex to be sited at Port Harcourt in Nigeria and which is expected to produce caustic soda, polyethylene, ethylene and other chemicals, is estimated to cost over ₦300 million, while the nitrogenous fertilizer factory to be built near the complex is estimated to cost over ₦70 million. It is this huge capital cost and the small size of local markets which have made it difficult to establish such factories, since the size of the basic chemical factory cannot be easily reduced as is the case with textiles and sugar factories. However other countries such as Gabon, Ghana and the Ivory Coast have also completed plans to establish large chemical complexes.

Building and construction materials

The range of building and construction materials produced in tropical Africa has increased tremendously since about 1960. Some of the materials, such as quarried stones, sand and gravels are widespread and are produced on site rather than in factories. Cement, tiles, asbestos, corrugated iron roofing sheets, locks and metal frames for doors and windows are, however, made in factories. The continued shortages of most manufactured building and construction materials, in spite of the increasing number of factories producing them, testifies to the very high demand for these materials and is responsible for the large sums of money which some countries still expend in importing such materials. Factories producing building and construction materials are usually located in the major urban centres which provide the market for the products, especially in the port cities, since most of them depend on imported raw materials. The major exceptions are cement and bricks, which have to be located at or near to limestone and clay deposits, only a few of which are close to the main urban centres. In addition to factory products, a large number of blacksmiths also fabricate metal frames for doors and windows as well as locks and keys from steel rods.

Most countries have at least one cement factory. In Nigeria there were seven cement factories in 1980, located at Nkalagu (near Enugu), Ewekoro (near Abeokuta), Shagamu, Ukpilia in Bendel State, Kano, Calabar and Sokoto. Yet the country continues to experience shortages of cement, resulting in delays in the construction of priority projects, such as school buildings for the Universal Primary Education Scheme. Outside Nigeria there are large cement factories at Atbara (the Sudan), Dondo (Mozambique), Loutete (Congo Republic), Harar (Ethiopia), Mombasa and Nairobi (Kenya), Takoradi and Nauli in Brong Ahafo (Ghana) and at Rufisque (Senegal) amongst others. There are also some large clinker-grinding plants which are located at important port-towns such as Port Harcourt, Lagos, Tema, Abidjan and Cotonou. Brick and tile factories exist in Mali at Bamako, Markala, Macina and Segou as well as in several other countries including the Sudan, Guinea, the Ivory Coast and Zimbabwe. In addition bricks are produced under obsolete methods in numerous other locations.

Metals and light engineering

Metal products consisting mainly of buckets and basins were formerly produced in small units by local craftsmen on the verandas of their houses. Later a few factories sprang up to produce steel drums for the export trade of palm oil and for distributing petroleum products and coal tar. Other products of such factories include 18-litre square tins for distributing vegetable and mineral oils and metal boxes for the packaging of the paint and mineral oil industries. Household utensils are still an important product of the metal industry in tropical Africa in spite of increasing competition from plastic goods.

In countries like Nigeria, Kenya and Zimbabwe which have relatively more developed industries, metal products and light engineering have become increasingly important because of the rising standard of living.

Products of this sub-sector of manufacturing such as corrugated iron sheets, aluminium sheets, nails, wire products, iron rods, metal pipes, storage tanks and truck bodies, are in great demand in the building and construction industry as well as in the transportation sector. Like the light engineering industries which assemble radios, bicycles and motor vehicles, these metal goods factories are all located within the largest urban centres which provide the necessary market for their products. The number of vehicle assembly plants is increasing and in 1980, Nigeria had five such plants located at Apapa, Kaduna, Badagry Road (Lagos), Ibadan and Enugu. Other plants include those at Tema, Cotonou, Mombasa and Salisbury. Radio assembly plants are more widespread, the larger plants being located in Abidjan, Tema, Kano, Port Harcourt, Nairobi, Lagos, Salisbury and Dar-es-Salaam.

Heavy industries

Steel has appropriately been described as the backbone of modern industry, although it appears more appropriate to describe it as the backbone of modern civilization. Factory engines, offices and residential buildings, furniture and household appliances, modern agriculture and transportation, and modern military equipment all depend on iron and steel products. Throughout tropical Africa the consumption of steel products has been increasing and all the import-substitution industries depend in varying degree on machinery and raw materials made from iron and steel. Yet, apart from Zimbabwe, no tropical African country has established a modern iron blast furnace, even though vast deposits of rich iron ore are being mined and exported! The high capital cost of blast furnaces and the high level of technology required to operate the plants have so far made it impossible for tropical African countries to establish this most basic industry.

Up till 1980, the development of heavy industry was largely concentrated in Zimbabwe, manufacturing being the largest single contributor to the GDP (22·3 per cent in 1976). The only modern iron and steel complex in tropical Africa is located at Redcliff near Que Que (Zimbabwe) where the iron ore for the industry is obtained. A blast furnace complex expected to cost over ₦1,000 million is under construction at Ajaokuta in Nigeria and may go into production before 1985. A direct reduction iron complex is also under construction at Warri in Nigeria. There are also several steel mills producing steel bars, wire nails and steel strips for the building industry from scrap metal.

Heavy engineering associated with the railways is carried out in some countries, notably Kenya (Nairobi), Zimbabwe and Nigeria. The manufacture of agricultural and industrial machinery is largely restricted to Zimbabwe which uses locally produced iron and steel

Pl. 14.5 An industrial power station in Salisbury, Zimbabwe

products as raw materials. Kenya and Nigeria also produce a small amount of the less sophisticated type of agricultural machinery. There is however a pressing need to commit more resources to the manufacture of agricultural machinery in order to update agricultural methods in the various countries. Other products of the heavy industry manufactured in Zimbabwe include glass, pottery, steel pipes and structural steel.

Factors influencing industrial location and development

Since the days of the industrial revolution in Europe, the relative importance of the traditional factors of industrial location and development, namely accessibility to power, raw materials, labour, market and availability of capital has undergone considerable change. In tropical Africa, the shift of emphasis from the semi-processing of primary raw materials to import-substitution industries has resulted in the location of most factories in large cities, especially the port cities, where the market for the products exist, rather than in areas where the raw materials are produced. The port cities are particularly suitable for import-substitution

industries, because most of these industries depend on imported raw materials, as well as imported machinery and skills; the port cities also have a pool of local semi-skilled and unskilled labour. Government policy and political considerations are a major additional factor influencing the location of industries in tropical Africa. In this section, we shall briefly consider these factors.

Power resources

The main sources of modern industrial power are coal, hydro-electric power and petroleum (oil and natural gas). Coal, the oldest and major source of power for heavy industry, is lacking in most countries although limited deposits occur in Zimbabwe, Zambia, Mozambique, Tanzania, Zaïre and Nigeria (see Fig. 12.4 and pp. 148–9). Tropical Africa is, however, very rich in potential hydro-electric power (see pp. 150–1). Crude petroleum and natural gas are mined in Nigeria, Gabon, Congo Republic and Angola and most countries now have refineries which produced diesel oil for generating electricity. In addition countries like Nigeria and Gabon also generate electric power from natural gas. The high capital costs of nuclear power stations have precluded the local utilization of the uranium mined in Niger, Gabon and the Central African Republic.

The importance of power in industrial location is obvious since manufacturing is carried out mostly in the larger cities, which have a regular supply of electricity. Indeed mining syndicates were obliged to generate hydro-electricity from local rivers in order to facilitate mining operations in such areas as the Jos Plateau, the Katanga Copper Belt and the Mount Nmiba iron ore mines of Liberia. The availability of good-quality coking coal is an important factor which has enabled Zimbabwe to establish the only blast furnace in tropical Africa. And in Nigeria, the availability of coal at Enugu has weighed heavily in the choice of Ajaokuta as the site for its proposed blast furnace complex. However, power can now be readily transported and is therefore not such an important localizing factor as it was during the colonial period or in Europe during the industrial revolution, except for such major power-consuming industries as the VALCO alumina smelter at Tema in Ghana.

Raw materials
Tropical Africa is rich in certain agricultural and mineral raw materials which formed the basis of the processing factories of the colonial period. However, these factories have steadily declined (see p. 164), and a large number of present-day import-substitution industries depend on imported raw materials. Currently, the location of raw materials is not an important determining factor except for bulky or perishable materials used in agriculture and for plants designed to upgrade some mineral ores before export. Industries which can be located far from the source materials include sugar refineries, vegetable oil factories, meat processing and plywood factories. It is however, not unreasonable to argue that the fact that most import-substitution factories are located in the major port cities, where imported raw materials are landed, suggests that accessibility to raw materials is still an important localizing factor in manufacturing.

Labour
An abundant supply of unskilled labour and some categories of semi-skilled labour exist in the cities where most industries are located. Unfortunately labour productivity in tropical Africa is very low because of the deplorable attitude to work. Dumont's observation that 'a typist for the Dakar government types an average of six to seven pages, double spaced, a day, less than a quarter of what an average French typist accomplishes for a salary that is equal if not higher' (Dumont, 1968, p. 68) applies to most countries of tropical Africa. The result is that production costs are very high in spite of low wages paid to unskilled and semi-skilled workers. The supply of skilled labour including technicians, engineers and managers is still

inadequate. The high cost of maintaining expatriate staff, especially from Europe and America, is a major problem facing manufacturing in tropical Africa.

Given the fact that labour can be readily obtained in most urban locations, availability of labour would appear to rank very low as a factor in the location and development of manufacturing. The price of moving skilled labour to some areas is however very high and therefore constitutes a limiting or localizing factor. Most manufacturing firms provide in-service training for their workers, that is in addition to the increasing number of trades schools and colleges of technology in the larger countries. However there has been very little achievement here although there is much talk about the transfer of technology to tropical Africa and other underdeveloped parts of the world. This has been attributed partly to the high incidence of illiteracy, the emphasis on education of the grammar school type and the fact that the Research and Development units of manufacturing companies are usually located in the headquarters of the parent companies in Europe, North America or Japan.

Markets
Apart from the semi-processing of raw materials, manufacturing in tropical Africa is mostly market-oriented. In the case of beer and soft drinks, the finished products are much heavier (bulkier) than the raw materials. It is therefore more economical to locate the factory at or near to the market for the finished products. Furthermore, treated water, which is the principal content of these drinks, is provided almost exclusively in areas of population concentrations which also provide markets for these products. Port-towns, favoured for reasons already given, are also major centres of population concentration, and therefore serve as effective market centres. The purchasing power of the people of tropical Africa is generally much higher in the port-towns and other cities where the wage-earners are concentrated.

The purchasing power of the smaller countries of tropical Africa has been compared to that of a medium-sized American or European city (Green and Seidman, 1968). Most countries are therefore unable to attract investment in certain areas of manufacturing since existing customs barriers have forced many factories to depend mostly on the internal market. For the same reason, a number of government financed manufacturing concerns operate at sub-optimal levels in many countries and have therefore been unable to make their costs break even. The small size of national markets has therefore slowed down the rate of industrialization since such markets are unable to support large-scale manufacturing such as iron and steel, fertilizer plants and the production of industrial gas.

Pl. 14.6 The telecommunications station at Longonot, Kenya

Capital

Availability of capital is a major factor influencing the development of manufacturing and its location since most investors want to locate factories at points of maximum net returns. At present the main sources of capital for industrial development are private foreign entrepreneurs and government funds which are usually channelled through national industrial development corporations. Capital from private domestic sources is still highly restricted since the vast majority of the people are poor and have little savings to invest in manufacturing. A marked change is, however, occurring in Nigeria where all foreign companies have been obliged to comply with the 1977 Enterprises Promotion Decree which requires that 60 per cent of their equity capital must be owned by Nigerian citizens and associations. All shares advertised for sale in 1978 and 1979 were over-subscribed. In addition an increasing number of wealthy Nigerian entrepreneurs have established factories manufacturing consumer goods.

As a rule, capital goods or equipment have been much less mobile than capital. And since tropical Africa depends almost entirely on imported machinery and technicians, this situation has slowed down the development of manufacturing. Because of the great cost of the purchase and installation of heavy capital goods, industries requiring such equipment are gen-

erally owned wholly by large multinational corporations or in partnership with national governments, and tend to be located in the already well-established industrial centres.

Government policy

The dispersal of manufacturing is now an important element of government policy in the larger countries such as Nigeria, the Ivory Coast, Ethiopia and Kenya. By encouraging dispersal, the governments hope to bring about a more even development in the various parts of the country and thereby reduce the influx of population into the cities. Experience has shown that the free play of market forces in poor countries such as those of tropical Africa tend to create regional inequalities and to widen rather than narrow those which already exist. For reasons of social justice and equity, especially in countries with a federal constitution, it has become necessary for governments to intervene to ensure a more even development to promote national integration. Government intervention in the location of industries has also been prompted by the desire to have strategically important industries located in a safe place.

In Nigeria, the creation of nineteen states in 1975 has proved to be an effective instrument in ensuring the dispersal of manufacturing industries since the state capitals have now become growing industrial centres. Furthermore, some government financed factories have been located in particular areas for political reasons and governments have tried to influence the location of industries through legislation on taxation, uniform rates of charges for petroleum products and the establishment of industrial estates where land can be readily obtained by manufacturing firms at a reasonable price.

Conclusion

The issue of the best location is basic to all human activities and for some manufacturing industries 'the location problem is to find the point where transfer costs are lowest' (Estall and Buchanan, 1967). We have therefore considered it unnecessary to treat transport as a separate location factor since transport costs are involved in considerations of accessibility to power, raw materials, market and labour. Indeed the pervasive role of transport is such that in Weber's view, location is a matter of transport costs. Considerations of

transport costs or points of maximum accessibility are certainly of overriding importance in the decision to locate most manufacturing industries in the main urban centres of tropical Africa.

References
Dumont, R. (1968), *False Start in Africa*, Sphere Books, London, pp. 87–8.

Estall, R. C. and Buchanan, R. O. (1967), *Industrial Activity and Economic Geography*, John Wiley Science Editions, Chichester, p. 24.

Green, R. H. and Seidman, A. (1968), *Unity or Poverty? The Economics of Pan-Africanism*, Penguin African Library, Harmondsworth, p. 58.

Sunday Times Lagos (1979), 25 March 1979, p. 1.

Thompson, V. and Adloff, R. (1958), *French West Africa*, George Allen & Unwin, London.

Webster, J. B. and Boahen, A. A. (1970), *History of West Africa (The revolutionary years – 1815 to independence)*, Praeger, New York, p. 261.

15　Transport and Communications

Transport involves the carrying or moving of anything (goods) or anybody from place to place, while communications involve the passing on of news, information or even an illness from one person to another or from place to place. The means of communication consist of all the means of transport such as roads and railways as well as special means such as the telephone, telegraph, radio and television. The above definitions are given in order to stress the great importance of transport and communications in our daily lives. Transport and communications are basic to the development of any economy and society, and it is a well-known fact that the most developed areas are those with well-developed transport and communications networks. Most of tropical Africa is still undeveloped because many areas are inaccessible. On the other hand, the most developed areas – the so-called economic islands – are those which are served by a dense network of roads and, in some cases, railways. In this chapter we consider the contemporary transport pattern, the problems of transport and communications and the various forms of transport currently in use.

Contemporary transport and communications patterns

The transportation and communications patterns in tropical Africa are a product of the colonial period and were designed to facilitate political administration and the implementation of the 'colonial economic pact'. According to this pact, the colonies were to provide export crops and other primary raw materials for the Imperial countries who in turn would provide manufactured goods to their dependencies. In consequence all areas of production of export commodities, such as timber, industrial crops and minerals, were linked by railways or roads, or both, to sea ports. The roads and railways of West Africa thus followed a north–south route from the interior to the ports of the Gulf of Guinea and an east–west route to the Atlantic ports west of Cape Palmas. In East Africa the transport routes ran in a west–east direction from the Great Lakes region to the Indian Ocean ports and in Central Africa the roads and railways ran east and west from the Katanga and Zambian mining districts to the Indian Ocean and Atlantic coasts respectively. Rural areas producing only

food crops received very little attention in the development of transport routes and remained largely isolated except where an 'economic route' happened to pass through it.

Some colonial powers enforced the colonial economic pact so rigidly that they refused to use the shortest or most economical route if it passed through the territory of another colonial power. In West Africa, for example, the French refused to allow Guinea, Senegal or Upper Volta to use shorter or natural routes passing through English-speaking territories. Landlocked countries like Niger and Upper Volta were made to construct rather circuitous routes in order to use the ports of Cotonou and Abidjan in Benin Republic and the Ivory Coast respectively, instead of the ports of Lagos (Nigeria) and Accra (Ghana) which were nearer to a greater part of these French-speaking countries. Roads were constructed to bypass the Gambia River which is a natural outlet to southern Senegal and no attempts were made to build roads to link Guinea with Sierra Leone and Liberia, both of which provide the natural outlet to eastern Guinea. In Zaïre, the belated decision in 1931 of the Belgian colonial government to link Katanga with the Benguela railway was made as a concession to the Portuguese administration of Angola in return for a grant of land by Angola to Zaïre to enable the latter to widen the Matadi strip (Fitzgerald, 1957). Before then, the Belgians preferred to use the Zaïre River route which lay within Belgian territory, even though this involved constructing three short railways to bypass the waterfalls obstructing through navigation along the river. The result was that much time and money were lost in the process of transhipping cargo from rail to river boats and vice-versa at several points.

During the colonial period telecommunications fared little better than transport. Communication links were confined to the territories of a particular metropolitan power. Neighbouring countries like Nigeria and Niger Republic had no direct telephone connections because they were administered by rival colonial powers. In consequence a call from Lagos to Niamey had to go first to London for a connection to Niamey through Paris! Calls from Lagos to Accra passed through London only, since both countries were administered by Great Britain.

Today, about twenty years since most tropical African countries became independent, the colonial patterns of transport and communications persist in most countries, although remarkable changes have occurred in a few countries such as Nigeria, Tanzania and Zambia. The persistence of these patterns in most countries is related to three major factors:

1. the continued domination of the economy by former metropolitan countries;
2. the poverty of most countries in tropical Africa and
3. the operation of basic conditions affecting transport development (in other words transport networks change or develop only when their users dictate such an expansion).

The first two factors have already been discussed in other parts of this book. All we need add here is that the marked developments which have taken place in the transport and communications sectors of the economies of a few countries like Nigeria and Tanzania have been made possible either by the material wealth of the country as in Nigeria or by seeking foreign aid from non-Western countries as in the case of Tanzania (see p. 184). The third factor is discussed below.

Conditions which affect transport development

Transportation and communications systems are created or improved only when there is a demand which the new systems will satisfy. Thus during the colonial period, railways and roads were built to replace footpaths and canoe transport because the colonial economy created a demand for bulk transportation of industrial raw materials from the hinterland to the coastal ports for shipment to Europe. In the same way, in various countries, notably Nigeria, Kenya and the Sudan, the need to promote national integration and local economic development since independence has created a demand for more roads and communications networks; new roads are being built and existing roads and communications networks are being improved. It was while reviewing similar situations that Edward L. Ullman (1956), an American geographer, postulated that the three conditions that affect transport development are 1. regional complementarity, 2. intervening opportunity and 3. spatial transferability. We now proceed to examine how these conditions apply to tropical Africa.

Regional complementarity is partly created by areal differentiation which results in the supply of different products. But before any two different regions interact, there must be a demand or deficit in one region and a supply or surplus in the other region. It is the complementarity of supply and demand that brings about movements and interactions. The colonial period

transport routes, as observed earlier, were largely developed to connect the areas of supply of raw materials to the coastal ports for shipment to Europe. In the same way in the 1970s the great demand for petroleum products in the far north of Nigeria generated a large traffic of oil tankers from the oil refineries of Port Harcourt and Warri and subsequently prompted the construction in 1978 of a crude-oil pipeline from the Niger Delta oilfields to the new refinery at Kaduna.

Examples abound to show that the volume of flow or the traffic generated between two regions by complementarity may be greatly reduced by the occurrence of an intervening opportunity or an alternative source of supply or demand as the case may be. The export of palm oil from the eastern states of Nigeria to England, for example, stopped in 1970 because of the alternative demand provided by local factories in the Lagos and Port Harcourt industrial areas. The Nigerian Railway Corporation lost its groundnut and raw cotton cargo and the revenue from them when an alternative demand for these industrial crops developed from factories located close to the rural areas of production.

The third condition for spatial interaction and transport development is transferability or the constraints imposed on movement of goods by distance. Transferability is measured in time and money costs. Whenever these costs are excessive, interaction will not take place or will be minimal, in spite of perfect complementarity and the absence of intervening opportunities. There is usually a tendency to substitute local products for those non-local products that are difficult or very expensive to transport. Transferability conditions change over time in response to improvements in transportation which usually result in increased interraction and trade. The extension of the Port Harcourt–Enugu railway to Jos in 1927, for example, improved the transferability conditions for tin mined from the Jos mines by reducing drastically the time and cost of transporting tin ore from Jos to the port of export (see p. 182).

A model of the sequential development of a transport network

The Taaffe model of the sequence of transport route development in underdeveloped countries is considered in this section. The model is based on empirical work carried out in Nigeria and Ghana as well as in Brazil, Malaya and East Africa. With a few exceptions, the development of transport in African countries which have a coastal boundary has followed the sequence presented in the model. Four phases of transport network development are recognized

175

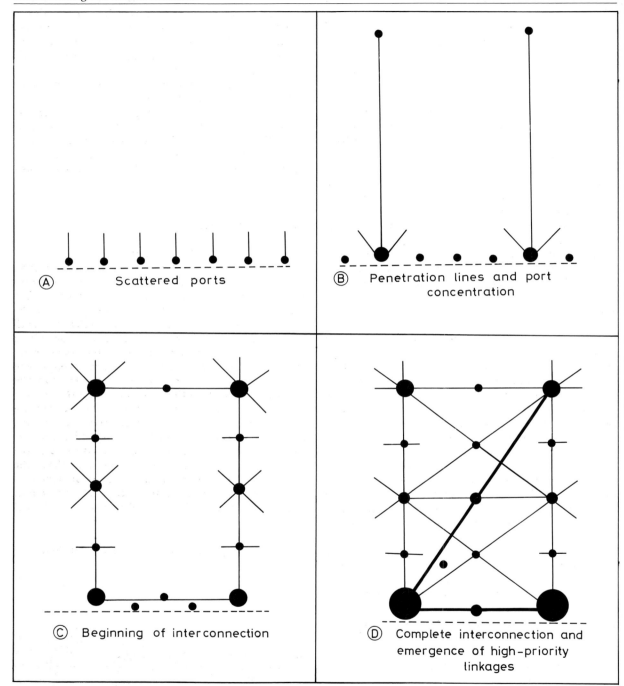

A Scattered ports

B Penetration lines and port concentration

C Beginning of interconnection

D Complete interconnection and emergence of high-priority linkages

Fig. 15.1 The Taaffe model of transport development (after Taaffe, Morrill and Gould, 1963, p. 504)

(Fig. 15.1). The first phase is characterized by the dominance of river and inland waterway transport, and a multiplicity of small primitive sea ports or coastal settlements (Taaffe, *et al.*, 1963). Some of these settlements had existed for many generations as fishing outposts while many others were established during the period of the slave trade and after. Up till the first few years of colonial rule, the hinterland of each port was small and there was very little direct contact between neighbouring ports. Many of these small ports have since disappeared.

Phase two of the transport development process features the construction of a few major lines of penetration to link selected coastal ports with inland centres of production of export commodities. Another major reason for constructing penetration lines in tropical Africa was the desire for political and military control of colonial territories. One important result of the emergence of penetration lines was the differential growth of coastal ports, and the subsequent decline of many primitive ports. In Nigeria this period started with the building of the western railway line from Lagos in 1895 and ended in about 1930 when the railway had reached the inland termini of Nguru and Kaura Namoda. The need to concentrate the meagre resources of that country in developing a few ports to handle modern shipping resulted in the decline of the ports of Calabar, Warri, Abonnema and Sapele and the complete extinction of the ports of Ikang, Forcados, Opobo, Bonny and Brass. This phase is still continuing in some countries since the discovery of new mineral deposits in locations far from existing transportation routes is still resulting in the construction of penetration lines from the ports nearest to such locations. Examples are the railway from Buchanan to the Mt Nimba iron-ore mines in Liberia built in 1962 (p. 142) and the new railway line from the new seaport of Owendo (near Libreville) to the rich iron-ore deposits of Belinga in north-west Gabon (still under construction in 1980).

The third phase witnesses the development of feeder roads direct to the major ports and the inland cities which serve as the interior terminals of the penetration lines. Several intermediate centres of commerce begin to grow up between the coastal and interior terminals. Rudimentary lateral interconnections start with the linking up of the major inland terminals. In Nigeria this phase featured the construction of such east–west roads as the Ibadan–Asaba road, the Kano–Potiskum–Maiduguri road and the Jos–Kaduna road.

During the fourth and last phase, the process of lateral linkage continues and inland towns, which are well served by road or railways or both, tend to grow rapidly at the expense of other less accessible towns. The few coastal ports selected as terminals of the early penetration lines continue to grow as the volume of trade generated inland also grows. Eventually all the major inland towns are connected with roads and as the volume of traffic between certain towns becomes very heavy, high-priority linkages begin to emerge, such as the Lagos–Ibadan expressway, the Port Harcourt–Enugu expressway, the Benin–Shagamu expressway and the Accra–Tema motor road. Extreme port congestion may follow depending on the state of the economy, as was the case in Nigeria between 1970 and 1978. This may lead to further expansion of existing port facilities and the resuscitation of some older ports which were abandoned during the second phase of port concentration.

Forms of transport

Primitive forms of transport

In the area of transport, the old and the new co-exist all over tropical Africa. Indeed vast areas of the region are still inaccessible to modern transport. We will therefore start our review of the state of development of the different means of transport and communications with the primitive or pre-colonial forms of transport which happen to be the only means still available in some rural areas. The more open grassland areas have always been better served by non-motorized transport than the forest belt where primitive forms of transport consist of walking and canoe transport in areas served by navigable rivers. The menace of the tsetse fly prevents the use of animal transport in the forested areas. The transport network in the grassland areas is based on the use of animals such as the ubiquitous donkey, the horse, the camel and in some areas the ox. It is thought that the use of animal transport, especially the horse, contributed much to the establishment and survival of

Pl. 15.1 Loading kola on to camels by the Sokoto River

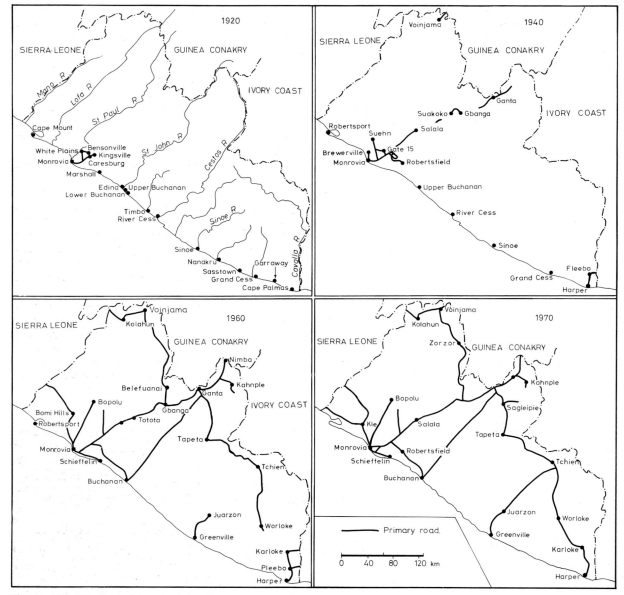

Fig. 15.2 The Taaffe model at work in Liberia

larger political units in the grassland areas of tropical Africa.

Market days provide suitable occasions to observe the continuing dominance of non-motorized forms of transport in the rural areas of tropical Africa. In the grassland areas, women are to be found walking in groups and carrying food items and other goods on their heads, while some men ride on donkeys or on horseback on their way to market. In the forest belt, the journey to market is still largely made on foot although bicycle taxis are now common, and along the coast and creeks,

the journey is made in small canoes, some of which are now fitted with small diesel engines.

Inland waterways transport

Inland waterways consisting of rivers, creeks, lagoons and lakes have been used in tropical Africa from time immemorial, and were particularly important along the coastal areas and in the forest belt. Rivers and creeks provided the first means of penetration from the coast into the interior. French penetration of equatorial Africa, for example, was through the Ogowe River. In

Nigeria, the Niger–Benue system and the Cross River provided important highways, as did the Gambia and Senegal Rivers in those respective countries. Navigable stretches of the upper and middle Niger are still important for local traffic and it was the estimated traffic potential of the Niger that encouraged the French colonial administration to embark upon the building of the Dakar–Niger, Conakry–Niger, the Abidjan–Niger and the Benin–Niger railways. The Congo, the Zambesi and the Rufiji were also important lines of communication in the early days of colonial rule and so were the coastal lagoons and creeks of West Africa in particular.

Today, inland waterways in general, and rivers in particular, have been overshadowed by roads and railways, in spite of the fact that river transport is relatively cheap, since tracks are not needed. The declining importance of river transport has been caused by a number of physical handicaps which have restricted the use of rivers for transportation. One of such handicaps is the occurrence of rapids and waterfalls which restrict navigation to only a few stretches. Along the Congo (Zaïre), which is the most important river, for example, navigation is interrupted by a series of waterfalls and rapids, namely the Gates of Hell, Ngaliema Falls, Livingstone Falls and the cataracts of the lower reaches of the river. The navigable reaches

have therefore been linked together by short railway lines which bypass the unnavigable sections (that is the Kongolo–Kindu, Uhundu [Ponthierville]–Kisangani and the Kinshasa–Matadi railways). Nevertheless, the use of the Congo River route entails considerable delay and cost because of the need to tranship goods at each of the five rail terminals. The second most important waterway, the River Niger, is also interrupted by falls and rapids so that navigation is only possible from Kouroussa to Bamako, Kulikoro to Ansungo, Niamey to Yelwa and Jebba to the sea, although the new Kainji Lake now makes it possible for large boats to travel from the coast to Niamey.

Only two rivers, the Gambia and the Benue, in Nigeria, are free of interruptions by waterfalls and rapids. But even these two rivers, as well as the navigable sections of other rivers, suffer from extreme fluctuations in water level during the dry season when most of the smaller rivers dry up completely. The result is that navigation is limited to only a few months in the year.

Another major handicap restricting the use of African rivers for transportation is the fact that navigable sections of most rivers flow through very sparsely populated districts which produce very little for export or for internal exchange. The result is that traffic on tropical African rivers is extremely small.

Pl. 15.2 The busy river port at Mopti, Mali

Some of the riverbeds have deteriorated considerably through silting caused by sand brought down by accelerated soil erosion in deforested watersheds. Traffic on such rivers has therefore been largely restricted to canoes and small boats which are still important for local traffic.

The relatively small Gambia River is navigable for most of its length, and enters the sea through one of the few good natural harbours in tropical Africa at Banjul (Bathurst). The river is still the major transport route in that small country where there are as many as 58 river stations. Unfortunately, much of its drainage basin lies in Senegal which prefers to evacuate the produce of the upper Gambia Basin by road to Senegalese ports. The Gambia River is therefore deprived of much of the traffic of its natural hinterland.

Along the coast, especially in East and West Africa, the lagoons and creeks still provide sheltered channels for coastal traffic. In Nigeria and the Republic of Benin, local traffic along the creeks includes staple foodstuffs, firewood, smuggled imported goods and passengers from the nearby coastal areas to the cities of Lagos, Porto Novo and Port Harcourt. In the past, there was a sizeable transhipment traffic in timber and palm oil along the creeks linking Lagos to the western delta ports of Sapele, Warri and Burutu. The rapid silting of the shallow channels of these creeks and lagoons has made them unusable by large coastal vessels.

The greatest volume of inland waterways traffic in tropical Africa takes place in Lake Victoria which is politically divided between Uganda, Kenya and Tanzania. The large concentration of the population of these countries along the lake shores (about 7·4 million people) and the varied agricultural products of the fertile lake shore districts provide adequate freight and passenger traffic across the Lake. In pre-colonial times, however, traffic across the lake was very limited partly because the small canoes and rafts could not weather the severe storms of this massive body of water and partly because of the hostilities between the various ethnic groups inhabiting the lake shores. Traffic and trade across the lake became important when the railway from Mombasa arrived at Kisumu in 1901 shortly after the commissioning of a 500-ton steamer. More steamers were introduced a few years later but the extension of the Uganda railway to Jinja in 1928 and to Kampala in 1931 resulted in considerable loss of lake traffic originating from the rich and densely populated agricultural districts of Sukuma, Buganda and Busoga. Traffic on the lake has suffered considerably in recent years because of increasing competition from road haulage. New ferries carrying railway trucks and carriages have, however, been introduced to enable the lake service to link the various arms of the railways.

Like Lake Victoria, the other large natural lakes of tropical Africa, Lakes Chad, Tanganyika and Malawi, are also international inland waters. Traffic on these lakes is, however, very localized and relatively insignificant. By contrast the large man-made lakes, notably Lake Volta in Ghana, Lake Kainji in Nigeria and Lake Kariba on the Zambia–Zimbabwe border, now permit low-cost water transport along their shores. Furthermore, by regulating the water volume below Kainji, the dam at Kainji has, for example, also helped to improve the navigability of the lower Niger below Bussa, while the canals and locks at Kainji allow cargo boats to get past the dam to and from the riverine port of Yelwa.

Railways

In tropical Africa, unlike Europe and North America, the railway came before the road; and in the early years of the railway era, political considerations were more important than economic ones in the choice of railway routes. It was only after the First World War that economic considerations became paramount. Indeed, with the exception of the mineral lines constructed after 1950, most of the railways were built in the hope that they would generate sufficient traffic to justify the cost. This hope was justified in several cases. In Nigeria, for example, the extension in 1912 of the western railway to Lagos resulted in a phenomenal increase in groundnut exports from 2,000 tons in 1911 to 19,290 tons in 1913. The Dakar–Niger and the St Louis–Dakar railways in Senegal also stimulated groundnut production as farmers moved to settle along the railways in areas which were formerly uninhabited wastelands. However, long stretches of most railways pass through virtually uninhabited country such as the Middle Belt of West Africa, central Tanzania and eastern Angola where very little or no traffic is generated. This situation has contributed much to the poor finances of some railways in tropical Africa.

With the exception of the private mineral ore railways such as the Bong Mining Company and the National Iron Ore Company railways of Liberia, and the Miferma (Iron Ore Company) railway of Mauritania, almost all the railways were built and are owned by the governments of the various countries. Most of these government railways were constructed during the colonial period when the territories were very poor and there was a deliberate effort to build the lines as cheaply as possible. Narrow gauges were selected and in order to minimize cost, circuitous routes were chosen to avoid the bridging of many large rivers. In some stretches the gradients were so steep that the load which the train could carry was greatly limited. Railway construction also suffered from lack of adequately skilled and even unskilled manpower and in East Africa the British colonial administration had to recruit almost 32,000

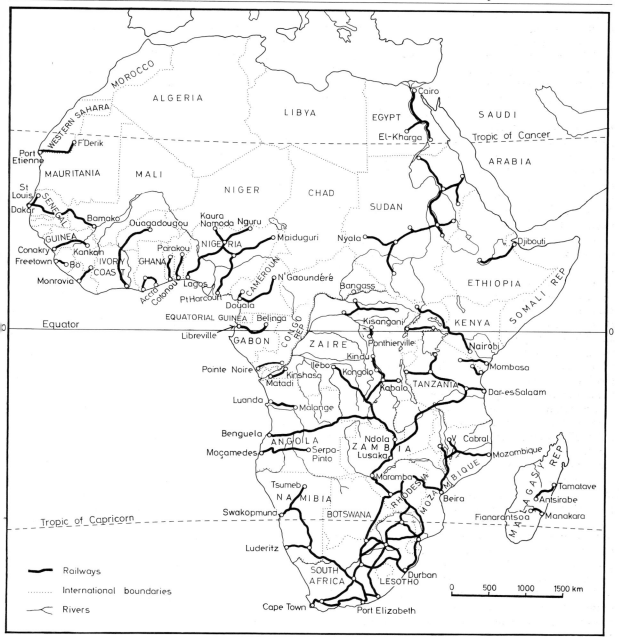

Fig. 15.3 The railways of Africa in the 1970s

Indian labourers to work on the Uganda railway (Morgan, 1973, p. 152). All the railways consist of narrow single tracks which are capable of carrying light loads and at very slow speeds. However, where the volume of available traffic is sufficient to justify greater investments, some stretches of a few national railways have been rebuilt to allow heavier trains and engines

and in Ghana, the line from Tarkwa to Takoradi has since been doubled to enable it to cope with the heavy traffic along this stretch.

The commissioning in 1975 of the new 1,860 km Tanzam railway from Dar-es-Salaam to Kapiri Moshi in Zambia has produced a major trans-continental railway link from Lobito in Angola to Dar-es-Salaam in

Tanzania. Apart from this new link and the older Lobito–Beira link through Zambia and Zimbabwe, the different railway systems of each country are generally unconnected. Unfortunately, future unification of the lines is greatly hampered by the great variations in gauges, couplings and brake systems. Yet there is a great need for such unification to promote trans-frontier rail traffic with mutual utilization of wagons, coaches and skilled personnel. The greatest difficulties appear to be created by the existing five different types of gauges – 1·435, 1·067, 1·000, 0·950 and 0·762 m – in the major main lines (Kampfe, 1973).

In spite of the shortcomings noted above, the railway, which is most suitable for bulk haulage over long distances, has played a major role in the economic development of tropical Africa. Before the Nigerian tin fields near Jos were linked by rail to Port Harcourt, it took as much as thirty-five days to transport tin ore from Jos to the coast for export (Hodder, 1959). Part of this journey involved carrying tin by headloads for a distance of over 320 km from Jos to the Benue River port of Loko, a journey which took twelve days! At Loko, the tin ore was loaded into barges bound for Forcados in the Niger Delta from where it was exported to England. The railway, which reached Jos in 1927, reduced this journey to about one day and made it possible for larger quantities to be transported. Railways have made possible the development of the vast copper reserves of Katanga and northern Zambia, the mining of iron ore in various parts of West Africa and constitute a major source of revenue to Mozambique from transit trade with South Africa, Zimbabwe, Zambia, Malawi and southern Zaïre.

The more important main line railways include:
1. The 1,280 km (800 mile) Dakar–Niger line from Dakar to Koulikoro, via Kayes. The construction of this 1·000 m line started in 1885 but did not reach Kayes until 1923, although the Kayes–Koulikoro stretch linking the Senegal River to the River Niger had been completed by 1906. It was this line that stimulated groundnut production in Senegal and resulted in the westward movement of population to the groundnut belt.
2. The 660 km (410 mile) 1·000 m gauge Conakry–Niger line from Conakry to Kaukau. This line, started in 1900, passes through very difficult country and was built at great cost of lives, materials and money. Steep gradients and sharp curves are common. The line reached Kouroussa on the upper Niger in 1911 and Kankan in 1914 and became the first of the four projected railways of French West Africa to link the River Niger to the coast. It therefore served as a temporary outlet for south-eastern Mali until the completion in 1923 of the Dakar–Niger link.
3. The 1,140 km (710 mile) Abidjan–Niger line from

Abidjan to Ouagadougou in Upper Volta. Construction started in 1903 but progress was very slow because of poor port facilities, lack of funds, steep gradients, difficult forest country and resistance to French colonization by some inland ethnic groups. By 1934 the line had reached Bobo-Dioulasso which remained the inland terminal until the end of the Second World War when the line was extended to Ouagadougou. This line provides a major link with the very densely settled Mossi country of Upper Volta which exports a large amount of agricultural labour to the Ivory Coast.
4. The railways of southern Ghana which consist of only 950 km of line of 1·067 m gauge, but carry almost as much tonnage per year as all the lines of French-speaking West Africa. In 1967–8 the tonnage carried by the Ghana railways was 84 per cent of that carried by the much longer Nigerian railways. The Ghana railways serve the gold mines of Obuasi and Prestea, the diamond mines of Oda and Kade, and the bauxite mines of Awaso as well as the rich timber forests and cocoa belt of south-western Ghana. Note that the Ghana railways serve only the southern third of the country.
5. The 3,200 km (2,000 mile) Nigeria railway (gauge 1·067 m) which consists of a western main line from Lagos to Kano and an eastern main line from Port Harcourt to Maiduguri. The older western line started from Lagos in 1898 and reached the important cocoa-growing centre of Ibadan in 1901. The eastern line was built in 1916 to link the Enugu coalfields to the new port of Port Harcourt. Both lines, which are characterized by numerous curves, were later extended to the far north to serve the groundnut and cotton-growing districts of Kano and Zaria respectively and the Jos Plateau tin mines.
6. The Cameroun railways. These consist of a short northern line (about 160 km) from Douala through difficult country to N'Kongsamba at the foothills of the Cameroun Highlands; and a central line which the Germans had planned to link Douala with Lake Chad. At the beginning of French rule, the central line had only reached Eseka, but was later extended to the capital city of Yaoundé. This central line now forms part of the trans-Cameroun railway to the northern terminal of N'Gaoundéré, with a branch line to the nearby rich bauxite deposits. The current plan is to further extend this 1·000 m line to link Sarh in Chad Republic and Bangui in the Central African Republic.
7. The short but important Congo–Ocean railway in Congo Republic which connects the Zaïre River port of Brazzaville with the ocean port of Point Noire. It has a 1·067 m gauge and covers a distance of only 520 km, some of which consists of very difficult country with steep gradients, especially in the Mayombe Plateau area where the line passes through twelve tunnels, including the 1,690 m long Mount Bembe tunnel.

8. The Zaïre railways, which are operated by five different companies, and consist of three different systems: (a) the 'portage' system, (b) the Bas-Congo du Katanga (BCK) system and (c) the short (136 km) and insignificant 0·615 m gauge Mayumbe Railway Company line from Tshela to the sea port of Boma. Portage is by a combined rail–water system in which the railways have been built to circumvent the rapids and falls along the Lualaba–Zaïre River. It also includes the 840 km long Vicicongo line built to link the Uele region of upper Zaïre to the Zaïre waterways at Aketi. The most important of the Zaïre railways is the BCK system with a line length of 2,600 km, 1·067 m gauge. It serves the rich mineral districts of upper Katanga and upper Zambia. Originally the BCK system formed part of the 'portage' system since its main line was connected to the Lualaba River port of Bukama. It continued to form part of the 'portage' system when the line was extended in 1927 to Ilebo (Port Franqui) on the Kasai River, resulting in the reduction of the rail–river route from 3,576 km (2,235 miles) along the Lualaba–Zaïre route to 2,752 km (1,720 miles) along the Kasai–Zaïre route through Ilebo. In 1931 the BCK main line was connected with the Benguela railway in Angola thereby reducing considerably the distance and time for transporting minerals from the copper belt to the sea port.

9. The Benguela International Railway which serves central Angola and the copper belt. Work started on this 1·067 m gauge line in 1903 but it took another fifteen years before the line reached the Zaïre border and another three years before it linked up with the BCK line in 1931. There are in addition three domestic railways in Angola of which the most important is the Luanda–Malanje line which serves the rich agricultural and mining districts of northern Angola. This line is only 425 km long but there are plans to extend it eastwards and eventually to the diamond-mining district of the town of Portugalia on the Zaïre border. The Moçamedes–Serpa Pinto line (756 km) serves the Huila Plateau in the south and has a branch line to the iron-ore fields of Cassinga. There is also a private short railway from Porto Amboim to the coffee district town of Gabela.

10. The Mozambique railways with a track length of over 3,500 km of 1·067 m gauge. About two-thirds of the entire rolling stock is used for international traffic which is the main source of revenue. The oldest line from Maputo (Laurenço Marques), built between 1886 and 1890, was extended in 1894 to link the then Boer controlled Transvaal Republic to the port of Laurenço Marques. It now serves the rich mining and industrial Witwatersrand district, which provided about 80 per cent of the rail traffic to the port until 1955 when the Malvernia line or the Limpopo railway linking Zimbabwe to Maputo was opened. By 1962, the Milvernia line was transporting almost as much copper from the

Pl. 15.3 The Congo–Ocean Railway

183

copper belt as the older Beira line built between 1893–6. The Beira line also serves southern Malawi and now carries considerable domestic traffic following the opening in 1950 of the Tete branch line which serves the coalfields of Moatize and the Sena sugar estates. The newest and longest railway in the country is the northern Mozambique railway from Nacala to Villa Cabral. It is basically a domestic line and unlike the Mozambique and Beira railways, has been operating at a loss for many years. The construction in 1970 of a branch line to link southern Malawi now provides the Nacala line with international traffic.

11. The Zimbabwe railways with a total line length of over 4,300 km. The main line links the capital city of Salisbury with the important southern city of Bulawayo and passes through the mining districts in the centre of the country. Important branch lines include the Bulawayo–Wankie coalfield line which is linked to the Benguela railway through Zambia and Zaïre, the Salisbury–Umtali line which links up with the Beira line and the line from Gwelo to the Mozambique port of Maputo. The link between Bulawayo and Kimberley makes it possible for landlocked Zimbabwe to use the South African ports of Cape Town and East London.

12. The Zambian railway system built primarily to serve the mines of the copper belt. It is connected to the Benguela railway and through Zimbabwe to the Maputo main line railway. In 1975 the Tanzam railway linking Zambia to the Tanzanian port of Dar-es-Salaam was opened to traffic. This new line, which passes through districts with very rough terrain, provides Zambia with uninterrupted access to the sea following the break with Zimbabwe. It was built by Chinese technicians and was financed with a loan of ₦300 million from China. The 1,600 km Tanzam line took four years to build.

13. Tanzania railways which consist of a main line from the sea port of Dar-es-Salaam to the Lake Tanganyika port of Kigoma. The most important branch lines are the Tabora–Nwanza line and the Dar-es-Salaam–Arusha line. The main line was built by the Germans before the First World War and has a gauge of 1·000 m. Between 1948 and 1978 the Tanzania railways formed part of the East African Railways.

14. The Kenya–Uganda railway which originally consisted of a 900 km 1·000 m gauge line from Mombasa to the Lake Victoria port of Kisumu. The line was built between 1896 and 1901. In 1931 Kampala became the terminal of the main line from Mombasa through Nairobi. Considerable difficulties were encountered in building the line across the Kenya Highlands and the Rift Valleys. The major branch lines include the 360 km extension from Kampala to Kasese, a line which was completed in 1956 and which serves the Kilembe copper mines and the tea- and coffee-growing districts of Toro. There is also a major branch line from Tororo, through

Pl. 15.4 Illegal passengers aboard the Mauritanian Railway

the cotton-growing province of Lango to Pakwach on the northern tip of Lake Albert. The Nairobi–Nanyuki branch line serves the former White Highland agricultural districts of Kenya.

15. The Sudan railways which maintain the longest operated line length of 4,750 km (1·067 m gauge). Unlike most countries of tropical Africa the railways still play a dominant role in the movement of goods and passengers especially during the rainy season when the unsurfaced roads in the south become impassable. There are two main lines, the older north–south line from Wadi Halfa on the border with Egypt to Sennar, and an east–west line from Port Sudan through Kassala and Sennar to Wau in Bar-el-Ghazal province. The Wadi Halfa–Khartoum line was built in 1897–9 and was extended to Sennar in 1906, and in 1956 the north–south main line was further extended to the Al Rusayris Dam on the Blue Nile. The first link between Khartoum and Port Sudan was through the Atbara–Port Sudan branch line opened in 1906. The oldest section of the east–west main line which reached Waw in 1962 is the Sennar–Al Ubayyid stretch which was opened in 1911. The extension to the Darfur provincial terminal of Nyala was opened in 1959.

Road transport

The development of road transport started after the main rail lines had been built, largely because in the absence of any form of wheel transport, it was uneconomical to build roads before the era of the motor car. In many countries, the first roads were built to serve as feeder lines to the railways and thereby extend their commercial hinterland. In French West Africa, for example, the inland terminals of the Abidjan–Niger and

Benin–Niger railways, which have still not reached the Niger River, were connected by road to the Niger Valley. Roads were also built to connect various sections of the national railway systems and to link up important towns not served by a railway to the nearest railway station. Thus, in Nigeria Oyo was linked to Ibadan, Sokoto to Gusau, and Katsina to Kaura Namoda. From 1905 the Nigeria railway maintained a road transport fleet for carrying goods and passengers to the nearest railway station and thus became a major pioneer of road transport development in the country.

Most of the early roads followed the old bush tracks linking existing settlements and were generally badly aligned, narrow and characterized by steep gradients. Only small rivers could be bridged and almost every major colonial road had at least one ferry consisting of wooden platforms carried on canoes or steel barges. Some of these early roads have since been rebuilt and their wooden bridges replaced with solid steel and concrete bridges, resulting in the withdrawal of many ferry services. However, the great majority of roads in tropical Africa, including those built in recent years by some local government councils, fit the description of early roads. Indeed vast areas, especially the very sparsely settled districts, are still inaccessible to motor vehicles and in such areas the footpath remains as important in the 1980s as it was before 1900.

During the early colonial period and up to the end of the Second World War, the construction, improvement and maintenance of roads other than railway feeders received little or no attention. This was partly caused by lack of funds and also by the deliberate policy to prevent or minimize road competition with the government railways, most of which were already operating at a loss. It was not until the early 1960s when most countries became independent that road development received a high priority in the various national development plans. Many new earth roads have been built while the more important inter-city roads have been tarred. At the beginning of the 1980s most roads are still surfaced with laterite and many are impassable after a heavy rainstorm. Tarred roads degenerate rapidly in the forest belt where the rainfall is very heavy and may become much worse than laterite roads because of poor maintenance. In many countries, some tarred roads have been described as death traps and it is widely believed that their poor surfaces and characteristic narrow bridges have contributed considerably to the high accident rate and the relatively short life of motor vehicles in tropical Africa.

The road systems of tropical Africa consist of separate national and local networks, similar in some ways to the railway systems. There is, however, an increasing number of international road connections especially in East, West and southern tropical Africa.

Currently an east–west trans-Africa highway from Nairobi to Lagos is under construction by the governments of the various countries through which the route passes.

Road transport, except in a few countries such as Mali and Guinea where the government controls all sectors of the economy, is largely organized on a small scale by individuals or by a group of blood relations. Return on investment is quick although the risks are also high because of the high accident rate. Passenger services provided by private operators are generally unsatisfactory especially in countries where the dual-purpose mammy wagon, which carries both goods and passengers, is still common. There is usually no scheduled departure or arrival time and often the vehicles are overloaded and in a state of bad repair. A number of private companies have, however, emerged in some countries in recent years to provide efficient and reliable passenger services to some of the major cities.

Road and railway competition

In some countries, notably Nigeria, the government railways operated fleets of lorries to feed the railways with goods and passengers. These road services were gradually discontinued as private road transport operators became numerous enough to compete effectively with the railway by offering direct long-distance services without breaking bulk at railway stations. In many countries the road has now emerged as the most important means of transporting goods and passengers for both short and long distances. The consequent loss of traffic has worsened the already precarious finances of most government railways, and in Sierra Leone the main-line railroad from Freetown to Pendembu was

Pl. 15.5 Cutting through tropical rainforest to make a road

185

closed down in 1972 because it had operated at an annual deficit of about Le 1·1 million (Leone, currency of Sierra Leone; ₦2·2 million) for many years.

The fear of road competition has always been a source of concern to many governments. Indeed, in some countries laws were made to stop lorries taking traffic from the railways and before 1930 road building was largely restricted to areas not served by railways. Some large towns already linked by a railway were not provided with a road link while the road distance for towns provided with both railway and road links was deliberately made to be much longer than the rail distance. This policy has since changed and it is now common to find major roads running parallel to railways, hence the increasing transfer of traffic to the roads, even for long-distance bulk cargo traffic for which the railways are traditionally considered to be more suitable.

Shorter transit time, regularity of service and flexibility in terms of choice of routes and door-to-door conveyance are the main advantages of road transport. Both the time spent at the railway terminal and the transit time are always much greater. Often the trains are late and a journey may be cancelled at short notice. Speed restrictions to about 65 km per hour on many lines are generally adhered to while road transporters ignore with impunity the speed limit of 56 km per hour for lorries and trailers. There are also the delays at intermediary railway stations. A journey by rail from Kano to Lagos, for example, takes about three times as long as the journey by road. Of course it is generally safer to travel by rail but the incidence of theft in railway coaches is much greater. Time-conscious travellers and shippers of perishable goods therefore prefer to use the road even though the cost of road transport is now much higher. In addition, the introduction of passenger bus services in place of the mammy wagon has made road transport much more comfortable than the rail passenger service in tropical African countries. And finally lorries and big trailers can carry out a door-to-door service unlike the railway.

Part of the problem with the shaky finances of government railways *vis-à-vis* the booming and fast-expanding road transport sector is the fact that the government establishes the upper limits on fares and freight rates chargeable by the railway while road transporters vary their charges according to the market situation. Another consideration is that while the railway company or corporation builds and maintains its own tracks, signal system and terminal facilities, the road transport operator simply puts his vehicle on highways built and maintained by the government and uses terminal facilities provided by local government authorities. The road transporter is therefore in a position to operate at a cost far below real costs and yet he is 'allowed' to charge up to 6 kobo per tonne mile in Nigeria, as compared with only 2·65 kobo per tonne mile which the railway is 'permitted' to charge (Oshosanwo, 1973).

The inherent problems of the railway should not create the impression that the railway age in tropical Africa is over. It continues to play a key role in transporting timber and mineral ore in many countries, especially Zaïre, Liberia, Zambia and Zimbabwe. More mineral lines are under construction and future modernization featuring the introduction of comfortable fast express services of the British or Japanese type may resuscitate passenger traffic especially in view of the very high accident rate on the roads.

Sea ports and shipping

Tropical Africa has a comparatively short and straight coastline with only a few narrow inlets and even fewer natural or hospitable harbours. River estuaries, which usually provide suitable shelter for ships, are often too shallow or blocked by offshore bars, while the great River Niger enters the sea through a confused network of narrow distributaries. The late penetration of Africa by European powers has often been attributed to what is described as the inhospitable and uninviting coasts. It appears difficult to sustain this view when the coasts of tropical Africa are compared with those of India and Australia. It is true that the coast of West Africa has very few inlets since the lagoons which occur along parts of the coast are often completely shut off from the sea. It is also true that the coral reefs which provide shelter for small crafts along the coast of East Africa also constitute an impediment to modern shipping. But there are a considerable number of natural harbours suitable for port development, especially along that part of the Indian Ocean coast lying south of the Equator. The more prominent of these harbours include Maputo, Kilindini (Mombasa), Nacala, Beira, Porto Amelia, Dar-es-Salaam and Quelima. The major concentration of good natural harbours occurs along the 2,790 km coastline of Mozambique. Along the Atlantic Coast, the only good natural harbours are Freetown, Lobito, Luanda, Libreville and Banjul.

Sea ports are both gateways and terminals for external trade. It is for this reason that countries that are not fortunate enough to have natural harbours have had to construct artificial ones, a fact which played an important part in the proliferation of primitive sea ports during the early days of shipping along the coasts of tropical Africa. In West Africa, for example, most of the 'sea ports' of the pre-colonial period consisted of open roadsteads which could not admit ships. The ships had to anchor offshore so that cargo might be discharged on to surf boats. The coastal chiefs held jurisdiction over the waters within their kingdoms and acted as middlemen in the trade between the inland people and European traders. According to Cowan (1935) trouble began immediately there was any attempt by European traders to proceed inland to trade directly with the inland people. The coastal chiefs constituted themselves into local port authorities, hence the proliferation of primitive ports especially in Ghana which had over twenty-five at the beginning of the colonial period.

In the colonial period scarce capital and skill were concentrated in developing a few ports suitably located to provide adequate facilities for modern shipping in order to serve the new colonial economy. Many new ports were created by building artificial harbours while some existing ports with natural harbours were developed. Most primitive ports, especially those not linked by road or railway to the hinterland, completely disappeared while some reverted to their original status as fishing settlements.

Space does not permit the discussion of individual ports. Three groups of ports, namely the ports of West Africa, the other Atlantic ports and the east coast or Indian Ocean ports, are therefore recognized for the brief discussion that follows.

One of the oldest and largest of modern ports in West Africa is the artificial port of Dakar which can accommodate thirty-three ships along its 4·8 km of quays and 225 hectares of protected waters. The surplus capacity of the port has increased since the disbanding of the former Federation of French West Africa. Other important modern ports in West Africa include Abidjan, the large artificial port of Tema, Cotonou, Conakry, Lagos and Port Harcourt. Unlike Dakar, the Nigerian ports of Lagos and Port Harcourt have suffered for years from chronic congestion, especially between 1972 and 1976 when over 200 ships used to wait for berthing space at Lagos. The opening of the new Tin Can Island port complex at Lagos (1978) and the redevelopment of the ports of Warri, Sapele, Koko and Calabar have helped to reduce the congestion at Lagos and Port Harcourt. Freetown Port, which has the best natural harbour in West Africa, has not been extensively developed owing to lack of funds and the small size of its trade. Limited hinterland is also responsible for the undeveloped state of the Gambian port of Banjul (Bathurst) which is served by a good natural waterway.

Of the other Atlantic ports of tropical Africa, the most important are Douala, Libreville, Point Noire, Matadi and Lobito. Douala is the main sea port of Cameroun and is blessed with a rich hinterland which includes southern Chad. The harbour is, however, shallow and a larger port is planned for Victoria. Libreville and Port Gentil serve the sparsely populated small country of Gabon which has rich timber, agricultural and mineral resources. None of the ports has good road connections with the hinterland and

none of them was chosen to serve as the outlet for the vast iron-ore fields of Belinga. A new port has been built at Owendo, 12 km south of Libreville, for the export of iron ore from Belinga which is being linked by the only railway in the country to the new port of Owendo. Of much greater importance is the artificial port of Point Noire built in 1934–9 and linked by rail to Brazzaville. The chief exports of Point Noire are timber, palm produce and minerals. Matadi, which is located on the Zaïre Estuary, is the only important ocean terminal for the vast and potentially rich country of Zaïre. The size of its trade has been adversely affected by the problems of navigating the Zaïre River and the resultant diversion of traffic from Zaïre to the ports of Lobito and Beira. The last important Atlantic port is Lobito which was opened in 1928 and serves as the major outlet for Katanga, the Zambian copper belt and northern Angola.

Along the east coast the most important ports are Maputo, Beira and Nacala, all in Mozambique, and the ports of Dar-es-Salaam and Mombasa. Maputo has an excellent natural harbour with several deep-water channels for large ocean vessels. Its 3 km waterfront takes up to twenty vessels at a time and in addition to general cargo, there are facilities for handling crude oil and timber. The modern port, opened in 1903, serves as the principal outlet for the Transvaal, Zimbabwe, Swaziland and sometimes Zambia. The tonnage handled at the port exceeds 11 million per year. Beira, the second largest port of Mozambique, has a comparatively shallow harbour and is more difficult to enter and leave, especially at low tide. It is a river port located about

Pl. 15.6 The natural harbour at Dar-es-Salaam

24 km from the open sea in the estuary of the Pungue River. Much of the transit trade to Zimbabwe formerly handled by Beira now goes through Maputo, but Beira is still the principal outlet for Malawi. The newest modern port in Mozambique is Nacala which was opened in 1947. The natural harbour of Nacala is described as the finest along the eastern coastline and one of the best in the world (Brandenburg, 1969). It is located in the deep and wide bay of Fernao Veloso which is about 13 km long and 3–6 km wide. Nacala serves the northern half of Mozambique and has recently been linked by rail to southern Malawi.

Dar-es-Salaam, the main sea port of Tanzania, has a sheltered but relatively small harbour with a narrow entry. In addition to serving the vast hinterland of central and north-western Tanzania, Dar-es-Salaam handles considerable traffic to and from Zaïre through the Lake Tanganyika port of Kigoma to which it is linked by rail. The opening of the 1,800 km long Tanzam railway in 1975 has further extended the port's hinterland to include the Zambian copper belt. The physical limitations of the port site are, however, unlikely to permit the level of development of facilities available in the naturally better-endowed port of Mombasa, which has a better and more spacious harbour. As the principal port of Kenya, Mombasa serves the rich agricultural districts of the Kenya Highlands and the Lake Victoria shores as well as land-locked Uganda.

Most of the ships using the ports of tropical Africa belong to foreign shipping companies, largely of British, French, Portuguese, American and Japanese origin. Indeed, until 1960, when most African countries became independent, only Liberia had a sizeable merchant fleet which consisted largely of foreign-owned vessels flying the Liberian flag. There are now several indigenous shipping companies, owned both by governments and private companies especially in Nigeria, Ghana and Ethiopia, the major ones being the Nigerian National Shipping Line and the Black-Star Line of Ghana.

Pipeline transport

One of the cheapest modes of transporting liquid products over long distances is by pipeline which now dominates the transportation of petroleum (crude and refined) and natural gas in some developed countries of the world. The problem with pipeline transportation, however, is that it still requires a large number of road vehicles and rail tank cars for onward transportation from the pipeline terminal. In tropical Africa the use of pipelines is largely restricted to transporting crude oil from oilfields to the crude-oil terminals. In 1980 the only exceptions were the crude-oil pipelines from Dar-es-Salaam in Tanzania to the oil refinery at Ndola in

Zambia, and the pipeline from the port of Beira in Mozambique to the oil refinery at Umtali in Zimbabwe. Pipelines also supply crude oil from Warri in the Niger Delta oilfields to the new refinery at Kaduna in northern Nigeria. Other pipelines in Nigeria which are expected to be in commission before 1982 are the Warri–Benin–Ore–Ikorodu line, the Lagos–Ikorodu–Ibadan–Ilorin line, the Port Harcourt–Enugu–Makurdi line and extensions of the Kaduna line to Jos, Gombe, Maiduguri and Kano.

It appears strange that, with the exception of Zambia, pipelines have not become popular in the transportation of petroleum to the landlocked countries of tropical Africa. Yet pipelines can be readily laid through creeks, rivers and swamps which usually prove a serious impediment to road construction. In addition, the supply of petroleum through pipelines is not only more steady and reliable (usually at a speed of 5–6 km per hour), but also more secure. The extensive damage done to roads and bridges by heavy-duty petrol tankers, which are also a major source of road accidents in countries like Nigeria, are well known and could be considerably reduced by the use of pipelines. Most landlocked countries are however too poor to afford a refinery that would necessitate the construction of a crude-oil pipeline; nor can they afford to build pipelines for refined petroleum. The Dar-es-Salaam–Ndola crude-oil pipeline serves a refinery located in an area of high petroleum consumption but was also constructed in pursuance of Zambian government policy to reduce economic dependence on Zimbabwe, Mozambique and South Africa.

Air transport

In view of the poor state of land transportation in tropical Africa, the importance of air transport for mail, passenger and high-value cargo cannot be over-emphasized. In general, however, emphasis has been on international services while domestic services are still not well developed, even in Nigeria where there has been an unprecedented demand for air transport since the oil boom of the early 1970s. In most of the other countries the high cost of air travel has largely restricted the number of customers to a small group consisting of senior government officials, diplomats and company executives.

With the exception of the smaller countries such as Gambia, the Republic of Benin and Rwanda, each country operates a national airline which has a monopoly over internal flights. In practice, however, it is only a few countries such as Nigeria, Ethiopia, Kenya and Zimbabwe that can afford to purchase outright a few large aircraft for domestic services. Most of these government airlines still operate at a loss and have virtually become service establishments rather than economic ventures. The only example of an efficient and profitable airline in tropical Africa is Air Afrique which is owned by OCAM (Afro-Malagasy Common Organization) – Cameroun withdrew from Air Afrique in 1971 to set up its own airline. Air Afrique is currently the only multinational airline in tropical Africa, following the break-up of the East African Airways in 1975. The bigger commercial firms and petroleum companies use small private planes or charter flights for their business.

The number of airports, almost all of which are owned and maintained by government corporations, has increased considerably since 1960. Each national capital city has an international airport of which the largest include Lagos, Dakar, Abidjan, Nairobi, Salisbury and Kinshasa. Nigeria now has six international airports although only two, Kano and Lagos, are commonly used.

Communications

In pre-colonial times, drumming was the standard form of communication over long distances in most parts of tropical Africa, and is still commonly used today in many rural areas. Drumming was used to summon village meetings and to announce the approach of an enemy. Coded messages were passed from one village to another by specialist drummers. Messages were also sent by specially composed poems through messengers who often recited the messages without necessarily understanding their meaning. These 'primitive' means of communication continue today largely because of the undeveloped state of modern communication systems, in spite of the widespread adoption of the transistor radio.

During the early colonial period the modern postal system was established and with the spread of education the demand for post offices and postal agencies increased. In addition to handling mail, the post office was also the base of early telecommunications which consisted of telegraph lines established to link each territory with the metropolitan country in Europe. Internal communications links within each territory were not fully developed until after the Second World War, when the telephone system was expanded and improved and when the introduction of the teleprinter resulted in considerable improvement in traditional telegraph techniques. Contact between the colonial territories, however, took place by way of large trunk line exchanges in Europe, a situation which remained unchanged until 1968 when the 4,000 km radio-electric link between Addis Ababa and Abidjan was opened. The African telecommunications development programme of which the

Ethiopia–Ivory Coast link represents the first stage, continues, and some countries, such as Nigeria, Kenya and Zimbabwe, have since established satelite telecommunications. However, for most countries, a telephone call from one capital city to another still has to be relayed through a European capital, usually London, Paris or Brussels.

Newspapers and the radio have literally revolutionized the communications situation in tropical Africa even though the literate group who read the increasing number of newspapers are still in the minority. Fortunately many newspapers publish a weekly edition in at least one African language. The position with the radio is happily much better following the establishment of many local sub-radio stations which broadcast news in local African languages, in addition to English, French or Portuguese broadcasts. Today the transistor radio is available in the most remote areas and many young nomadic cattle rearers in West Africa are commonly seen listening to local music and news while watching over their cattle. In addition to news, various announcements, including commercial advertisements, now get to most people through the radio rather than the drum. Television services are still not widespread since the number of people who can afford a set is greatly limited.

References
Brandenburg, F. (1969), 'Transport Systems and External Ramifications', in D. M. Abshire and M. A. Samuels (eds.), *Portuguese Africa – A Handbook*, Pall Mall Press, London, pp. 320–44.

Cowan, A. A. (1935), 'Early Trading Conditions in the Bight of Biafra', Part I, *African Affairs*, 34, pp. 391–402.

Fitzgerald, W. (1957), *Africa: A Social, Economic and Political Geography of Its Major Regions*, Methuen & Co, London, p. 298.

Hodder, B. W. (1959), 'Tin Mining on the Jos Plateau of Nigeria', *Economic Geography*, 35, pp. 109–22.

Kampfe, I. K. (1973), 'Unification of African Railways', *Applied Science and Development*, Institute for Scientific Co-operation, Federal Republic of Germany, 2, pp. 96–121.

Morgan, W. T. W. (1973), *East Africa*, Longman, London, p. 152.

Oshosanwo, M. O. D. (1973), *Economics of Rail Transport*, Workshop on Third National Development Plan, 1975–80, University of Ibadan, The Railway Printer, Lagos, p. 13.

Taaffe, E. J., Morrill, R. L. and Gould, P. R. (1963), 'Transport Expansion in Underdeveloped Countries: A Comparative Analysis', *Geographical Review*, 53, pp. 503–29.

Ullman, E. L. (1956), 'The Role of Transportation and the Bases for Interaction' in W. L. Thomas (ed.), *Man's Role in Changing the Face of the Earth*, University of Chicago Press, Chicago, pp. 862–80.

16   Markets and Marketing Systems

A market is a site where sellers and buyers assemble on specific days to exchange goods and services. Markets are indigenous institutions throughout West Africa, North Africa and in parts of the Nile Basin, Ethiopia, the Somali Republic and southern Zaïre. We shall refer to these indigenous markets as traditional markets which are distinct in many ways from the modern markets established in recent years in the major urban centres of various countries.

Traditional markets are not only important as centres for the exchange of goods, ideas and fashions, but also perform significant social and political functions in the community. Amongst many communities, local spirits are believed to live in trees located in and around market places where these spirits are believed to meet at night. Often, sacrifices are made to these market spirits to ensure peace in the locality. In Yorubaland, for example, the branches of trees in the market place are cut off when an *oba* (king) dies to ensure that market spirits join in mourning the *oba*. Amongst some ethnic groups, including the Ibibio, major social functions such as marriages, the end of confinement after childbirth and the laying of the ghost of the dead always terminate with an outing ceremony to the market place. The religious importance of traditional markets is therefore considerable. Indeed, it was the traditional market place that served as the main centre for preaching the Gospel by early Christian missionaries! Today the market place also serves as a meeting point for political campaigns and for advertising new products, including new varieties of seeds.

Origins and distribution of traditional markets

There are two main theories about the origin of market institutions. The first and most widely held theory is that markets develop because of the need of the individual to barter, resulting in the necessity for local exchange; that the division of labour encourages local exchange and the establishment of local markets, only a few of which eventually become important market centres associated with long-distance trade. The following two quotations illustrate this view:

Barter exists amongst the most isolated and inaccessible societies; and the wordless exchange of goods made without witnesses (silent trade) in the jungle in Asia, America and Africa is evidence of an economic need. As confidence grows between individuals exchanging their respective goods, local markets spring up . . . (ILO, 1953)

As an economy changes from a self-sufficient to a commercial or exchange system, there appear on the landscape facilities for the collection, exchange and distribution of commodities including goods and services produced in spatially separated, specialized production places. (Stine, 1962)

The second theory of market origins is that markets are brought about primarily by external trade in which complementary products are exchanged with foreigners, and that local markets grow up to serve the needs of long-distance trade. Those who support this

Fig. 16.1 The idealized sequence of events leading to the growth of markets

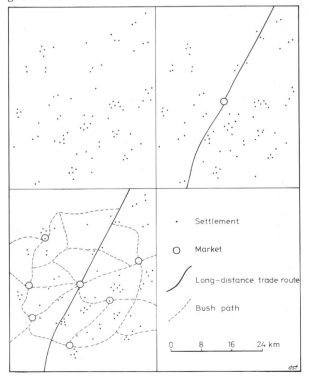

viewpoint argue that trade, with its associated market phenomenon, can never arise within a community. The sequence of development of local markets is presented as follows: 1. a trade route passes through a given district; 2. a market is established on this route and grows to become a major trade centre; 3. local markets develop around the main market. This sequence is presented in Fig. 16.1.

In West Africa, which has by far the largest number of traditional markets, the evidence in support of the second theory is overwhelming (Hodder, 1965). The most important markets in the area started and grew up as a result of the long-distance trade between 1. the forest belt of Guinea and the western Sudan and 2. the grasslands of the western Sudan and the Mediterranean world (across the Sahara Desert). Markets in the first group included Benin, Kumasi, Onitsha, Jega, Ouagadougou and Zaria, while markets involved in the trans-Saharan trade included Segou, Timbuktu, Katsina and Zinder. There were also similar markets along the coast at the points of contact between the farmers of the forest belt and the coastal fishing groups such as the Ijaw of the Niger Delta and the Kru of the Ivory Coast. Important trade goods in West Africa included gold, kolanuts, slaves, leather goods, gun powder and cotton cloth.

Traditional markets in Ethiopia and the Horn of Africa are also associated with external trade. In the Somali Republic, for example, Lewis reports that caravans laden with goods continually traverse the country, especially during the season of the coastal fairs, when the produce of the interior is traded for imports brought from Aden and India (Lewis, 1955, p. 79). Today, many of the modern towns in that country have developed from market villages established along these caravan routes. The Galla people of Ethiopia also have many traditional markets and are known to have been involved in long-distance trade with the coastal areas of the Somali Republic in pre-colonial times.

In the northern parts of the Sudan, including the Gezira district, traditional markets are associated with both long-distance trade and with the need for the local exchange of products between the contrasted communities of the Nile Valley and the arid hinterland (Culwick, 1951, p. 24). In its natural state the Sudanese environment does not support self-sufficient peasantries, with the result that from time immemorial, the local people have developed a strong 'trading mentality', with the exception of the pastoralists. Markets, which are important foci of economic activities and social life in northern Sudan, are therefore rooted in the history and culture of the area.

In East Africa rural markets are very few and much less developed compared with those of West Africa. In the past only a few ethnic groups such as the Kikuyu of Kenya and the Ganda of Uganda had some weakly developed traditional markets which were based largely on long-distance caravan trade, although the Kikuyu also traded with their own ethnic sub-groups and with neighbouring peoples. Kikuyu trade with large caravans was not conducted at fixed market places as in West Africa. The caravans had to seek the Kikuyu and arrange a time and place for holding a market. This would usually be attended by hundreds of men and women laden with the superfluous produce of their fields, which they were very glad to dispose of. Trade with their Masai neighbours was carried out by assembling at the frontier; Kikuyu traders were conducted by Masai friends to meet Masai traders in the villages where they exchanged their field crops for sheep and cattle; after this they were escorted back to the frontier by these friends. Those Masai who wanted to enter Kikuyuland for the purpose of trade adopted the same method. In other parts of East Africa, there were no local markets and no regular internal trade before the colonial period. Local markets were established by the government after 1900, and most of them after the Second World War (Jones, 1972, p. 209). The prominent position of alien traders, mostly Arabs and Asians, in the commerce of East Africa is largely due to the poor development of traditional markets in the sub-region.

The total absence of traditional markets in southern and Central Africa is not only difficult to explain, but has proved to be a great disincentive to local trade and production. In Botswana, where about 85 per cent of the population live in rural areas and where livestock production accounts for over 80 per cent of the total agricultural output, there are no traditional markets. The practice in this country is for anyone who wishes to sell or buy anything to inquire among his neighbours until he finds a customer, after which the transaction is concluded directly between them (Schapera, 1953, p. 29). Indeed as late as 1978, the government had established only three markets: in the capital, Gaborone (32,700), Francistown (24,000) and Mochudi. There were no markets in the other two urban centres of Lobatse (15,000) and Selebi-Pikure (21,000) nor in the major villages of Molepolole, Kasane and Maun. There is also no evidence of the existence of traditional markets in Zambia, Namibia, Zimbabwe, Swaziland, Lesotho and South Africa.

Finally, although North Africa is outside tropical Africa, it is important to record that the large number of traditional markets in this sub-region is associated with long-distance trade with Europe in the north and the West African Sudan in the south. In Morocco, for example, there were no towns before the colonial period. The scattered rural population of the country

Pl. 16.1 Fruit seller at Dar-es-Salaam market

was served by a large number of traditional weekly (periodic) markets called the *suq*, which are still held in the open, at predetermined sites, and which are completely deserted during the rest of the week. The Moroccan *suq* meets in the morning for a few hours, after which the market begins to break up, so that by nightfall the site is completely empty again. The *suq* is therefore a rural periodic day market (Mikesell, 1958).

Whatever the origins of rural periodic markets, an element of specialization is necessary for its survival. Specialization results in the emergence of part-time and full-time traders to serve a predominantly farming population. Since rural markets and some urban markets meet once in four or eight days, full-time traders are obliged to move about from one market to another in order to stay in business. Such traders are therefore essentially itinerant. It is also reasonable to argue that a minimum threshold population is necessary

to sustain a stable market and that *ipso facto*, markets cannot develop in very sparsely settled areas such as are to be found in the rural areas of Botswana, Namibia and Zambia.

Types and location of markets

Markets in tropical Africa can be classified in terms of the size of the population attending, the market's physical form, the order and kind of goods, the location and the timing or periodicity. In this section we consider the two most basic geographic attributes of the markets, namely their periodicity or timing and their location. On this basis, there are five major types of traditional market: 1. urban daily markets, 2. urban night markets, 3. rural daily markets, 4. rural periodic night markets and 5. rural periodic day markets.

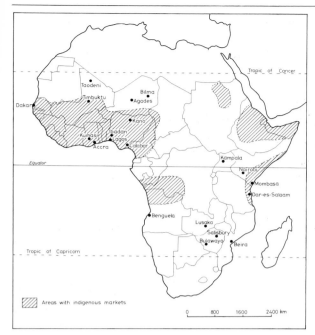

Fig. 16.2 Areas with indigenous markets

The rural periodic day market is by far the most common. Its main function is to serve as a centre for the exchange of commodities for a dispersed but sedentary population engaged primarily in farming, collecting and crafts. The frequency of market meetings varies considerably, depending on historical and social factors, but in most cases, the markets meet every four days or every eight days. On each market day, numerous itinerant or mobile traders converge on the market place from different directions. The local rural population, who spend the other days of the week on their farms, also converge on the market square. Those of them who are so inclined, also occasionally attend any of the long-distance urban daily markets. The vast majority of rural people, however, prefer to attend the periodic day markets rather than travel long distances to daily markets which are usually located in urban centres. Thus most visitors to rural markets willingly submit themselves to the discipline of time in order to be in a position to free themselves from the discipline of space (distance) (Stine, 1962).

Accessibility is a major consideration in the location of rural markets and in some countries, the critical factor is the availability of a reliable source of water supply. Although some markets are located within village settlements, it is surprising that the size of the population of rural settlements appears to have no influence on the choice of most market sites. Indeed many of the larger markets are not located in villages but at road junctions, usually lying between two or

three villages (Scott, 1972). In Yorubaland, this situation has been attributed to general insecurity resulting from local warfare. In this part of Africa, where markets have existed from time immemorial, it was the practice during inter-village wars for women, who still dominate the market scene in Yorubaland, to meet and trade on neutral ground, while the opposing warriors remained at a distance on either side.

A large number of traditional markets are located close to a shrine or religious sanctuary in the belief that the markets will be protected by sacred authority. It is also generally accepted that any men, including warriors, who disturb the peace of the market will be visited by misfortune. Additionally, the location of markets between rather than within village settlements ensures that the markets are readily accessible to several communities and further emphasizes the fact that markets are common property.

There are many instances in which the market, originally located in an open clearing, has in fact created the village, usually at the expense of existing neighbouring villages. This is often the case when a major road suitable for cars passes through the market site. Villages created by markets come into being as a result of the need to store on the site some trade goods which are bulky and therefore cumbersome to move about. Stores of different types are built and watched over by a nucleus population which subsequently grows as people desert the older villages to build houses near the road. Examples of villages created by roadside markets abound in Yorubaland and include Akinyele and Ojo on the road from Ibadan to Oyo (Fig. 16.3).

The distance which rural people can or are willing to travel, given the means of transport at their disposal, is important in the spacing of rural markets. In Yorubaland, most hamlets and villages are located about 8–10 km from a market, and this compares favourably with the average distance of 11 km observed in preindustrial Europe. 10 km appears to be the convenient maximum distance to walk from home to market and back within the same day. In localities where animal transport is used, the greatest distance that people are willing to travel to a market increases to 15–20 km. It is also a fact that markets which meet on the same day are usually physically further apart from each other.

Periodicity and the market ring system

Before the imposition of the seven-day week by the colonial powers, most of black Africa operated a four-day or an eight-day week. In West Africa, periodic day markets operated on a ring system which continues today (Hodder, 1965; Eighmy, 1972). Each market ring is composed of a complete and integrated sequence of markets taking place over a period of four days or multiples of four days. Amongst the Ibo of Nigeria, the four market days are *Eke*, *Orie*, *Afo* and *Nkwo*, in that order. The Ekiti Yoruba four-day week is also market oriented and is made up of *ojọ oja* (market day), *ojọ keji oja* (market's second day) *ojọ kẹta ọja* (market's third day), and *oja d'ọla* (market day is tomorrow).

Periodic markets are a characteristic feature of the rural landscape of pre-industrial societies and were once very common in Europe. They serve a predominantly agricultural population which can only afford to attend the market once in a while. Specialized periodic markets are also common in some urban centres, notably in Yorubaland, a good example being the famous Oje cloth market in Ibadan City which takes place every sixteen days. In general terms, the periodic markets survive because the professional traders in rural areas have to move from one market site to another in order to obtain a threshold (minimum) population of buyers to keep them in business. The urban trader, on the other hand, is able to remain fixed in one location throughout the week because the minimum threshold population is available in the city. It follows that the greater the population of effective buyers of a commodity, the greater the chances of the market becoming a daily one since the trader (dealer) will become fixed at a particular site instead of moving from one periodic market to another.

A market is not only a source of income but also an important symbol of prestige to the village in whose territory it is located, hence the tendency towards market proliferation in certain parts of West Africa. However, since the people recognize that a minimum threshold population is required for any market to survive and prosper, it is usual for neighbouring villages or groups to arrange to hold their markets on days that will prevent clashes. Markets that meet every eight days are of a higher order than four-day periodic markets and generally attract a much larger population of buyers and sellers. Also, in keeping with the central place theory, the eight-day markets are less numerous and more widely spaced out than the four-day markets. A few first-order periodic markets or regional fairs such as the Abagwu market at Uzuakoli or the market at Uburu, near Afikpo (both in Iboland), are still held every twenty-four days. These first-order markets usually go on continuously for four days at a time and draw traders from distances of over 700 km.

The Akinyele market ring, which is located a few km north of Ibadan city, is shown in Fig. 16.3. There are eight markets in the ring, seven of which take place on successive days, so that there is one market-free day, after which the cycle begins again. It is clear

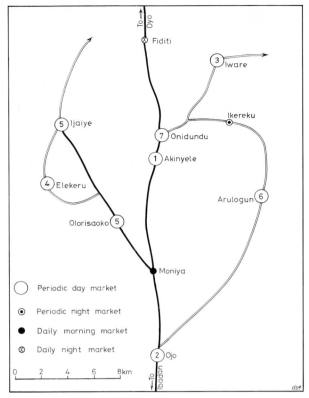

Fig. 16.3 The Akinyele market ring, Nigeria

from the order in which the markets meet that the ring operates in such a way that successive markets are not normally adjacent markets. The arrangement ensures that no hamlet or village is far from a market for more than three days. Full-time traders attend most of the markets while part-time traders attend at least two markets during the eight-day cycle (Hodder, 1961).

Characteristics of market sites

Most rural periodic markets consist of clearings measuring a few hundred sq m along the side of a road or bush path where buyers and sellers meet for about four hours on the market day. In the larger district markets, which meet for longer hours, there are usually a few crude shelters of thatched roofs supported by wooden poles. Such shelters are usually erected by the sellers, some of whom prefer to protect themselves from rain and the rays of the sun by using locally thatched mats of grass or palm leaves. In recent years, an increasing number of markets have been taken over by local government councils who provide more permanent stalls covered with corrugated iron roofs. Lock-up stores built with concrete are now a common feature

194

of all urban and some rural markets which are also provided with slaughter slabs.

Extreme congestion and deafening noise caused by endless haggling over prices are the most common characteristic features of African markets. Often the market population overflows into the road making it extremely hazardous to drive a car through the market site. But in spite of the apparent confusion that strikes the visitor, there is a definite order in the location of stalls for different goods and services as well as in the conduct of market affairs. Specialization of commodities in distinct areas is a feature of all markets and is carried out to such an extent that separate spaces or stalls are allocated to sellers of pepper, okra, dried fish, yams, cassava, textiles, rice, printed cotton cloth, locally made cloth and manufactured consumer items. Since women dominate the trade in local foodstuffs while some ethnic groups specialize in such commodities as stock fish, singlet garments and fresh fish, there is also a marked specialization by sex and ethnicity in most markets. Amongst other things, specialization by area facilitates price regulation and the enforcement of rules among members of commodity unions. Serious undercutting is made difficult and for some commodities such as garri, yams and kolanuts, bulking and loading into lorries is facilitated.

Poor sanitation is probably the most serious problem of African markets, especially those in urban areas. As a rule the market place is swept at the close of each day's business. This aspect of sanitation presents no problems in rural periodic markets. However, in urban daily markets, the amount of solid waste generated each day is often much more than the local government health department can cope with. This is particularly so during the rainy season when the market places become muddy and extremely filthy. Most urban markets are not provided with piped water nor with adequate public conveniencies. It is indeed very depressing to see food traders display their wares close to huge rubbish heaps and choked drainage channels or to watch fresh meat and fish on display being surrounded by an army of flies.

Market administration

The market is a public institution located on public land which is traditionally vested in the chief-in-council. Each major Yoruba town has a main market, the *oja oba* (the king's market) which is normally located in front of the house of the *bale* or *oba* of the town. Other markets in the town can only be opened after the performance of several rituals by palace servants on behalf of the *oba*. In the Bunyora Kingdom of Uganda, all traditional

Pl. 16.2 Up-country market in Kenya

markets 'belonged' to the king who had the sole right of appointing market masters. Even amongst the so-called stateless societies of south-eastern Nigeria, the village elders were charged with the responsibility for law and order in the market place.

A large number of markets in Africa were established as part of a deliberate policy to stimulate the use of money as well as to generate revenue. Such markets have therefore always been administered directly by or under the supervision of government agencies. Indeed, for the same reasons, indigenous market systems had to be regulated by the colonial administrations. Today almost every market is directly under the control of the local government which is responsible for appointing the market master, whose primary duty is to take charge of the general running and sanitation of the market place. Market tolls constitute an important source of revenue to some rural local government councils. Disturbances in the market place, formerly dealt with by palace servants, are now handled by the police. Trade disputes are, however, still referred to market elders in the first instance.

At the commodity level, the various traders in most urban markets are organized into associations each of which has a chairman or president who is responsible for the day-to-day administration of the association. Some of these urban traders' associations have been largely responsible for regulating the supply of some basic food items, thereby creating artificial scarcity and high prices with a view to increasing the profit margin of their members.

The larger modern metropolitan markets such as the multimillion-naira covered markets at Onitsha, Surulere (Lagos) and several others under construction are administered as corporate institutions.

Markets in the chain of distribution

In a predominantly but increasingly sophisticated rural setting markets play a very important role in the movement of goods from producers to consumers. We recognize for this purpose three marketing channels: 1. trading involving produce of the immediate locality, 2. the marketing of goods originating from specialized long-distance producing areas and 3. the distribution of manufactured goods, most of which were until recently imported from overseas. Commodities that are produced and marketed over a wide area include yams and garri in the forest belts, and maize, guinea corn and millet in the grassland areas. Such commodities are taken by producers to nearby periodic markets where the goods are collected, bulked and sent to the towns. Often the producers bypass the periodic markets and travel directly to sell their crops in urban daily markets.

Commodities like rice, kolanuts and dried fish, which are produced far away from the place of consumption,

are often collected and distributed by big-time urban foodstuff wholesalers. Wholesalers operate through agents stationed at the source of supply which they visit only occasionally and the supplies are usually delivered by lorry, some of which are owned by the wholesalers. Some food contractors supplying institutions such as the prisons and the universities also travel to distant markets to buy foodstuffs which are bulked and transported by lorries to the cities. Most contractors however obtain supplies from wholesalers who also sell in bulk to urban and rural retailers.

The marketing of export crops like palm kernels and cocoa follows the same channels as for foodstuffs originating from distant areas, but in this case the final purchaser and bulking agent is the Produce Marketing Board. In most countries textile mills and other factories buy raw materials such as cotton and groundnuts from the marketing boards and not directly from the small-scale producer. Manufactured goods, on the other hand, including those still imported from abroad, are distributed through agents and large commercial houses based in the cities. In countries such as Ghana and Nigeria, the distribution of manufactured goods is now restricted to indigenes or to companies in which at least 60 per cent of the share capital is owned by the citizens. In most other countries, aliens, notably Europeans and Asians, still control the wholesale and retail trade in manufactured goods. The distribution of such goods to the rural consumer follows the channels shown in the lower half of Fig. 16.4.

Fig. 16.4 Distribution channels for long-distance commodities

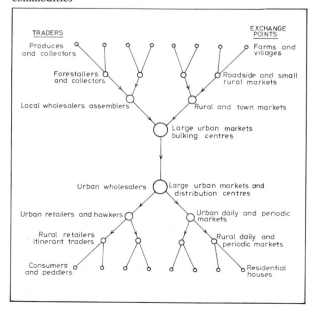

The traders

The large number of traders who supply and distribute goods and services in African markets fall into four categories, namely: 1. part-time traders, 2. professional petty-traders, 3. the big African traders and licensed buying agents and 4. the big trading firms, mainly exporters and importers.

Part-time traders, consisting mostly of women, include forestallers, collectors, peddlers and retailers handling local farm produce. In West Africa, forestalling points, which may be up to 2 km from the market place, are common along roads leading to rural periodic markets and even to urban daily markets. The forestallers are women who try to persuade women going to the market with farm produce to sell the items to them at slightly lower prices than those obtaining in the market. Each forestaller concentrates on one or two items and as soon as she has collected as much as she can afford to handle, she takes the items to the market to sell. Itinerant collectors go from one rural market to another to buy food items or export produce, such as palm kernel, which they bulk and transport for sale in urban markets or to licensed buying agents. Like women traders who retail local food items in rural markets, forestallers and collectors also combine trading with other occupations, mainly farming and crafts. Peddling of food items in the mornings and evenings is carried out by young children who go from house to house in the cities while young male adults dominate the peddling trade in manufactured goods.

Professional petty-traders are by far the most numerous and the most effective in the distribution of staple food crops and general merchandise. The small capital required to start petty trading (often less than ₦200 and the lack of alternative employment opportunities are largely responsible for the large number of people in the retail trade. The market women or market mammies of West Africa are professional petty-traders who deal in a wide range of merchandise or foodstuffs. Their wares, which are neatly displayed in stalls or in the open market place, have no price tags and weighing scales are rarely used except in the 'new' markets of East and southern Africa. Most of them depend on family labour and do not keep records of their sales. Some market women and male petty-traders are, however, very wealthy and have become very influential in politics and other spheres of public life.

The big African traders, such as the influential market women, are found mostly in West Africa. In

Pl. 16.3 Market woman at Bida market, Nigeria

other parts of tropical Africa, large-scale trade involving the long-distance transfer of goods is still controlled by Syrians, Lebanese and Indian traders. Some of them specialize as produce-buying agents while others are wholesalers dealing with staple food crops or with manufactured goods. Most traders in this category have standing arrangements with transporters to convey on a regular basis assembled commodities from rural areas or from the sea port to urban markets. Like the Syrian and Lebanese traders, the big African trader depends mostly on family labour. Those of them who are importers have been largely responsible for the increasing incidence of smuggling in the various countries.

Finally, we have the large exporting and importing trading firms which are heavily capitalized and still control the wholesale and retail trade in general merchandise in all countries except Ghana, Nigeria and Uganda. These big trading firms include the Compagnie Française de l'Afrique Occidental (CFAO), the Société Commerciale de l'Ouest Africain (SCOA), the United Africa Company (UAC) and John Holts. These foreign trading firms supply goods directly to African and some Asian retail traders. They also serve as licensed buying agents for agricultural exports or as direct exporters in some countries.

The changing market scene

The market landscape of tropical Africa has witnessed considerable changes since about 1950. On the one hand, a large number of periodic and daily markets have been established in those cultural areas where no markets existed before the colonial period. On the other hand there has been a decrease in the number of periodic markets in those areas where the market is an indigenous institution. In such areas, an increasing number of people now go to the market on bicycle, motor cycle or by lorry, and this means that longer distances can be covered, especially by itinerant traders. Rural areas have become more accessible so that an increasing number of rural people can now travel to town and back in the same day. One consequence of this is that many of the smaller periodic markets have disappeared. Markets in peri-urban areas in particular have been swallowed up by urban development so that some of them have become daily markets which now serve as forestalling points where foodstuffs are purchased early in the morning for resale in the nearby central city markets.

Periodic markets in most small urban centres have become daily markets since such urban centres now have a large enough population of wage-earners to support them. In addition the market landscape has featured the development of retail shops or lock-up stores within the market squares. Large modern market complexes are also being constructed in Nigeria at great expense to serve the larger metropolitan areas such as Ibadan, Onitsha and Sokoto.

However, the vast majority of tropical African peoples still live in rural areas, where farming is still the main occupation. In an ever-increasingly monetized economy, the importance of rural periodic markets must be recognized in planning for rural areas. Basic physical facilities at these rural markets are overdue, and must be provided since these markets yield considerable revenue in the form of market fees payable to the local government councils of the area in which the markets are located.

References

Culwick, G. M. (1951), *Diet in the Gezira Irrigated Area, Sudan*, Government Printing Press, Khartoum.

Eighmy, T. H. (1972), 'Rural Periodic Markets and the Extension of an Urban System: A Western Nigeria Example', *Economic Geography*, 48, pp. 299–315.

Hodder, B. W. (1961), 'Rural Periodic Day Markets in Part of Yorubaland', *Transactions of the Institute of British Geographers*, 29, pp. 149–59.

Hodder, B. W. (1965), 'Some Comments on the Origins of Traditional Markets in Africa South of the Sahara', *Transactions of the Institute of British Geographers*, 37, pp. 97–104.

ILO (1953), 'Indian Markets and Fairs in Latin America', in *Indigenous Peoples*, International Labour Organization, p. 65.

Jones, W. O. (1972), *Marketing Staple Crops in Tropical Africa*, Cornell University Press, New York.

Lewis, I. M. (1955), 'Peoples of the Horn of Africa', *Ethnographic Survey of Africa*. Southern Africa, Part 3, International African Institute, London.

Mikesell, M. W. (1958), 'The Role of Tribal Markets in Morocco', *Geographical Review*, 48, pp. 494–511.

Schapera, I. (1953), 'The Tswana', *Ethnographic Survey of Africa*. North Eastern Africa, Part 1, International African Institute, London.

Scott, E. P. (1972), 'The Spatial Structure of Rural Northern Nigeria: Farmers, Periodic Markets and Villages', *Economic Geography*, 48, pp. 316–32.

Stine, J. H. (1962), 'Temporal Aspects of Tertiary Production Elements in Korea', in F. Pitts (ed.), *Urban Systems and Economic Development*, Euguene, Oregon.

Section E
Aspects of Change in the Political Process

17 Legacies of the Slave Trade and the Colonial Imprint

The slave trade and European colonization affected all Africa and together have had a lasting imprint on intergroup relations, the population distribution, the economy and the politics of contemporary Africa. The slave trade and slavery were sanctioned and extolled from the economic and moral point of view by majority opinion in 'civilized' Europe just as European colonial powers saw nothing wrong in depriving Africans of their land, even by force of arms. Indeed some Europeans considered the slave trade and the occupation of African land to be beneficial to Africans in the belief that both slavery and colonization made it possible for Africans to be brought into the orbit of 'superior' European civilization. The slave trade ended at about the end of the nineteenth century while the period of colonization for most countries ended before 1965. In this chapter we shall review the legacies of the slave trade and the impact European colonization had on the cultural landscape, the economy and aspects of life of the people of contemporary tropical Africa.

Tropical Africa has a long history of trade and state formation dating back to the eleventh century AD or earlier. This is particularly true of West Africa and the coastal areas of East Africa, both of which had considerable trade contacts with the Arab world and southern Europe. Important pre-colonial states in tropical Africa include Ghana, Songhai, Bornu, Ashanti, Benin and the Fulani empires of Macina and Sokoto-Gwandu in West Africa; Ethiopia, Buganda and the Madist State of Sudan in East Africa; and Chokwe, Barotse and Bamangwato in southern Africa. Many of these states declined and gave way to successor states but some survived to confront the colonial invaders whom the people resented as intruders. The history of tropical Africa does not date from the colonial period, as some European historians would want us to believe, although we accept that documentary evidence is largely restricted to the colonial period. The period of the slave trade and the colonial period can be considered to constitute political and economic 'accidents' or interruptions in the historical evolution of modern tropical Africa. They were accidents in a sense similar to that of the Quaternary Ice Age in the landscape evolution of Europe and North America. And just as the Ice Age left behind lasting impressions on the physical landscape of Europe and North America, the slave trade and the colonial period have also left their legacies.

The two slave trades

It is usual to distinguish between the trans-Saharan or Arab slave trade and the trans-Atlantic or the European slave trade. The trans-Saharan slave trade, which apparently continues today in some form or another, started long before the slave trade across the Atlantic. It involved the forced migration of African Negroes, originating mostly from East Africa and the Sudan, to the Muslim countries of North Africa, Arabia and southern Europe. In terms of the number of slaves involved, it was on a much smaller scale than the European slave trade. This started as a trickle during the late fifteenth century, when an average of less than 700 slaves were exported per year, but assumed an alarming proportion in the eighteenth century when almost 60,000 slaves were landed in the Americas every year.

The difficulties of moving large numbers of people across the desert contributed to the relatively small number of slaves involved in the slave trade across the Sahara. The cost and problems of feeding and providing water for the slave caravans were enormous. Fortunately slaves made up only one of several items of trade across the Sahara whereas slaves constituted the only item of trade from Africa to the Americas. Arab traders therefore invested more on articles of small bulk and high value which in addition were neither perishable nor in need of food and water as was the case with slaves. The low level of shipping technology at the time also created considerable difficulties in shipping slaves to the Americas. However, on the whole, it was easier to move larger numbers of men by sea to the Americas than it was by caravan across the Sahara Desert. The vast majority of Africans sold into slavery before 1870 went to the Americas where the number of slaves landed between 1445 and 1870 is estimated to be about 10 million.

Pl. 17.1 Tuareg slave hunters with their captives

Effects of the slave trade on population and settlement

In a recent study of the Atlantic slave trade, Philip Curtin (1969) has come to the conclusion after a detailed analysis of massive data from various sources, that the number of Africans landed in the Americas during the period of the slave trade was closer to 9·5 million rather than the more commonly accepted figure of 14 million. About 60 per cent of these slaves originated from West Africa. The rest came from Gabon, the Congo Basin, Angola and Mozambique. The total loss of population was however much higher than the 10 million or so slaves which landed alive in the Americas. First, an average of about 15 per cent of slaves died on the voyage between Africa and the Americas. Secondly, a large number died during the long treks between the point of capture and the coastal ports of storage and shipment, especially where they had to travel several hundred km on foot. The third and major cause of death was occasioned by local warfare which became the principal means of obtaining slaves (war captives) in many parts of tropical Africa. The total loss of population caused by the slave trade has been estimated to be well over 60 million people. In this section we consider the implications of these losses on population growth as well as the effects of slave raids on the spatial distribution of population and the location and character of human settlements.

There is no doubt that Africa is today the least populated of the continents except Oceania because of the large-scale depopulation of the continent during the period of the slave trade. In 1650, for instance, the population of Africa was estimated to be 100 million, compared with 103 million for Europe and 257 million for Asia. Two hundred years later, that is in 1850, the population of Africa was still about 100 million whereas the population of Europe was 274 million and that of Asia about 656 million. Today, Africa has only about 10 per cent of the world population, whereas in the seventeenth century Africa had about 20 per cent of the world population or about the same as the population of Europe. The population of Africa therefore remained at best stagnant during the period of the slave trade. It is thus obvious that but for the slave trade, the population of Africa, which today has a growth rate of 3 per cent, would have been much greater than it is.

The fact that the slave trade, like modern migrations, was selective of age and sex is important in assessing its effect on population growth in tropical Africa. Most slaves were between the ages of 15 and 35, about two-thirds being males. In March 1722, for example, the Cape Coast agents of the African Company in London were instructed to get ready cargoes of 600 slaves, each of which should consist of:

good merchantable negroes, two-thirds males, one-third females, six-sevenths of each cargo to be about 16 and 30 years of age, and upon no account exceed 30 years, one-seventh boys and girls of which none should be under 10 years of age. (Boahen, 1964)

The demographic characteristics of the slave population as represented by the above quotation and also the fact that most of those who died during the civil wars were young male adults suggest that there was a marked decline in the growth rate of the population during the period of the slave trade. Fage (1969) has, however, argued that except during the eighteenth century when the export of slaves reached its peak, the natural increase in population was consistently higher than the loss due to the forced migration of the slaves, and that at worst the total population remained static. His conclusion is based on the premise that African societies were polygymous and that the number of women of child-bearing age exported as slaves was much less than the men. These two facts, he argued, made it possible for many more children to be born during the period than would have been the case if more women had been exported.

Fage's arguments appear logical on the surface. They fall flat however in the face of evidence from contemporary Africa where there are examples of declining populations amongst some groups such as the Nupe who are still polygamous. Furthermore, his arguments appear to ignore the high incidence of infertility and partial infertility in tropical Africa (Romaniuk, 1968), or of the high rate of infant mortality. Our conclusion is that the slave trade resulted in an absolute decline of the population and that it adversely affected its growth rate.

The effects of the slave trade on the population of tropical Africa are more obvious when we come to consider the spatial distribution of population in the region. Vast areas of land in the Middle Belt of West Africa, eastern Zaïre, Angola, Gabon and Tanzania, to mention a few, remain very sparsely populated today with population densities of less than 6 persons per sq km (15 per sq mile). Vivid accounts of the destruction occasioned by slave raids are available in the journals of early European explorers including David Livingstone, Hugh Clapperton and Henry Barth. In the course of these raids and slave wars, towns and villages were sometimes completely destroyed and in some districts, the entire population was carried away into slavery or driven to seek refuge in inaccessible hilly or forest areas. Large-scale depopulation of vast areas meant that the remaining population was too small to tame the environment, resulting in greater infestation by the tsetse fly. Such infested districts therefore had to be abandoned for new and healthier areas.

In some areas, the general insecurity of the period resulted in the concentration of people in and around cities which were ruled by powerful chiefs who were able to offer protection against slave raids. Such was the case in the powerful states of Kano, Zaria and the Mossi Kingdom with headquarters at Ouagadougou (Wagadugu). Today, these areas stand out as islands of high population densities surrounded by vast areas which are very sparsely populated.

Defence was a major consideration in the siting of human settlements which at this period were generally located on inaccessible hill tops or in forested areas. Many villages were relocated away from navigable waterways while most grassland settlements were fortified with walls and moats. Hill villages, such as Idanre, Oke-Iho and Efon Alaiye, abound all over Yorubaland, as well as in the region of the Jos Plateau, the Adamawa Highlands and parts of East and Central Africa. Building space was restricted both on the hills and within the walled settlements, and dwellings were usually crowded to allow as much land as possible for cultivation. Today, the walls have fallen into disrepair and settlements have dispersed beyond the walls, just as many hill villages have since been relocated on more accessible sites.

Effects of the slave trade on the economy
The extensive destruction of life and property, as well as the fear, insecurity and misery caused by the slave trade, disrupted normal economic activity and overall progress in tropical Africa. It is therefore absurd to argue, as some European historians have done, that the slave trade was beneficial to Africa because it stimulated trade in other goods and that it encouraged the production of foodstuffs for sale to slave ships. It is even more absurd to suggest that it was the guns provided in the course of slave trading that made it possible for some African rulers to establish and sustain effective government over large territories (Fage, 1969, p. 90). We also consider it uncharitable to suggest that the economy of some areas profited from the export of the equivalent of their natural growth in population because the resultant loss of population reduced the demand on available foodstuffs and thereby reduced the incidence of starvation! This period was one of economic stagnation for tropical Africa although, admittedly, some coastal chiefs made fortunes from the sale of fellow Africans.

Starting first with agricultural production, we find that farming suffered considerably from the loss of a sizeable proportion of young adult males. The consequences of such a loss can be seen in parts of rural Nigeria today, where large-scale migration into the cities has created serious shortages of agricultural labour. Furthermore, because villagers feared they might be captured by slave raiders, farming was usually restricted land within the village walls. Insufficient of warfare, the only safe area to cultivate was the restricted land within the village walls, Insufficient farmland on hill settlements also prompted the adoption of terrace agriculture in many parts of tropical Africa. Considerable energy and time were therefore expended in constructing terraces on hill slopes because the people were afraid to descend from their hill outposts to cultivate the extensive surrounding plains which were often better watered and more fertile.

The suggestion that the demand for foodstuffs for feeding slaves on the long voyage to the Americas stimulated food production and therefore brought some money into the pockets of local farmers is questionable. In any case such gains were minimal and restricted to a few coastal areas. The situation created by slave raids often led to severe famines which resulted in further loss of life. There was little food for sale and much of the food supplied to slave ships came from farms or 'plantations' such as those at Calabar, which were cultivated by the use of slave labour.

Abundant evidence exists to show that, rather than encourage cash crop farming, European slave traders tried to prevent it. In 1751, for example, the British Board of Trade ordered Thomas Melvil, the Governor of Cape Coast Castle in Ghana, to stop the cultivation of cotton by the Fanti people. The argument put forward was that:

The introduction of culture and industry among the Negroes is contrary to the known established policy of this country; there is no saying where this might stop, and that it might extend to tobacco, sugar and every other commodity which we now take from our colonies; and thereby the Africans who now support themselves by wars, would become planters and their slaves be employed in the culture of these articles in Africa, which they are employed in, in America. (Boahen, 1968, p. 113)

It is significant that at the time of this 'order' Britain had not assumed political control over the Fanti people. It is also important to note that the British Board of Trade and indeed all Europe found that it was in the interest of their national economy for Africans to continue to support themselves by slave wars rather than by agriculture and trade. It was also partly in consideration of their national economy under changing situations and partly for humanitarian reasons that European powers found it necessary in the latter part of the nineteenth century to suppress the slave trade so that Africans could then settle to produce rubber, cocoa, palm oil and so on for export to Europe.

The fact that a wide range of food crops cultivated in tropical Africa was introduced during the period of the slave trade has often been considered to be an economic benefit which Africa derived from the slave trade. The crops in question include cassava, sweet potatoes, maize, lima beans, pawpaw, tomato, groundnut and pineapple, all of which were introduced from tropical America by the Portuguese. It is true that indigenous food crops cultivated in tropical Africa proved inadequate to meet the food demands of the slave ships. It is also true that today there is no part of tropical Africa that does not depend very much on one or more of these crops. Their introduction into tropical Africa was, however, incidental and was aimed at boosting the slave trade rather than the economy of the African peoples. In any case these crops would have been introduced later, given the pattern of crop diffusion all over the world, as indeed was the case with cocoa and para rubber. We also note that it was only after the period of the slave trade that these new crops spread from the coastal parts to the interior areas of tropical Africa.

For local manufacturing the period of the slave trade was a period of technological stagnation in tropical Africa. During the sixteenth century, the state of industrial development in tropical Africa was comparable to that of Europe or Asia, especially as far as the charcoal iron industry and the manufacture of cloth are concerned. Cottage industry predominated at that time and the quality of various crafts and iron implements made from locally smelted iron ore testify to the fact that parts of tropical Africa, especially the grassland areas, were not lagging behind in manufacturing. The industrial revolution started in England during the late eighteenth century, when the factory system led to the rapid growth of industrial towns. Tropical Africa at that time was, however, witnessing the peak of the slave trade which in many ways helped to sustain the cotton factories of Manchester. Thus, while the African textile industry stagnated, the European cloth industry was able to expand and copy fashionable African patterns. Eventually, European cloth and other manufactures like hoes, machetes, spears, beads and various household utensils flooded African markets and virtually eliminated locally made products which were relatively inferior in quality and very expensive in terms of the time used in fabricating them.

The industrial history of Japan, which has today emerged as an industrial giant, is relevant to an assessment of the role of the slave trade in the technological stagnation or even regression in tropical Africa. Before the Second World War and indeed up to about 1950, Japanese manufactures were ridiculed and branded as inferior to European goods. Today the Japanese dominate the field in the production of high-quality precision goods such as watches, electronics, automobile engines and cameras. In Nigeria, for example, about 90 per cent of the taxis in the major cities in 1978 were Japanese, compared with the situation in 1958 when almost all the taxis were British-made cars. The experience of Japan suggests that but for the technological stagnation caused by the slave trade, tropical Africa could have made considerable progress in the field of manufacturing. The abandonment of the local iron-smelting industry and the decline of the textile and salt-making industries must therefore be seen as clear evidence of technological regression in tropical Africa.

Local and long-distance trade also suffered during the period, because of the general state of insecurity. The mutual need to hold markets was, however, recognized by most ethnic groups especially in West and East Africa. In Yorubaland, for example, women were allowed considerable immunity from attacks even in times of war (see p. 193). The fact that women predominate today in all facets of marketing in Yorubaland is thought to date back to this period. Important slave traders, however, carried out some long-distance trade featuring the sale of salt, natron and cloth from the Sahel region in exchange for kolanut, gold and some European goods from the forest belt.

Some European historians have argued that the slave trade stimulated trade in other commodities, since, according to them, it brought an increasing number of European buyers of ivory, gold, palm oil and other African products, besides slaves. They also point out that in exchange for slaves, European traders brought textiles, firearms, trinkets, farm implements and alcoholic drinks which were highly prized by Africans. It should, however, be realized that these goods were luxury items which the coastal chiefs accumulated and used in exchange for slaves from the hinterland. The majority of the population did not benefit from such trade.

Colonial powers and colonial policies

A colony is a territory or country developed by people from another country and which is fully or partly controlled from the mother country. It is in this sense that we describe the period starting from about 1890 and ending in the early 1960s for most countries as the colonial period in tropical Africa. In a discussion of the impact of colonialism in Africa, it is, however, important to distinguish those countries of High Africa such as Angola, Kenya and Zimbabwe where Europeans established permanent settlements, from those countries such as Nigeria, Mali and Uganda, where Europeans never intended to settle permanently.

During the 'Scramble for Africa' by European powers which started from about 1885 and ended at the beginning of the First World War, the important colonial powers were France, Britain, Germany, Portugal and Belgium. By 1918, Germany had been pushed out of tropical Africa, her territories being taken over by France and Britain. Our brief discussion of colonial policies is therefore restricted to those of France, Britain, Portugal and Belgium. The techniques of administration adopted by each colonial power were fundamentally different both in theory and practice, and, as might be expected, these policies were to have a great impact on the pace and character of the economic, social and political development of the various territories.

France occupied the largest land area in tropical Africa although the population of her African subjects was much less than that of Great Britain. The method of administration adopted by France was that of direct rule, whereby all French territories were considered to be an integral part of Greater France. In all territories, Frenchmen occupied all the important administrative positions and Africans were only trained for subordinate posts (Whittlesey, 1964). Traditional rulers were replaced by French administrators and all land in each territory became state land. As provinces of overseas France, territories like Senegal and the Ivory Coast elected deputies to sit at the French National Assembly in Paris. The result was that on the eve of independence, the French territories were economically and administratively completely dependent on French personnel, a situation which has continued even up to 1980 – about twenty years after independence!

By contrast, Great Britain adopted a policy of indirect rule in most of her African territories except in Kenya and Rhodesia (Zimbabwe) where permanent white settlements had been established. In West Africa, for example, the essence of British colonial policy was to guide the colonial territories to responsible self-government within the commonwealth in the shortest possible time. Each territory was therefore administered as a distinct political entity which had to pay its way and balance its annual budgets without any subvention from Britain. Traditional rulers were recognized as administrative agents of the colonial government. Furthermore, the British, unlike the French and Belgians, refused to alienate African land to European planters, arguing that Britain was morally obliged to protect the natives and their land from exploitation by foreign capitalists. Unfortunately, this principle was not upheld in British East Africa where the climate favoured European settlement in Kenya and parts of Tanzania, nor in the then Rhodesia. The ambivalence of British colonial policy in West and East Africa confirms the view that European powers did not scramble for territories in Africa because they wanted to carry out charitable works for Africans, but because of economic interests and fears of the political intentions of rival powers (Crowder, 1970).

Next to France and Britain came small Portugal, which happens to have been the first European power in Africa and the last to grant independence to her territories. Like France, Portugal adopted a policy of direct rule, and as well as eliminating traditional rulers, went further to demand that the natives must abandon their languages and adopt Portuguese to qualify as civilized. As late as 1965, Portugal continued to insist that Guinea-Bissau, Angola and Mozambique were 'overseas provinces' of Portugal. However, these territories were only provinces of Portugal in name and not in fact, since Portugal, which is still the poorest and most undeveloped country in Europe, was unable to afford the capital to invest in her colonies. At the same time Portugal relied heavily on raw materials obtained through the use of forced labour from her 'overseas provinces' which also provided her with markets for her industrial goods.

Curiously, and to the great annoyance of the educated élite in Angola, Mozambique and Guinea-Bissau, as late as 1963 Portugal continued to parade herself as a successful colonial power which had no political or racial problems. This political illusion was derived from the Portuguese policy of individual assimilation, whereby educated Africans were accorded social and political acceptance as fully-fledged Portuguese citizens. But the number of *assimilados* in each colonial territory was always less than the number of Portuguese settlers and traders. Indeed after over sixty years of colonial rule, there were only 37,870 *assimilados* in Angola in 1960 out of a total African population of about 4,670,000, compared with the white settler population of about 172,530 (Abshire and Bailey, 1969). The situation in Mozambique was even worse since only 0·5 per cent of the African population (6,603,650) qualified as *assimilados* compared with 0·8 per cent for Angola. In any case racial discrimination against the *assimilados* was commonplace as was the practice of forced labour.

In the early 1950s, when Britain was preparing to grant independence to her colonies and when France had accepted that the concept of 'overseas France' was no longer tenable, Portugal still stuck rigidly to the policy of gradual assimilation and rejected outright the question of granting independence to her colonies. In 1960, Portugal found excuses to justify her African policy by arguing that independence had led to Communism in Ghana and the Republic of Guinea, and to bloody chaos in Zaïre (Duffy, 1964). The position of Portugal in that year was clear from a declaration made in Mozambique by the head of the ruling political party, the National Union, that 'Portugal is in Africa and will remain in Africa' (Duffy, 1964). The following

year, the Angolan rebellion started and was followed by armed resistance in Mozambique and Guinea-Bissau. The war of liberation in the three territories continued into the 1970s and played a major role in the overthrow of the Salazar dictatorship in Portugal and the eventual granting of independence to Guinea-Bissau (1974), Mozambique (June 1975) and Angola (November 1975).

The fourth colonial power in effective occupation of African territory after the First World War was Belgium. Unlike the other colonial powers, Belgium had no official colonial policy in her territory in the Congo (Zaïre). In practice, however, the Belgian pattern of administration contained elements of British, French and Portuguese policies. In 1885, for example, the government declared that no one might dispossess natives of the land they occupied but that all vacant land should be considered as belonging to the State (Ryckmans, 1964). Like the British, the Belgians in the Congo recognized the authority of traditional rulers, although the government had to review this policy when it discovered that there were too many chiefs (about 6,000 in 1917), many of whom had no authority over any group of people. Also like Portugal, as late as 1955, Belgium did not believe in granting political rights to either Africans or European settlers in the Congo. The government at Brussels decided to hold the balance between European interests, the 'evolved' Africans and the vast 'tribal masses', in the vain hope that this would prevent political friction.

Like Portugal, Belgium pretended that there was no colour bar between European settlers and the 'evolved' Africans and as in the Portuguese territories this class of Africans was kept to a minimum. Indeed the guiding principle of Belgian colonial administration in the Congo was the slogan 'no élites, no problems'. Africans were therefore denied the opportunity to study beyond secondary-school level and were forbidden to travel outside the territory to study in any other country. It is therefore not surprising that as of 1955, there was not a single African in Belgian Congo who had obtained a university degree, except perhaps in divinity. The result was that at independence in 1960, the Congo found itself unable to provide the local manpower for its civil service and various sectors of the economy.

Effects of colonialism on economic development

Although the countries of tropical Africa have become independent of European rule, almost all of them are still tied to the economic apron-strings of their former colonial overlords. Besides, the pattern of development in agriculture, industry and other sectors of the economy has not changed much since independence. In this section we shall examine the changes that occurred in the local economies during the colonial period as well as the type of economic foundations which the newly independent countries inherited from the period.

The economic principle which applied to all territories in tropical Africa was that each territory must be self-supporting by providing minerals and industrial crops for the governing power, which could in turn supply the territories with manufactured goods. Of course the prices paid for agricultural products and minerals from the colonies as well as prices which the Africans paid for manufactured goods were decided by the European trading firms. The French, Belgians and the Portuguese enforced this colonial pact – as the French termed the principle – more rigidly than the British. In all territories, Africans were compelled to work on roads, ports and railways to facilitate movement of crops to Europe, and in Portuguese and some French territories, the Africans were forced to cultivate the crops needed by the metropolitan country.

New industrial crops, including cocoa, coffee and cotton, were introduced during the colonial period when the production of palm oil and groundnuts was also stimulated. The high prices in the world market for these crops brought considerable income to African farmers who were largely responsible for industrial crop production in British colonial territories. In French and Belgian territories, large areas of land were alienated to foreign companies for establishing plantations of cocoa, rubber, coffee and oil palms. The development of food crops received little or no attention from the colonial administrators in spite of the periodic famines that featured all over tropical Africa. Indeed, outside those areas producing industrial crops, the colonial period made little impact on African agriculture. Today, African farmers still use the same implements and cultivate about the same size of farmland as their ancestors did before the colonial period. Further proof of the neglect of food crop production is the fact that in most countries even such basic food items as maize, vegetable oils, rice and meat have to be imported to supplement local production, especially in West and Central Africa.

The colonial administrators did not initiate but merely accelerated the change from subsistence to export-based agriculture. With the abolition of the slave trade European traders turned their attention to palm oil, rubber, cotton and other tropical industrial crops, most of which were introduced long before the colonial period. What colonial governments achieved in this direction was to intensify the production of cash crops by imposing taxes to be paid in cash as well as by forcing some Africans to cultivate such crops on their farmlands or to provide labour on European-owned plantations.

Industrial development was suppressed as being contrary to the economic interests of the metropolitan

countries just as the British Board of Trade had discouraged cotton cultivation in Ghana in 1951. The result was that indigenous manufacturing technology, which had been disrupted during the slave trade, was further handicapped and eventually suffered total eclipse. An increasing range of manufactured goods was supplied to the colonies while goods from countries like Japan and Germany were debarred from entering territories like Nigeria and Ghana. Today some countries have not moved much further in the field of industrialization, but still supply raw agricultural products to Europe in return for industrial goods.

The greatest impact of the colonial period on the economy was in the commercial sector where a large number of African middlemen traders emerged to participate in the export trade in produce and the retail trade in imported merchandise. But here again, Africans were completely dependent on European shippers and merchants who monopolized the export trade in industrial crops and the wholesale trade in manufactured goods. The major firms gave credit facilities to Indian, Syrian and Lebanese traders who then sold in smaller quantities to African retailers! In this way the commercial sector came to be controlled by aliens who repatriated most of their profits. It is this situation, which persisted even after ten years of independence, that Ghana, Sierra Leone and Nigeria have since 1969 sought to reverse by restricting various businesses to indigenes. In the French-speaking countries, however, the retail trade is still dominated by Frenchmen, Lebanese and Syrians.

The racial problem in East Africa and Zimbabwe is a legacy of the colonial period. The white settler problem in East Africa no longer exists but remains a major political issue in Zimbabwe. East Africa, however, has a large Asian population, totalling in 1970 about 300,000. Asian merchants were known in East Africa long before the colonial period, but the Asian community was greatly increased when the British colonial government recruited thousands of Indians to work on the Kenya–Uganda railways. Over the years the Asians came to dominate the commercial life of all the East African countries and continue to do so to this day, except in Uganda, where thousands of Asians were expelled during the Idi Amin administration.

The impact of foreign religions and colonialism on education
Much of the changes affecting the society and economy of contemporary tropical Africa can be attributed to the role played by two foreign religions, namely Islam and Christianity. Islam became firmly established before the colonial period, that is during the period of the slave trade, but extended its sphere of influence to other areas during the colonial period when Christianity

became firmly established in most coastal areas. Both the colonial governments and the missionaries of Islam and Christianity played a very important role in the spread of a western type of education in tropical Africa. Today, the two greatest legacies of the colonial period are that English or French is the official language of most countries and the fact that the educational systems of the various countries are based on the patterns existing in the metropolitan countries in Europe.

Before considering the impact of Islam, Christianity and the colonial governments on education and general social change, it is worth pointing out that in general, Islam has become more attractive to Africans than Christianity. This is because Islam does not demand revolutionary changes in social life nor does it undermine family and communal authority to the extent that Christianity does. Furthermore, during the colonial period, the apostles of Islam were fellow Africans whereas the Christian missionaries were Europeans who were considered to be agents of the colonial powers. The open condemnation and suppression of African cultures by Christian missionaries also made them unpopular and unacceptable in many districts. The cause of Christianity was, however, greatly advanced through the schools and hospitals which the missionaries built and administered, especially in the British colonial territories.

Apart from the Koranic schools which existed in those parts of tropical Africa which had already adopted Islam, there was very little formal education in pre-colonial Africa. Koranic schools exist today but are still very few in number and have made no significant contribution to the manpower requirements of the various countries. It is education of a western type that has been adopted by both Christians and Muslims as well as by the vast majority of Africans who still practise aspects of traditional religions.

In all the colonial territories, the educational policy was to train as many Africans as the government considered necessary to supply middle-level manpower in administration and the schools. The idea of education for the purpose of uplifting the mind did not exist and was even considered to be dangerous since it produced the élites that constituted a thorn in the flesh for the colonial administrators. In the Belgian Congo, for example, no university education was provided and moreover, no person was allowed to travel outside the territory for the purpose of furthering his education. Many West Africans, however, found their way to Europe and the United States although the British in Nigeria refused to accord recognition to degrees awarded by American universities. The foundations for primary and secondary education were however laid during the colonial period, even though school enrolment was minimal.

Christian missionaries played a prominent role in the development of formal education throughout tropical Africa. In the Belgian Congo and the French colonial territories, Roman Catholic missionaries were responsible for almost all formal instruction in schools, although, as from 1903, the majority of children in French West Africa went to government schools. In the British colonial territories, on the other hand, almost all the schools were owned and run by Christian missions, notably the Roman Catholic, Anglican, Methodist, Presbyterian, Baptist and, much later, the Lutheran Church. A number of African separatists churches and the Ahmadiya movement in Islam also established schools during the second half of the colonial period. A few government schools existed in British territories, especially in the Muslim areas where some traditional rulers did not welcome the establishment of Christian mission schools. Government policy of allowing missionaries to own and administer schools was mostly responsible for the much greater proportion of educated Africans in British territories as compared with French, Belgian or Portuguese territories. The restriction of Christian missions in the northern provinces of Nigeria also meant that today the north still remains far behind the south in educational development.

Western education has tended to make the African more discontented with his traditional environment. School-leavers have therefore tended to reject African traditional life in preference to urban life, hence the increasing migration of educated Africans to the fast-growing cities of the new nations of tropical Africa. The development problems posed by rural–urban migrations are considerable, particularly in the face of increasing labour shortages in growing rural areas. Many people, notably politicians, have blamed this situation on the current élitist type of education in which much emphasis is placed on paper qualification. Often such critics have no meaningful suggestions to offer apart from expressing the view that the urban unemployed should go back to the land. The dilemma today is that the colonial type of formal education has come to stay since those who condemn it do not prevent their children from going to school. There is, however, a great need to place more emphasis on technical education as a step towards a more effective use of the manpower of tropical Africa.

References

Abshire, D. M. and Bailey, N. (1969), 'Current Racial Character of Portuguese Africa', in D. M. Abshire and M. A. Samuels (eds.), *Portuguese Africa – A Handbook*, Pall Mall Press, London; Praeger, New York, pp. 202–15.

Boahen, A. (1964), *Topics in West African History*, Longman, London, p. 12.

Crowder, M. (1970), 'The Colonial Imprint', in J. Paden and E. Soja (eds.), *The African Experience*, vol. I, Northwestern University Press, Evanston, pp. 233–49.

Curtin, Philip D. (1969), *Dimensions of the Atlantic Slave Trade*, University of Wisconsin Press, Madison.

Duffy, J. (1964), 'Portugal in Africa', in P. W. Quigg (ed.), *Africa: A Foreign Affairs Reader*, Praeger, New York, pp. 86–98.

Fage, J. D. (1969), *A History of West Africa*, Cambridge University Press, Cambridge, ch. 6, pp. 81–95.

Romaniuk, A. (1968), 'Infertility in Tropical Africa', in J. C. Caldwell and C. Okonjo (eds.), *The Population of Tropical Africa*, Longman, London, pp. 214–24.

Ryckmans, P. (1964), 'Belgian "Colonialism"', in P. W. Quigg (ed.), *Africa: A Foreign Affairs Reader*, Praeger, New York, pp. 71–83.

Whittlesey, D, (1964), 'British and French Colonial Technique in West Africa', in P. W. Quigg (ed.), *Africa: A Foreign Affairs Reader*, Praeger, New York, pp. 57–70.

18 Political Boundaries and Boundary Problems

In Africa the state boundary, which is a line, as distinct from the frontier, which is a zone, is a relatively recent phenomenon. A boundary has to be surveyed, drawn on a map and demarcated on the ground. If we accept this definition of a boundary, it follows that there are only a few boundaries in tropical Africa since the boundary agreements between the colonial powers only succeeded in defining the frontiers of their various territories. Often these boundaries were agreed upon hurriedly in Europe and without the aid of accurate maps or adequate knowledge of the locality. However, the fact that many colonial field officers met and signed agreements with local rulers in the process of making territorial claims suggests that some boundaries did, to some extent, have regard to existing ethnic and political groups. But some of the larger kingdoms were not long established nor permanent. Some empires were expanding while others were declining at the time. The frontiers were therefore in a state of flux with the result that the territorial claims of some local rulers were questionable. In consequence, many of the boundaries, as we shall see, cut across ethnic territories. It is largely for this reason that African boundaries have been described as artificial. Many boundary disputes have already given rise to armed conflict between some of the newly independent countries. We therefore intend to examine first the problems of international boundaries before discussing the equally serious problems posed by boundaries separating the territories of different ethnic groups and of different villages within the same country.

Types of political boundaries

Most boundaries in tropical Africa have been described as artificial, and this situation has been blamed on the colonial powers. These so-called artificial boundaries have persisted twenty years after the exit of the colonial powers and there is no likelihood that they will be altered in the foreseeable future. Their character was largely determined by the manner in which they were created, since they had to be of a type that could be easily agreed upon around the conference table. Unfor-

tunately it has not been easy to delimit such boundaries on the ground. The common types used in Africa were: 1. astronomical lines, 2. mathematical lines and 3. relief features, notably rivers and watersheds.

According to Michael Barbour (1961), astronomical lines make up about 44 per cent of the boundaries of tropical Africa, while mathematical lines and relief features make up 30 per cent and 26 per cent, respectively. Astronomical lines are parallels of latitude or meridians (lines of longitude). As boundaries, they are very easy to select when little information is available, but they are not easily defined on the ground, since they are not related to any physical features. Moreover, astronomical line boundaries create considerable problems when they pass through populated areas, since they do not take account of the people living in these areas. Fortunately this type of boundary has been used mainly in sparsely populated areas. Typical examples include that portion of the boundary

Fig. 18.1 Types of boundaries

between Kenya and the Somali Republic which follows longitude 41°E, the boundary between Botswana and Namibia which follows longitude 20°E in the south and then latitude 22°S before it turns along longitude 21°E, and parts of the Zambia/Zaïre boundary.

Mathematical lines consist of straight lines or arcs of a circle and are usually defined in relation either to relief or human features. A straight line between two towns such as Calabar and Yola (see p. 211) or between two hilltops is an example of a mathematical line. Mathematical lines, especially the straight ones, present similar problems to astronomical lines with respect to the human population. With the exception of the small stretch formed by the River Yobe, the long boundary separating Nigeria from Niger Republic consists of mathematical lines. Other examples include the boundary between Nigeria and south-western Cameroun, between Uganda and Kenya, and a considerable stretch of the boundary between Ghana and the Ivory Coast. In a number of instances, mathematical lines have been used to fill the gaps between other types of boundaries.

The third type of boundary consists of those which make use of relief features, the most common of which are watersheds and rivers. The use of mountains and lakes as boundaries is also common in East Africa. Watersheds were considered to be suitable as boundaries during the scramble for Africa because early European exploration was mainly concerned with 'discovering' the sources and drainage network of the various major rivers, of which only the mouths were known and mapped. There was very little or no idea of the nature of these watersheds, nor of the land through which the rivers flowed. In 1894, for example, the claims of King Leopold of Belgium that his authority in the Congo Basin extended to the watershed (or mountain ridges) of the adjacent basins, including that of the Nile River, were recognized by Great Britain. The present boundary between Zaïre (formerly the Belgian Congo) and Zambia lies partly along one of these watersheds. Other examples of watershed boundaries include the boundary between the Sudan and Zaïre, the western part of the boundary between Malawi and Mozambique and a part of the boundary between Zaïre and Zambia. The boundary between Zambia and Malawi lies along the watershed separating the Luangwa River and the Lake Malawi Basin, while much of the boundary between the former British Cameroon (now western Cameroun) and the rest of Cameroun Republic lies along the Adamawa range of hills which form a major watershed in the area.

Unfortunately many watershed boundaries have proved unsatisfactory for two main reasons. First, many African watersheds are ill-defined because they consist of gently sloping and open landscapes. The absence of physical barriers along some watersheds is largely

responsible for the fact that such watersheds serve as centres of population and not as barriers to population movements. The second reason is related to the first since boundaries passing through watersheds with no relief features often cut across ethnic territories and do not therefore make any allowance for the inhabitants of the area. The delimitation of some watershed boundaries has therefore proved to be very difficult.

Pl. 18.1 The Zimbabwe/Zambia border bridge over the Victoria Falls

Given the state of geographical knowledge of tropical Africa at the time of the scramble for Africa by European powers, it is not surprising that rivers were often considered to be good natural boundaries. Amongst other attributes, rivers are clearly defined on the ground and are relatively permanent features, even though sections of many river courses do change from time to time. However, in some parts of tropical Africa, rivers were chosen as boundaries before their courses were known. Provisions were therefore made in some of the treatises signed in case the river followed a course different from that expected (see Barbour, 1961, p. 310). Rivers form the current boundaries between Zaïre and Congo (Brazzaville), Zimbabwe and Zambia and parts of many other boundaries all over tropical Africa.

The main problem with using rivers as boundaries is that they tend to attract population, especially in semi-arid areas, and do not serve as barriers to population movement. Apart from being the main source of water supply, rivers are used for transport and fishing while their floodplains provide the most suitable farmland in arid and semi-arid zones. The boundary is usually taken to follow the centre line of the river, the line of deepest channel or one of the banks of the river.

International boundaries and associated problems

There is no type of boundary – astronomical lines, mathematical lines or boundaries based on relief features – which does not suffer from the defect of cutting across and thereby dividing the traditional territories of many African peoples. This situation was caused partly by the hurried way in which the boundaries were made and partly by the limited state of knowledge about the geography of tropical Africa. In the case of the origin of the Nigeria–Cameroun boundary, for example, the only maps available in 1885 were the British Admiralty charts. The boundary between Nigeria and Cameroun, as agreed between Britain and Germany, was a line from the Rio del Rey Estuary to a point marked 'rapids' on the British Admiralty charts. This arbitrary line was about 256 km (160 miles) long. In a commentary on the origin of this boundary Sir Claude MacDonald of the British Foreign Office, appointed Governor of the Oil Rivers Protectorate in 1891, wrote as follows:

In those days we just took a blue pencil and a ruler and we put it down at Old Calabar and drew a line up to Yola. The following year I was sent to Berlin to endeavour to get from the German authorities some rectification of the blue line . . . [and] . . . my instructions were to grab as much as I could. (Nugent, 1914)

According to MacDonald, he was provided with the only available map, which was a naval chart, with all the soundings of the sea carefully marked out, to take to Berlin. The rest of the map was blank except for a river Akpayoff which started near the Calabar River and meandered for 1,280 km (800 miles) on the map. That river was to be the negotiated boundary, but it later turned out not to exist, and the only river in that area was only 5·6 km (3½ miles) long!

In a review of the evolution of the boundaries of Nigeria, Prescott (1959, p. 81) has reported that the boundary between Nigeria and Dahomey, now the Republic of Benin, was not closely described because the local tribes were themselves contesting the area, and

did not therefore agree on the boundary. Another reason given was that the British authorities had only a very limited knowledge of the geography of the coastal hinterland. The boundary was therefore arbitrarily taken to lie along longitude 2°E and, like most other boundaries created at that time, it was intended to be temporary, its functions being 'simply to prevent the territory falling under the control of another European country'. Evidence from other parts of tropical Africa also confirms that during the early colonial period, official international boundaries did not serve as barriers to trade or movements of people. Wherever a boundary which had been accepted by two colonial powers appeared to disrupt the way of life of local people, efforts were made to minimize the problems arising from the division. Thus in the case of the boundary between British and French Somaliland, there was a clause to the effect that 'the subjects of both parties are at liberty to cross frontiers and graze their cattle, but wherever they go, they must obey the Governor of the country where they are, and the wells remain open for both countries' (Hertslet, 1909).

There were, however, many cases in which European powers refused to take into account the convenience or views of local peoples, even when information was made available to them by their field officers. In 1898, for example, both the French and the British knew that Nikki was the capital of the Hausa state of Borgu when they agreed to assign Nikki to France and allocate most of Borgu to Britain. Indeed, five years earlier, in 1893, the French had included Borgu in their newly proclaimed protectorate of Dahomey, without first signing a treaty with Borgu. However, Britain had earlier claimed Borgu by virtue of the treaty which the Royal Niger Company had signed with Bussa. The French position was that the chief of Bussa was subordinate to the chief of Nikki, who alone had the authority to sign treaties and in any case Nikki, the capital of Borgu, was in French territory. It turned out that in making this claim, France had not yet met and signed a treaty with Nikki. An attempt was made in 1894 when a French commissioner arrived in Nikki only to discover that the British had already signed a treaty five days earlier. Yet at the Anglo-French Convention of June 1898, Nikki was assigned to France!

A recent review of the contemporary political situation in Uganda by Ali Mazrui (1979) shows clearly some of the implications and consequences of the arbitrary political boundaries of tropical Africa. The former military ruler of Uganda, General Idi Amin, belongs to the Kakwa ethnic group, whose territory was split by colonial boundaries so that the group is now represented in three countries, Zaïre, Sudan and Uganda. Idi Amin himself comes from a border village near the Sudan. We agree with Ali Mazrui that the contemporary history of Uganda could have been different if the British colonial office had accepted the recommendation of its field officers that the West Nile district of Uganda be included in Sudan. Idi Amin would have been a Sudanese citizen and the political developments in Uganda since independence might have taken a different course. The alternative decision turned out to be advantageous to Idi Amin who reportedly recruited into the Ugandan army a large number of loyal members of his ethnic group from the Sudan and Zaïre. It is also relevant at this point to observe that the protracted but abortive war of secession against the Arab-dominated central government at Khartoum by the predominantly African negroid peoples of southern Sudan drew considerable support in men and materials from the Kakwa people of Uganda.

The eastern borderlands of Nigeria and Cameroun consist of a range of rugged highlands and therefore provide a good example of a natural boundary zone. But rather than serve as a barrier to human movements, the rugged highlands became a refugee zone for dozens of small ethnic groups such as the Margi, Kilba, Batta, Verre and Mambila, each of which occupies a restricted but contiguous territory. The most widespread groups in the borderlands are, however, the Fulani and Hausa who are newcomers to the region. The Fulani were attracted to the area because they found the tsetse-free highlands to be good for grazing their cattle while the Hausa are mostly itinerant traders. During the *Jihad* (Holy War) which swept the Fulani to power over a large part of northern Nigeria, Adamawa and parts of northern Cameroun were subdued by the Fulani of Yola. The British–German boundary arrangement not only split many ethnic group territories into two, but also placed certain parts of Fulani-controlled territory in German Cameroun, while the greater half remained in Nigeria. Many chiefs in the German areas, however, remained loyal and continued to pay tribute to the Fulani rulers in British Nigeria, and although the Germans were irritated by this practice, they were unable to destroy Fulani native administration in the Cameroun.

It is common to describe boundaries which follow natural features such as rivers, mountain ranges and watersheds as natural boundaries as distinct from 'artificial' boundaries. However, all political boundaries are created by man and the facts presented so far show clearly that so-called natural boundaries are often no less artificial than straight lines. Furthermore, international boundaries in tropical Africa have often been described as artificial, largely because they were created by European colonial powers. Yet since independence no governments or secessionist groups have been able to alter any of these boundaries. When faced with secessionist threats, each government has

invoked Article 3 of the Charter of the Organization of African Unity which accepts the existing boundaries of each country as inviolate. Attempts at secession in Zaïre, Nigeria, Sudan and Ethiopia have failed and are not likely to succeed elsewhere largely because there are potential secessionists in almost every country.

It is also paradoxical that the free flow of people and goods between countries has become more restricted since independence. This is partly a result of a sudden development of boundary consciousness by the various young countries which have been much occupied with problems of internal security. Indeed in many countries political instability has often resulted in the closure of boundaries with neighbouring countries. Suspected and genuine cases of subversion by political refugees in neighbouring countries have tended to result in greater restrictions on the movements of people and even in the expulsion of aliens in some countries. However, increasing boundary consciousness has also been caused by the desire of each country to raise revenue through import and export duties. The fact that many international boundaries cut across ethnic territories has contributed considerably to the high incidence of smuggling.

The inescapable conclusion is that the so-called artificial boundaries of the colonial period have come to stay. Attempts to alter existing boundaries, even for the purpose of seeking to enable such ethnic groups as the Ewe of Ghana and Togo, the Masai of Kenya and Tanzania or the Luval of Zambia and Angola to be within one country instead of two as at present, will be most unlikely to succeed. Future efforts to facilitate the movements of people and the free flow of trade and capital appear to lie in establishing and maintaining effective regional economic communities on the lines of the Economic Community of West African States or the recently defunct East African Community.

Internal boundaries

At independence, the various countries of tropical Africa inherited not only the international but also the internal administrative boundaries of the colonial period. We have already discussed the human problems associated with international boundaries and the inherent difficulties of altering them. Similar problems occur with many internal boundaries, and although many more administrative districts and provinces have been created in many countries since independence, it has not been easy to alter the inter-group boundaries dating from the colonial period, as well as those internal boundaries which split the territories of some ethnic groups and thereby place them in two or more districts.

Pl. 18.2 Soldiers manning the border between Zimbabwe and Mozambique during the pre-Independence war

In 1967 in Nigeria, for example, twelve states were created out of the three states of the colonial period and in 1975 seven more states were created. Curiously, the basis for creating these states was the colonial period districts, the boundaries of which were established before 1920. This is a great credit to the field officers of the early colonial period whose task it was to advise on the delimitation of district and provincial boundaries.

In establishing the internal administrative boundaries, the colonial governments were fully aware that one of the main causes of inter-group warfare and bloody clashes between clans and villages was the conflicting claims for land. Indeed the immediate reason for establishing these boundaries was to prevent further boundary disputes. In the process some villages and groups ended up with vast areas of land which they had acquired by conquest while others had to be content with the little land on which they were able to establish an effective claim. In the course of time the boundaries have contributed to the existence in some countries of pockets of very densely populated areas surrounded by extensive areas which are very sparsely settled or virtually uninhabited, but which belong to other villages or ethnic groups.

Although the internal boundaries helped to define the limits of ethnic and village territories, boundary disputes between villages and ethnic groups were not uncommon throughout the period of colonial rule and

even to this day. Indeed some ethnic groups, such as the Tiv of the Benue Valley of Nigeria, continued to expand their territory as if they had no concept of boundaries. Frequent border raids by the Tiv continued and in 1912 the Nigerian Government decided to build the Munshi (Tiv) boundary wall, consisting of a three-foot (0·9 m) high rampart with a ditch, from which the material was excavated on one side. The wall later proved ineffective because the Tiv did not only 'climb over the wall', but also migrated in large numbers in other directions (Bohannan and Bohannan, 1962).

In each of the countries formerly under British rule, there are three different categories of administrative units, namely, the district, the division and the province. The district is made up of a number of village territories or clans while the division consists of several districts. Two or more divisions make up a province. Each unit has administrative headquarters. In some countries there is still a higher unit called the region or state. Many more units of all categories have been created in some countries since independence with a view to making the government much closer to the people. In this process of decentralization, boundaries between villages and regions or states have posed the greatest problems. We now proceed to explain the background and the resulting problems.

Village boundaries denote the smallest areas throughout tropical Africa and were based mostly on a chief's area of jurisdiction. One of the problems associated with this definition of the village boundary was that a chief's jurisdiction was and is still over people who acknowledge him as chief rather than over a given area of land. Thus there were situations in which people lived in territories claimed by other groups and yet acknowledged a chief in an adjacent territory. There were also situations in which dissident groups abandoned a village to establish another village in a territory claimed by the parent village, even though the dissidents refused to recognize the authority of the parent village head. Village boundary disputes have continued today in the form of protracted litigation, and instances of open confrontation, resulting in loss of life, are still common. The main cause of these boundary disputes is the quest for more farmland and sometimes the desire to ensure that the compensation for land acquired by government for development purposes is paid to one village rather than another.

State boundaries have also posed considerable problems in countries such as Nigeria where the federal system of government has been adopted. This is because some internal state boundaries, like many international boundaries, cut across ethnic territories. The 1906 boundary between the former eastern Nigeria and the former northern Nigeria, for example, was a straight line drawn along latitude $7°10'N$, and cut across the ethnic territories of the Ibo, the Idoma and the Tiv, resulting in small Ibo populations in northern Nigeria and small Idoma and Tiv populations in eastern Nigeria. The western part of the boundary which divided northern Nigeria from western Nigeria also cut across the Yoruba ethnic territory such that Ilorin and Kabba Provinces were included in northern Nigeria. Further the boundary between western and eastern Nigeria cut across the Ibo and Ijaw ethnic territories.

There is no doubt that these regional or internal state boundaries were drawn up when much of the country had not yet been explored. From 1917, some of the boundaries were revised, notably that between northern and eastern Nigeria. However, the revised boundaries still left small Ibo groups in northern Nigeria and Igalla as well as Tiv minorities in eastern Nigeria. The problem surfaced during the early years of independence when the various regional (state) governments started to regard the state boundaries as if they were international boundaries. Some leaders of minority groups created in the various states expressed the desire to be transferred to the states in which the bulk of their ethnic population was assigned, but were ignored. This has not been resolved since the boundaries of the present nineteen states were based on the district boundaries drawn up during the colonial period.

Finally, there was another category of internal boundary in such countries as Kenya, Zimbabwe and Zambia where the land of some ethnic groups was alienated by the colonial governments and reserved for European settlers. All of these countries have since become independent with the result that administrative units are no longer reserved for whites or Africans. However, the problems created by segregation in the colonial period have still not disappeared, at least as far as spatial inequalities in development are concerned. This situation has arisen largely because European reserves were usually located in areas served by existing major roads and railways and were therefore more accessible and attractive for development. As a result the major towns grew up in the European reserves which also included the important mining districts. The former European areas are therefore the industrialized parts of these countries and are also agriculturally better developed. Boundary changes are not necessary in such situations since the restriction of movements of citizens no longer exists. Boundary disputes between villages and ethnic groups however continue to present problems as in other countries.

To this day, ethnic consciousness persists and so does the attachment of ethnic groups to their own particular territories. However, there are signs that the new generation is becoming less attached to their ethnic territories since an increasing number now live and die outside their areas of origin. With the current rapid rate of urbanization, ethnic consciousness and close links with ethnic territories will hopefully weaken and give way to national consciousness. More administrative units may continue to be created for the purpose of getting the government closer to the people. Boundary disputes are also likely to continue, but, with luck, on a much reduced scale.

References

Barbour, K. M. (1961), 'A Geographical Analysis of Boundaries in inter-Tropical Africa', in K. M. Barbour and R. M. Prothero (eds.), Essays on African Population, Routledge and Kegan Paul, London, pp. 303–23.

Bohannan, L. and Bohannan, P. (1962), The Tiv of Central Nigeria, International African Institute, London, p. 54.

Hertslet, E. (1909), The Map of Africa by Treaty, vol. I, 3rd ed., HMSO, London.

Mazrui, A. A. (1979), 'Ethnicity, Power and Population in Eastern Africa', in R. K. Udo et al. (eds.), Population Education Source Book for Sub-Saharan Africa, Heinemann, London, pp. 296–304.

Nugent, W. V. (1914), 'The Geographical Results of the Nigeria–Cameroun Boundary Demarcation Commission, 1912–13', Geographical Journal, 43, pp. 630–48.

Prescott, J. R. V. (1959), 'The Evolution of Nigeria's Boundaries', Nigerian Geographical Journal, vol. 2, no. 2, pp. 80–104.

19 The Process and Problems of National Integration

Introduction

The thirty-seven countries of tropical Africa are independent political entities (with the exception so far of Namibia), and each independent country has a defined territory, a national flag and anthem, and a recognized government. These countries are sometimes referred to as states and it is usual to talk about the head of state of Zaïre or Senegal paying a state visit to Nigeria or Tanzania. It is also common to refer to these countries as nations. It is therefore worth defining the terms state and nation to ensure that they are properly understood.

A state is a specified territory organized politically in an effective manner by an indigenous, or resident, people with a government in effective control of the area. The term may refer to a single country like Ghana or Kenya or, as is the case in Nigeria, to a unit of regional government such as Oyo State or the Cross River State. At present, Nigeria is made up of nineteen states but has only one head of state, because, as far as world bodies such as the United Nations or the Organization of African Unity are concerned, Nigeria is one political unit with a single national flag and one national anthem. There have also been city states such as in ancient Greece or in Hausaland and the Niger Delta during the pre-colonial period. The city states of Greece included Sparta, Athens and Crete, while those of pre-colonial Nigeria included Kano, Zaria, Ife, Abeokuta, Bonny and Abonnema.

It is common practice to equate a state with a nation, which we define as a population group which occupies a distinct territorial area and which regards itself as a political community because its members are bound by historical ties or share a common sentiment, ethnic kinship and often a common language. Ideally the state and the nation should be identical, and this indeed is the case with nation states such as ancient Benin, and the early kingdoms of Ashanti, Buganda and Barotse. There is, however, no nation state in contemporary Africa, since all the countries and even the states of Nigeria consist of two or more national groups. This is indeed the basic problem facing national integration in African countries where the main cementing factors are the national flag, the national anthem and a common official language imposed on the country by the former colonial rulers, and adopted on independence for the purpose of promoting national integration.

In Africa the term nationalism has often been identified with anti-colonialism or anti-European activities. Nationalism is however the desire of cultural, linguistic or religious groups to achieve a political status that would give them some measure of self-government to enable them to protect and deepen their cultural identity (Pounds, 1972). In tropical Africa, as indeed in other parts of the world, a common language or common religion or even common ethnic origin is not a sufficiently cohesive factor to establish national unity. Most African countries consist of two or more indigenous peoples speaking a variety of languages and professing different religions. Furthermore, the ethnic territories of such groups as the Hausa, Yoruba, Ewe, Tonga and Tutsi were shared between two or more colonial powers and these divided territories have since become independent countries. The obvious signs of social cohesion which make for national consciousness, namely a common language, common religion or common ethnic origin, therefore do not exist in any single African country.

The process of national integration

National integration involves political as well as territorial integration. The desire to achieve both dimensions has been the major preoccupation of the leadership of African countries since independence, and still constitutes the major obstacle to nation building. Political integration is concerned with bridging the gap between the minority but increasing indigenous élite and the vast majority of the rest of the population – the so-called masses. The problem of political integration is widespread but more pronounced in countries such as Liberia and Sierra Leone where the majority of the population has been dominated politically and economically by a culturally differentiated minority group, such as the Creoles of Freetown and, until recently, the Americo-Liberians of Monrovia. The survival during the colonial period of political domination of the majority by the minority, such as the case of the Fulani oligarchies in northern Nigeria, or Tutsi domination of the majority Hutu in Rwanda and Burundi, also created considerable problems of political integration at independence.

Structural social inequalities have increased in all countries since the end of the colonial period and constitute a major threat to political integration. In a situation of comparatively rapid social and economic development, the gap between the rich and the poor has tended to widen. The minority élites of the colonial period have continued to dominate the economy and politics of the various countries. It is true that their number is increasing but the élites still constitute a small proportion of the entire population, the rising expectations of whom must be met if more military coups are to be prevented.

The second dimension of national integration is horizontal in character and is identified as territorial integration. Currently, territorial integration poses the most serious problem to national integration in several countries, and is manifested through the series of attempted or planned secessions in countries such as Nigeria, Zaïre, Ethiopia, Ghana and the Sudan. Every country in Africa is made up of two or more distinct ethnic groups, each of which occupies a distinct contiguous territory and has distinct customs, languages and beliefs. Often the larger and politically better organized groups such as the Ashanti of Ghana, the Edo of Nigeria and the Ganda of Uganda enjoyed considerable autonomy and independence under the system of indirect rule during the colonial period. Today, for example, many people in Nigeria still think of themselves first as Yoruba, Hausa, Ibo, Edo or Igbirra and secondly as Nigerians. Furthermore, there has been a persistent tendency for political aspirants to exploit ethnic (tribal) feelings in their efforts to get elected to serve in the national (not ethnic) legislatures. There has also been a marked tendency to exhibit tribal sentiments (nepotism) in the matter of public appointments and the award of scholarships. These tendencies have come to be collectively referred to as tribalism, which has rightly been considered to be the most problematic aspect of national integration in tropical Africa.

Secessionist tendencies have been encouraged by the increasing manifestations of spatial or regional economic inequalities which, like structural social inequalities, have become more pronounced since independence. The concentration of government development projects in a few areas, often the home districts of members of the politically dominant groups, has tended to create disaffection amongst some minority groups who complain of discrimination in various spheres of public life. The situation is worse in those countries where the main source of government revenue consists of mineral or agricultural exports produced in the home territories of aggrieved ethnic minorities. In Nigeria, for example, the persistent demand for and the subsequent creation of more states in 1967 and 1975 was based on the belief that more states would mean more even development, resulting in the creation of a greater sense of belonging amongst disadvantaged groups. The break-up of the old Western Nigeria, for example, into five states can be considered to be a form of internal political disintegration or 'secession' aimed at achieving lasting national unity.

Given the large number of ethnic groups in most countries and the absence of basic unifying principles, the major foundation for national unity in each country was the collective loyalty to the political movement that dominated the scene during the struggle for independence. After independence, parliamentary opposition, made up largely by minority groups, came to be increasingly associated with anti-national feelings, and was generally ruthlessly suppressed. Hence the emergence of the one-party state in most tropical African countries, the governments of which progressively degenerated into dictatorships. Supporters of the one-party state have often argued that the system makes it possible to pool together the country's manpower resources for effective development rather than indulge in the luxury of lengthy parliamentary debates. The one-party system usually succeeded in lessening political conflict only for a while as was the case in Ghana and Mali. It also created underground opposition groups which have contributed towards military intervention in the politics of African countries.

Stages in the struggle for independence

Given their common experience as colonial territories and the fact that each country is made up of many ethnic groups, it is not surprising that the path towards national integration has been basically the same. In the first stage there was very little criticism of the colonial administrations by the African population, even though many ethnic leaders and the then few educated élite resented the high-handedness of many colonial officers. As the number of graduates from the predominantly missionary-controlled educational institutions increased, a sizeable opposition against the colonial governments grew up especially in territories like Kenya and Rhodesia (Zimbabwe), where African land had been forcibly taken over and given to white settlers. A number of committees of intellectuals, advocating limited reforms, were formed in various territories. Youth movements and pressure groups representing local religious and economic interests were organized for political action, seeking to displace the colonial governments. Early politically oriented organizations included the National Congress of British West Africa, formed in 1917, the Nigerian National Democratic Party of 1923 and the Kikuyu Central Association of 1928. In Senegal local Africans such as Blaise Diague of the Serer tribe had featured in political activities as early as 1914 when he was elected to serve as the first African Deputy in the French Assembly in Paris. He later became the mayor of Dakar in 1924.

The second stage came in the 1940s and particularly after the Second World War when organized political activity became very pronounced in the colonial territories of tropical Africa. Some of the more prominent political associations of this period which were basically of the congress type include:

1. The Kenya African Union (KAU) formed in 1944. This was basically a Kikuyu tribal movement although it tried to serve as an all-Kenya movement and stood for self-government for all Africans in Kenya.
2. The Nyasaland African National (NAC) founded also in 1944 to protect African interests by seeking to prevent government from passing discriminatory laws and recommending to government legislation that would benefit Africans.
3. The National Council of Nigeria and the Camerouns (NCNC) also formed in 1944 and whose membership was open to trade unions, professional associations, and tribal unions. The objective of the NCNC was internal self-government for Nigeria and the British Camerouns.
4. The Rassemblement Démocratique Africain (RDA) formed in 1946 and whose membership was open to every national group in French West Africa.

Other similar associations were formed in Northern Rhodesia (Zambia) (1946), Ghana (1947), Uganda (1952) and Southern Rhodesia (Zimbabwe) in 1957.

The next and final stage in the fight against colonialism was the emergence of political parties. Naturally, these parties grew up from the then existing ethnic cultural unions and political associations. Unfortunately, the increasing rivalry between major ethnic groups meant that political parties in each territory came to be identified with particular ethnic groups. Some political parties attempted to involve citizens from all ethnic groups and did enjoy support from several such groups. The survival or not of these multi-ethnic parties depended very much on whether or not the leaders of the component ethnic groups were satisfied with the manner in which political patronage was distributed.

Ethnic power struggles in Nigeria

The large size and varied ethnic composition of the population combine to make Nigeria very representative of the African political scene. A brief review of the process and problems of national integration in

Nigeria is therefore presented to illustrate the trends of political developments since the closing years of the colonial period. There are about 200 ethnic groups in the country, each of which occupies a contiguous territory and has a different language. The largest ethnic groups are the Hausa–Fulani (12 million), the Yoruba (10 million) and the Ibo (8 million). Each of these three major groups happens to be politically dominant in only one of the three main political units – the northern, western and eastern regions – which were to become the three states of Nigeria at independence in 1960. This geographical fact was to prove of great advantage to the first generation of Nigerian politicians each of whom drew their support almost exclusively from their ethnic territory. At the same time it posed serious problems for creating national consciousness.

Party politics in Nigeria became prominent during the last decade before independence and came to an abrupt end in January 1966 when the military took over political power for a period of almost fourteen years (January 1966 to September 1979). This review is restricted to the period ending in 1966 largely because events during the first few months after the resumption of politics in October 1978 have confirmed that little or no change can be expected in the pattern of political support and voting behaviour among Nigerians. The same type of personal and ethnic feuds which destroyed the Nigerian Youth Movement in 1941 have already featured in some of the political parties of the post-military era.

Before independence, the three major political parties in the country were each identified with one of the three major ethnic groups. The National Council of Nigerian Citizens (NCNC) which started in 1944 as the National Council of Nigeria and Cameroons was the only party which strived to stay national in outlook although it came to be dominated by and identified with the Ibo of eastern Nigeria. The Action Group (AG), founded in 1951, was similarly identified with the Yoruba of western Nigeria while the Northern Peoples Congress (NPC) was identified with the Hausa–Fulani of northern Nigeria. The political creed of the NPC was 'North for Northerners, East for Easterners, West for Westerners and the Federation for all' and is very relevant to an understanding of the politics of the time.

In each of the then three states of the Federation of Nigeria, there was at least one opposition party led and supported by members of minority ethnic groups. The government party in each state was dominated by the majority ethnic group. It was over the struggle to control the Federal Legislature that the three major groups stepped on each other's toes. The position taken by each minority group in the political drama that ensued depended very much on what its leaders considered to be in the best interest of the group. As a

Pl. 19.1 Soldiers of the Nigerian Federal Army examine captured Biafran weapons during the Biafran War, 1967–70

rule candidates for parliament had to be indigenes of the constituency. Other Nigerians who had spent even up to twenty years as residents in a given constituency were still considered to be 'aliens' who could not be supported at the polls. Politically minded 'aliens' were normally expected to go to their home districts to canvass for votes. Thus, when in 1951 the NCNC won the election over the predominantly Yoruba-dominated Western Nigeria House of Assembly, many prominent Yoruba politicians became extremely embarrassed at the prospect of the Ibo leader of the NCNC being appointed the premier of a Yoruba state! Hence the infamous episode of mass 'carpet-crossing' in which many Yoruba parliamentarians deserted the Ibo-led NCNC to join the Yoruba-led Action Group. The result was that the Action Group, which was defeated at the polls, ended up forming the government at Ibadan while the NCNC, which won the election, was forced to form the official opposition.

It is possible that a similar situation might have arisen at Enugu if a Yoruba-led party had won the election in the Eastern Region of Nigeria. Indeed having been cheated of the position of Leader of Government Business (premier) in the Western Region, the Ibo

NCNC leader returned to Enugu and successfully displaced the non-Ibo Leader of Government Business, thereby precipitating a crisis within the NCNC. It was after this unfortunate incident that the NCNC, like the Action Group, became more of a tribal than a national party. Thus, throughout the pre-1966 period of party politics ethnic consciousness and considerations hampered the emergence of a Nigerian nation. There are strong indications that the politics of the Second Republic may not be very different since the political leaders of the First Republic are also the leaders of parties formed in 1978.

Ethnic rather than national consciousness and the desire of the major groups to dominate the politics of the country have been largely responsible for the failure of the three post-independence censuses of 1962, 1963 and 1973. Under the Nigerian constitution, the basis of representation in parliament is size of population. Given the ethnic pattern of voting at elections, and the fact that the political party in power always won the elections in its area of authority, it became obvious to Nigerian politicians that the only way, other than a military coup, to maintain or change political control of the Federal Legislature was by manipulating the population census. It is noteworthy that the NPC, which dominated the politics of the Northern Region of Nigeria and which controlled over 50 per cent of the seats in the Federal Legislature, readily accepted the rejected 1962 census and the controversial census of 1963. The NPC was able to do so because the two censuses confirmed the numerical superiority of the Northern Region over the two southern regions (Eastern Nigeria and Western Nigeria), since this meant that the NPC was guaranteed continued control of the Federal Legislature. The Action Group and the NCNC, on the other hand, rejected the census figures because these two southern parties had hoped that the census would show that there were more people in the two southern states than in Northern Nigeria (Udo, 1968). The political crisis that followed on the wake of the census dispute culminated in the breakdown of law and order in Western Nigeria during the latter part of 1965. It was this situation that provided the excuse for military intervention on 15 January 1966.

The worst phase of ethnic rivalry and hatred was yet to come; because although the January 1966 coup was heralded with fanfares in all parts of the country, the rejoicing lasted only a few days. People became disillusioned when details of casualties in the military uprising were known and they were gripped by a feeling of fear and suspicion. The leaders of the coup were found to be mostly of the Ibo ethnic group while almost all the senior army officers killed were non-Ibo. Furthermore, the Yoruba and Fulani premiers of Western and Northern Nigeria, respectively, as well as the federal prime minister who was Hausa, were killed, while the two Ibo premiers of Eastern and the newly created Midwestern Nigeria were spared. And to crown it all, the most senior army officer, who was eventually selected to head the Federal Military Government, was Ibo. The turn of events was too much for a country in which the major ethnic groups were already very suspicious of one another. Most Nigerians came to see the coup as an attempt by the Ibo to dominate the country.

An uneasy calm prevailed until towards the end of May 1966 when a carefully co-ordinated plan to eliminate all eastern Nigerians in Northern Nigeria was carried out simultaneously in almost all the cities of Northern Nigeria. Thousands of civilians of eastern Nigerian origin, largely Ibo, living and working in the north, were massacred. It was at this stage that the Ibo-controlled government of Eastern Nigeria started making plans to secede from the Federation. Various unsuccessful attempts were made to reconcile the Ibo and thereby preserve the unity of Nigeria. Unfortunately in September 1966 there occurred a second barbaric massacre of more Ibo in Northern Nigeria, following reports that the Ibo had also embarked on killing people of northern origin as a reprisal for the earlier massacres of May. The stage was set for a civil war and in a frantic effort to prevent it, the Federal Government created twelve states in Nigeria on 27 May 1967, thereby dividing Eastern Nigeria into three states. The Ibo rejected the new federal structure and proceeded to proclaim Eastern Nigeria as an independent Republic of Biafra. This was the immediate cause of the civil war which lasted till 15 January 1970, when Biafra formally surrendered to federal troops.

Obstacles to national integration in East and Central Africa

Kenya

The ethnic diversity of the populations of the countries of East and Central Africa is similar to that of Nigeria and so are the problems created by ethnic consciousness and rivalry in the process of political unification at the national level. In Kenya, for example, leading politicians have often exploited ethnic sentiments to discredit their rivals in the political race for power. There are four major ethnic groups in the country: the Kikuyu of central Kenya who number about 2·20 million and who organized the nationalist guerrilla warfare, the so-called Mau Mau insurrection, against the British colonial administration; the Luo (1·52 million) of the Nyanza Lake district; the Luhya (1·45

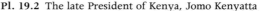

Pl. 19.2 The late President of Kenya, Jomo Kenyatta

million); and the Kamba (1·20 million). It is perhaps not surprising that the Kikuyu have dominated the politics of Kenya since independence. However, the Kikuyu appear to have grabbed more than their fair share of the national cake and have thereby caused considerable internal dissension. Furthermore, Kikuyu leadership under the late Jomo Kenyatta tended to become rather dictatorial and very resentful of Luo intellectuals, his former ethnic allies.

It was as far back as 1944 that the first country-wide political organization, the Kenya African Study Union (KASU), was formed on the advice of the British Governor of Kenya (Odinga, 1968, p. 97). The organization later became the Kenya African Union (KAU) which in 1946 came under the dynamic leadership of the prominent Kikuyu politician, Jomo Kenyatta. The KAU under Kenyatta tried to unify the Africans against continued British rule but did not receive much support from some Luo leaders (notably Tom Mboya) of the Nyanza district. The strength of KAU lay chiefly among the Kikuyu, that is Jomo Kenyatta's ethnic group. The rather moderate political programme of KAU was altered in 1951 when some of the moderate members were voted out of office and when the Africans first made a demand for total independence from Britain. In 1952, the uneasy British colonial administration declared a State of Emergency and proceeded to ban KAU. Jomo Kenyatta was arrested on charges of managing the Mau Mau insurrection, and the following year he was sentenced to seven years' imprisonment. About 13,000 people were dead and 80,000 in detention

when the Mau Mau was crushed in 1959; but the suppression of the rebellion also signalled the end of white supremacy in Kenya, and indeed in East Africa (Lonsdale, 1971).

In March 1960 a new party was formed, the Kenya African National Union (KANU), in effect a revival of KAU. KANU was dominated by the Kikuyu and the Luo, the two largest ethnic groups in the country. As in Nigeria, each leader of KANU, whether Kikuyu or Luo, had a tribal base. KANU was highly resented by the minority ethnic groups who in August 1960 proceeded to form another party, the Kenya African Democratic Union (KADU), which came to be known as the party of the small tribes. When in 1961 KANU won eighteen out of the thirty-three African seats in the general elections the party demanded the release of Jomo Kenyatta before it would form a government. The colonial administration rejected the ultimatum and the minority party KADU, led by Ronald Ngala, eventually formed a government. Fortunately for Kenya, at least for a time, KADU later agreed to form a coalition government with KANU, thereby making it possible for Jomo Kenyatta to become Leader of Government Business a few months after his release from detention.

Independence came in 1963 but early in 1964 the foundations of national unity were shaken by a mutiny of the army. The emergence of a one-party state at independence failed to promote the much-desired goal of national integration owing to internal dissensions within the party. There were open criticisms of the government for concentrating development projects in

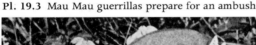

Pl. 19.3 Mau Mau guerrillas prepare for an ambush

Kikuyu territory and for favouring Kikuyu in public appointments even in the university. Kenyatta did not take kindly to public challenge of his authority and policies, and reacted by becoming increasingly dictatorial. He subsequently clashed with the Luo leader Oginga Odinga whom he later imprisoned and prevented from participating in politics. Further, as in Ghana, many prominent Kenyan politicians who had fought for independence were progressively assassinated by pro-Kenyatta fanatics. Kenyatta died in 1978 and was succeeded by a president from one of the minority ethnic groups. It appears, therefore, that the threat of secession from dissatisfied minority groups has been contained, but events since independence have not created much sense of commitment to the Kenyan nation by all the ethnic groups.

Rwanda and Burundi

A rather complicated situation exists in both Rwanda and Burundi, both of which experience severe population pressure on available farmland, which is the main natural resource of the two countries. Both countries have a lot in common, not only because they were formerly administered as colonial territories of Belgium, but also because of their rugged landscapes and the ethnic composition of their populations. Rwanda has a population of 3·68 million, while Burundi has a population of 3·34 million. These two countries therefore rank amongst the smallest in tropical Africa.

The three major ethnic groups in both countries are the Hutu, the Tutsi and the Twa, each of which is extremely conscious of its ethnic identity. The two larger groups, the Hutu and the Tutsi, compete for political control while the much smaller Twa group is mainly concerned with struggling to survive as a distinct ethnic group. Such a situation cannot, and does not, favour the emergence of national consciousness.

In both Rwanda and Burundi, the Hutu constitute the overwhelming majority, but have for generations been subjected to political domination by the minority Tutsi who make up only 10 per cent of the population of Rwanda and 15 per cent of the population of Burundi. The situation is complicated by the fact that the Tutsi minority openly despise the Hutu majority in much the same way as the British settler minority despised the Africans in colonial Kenya! It is not surprising therefore that with the approach of independence and the emphasis on majority rule, the despised Hutu began to exploit the powers of their numbers while the minority but aristocratic Tutsi began to feel insecure about the future. In 1959, the Hutu of Rwanda successfully rebelled against their Tutsi overlords. An estimated 20,000 lives were lost during the rebellion while an estimated 100,000 refugees fled to neighbouring countries (Mazrui, 1979). Hutu majority rule in Rwanda

was therefore established at great cost to human life. The maintenance of Hutu administration was to cost even more lives during the first decade of independence owing to repeated raids by Tutsi refugees, seeking to regain political control, resulting in further massacres of Tutsi within Rwanda. The republican government established in 1961, just before independence, found it difficult to enhance national unity since members of the Tutsi ethnic groups could not be trusted in view of the continuing raids by Tutsi refugees from neighbouring countries. There has, however, been considerable lessening of tension between Hutu and Tutsi since about 1975, but it will take some time before the wounds of the civil disturbances are healed.

Tutsi minority rule has continued in Burundi, but also at great cost to human life. As a result of the Hutu ascendancy in Rwanda, the Tutsi rulers of Burundi became scared of the future and rather repressive of the Hutu majority, especially after the assassination in October 1961 of Premier Rwagasore who had earlier carried out an extensive campaign for national unity so as to prevent confrontation between the Tutsi and the Hutu. Although the monarchy served as a stabilizing force during the early years of independence in Burundi, the fact that the king appointed eight consecutive governments between 1962 and 1965 is clear evidence of the political instability that existed in the country. Efforts by the king to promote unity included allotting ministerial posts in almost even proportions between the Hutu majority and the Tutsi minority ruling group. The assassination of the Hutu prime minister in 1963 worsened the delicate political situation as the minority Tutsi progressively took control of the government. What followed was the abortive Hutu uprising against the Tutsi in 1965 which was ruthlessly suppressed, when at least eighty Hutu leaders were executed.

Burundi became a republic in 1966, following the deposition of the ruling king, Ntare V, and a concerted effort was made to reconcile the Hutu and Tutsi by the republican prime minister, Michael Micombero, himself a Tutsi. Unfortunately his efforts ended suddenly in October 1969 when the Hutu attempted to overthrow his government in another abortive coup. Another period of bloodshed and repression of the Hutu followed. Worse was yet to come. In April 1972 the Hutu, backed by Hutu refugees from Tanzania, staged a major uprising to oust the Tutsi from power. Obviously tired of the repeated Hutu threat to their continued political domination of the country, the Tutsi decided to teach the Hutu a lasting lesson. About 100,000 people, mostly Hutu, were killed in the organized massacre of Hutu, and the general confusion which ensued. The ethnic problem in Burundi is therefore a major obstacle towards achieving national unity.

Zaïre

Another country which has experienced serious problems of national integration is Zaïre which became independent on 30 June 1960 only to be confronted with the secession of Katanga about two weeks later, and another secession attempt in the Kasai Province. The secessionist movement in Kasai was crushed by the central government troops of Lumumba, but the Katanga rebels under Moise Tshombe received substantial support from the European-controlled mining interests, and were able to sustain their rebellion until January 1963 when Tshombe agreed to end the secession. Several other revolts occurred after the murder in Katanga of Lumumba, the first prime minister, in January 1961 and continued until 1967, when General Mobutu introduced a new constitution with himself as president.

Political instability and military coups

Since 1960 when most countries in tropical Africa became independent of colonial rule, about twenty-five of these countries have experienced one or more military coups. Often the coups have been provoked by political instability created by ethnic power struggles for political control and in some cases the excuse for military intervention was the deteriorating economic situation resulting in mass unemployment in the cities and general dissatisfaction among the people. In all cases, the army has pledged to restore political and economic stability and to promote the process of national integration. Often each coup has been followed by a counter-coup which was sometimes prompted by ethnic dissensions within the army, disaffection of junior officers or the inability or failure of the army rulers to correct the political and economic evils which in the first instance provided them with the excuse to overthrow the legal governments (First, 1971, pp. 19–20).

The performance of military administrations in the various countries, notably Ghana, Nigeria, Zaïre, Uganda and the Republic of Benin, shows clearly that a solution to the political and economic problems of the young countries of tropical Africa will only be found with patience and careful planning. Indeed in most cases, the army rulers have not performed better than the maligned ousted politicians. This is not surprising since the members of the armed forces are themselves part and parcel of the system which they attempt to change. Apart from the peculiar problems of the economy of tropical African countries dating from the colonial period with a heavy dependence on foreign capital goods and foreign technology – a situation which army rulers cannot change overnight – we find that once in power, the army rulers have generally fallen victim to the same set of social and political evils which they condemned. Indeed, some army rulers have been so corrupt that they have amassed much more wealth in a shorter period of time than any politician could do. Furthermore the army governments have generally tended to make life more comfortable for soldiers at the expense of other citizens. Defence expenditures have sky-rocketed while basic social services, including education and health, have suffered. Shortages of essential commodities have increased in some countries and, given the pattern of military expenditure, the rate of inflation has risen. These are some of the reasons which have made an increasing number of people weary of army rule and which have provided excuses for counter-coups.

Yet, by the very nature of its organization, a disciplined army offers the hope of infusing national consciousness into the diverse ethnic groups of the countries of tropical Africa. In seeking to achieve this important and basic goal, the army must of course recognize that national consciousness cannot be accomplished by force. Deliberate efforts to reduce regional economic inequalities, liberalize education and make members of the various ethnic groups feel a sense of belonging are what is required. The army is really not cut out for such programmes, hence the need for the military to withdraw from the political scene at the earliest opportunity. Fortunately, after two decades of military rule and misrule, both the military and the people appear to have had enough of the army meddling in politics. It is this situation that offers some hope that the next set of politicians will endeavour to carry out policies that will make for rapid economic development, social justice and above all promote national integration and therefore ensure continued political stability.

References

First, R. (1971 ed.), 'Political and Social Problems of Development', in *Africa South of the Sahara 1971*, Europa Publications, London, pp. 19–20.

Lonsdale, J. (1971 ed.), 'Recent History of Kenya', in *Africa South of the Sahara 1971*, Europa Publications, London, pp. 404–6.

Mazrui, A. A. (1979), 'Ethnicity, Power and Population in Eastern Africa', in R. K. Udo *et al.* (eds.), *Population Education Source Book for Sub-Saharan Africa*, Heinemann, London, pp. 296–304.

Odinga, O. (1968), *Not Yet Uhuru*, Africa Writers Series, Heinemann, London, p. 97.

Pounds, N. J. G. (1972), *Political Geography*, McGraw-Hill, New York, p. 6.

Udo, R. K. (1968), 'Population and Politics in Nigeria', in J. C. Caldwell and C. Okonjo (eds.), *The Population of Tropical Africa*, Longman, London, pp. 97–105.

20 Economic Integration and African Unity

In 1965, when almost all the countries in tropical Africa had become independent of colonial rule, the region was politically more fragmented than it was during the colonial period. In West Africa, for example, the colonial-period Federation of French West Africa was broken up into nine independent countries, while the four English-speaking countries of Gambia, Sierra Leone, Ghana and Nigeria drifted further apart following the dissolution of several common services, including the West African Currency Board, the West African Frontier Force and the West African Airways Corporation. The foundations of regional integration in East Africa, which were laid by the British, remained, albeit in a shaky form, until the final break-up of the East African Economic Community in 1978. The shaky Central African Federation of Malawi, Zambia and Rhodesia (Zimbabwe) also broke up even before the first two countries obtained independence from Britain. The position today is that the 'balkanization' of Africa, which is commonly blamed on the colonial powers, has been upheld and rendered more problematical by indigenous African politicians. Inter-country movements of people and goods have become more restricted since independence, while the ties with the maligned metropolitan countries remain strong!

It is indeed strange and disturbing that the progressive disintegration of Africa was taking place at a time when the older and more developed countries of Europe and the Americas were coming closer together to form common markets and strong military alliances. It is also unfortunate that an admirable attempt made by the United Nations Economic Commission for Africa (ECA) in the early 1960s to bring about the formation of an economic community in West Africa ended in failure. And yet Africa is in great need of some form of economic unity to enable co-ordinated planning of the development of her vast natural resources. Today, Africa remains poor and heavily dependent on Europe, America and Japan largely because it is divided into too many mini independent countries. The result is that human and physical resources, and markets, are also divided by artificial but effective political boundaries. This chapter presents the case for economic integration and political unification and also reports on progress.

The case for economic and political integration

The late President Kwame Nkrumah of Ghana was by far the best-known advocate of African Unity. He held the view that unless Africa was united under an all-African Union Government, there could be no solution to her political and economic problems. Nkrumah was fully aware of the enormous problems confronting his proposals which most of his opponents, as well as some friends, considered to constitute 'a policy of the impossible' (Nkrumah, 1963, p. 170). Many of his contemporaries, including the late Prime Minister Tafawa Balewa of Nigeria, the late President Jomo Kenyatta of Kenya and President Houphouët-Boigny of the Ivory Coast, also appreciated the need for some form of economic union to be followed much later by political union. However, like most contemporary African politicians, they thought that Nkrumah was in too much of a hurry. Their view was that each country should first consolidate its independence by resolving the difficult problem of national integration. Nkrumah, on the other hand, insisted that now was the time for political unity and charged that 'to suggest that the time is not yet ripe for considering a political union of Africa is to evade facts and ignore realities in Africa today' (Nkrumah, 1963).

In 1970 there were only five countries in Africa south of the Sahara with populations greater than 10 million, twenty-nine with less than 5 million and thirteen with less than 2 million. Most countries are therefore so small and are so extremely poor that they cannot maintain a permanent mission at the United Nations. Furthermore, all countries, with the possible exception of Nigeria, still depend very much on 'foreign aid' for financing capital projects. Indeed some French-speaking countries are unable to balance their budgets without subvention from the French Treasury with which most of them still maintain Operation Accounts. It is true that each of these economically backward mini countries has a vote in the United Nations. But it is also a fact that both the United States of America and the Soviet Union, each of which has a population of over 200 million and one vote in the United Nations, play a more decisive role in that world body than the combined forces of the 36 independent countries of tropical Africa. The size of the territory and of the population of a country are certainly factors to reckon with in the world economic order and world politics. Political independence is certainly a necessary but not a sufficient condition for effective participation in world politics. An all-African Union Government or an Africa made up of four governments in East, West, Central and southern Africa could be a great force to reckon with both politically and economically. The case for economic and political integration in tropical Africa is a strong one. Indeed the issue is so basic that an increasing number of Africanists hold the view that the only choice open to African peoples and governments is 'unity or poverty' (Green and Seidman, 1968).

At present no African country, with the possible exception of Nigeria, is economically large enough to evolve a modern economy on its own. However, Africa as a whole has vast resources and a large population comparable with the United States and the Soviet Union. The problem is that the continent and its resources are split among more than forty independent countries. Currently tropical Africa is the leading world producer of cocoa, sisal, palm oil, and an important producer of groundnuts and coffee. The mineral wealth is also extensive, Africa being the leading world producer of gem diamonds, cobalt, gold, columbite antimony, manganese and phosphate rock. The power resources are impressive because although the coal resources are limited, tropical Africa has the greatest water power potential in the world. Economic integration and some form of political union is necessary for the effective and planned development of these vast resources for the benefit of African peoples.

Apart from the issue of divided resources, political fragmentation has created very small domestic markets for each country. Today the cash market of most countries like the Republic of Benin, Togo, Botswana, Burundi and Guinea-Bissau are considered to be comparable to that of a medium-sized American or European city. Many manufacturing industries established in these countries have therefore had to operate at sub-optimal levels and therefore hardly make any profit. Government investments in small tariff-protected industries, in the continuing process of modernizing the local economy, have often turned out to be a drain on scarce resources rather than serving as a base for further development.

The restricted market for manufactured goods is created largely by the existing trade barriers set up by most countries to generate revenue from import and export duties. For commodities like beer, soft drinks, flour and printed cotton, in which the demand exceeds the supply, as is the case in Nigeria, there is no problem

whatsoever. But there are many industrial plants, such as the huge modern plywood factory in Gabon, the Tema lorry assembly plant in Ghana and a number of oil refineries in the smaller countries, which are operating below full capacity because the national markets are too small. Some countries have reacted to this situation by building small factories which have turned out to be inefficient and rather expensive to operate. Such factories have been able to survive because of high import duties imposed on foreign goods, most of which are not only cheaper but of much better quality.

It is common knowledge that the market problem can be resolved through the formation of a free trade area, a customs union or, better still, a common market. This would make possible the replacement of the many small inefficient oil refineries by a few suitably located large ones which would provide the basis for modern petrochemical complexes producing numerous by-products essential for both the manufacturing and agricultural sectors. Specifically, it would make it possible for Nigerian manufactures to earn free entry to the Republic of Benin, Niger and Cameroun and *vice versa*. The current situation whereby the Republic of Benin imposes a higher import duty on cigarettes made in Nigeria as compared with cigarettes made in France would thereby cease. It is indeed sad that such a trade restriction has in turn resulted in the Nigerian Tobacco Company restricting the amount of leaf tobacco produced by the Nigerian farmer.

Today, the economy of the countries of tropical Africa continues to be vulnerable to the fluctuations in world prices due to their over-dependence on the export of primary products. The increasing use of synthetic raw materials suggests that the future of primary products is very uncertain. African countries would do well to expand their domestic markets for such primary products if they are to avert serious economic crises. Fortunately many countries are now expanding their industrial sector by utilizing these products in local factories. But apart from the limitations imposed by small domestic markets, some countries, such as the Ivory Coast, Kenya and Tanzania, do not have adequate generated power to support large-scale manufacturing. Neighbouring countries such as Ghana and Uganda, however, have power installations which are not fully utilized because of inadequate demand. Economic co-operation would certainly make for better planning and a more effective use of the power resources of tropical Africa for the overall benefit of the people.

The case of the iron and steel industry demonstrates clearly the need for economic and possibly some form of political union. Iron and steel constitute the backbone of modern industry and even agriculture has come to depend more and more on iron and steel products. But no country in tropical Africa except Nigeria has the market or the capital to support a modern integrated iron and steel works. Yet tropical Africa has large deposits of high-grade iron ore in Mauritania, Sierra Leone, Guinea, Liberia, Angola and Zimbabwe, as well as smaller deposits elsewhere. A combined market of all the countries in West Africa, for example, would be more than adequate for one or two steel works in view of the growing demand for iron and steel products for industrialization. At present, in West Africa Ghana has built a steel mill to produce 40,000 tonnes per year from scrap and eventually from local iron ore, while Nigeria has a small steel mill at Enugu which also uses scrap but operates at a loss! Nigeria, which has very little iron ore, is currently constructing a ₦641 million steel complex at Ajaokuta in Kwara State, while Niger Republic has planned a small iron factory based on local iron ore near Say to produce 20,000 tonnes of reinforcing rods and cast iron every year. Joint production of iron and steel, making use of low-cost but high-grade ore from Mauritania, Liberia and Sierra Leone would be more beneficial to all and would create more employment and more opportunities to train local technologists; that is in addition to conserving considerable foreign exchange.

West Africa also has sufficiently abundant resources to sustain a large efficient chemical industry which could produce fertilizers to make possible the much talked about revolution in agricultural production. Togo has over 50 millon tonnes of high-grade phosphate deposit, which is now shipped in crude form to be manufactured in other countries. That country, however, does not have enough power to support a large fertilizer factory. Fortunately, the neighbouring country of Ghana has excess power and since 1972 has been selling electricity to Togo. Economic integration would provide better terms for the sale of electricity not only from Ghana but also Nigeria which has since started generating power from its vast wealth of natural gas.

Shortage of local capital to develop local mineral resources has led to unhealthy competition in offering favourable terms to attract foreign investors who also provide much-needed technological skills. Most governments have been obliged to levy extremely low taxes on mining companies, thereby curtailing the national income from the mining sector. In their desire to attract investors, African governments are also known to have invested substantial local and borrowed resources in developing basic infrastructure to serve the mining sector rather than the agricultural sector which employs the vast majority of the people.

It is the weak bargaining position of these poor mini countries that has made it possible for large multinational corporations, such as Unilever and Lonrho, to continue to exploit them. By extracting minerals, such as bauxite in Guinea, and smelting it in Cameroun or Ghana, large foreign firms have been able to play one country against another in order to obtain more favourable tax and royalty agreements. In all such cases, the affected African countries, which have neither the capital nor the skilled personnel to mine or smelt the ore, lose considerable sums of money in the process. It has indeed been suggested that the main reason why France supported the abortive attempt by Biafra to secede from Nigeria was because France believed that it would obtain more generous terms for exploiting crude oil from small Biafra than it could hope to get from the larger and economically powerful united Nigeria. Some form of economic or political union would certainly be of great advantage to the countries of tropical Africa and would eventually lessen their great dependence on Europe and North America.

Past attempts at political unification

The earliest attempts at political unification of the balkanized countries of tropical Africa were linked with the French colonial policy of direct rule, whereby all French territories overseas were regarded as integral parts of the French Republic. Accordingly, by a decree promulgated as early as 1904, French territories in tropical Africa were constituted into two federations. These were the eight-territory Federation of French West Africa made up of Senegal, Mauritania, Guinea, Sudan (Mali), Dahomey (Benin), Niger, the Ivory Coast and Upper Volta; and the four-territory Federation of French Equatorial Africa, made up of Chad, the Central African Republic, Gabon and Congo (Brazzaville). Each territory had its governor, who was responsible respectively to the governor generals resident at Dakar for West Africa and at Brazzaville for Equatorial Africa. The two governor generals were in turn answerable to the Minister for the Colonies and to the French Parliament.

Under the 1946 constitution of the French Republic, the territories making up the two French African federations were given direct representation in the French National Assembly. African politicians in the Paris Assembly were, however, not satisfied with the handling of African affairs in the Assembly. This contributed to the formation of the first two political parties which cut across territorial boundaries to embrace almost all the French-speaking countries of Africa. These parties were the Rassemblement Démocratique Africain (RDA) in 1946 and the Indépendents d'Outre Mer (IOM) in 1948. At the IOM Congress of 1953, held at Bobo-Dioulasso, the formation of a Federal Republic of French West Africa was proposed. But shortly after the meeting, Senghor of Senegal favoured the creation of two states in French-speaking West Africa, each with a premier and a parliament to be located at Dakar and Abidjan. However, in 1956 the French Government promulgated a decree, the *loi cadre*, which prepared the way for internal autonomy in each of the twelve territories of French tropical Africa, thereby effectively undermining the two federations. Rivalry between Senghor of Senegal and Houphouët-Boigny of the Ivory Coast (the architect of the *loi cadre*) contributed to the break-up of the French African Federations of the colonial period (Thompson and Adloff, 1958, pp. 83–107). Of course France was very happy about this development and took an active part in encouraging the emergence of mini independent countries which would be obliged to depend on French financial and administrative support after independence.

The general enthusiasm for political unification however continued amongst some countries of French West Africa after the first few months of independence. Unfortunately, but understandably, the various countries started to drift apart as each became more concerned with its internal security, national integration and economic development. The collapse in 1960 of the Mali Federation proved to be a major setback to advocates of political unification.

Another major attempt at political unification in the colonial period, this time by the British, was the formation in 1953 of the ill-fated Central African Federation of Northern Rhodesia (Zambia), Southern Rhodesia (Zimbabwe) and Nyasaland (Malawi). This Federation was formed before independence and is therefore similar in some respects to the Federation of French West Africa which also broke up at the eve of independence from France. Massive African hostility to the Central African Federation stemmed largely from the fact that Africans saw it as a device for strengthening and extending white minority political domination over the area. Many of the fears expressed by Africans who formed the vast majority (96 per cent) of the population in the federation were in fact justified by

subsequent developments. About 56 per cent of all new investments, mostly in industry between 1953 and 1963, for example, went to Southern Rhodesia. Political union also made it possible for the use of Northern Rhodesia's favourable trade balance to import capital equipment to develop more industries in Southern Rhodesia, including the construction of the largest integrated iron and steel complex in tropical Africa.

There were sound economic arguments in favour of the federation since the economies of the three territories were in many respects complementary to one another. Nyasaland (Malawi) was poor in physical resources but had a plentiful supply of cheap unskilled labour which was in great demand in the mines, factories and farms of Southern Rhodesia. Northern Rhodesia had a thriving copper-mining industry but very little development in manufacturing and agriculture. It also had a large pool of cheap labour. There was, however, a major political factor, namely, the racial policies of Southern Rhodesia which made the union unrealistic right from the start. It is not surprising, therefore, that in spite of certain obvious economic advantages to the three territories, the federation finally broke up in 1963.

In 1958, shortly after Guinea had opted for independence from France, the country entered into a political union with Ghana, which had achieved her independence a year earlier. This union was unique for two reasons. It was the first attempt at political unification by two independent African countries and secondly it was the first major attempt at some form of collaboration between an English-speaking and a French-speaking African country. Two years later the Republic of Mali joined to form the Ghana–Guinea–Mali Union, a few months after the collapse of the Mali Federation. The union assumed the name of Union of African States (UAS) and was expected by its founders to form the nucleus of the United States of Africa (Nkrumah, 1963, p. 142). Membership was open to every state or federation of African states which accepted its aims and objectives. No other state joined the Union up to the time of the fall of Nkrumah in 1966,

Table 20.1   Area and population of the Central African Federation (1953–63)

Territory	Area (sq km)	Total population	Africans	Europeans	Others
Northern Rhodesia (Zambia)	752,610	2,183,100	2,110,000	66,000	7,100
Southern Rhodesia (Zimbabwe)	389,360	2,481,200	2,290,000	178,000	13,200
Nyasaland (Malawi)	118,480	2,596,600	2,580,000	6,800	9,800
Federation	1,260,450	7,260,900	6,980,000	250,800	30,100

*Figures for 1956.

from which time the Union may be considered to have ceased to exist.

Another serious attempt to form a political union was made in January 1959 when Senegal, Dahomey (Benin), French Sudan (Mali) and Upper Volta met to draw up a plan to form a federation with headquarters at Dakar. The federation was formally established on 25 March 1959, by which time Dahomey and Upper Volta had been persuaded to withdraw by Houphouët-Boigny who had argued that political unity should be left to the next generation (McKay, 1964, p. 105). Instead, Houphouët-Boigny convinced Upper Volta and Dahomey along with Niger Republic to join with the Ivory Coast to form a loose economic arrangement called the Conseil de l'Entente in the middle of 1959. The political union of Senegal and the French Sudan assumed the name of Mali Federation. It was a short-lived union because the leaders and political parties in the two member countries had different concepts of political unity. Senegal, the richer and more developed country, wanted a loose federation while the French Sudan (Mali) insisted on a unitary form of government. The result was that in August 1960, the union abruptly ended when Senegal decided to secede. The Sudanese Republic, however, proceeded to adopt the name of Republic of Mali, and on 24 December 1960, Mali joined with Ghana and Guinea to form the Union of African States.

Alternatives to political union

The break-up of the Mali Federation, the fate of the Union of African States involving Ghana, Guinea and Mali and the abortive attempt by Biafra to secede from Nigeria and of Katanga to secede from Zaïre, all go to emphasize the difficulties inherent in attempting to alter the existing political boundaries of tropical Africa. It appears that although most governments have accepted in principle and made public pronouncements about the urgency for political union, many are still unwilling to make the sacrifices that such a union would entail. What then are the alternatives, if any, to political unification? Most countries consider some form of economic integration to be the first step towards inter-state co-operation and eventual political union.

Economic integration can take any of the following forms depending on the degree of co-operation required:

1. a free trade area which involves the abolition of tariff restrictions among the participating countries, but leaves each country to establish independent tariffs against third countries;
2. a customs union involving the abolition of internal barriers to trade and adoption of a common tariff against third countries;

3. a common market in which restrictions on both trade and factor movements are abolished;
4. an economic union which combines the abolition of restrictions on commodity and factor movements with harmonization of national economic policies;
5. total economic integration in which monetary, fiscal, social and other policies are unified and in which a supra-national authority takes decisions binding on all member states.

About twenty years after the independence of most tropical African countries, the whole region has still not been constituted into a free trade area. Yet the free trade area is considered to be the simplest form of economic integration to negotiate. Several attempts have, however, been made to form customs unions and common markets embracing groups of countries.

The East African Community

This was probably the most effective of the customs unions of tropical Africa. It ceased to exist in 1978. Its history dates back to the establishment in about 1925 of the East African Common Market for the purpose of uniting Kenya, Uganda and Tanganyika behind a common tariff-wall designed to protect agriculture in the then White Highlands of Kenya (Green and Seidman, 1968, p. 141). It became very effective only with the creation in 1948 of the East African High Commission which immediately started to operate joint services in the fields of transport and communications, research and education, resulting in a sharp rise in inter-territorial trade. When Tanganyika became independent in December 1961, the basis of co-operation changed. However, the governments of the three countries recognized the need for the continued maintenance of existing common services and therefore decided to replace the High Commission with the East African Common Services Organization which came into being in 1961 (O'Connor, 1971). Several joint ministerial committees were created but there were no provisions for monetary policy, harmonization of taxation or for integrated economic planning.

In 1964 and again in 1965, the Common Services Organization was in danger of breaking up because of the following factors:

1. The benefits derived from the union were largely in Kenya's favour while Tanzania was the net loser. Industries which could be supported by single territorial markets were heavily concentrated in Kenya. Furthermore the location of the headquarters and the main operating units of each common service in Kenya brought disproportionate benefits to Kenya.
2. The agreement signed in 1964 at Kampala, providing for the relocation of certain industries and joint measures to protect new industries in Uganda and

Tanzania from competition by Kenya, were badly implemented and led to bitter disputes.

3. There were increasing ideological differences between the three member countries, especially Tanzania and Uganda.

Fortunately good counsel prevailed and after a series of negotiations supported by outside consultants, the Common Services Organization was reconstituted in December 1967 as the East African Community with headquarters at Arusha in Tanzania. Provision was made in the Treaty of 1967 for admission of new members. Ethiopia, Zambia, the Somali Republic and Burundi had made formal applications for membership long before the Community broke up in 1978.

The West African Customs Union
This was comprised of all former territories of French West Africa with the exception of Guinea and was formed in 1959. The union aimed at protecting the trade patterns of the colonial period as well as to encourage the local production of consumer goods. Although some effort was made to redistribute a portion of revenue derived from import duties, the details of this delicate issue had not been properly worked out and agreed upon. There was no attempt to adopt uniform tariff rates against third countries. Within a few years the customs union had failed although the member states were able to preserve some features of a free-trade area for natural products and manufactured goods (Plessz, 1968). Specifically the main reasons why the West African Customs Union failed were:

1. The lack of basic political understanding among member countries. The Ivory Coast, which is by far the richest country in the group, with about half of the union's export and tax revenue, was unwilling to continue to subsidize the weaker countries, especially Senegal.

2. The absence of appropriate centralized customs administration. The landlocked states of Mali, Upper Volta and Niger were not happy about the allocation of customs revenues at the ports, an arrangement which deprived them of income from the re-export trade. The issue of re-locating some consumer goods industries to replace coastal concentration in Dakar in particular resulted in a stalemate.

The West African Economic Community (1967–68)
One of the on-going programmes of the United Nations Economic Commission for Africa (ECA) which was established in 1958 is the promotion of economic co-operation and integration between the member states. In executing this programme the ECA divided Africa into four sub-regions, North, West, East and Central. The first step towards achieving a continental economic unification was to organize sub-regional economic

unions. It was in pursuance of this objective that the ECA carried out some studies on the economy of West African States (Plessz, 1968, p. 53) and subsequently arranged a series of meetings and consultations which resulted in the formation of the West African Economic Community at Accra in May 1967. Four English-speaking countries, Nigeria, Ghana, Sierra Leone and Liberia, as well as the eight French-speaking countries, signed the Accra agreement. The first meeting of the Interim Council of Ministers took place at Dakar in November 1967 and in April 1968 the heads of state met in Monrovia to sign the Protocol establishing the community. Nothing more was accomplished after the Monrovia meeting with the result that this admirable effort by the ECA to bring about economic integration in West Africa ended in failure.

The Equatorial Customs Union
This was formed in 1959 following the break-up of the Federation of French Equatorial Africa of the colonial period. Its main purpose was to ensure that goods and capital would continue to move freely within the territories of member countries. Amongst other things, the union sought to rationalize and harmonize tax and tariff systems of the four member states (Europa, 1971).

In 1961 arrangements started for the gradual inclusion of Cameroun and in December 1965 the Equatorial Customs Union was transformed at Brazzaville into the Central African Economic and Customs Union (UDEAC) made up of Chad, the Central African Republic, Cameroun, Gabon and Congo (Brazzaville). The provisions of the Brazzaville treaty included the following:

1. The creation of a customs union constituting the five countries into a free trade area in which there is free movement of persons, merchandise, services and capital. A common external tariff, additional to previous duties and fiscal charges, is levied on all imports into the area, except on goods from members of the European Economic Community (EEC) and from Madagascar.

2. The establishment of a solidarity fund of 20 per cent of all customs receipts to be paid as compensation to the landlocked states of Chad and the Central African Republic. This arrangement was adopted to avoid defining policies for the allocation of industries and to ensure that the interior states obtained an obvious net gain from the Union.

3. The joint allocation of industries requiring markets in at least two states such as the oil refinery at Port Gentil, Gabon which is a joint enterprise. The Executive Council decides on measures to harmonize development plans and transport policies.

4. The adoption of a uniform tax system.

5. The acceptance of one Central Bank as the sole issuing bank for the five countries.

So far UDEAC has not faced any serious problems of ideological differences or internal rivalry similar to that between Senegal and the Ivory Coast. UDEAC is therefore one of the few attempts at economic integration made in the 1960s surviving into the 1980s.

Barriers to political and economic integration

The failure of many attempts at political and economic union in tropical Africa suggests that there are some factors which tend to work against any form of integration. One such factor is the economic and sometimes political chains dating from the colonial period and binding many countries to the economic apron strings of their former colonial rulers. Most countries have defence pacts with European powers and sometimes provide for military bases and standing armies of alien powers on their territories. Colonialism in many countries has been replaced by neo-colonialism, which constitutes a major hindrance to economic and political integration.

A good example of one of these economic restraints is the existence of separate monetary zones, namely the franc, dollar and sterling zones. At independence, the various colonial powers, especially Britain and France, tried to ensure that the new states remained in monetary zones centred on London, Paris or Brussels. In the case of France, membership of the franc zone meant *de facto* retention of decisions on monetary supply and credit by the Central Bank in Paris. For operational convenience French-speaking Africa was divided into three separate monetary unions for West Africa, Central Africa including Cameroun, and Malagasy, each group having one Central Bank. Each of these group Central Banks has an Operation Account with the French Treasury and is given in return automatic overdraft facilities for use in times of foreign exchange shortages. Implicit in this arrangement is the fact that France may use the reserves of African members to settle her balance-of-payments accounts with countries outside the franc zone. Certainly, the problems of obtaining foreign exchange have contributed to the small volume of trade between neighbouring African countries in different monetary zones, such as Nigeria and the Republic of Benin, Angola and Zaïre or Sierra Leone and Guinea. The result is that many countries continue to maintain a trade pattern which is not very different from what it was during the colonial period.

On the whole the economic chains binding the French-speaking countries to France have been much greater compared with the position of the English-speaking countries. Indeed it is widely believed that it was the desire by France to ensure her continued domination of the economy of her former African territories that made her support, and even encourage, the break-up at independence of the Federation of West Africa and that of Equatorial Africa. At present many French-speaking countries still depend on 'aid' from Paris to subsidize their budgets. Some of these countries are fully aware that the profits that accrue to France as a result of existing trade and monetary arrangements are far greater than what is given to them in 'aids'. They appear to be helpless in breaking the chains that France has put round their necks. It is proper to mention that France gives preferential treatment to primary exports from French-speaking African countries. But what these countries need now is trade on fair terms rather than aid or preferential treatment, both of which have resulted in too much economic dependence on France. The resulting current feeling of security which is essentially false would then be replaced by one of self-reliance. This is best achieved through a regional and possibly an all-African common market, not through being an associate member of the European Economic Community.

It has often been argued that one major reason why there is little trade between countries like Nigeria, the Republic of Benin and the Ivory Coast is the fact that the basis for trade does not exist, since these countries produce similar crops for the domestic as well as the export market. This argument is no longer tenable today since some countries such as Nigeria and Ghana now consume all their palm oil and palm kernels as well as cotton and a large proportion of rubber and groundnuts in local factories. Indeed, Nigeria has become a net importer of palm oil since 1974 and has often had to temporarily close down several textile factories because of the shortage of locally-produced cotton wool. A basis therefore exists for trade in primary products, but more so in many manufactured goods produced in the larger industrial areas of Lagos, Dakar, Abidjan, Nairobi and Accra–Tema.

The poor state of transport and communications between states is a major disadvantage. However, this factor should not be overemphasized because large countries like Nigeria, Sudan and Zaïre still survive as single political units, even though many areas are not readily accessible to motorized transport and even though postal services and telecommunications remain very unsatisfactory. There are no international or transcontinental roads or railways, although the Lagos–Nairobi–Mombasa motor road is now under construction. No English-speaking country has so far been linked by railway to any French-speaking country and, besides, roads linking one country to another are circuitous and poor towards the borders. Air services between some countries are few and expensive. Extensive development of inter-state transport is necessary for the expansion of trade between the various countries.

Intense parochial nationalism and the fear of economic and political domination of the smaller states by the larger and richer states constitute the most serious barriers to economic and political integration. For the newly independent states of tropical Africa as indeed for all governments, the maintenance of territorial integrity and of national sovereignty followed by improvement of the quality of life of the people are the most fundamental objectives. Smaller countries, as well as landlocked countries, are afraid to forego their independence since, as in the case of Tanzania in the East African Community, they may be the net loser in the resultant integrated economy. Political unity implies loss of political power to some politicians, who would be obliged to play relatively less prominent international roles in a Union Government. On the other hand disintegration or secession means creating important political positions for more people! It is also a fact that some of the wealthier countries are hesitant to enter into a union in which their potential wealth may be tapped to develop countries which are less endowed with natural resources.

Existing supra-national organizations

With the exception of the Central African Economic and Customs Union (UDEAC), all the supra-national organizations discussed under the section dealing with alternatives to political unification have since ceased to exist. But the desire for some form of economic and political unification remains very strong amongst some states. We shall therefore end this chapter by discussing briefly the few existing supra-national organizations, some of which may eventually form the basis for regional political unification and possibly an all-African political union. The organizations considered are 1. the Conseil de l'Entente, 2. the Chad Basin Commission, 3. the Niger River Basin Commission, 4. the Organization of Senegal River States (OERS), 5. the Economic Commission of West African States (ECOWAS) and 6. the Afro-Malagasy Common Organization (OCAM).

The Conseil de l'Entente
Founded in 1959, the Conseil de l'Entente (that is, Council of Understanding), usually called the Entente, is a political and economic association of five states – the Ivory Coast, Niger, Upper Volta, the Republic of Benin and Togo. There is complete freedom of trade between

member countries and a unified system of external tariffs and fiscal schedules. In 1961, the member states signed agreements with France covering defence, civil aviation, higher education, cultural relations, economic affairs and postal and telecommunications. Upper Volta did not sign the defence agreement. The Entente is therefore very much a neo-colonialist organization which may disappear when the ECOWAS takes off. At present some member states have not made the agreed regular payments of 10 per cent of total customs revenue to the Entente solidarity fund.

The Chad Basin Commission
This was formed in 1964 to co-ordinate projects aimed at the social and economic development of the member countries of Cameroun, Chad, Niger and Nigeria, and thereby prevent conflict among countries which border the lake in their efforts to exploit the water resources of the Lake Chad Basin. It is specifically charged with the exploitation of the subterranean and surface water resources in relation to agricultural development (irrigation), animal husbandry and fisheries. A scientific survey of the water resources of the basin has since been completed with the help of UNESCO and some irrigation projects have been started in Nigeria and Chad. Landlocked Chad is also to be linked up with other countries by a railway extension from Maiduguri in Nigeria to N'Djamena and by another railroad from N'Gaoundéré in Cameroun to Southern Chad.

The Niger River Basin Commission
The Republic of Benin, Cameroun, Guinea, the Ivory Coast, Mali, Niger and Upper Volta are the present members of the Niger River Basin Commission which was formed in 1963 and which has its headquarters at Niamey in Niger Republic. The formation of this Commission, like that of the Chad Basin and the Senegal River Valley, is a clear testimony of the growing awareness amongst African statesmen of the great need for economic and political co-operation between states, especially those served by international rivers or lake basins. It is therefore curious to notice that Nigeria is not a member of the Niger River Basin Commission even though one-third of the Niger River and almost the entire length of its main tributary, the Benue, flow through Nigerian territory. Indeed in 1977–8, the Nigerian National Electric Power Authority reported a major drop in the water level of Lake Kainji on the Niger River, resulting in extensive power cuts over a large part of the country which receives power from the Kainji hydro-electric power station. A Niger Waters Agreement in which Nigeria is represented, similar to the Nile Waters Agreement between Egypt and the Sudan, appears to be overdue. So far, the work of the Niger River Basin Commission has consisted of a survey

aimed at improving navigation and general economic development along the River Niger.

The Organization of Senegal River States (OERS)

The youngest of the several mini unions that have characterized the West African sub-region since independence is the Organization of Senegal River States (OERS) which was founded in 1968 to replace the Senegal River Basin inter-state committee of 1963. The four member states – Mali, Senegal, Mauritania and Guinea – have a combined population of only 14 million, the earning power of which is still too small to support large-scale manufacturing industries. The aims and purposes are similar to those of other organizations in West Africa and include the encouragement of co-operation and solidarity as well as the maintenance of peaceful and friendly relations between member states. The Council, which has its headquarters at Dakar, is charged with the responsibility for initiating, executing and controlling projects aimed at developing the Senegal River Basin. Economic independence and social progress of member states are expected to be achieved through coordination of planning and action in the areas of agriculture, education, transport, trade and public health. The physical and manpower resources of the OERS are however rather limited to permit the realization of its laudable objectives. The real hope for the future lies in integrating its programmes with those of the larger union of the Economic Community of West African States (ECOWAS).

The Economic Community of West African States (ECOWAS)

The four existing supra-national organizations already considered in this section involve only countries in the West African sub-region. They provide ample evidence of the continuing desire for economic integration. The birth of the Economic Community of West African States (ECOWAS) in Lagos on 28 May 1975 was therefore a great event, and it did not come too soon. On that day, all fifteen heads of states in the sub-region met and signed the 65-clause treaty which is expected to promote co-operation and development in all fields of economic activity as well as in social and cultural matters. It aims to raise the standard of living of its peoples, increase and maintain economic stability and contribute to the progress and development of the African continent. In order to achieve the above objectives the treaty provided for the progressive elimination between member states of customs duties and other charges on imports and exports, the establishment of a common customs tariff between third countries, the free movement of people (without visas), services and capital, the establishment of a fund for co-operation, compensation and development and the harmonization of economic policies. ECOWAS is in effect a resuscitation of the West African Economic Community which became moribund after the 1968 meeting of heads of states at Monrovia. Negotiations to resuscitate it started in 1972 between Eyedema of Togo and Gowon of Nigeria.

With a total population of over 120 million and its great wealth of natural resources, the West African sub-region is well equipped for meaningful and effective economic development. Organizations such as the Niger River Basin Commission, the Senegal River Commission and the Chad Basin Commission may have to cease or be constituted into development authorities within ECOWAS, although the present attitude appears to be that such organizations could continue to exist provided their objectives were not inconsistent with those of ECOWAS. There are great hopes that ECOWAS will succeed. However, as of 1981 citizens of member states are still awaiting the abolition of visas and entry permits to enable the free movement of people and trade goods within the sub-region.

The Afro-Malagasy Common Organization (OCAM)

Like the ECOWAS, the Afro-Malagasy Common Organization is an economic union of fifteen member states, but unlike ECOWAS, all member states of OCAM are former colonial territories of France. It was founded in 1965 to replace the African and Malagasy Organization for Economic Co-operation (OAMCE) of 1961, which had relied heavily on French official experts and private capital and was unable to achieve much in terms of co-ordinated economic development. The member countries are the Ivory Coast, Senegal, Togo, the Republic of Benin, Upper Volta and Niger from the West African sub-region; the five countries of UDEAC (that is former French Equatorial Africa) and Zaïre, Rwanda, Mauritius and Malagasy. The declared purpose of OCAM is to accelerate the political, economic, social, technical and cultural development of member states within the framework of the OAU. It aims to achieve this through the harmonization of customs regulations, the setting up of an African Common Market, the suppression of subversion in African states, the creation of stabilization funds in support of steady prices and the harmonization of taxation and investment codes. Achievements of OCAM, which like other similar organizations has experienced considerable problems, include the signing and ratification of a Common Sugar Market agreement and the operation of Air Afrique with headquarters at Abidjan. OCAM coffee-producing countries now operate as one unit for the purpose of operating the International Coffee Agreement.

Note

The former French Equatorial Africa consisted of Chad, Cameroun, Gabon, Congo and the Central African Republic.

References

Europa Editorial Board (1971), *Africa South of the Sahara 1971*, Europa Publications, London, p. 117.

Green, R. H. and Seidman, A. (1968), *Unity or Poverty? The Economics of Pan-Africanism*, Penguin African Library, Harmondsworth.

McKay, V. (1964), *Africa In World Politics*, Macfadden-Bartell Corporation, New York.

Nkrumah, K. (1963), *Africa Must Unite*, Panaf Books Ltd, London.

O'Connor, A. M. (1971), 'Geography and Economic Integration', in S. H. Ominde (ed.), *Studies in East African Geography and Development*, Heinemann, London, pp. 73–85.

Plessz, N. G. (1968), *Problems and Prospects of Economic Integration in West Africa*, McGill-Queen's University Press, Montreal, p. 58.

Thompson, V. and Adloff, R. (1958), *French West Africa*, George Allen & Unwin, London. Ch. 5 deals with political parties in the region.

Glossary

assimilado – An African in Angola, Guinea-Bissau or Mozambique who during the colonial period was allowed to become a Portuguese citizen as distinct from a colonial subject.

banket – Dutch word meaning confectionery. Used to describe the thin bands of quartz-pebble conglomorates or 'reefs' in which gold occurs in South Africa. The weathered conglomorate resembles an almond confection.

bidonvilles – Literally 'towns built of tin cans'. Shanty towns in the suburbs of large cities.

boundary – See frontier.

crude birth rate – This is the simplest measure of actual fertility. It is calculated by dividing the total number of live births during a given year by the total male and female population as of July 1st of that year, and multiplying by 1,000 persons.

crude death rate – The simplest measure of mortality, it is calculated by dividing the total number of deaths (after live birth) during a given year by the total male and female population as of July 1st of that year, and multiplying by 1,000 persons.

dambo – A waterlogged area along a water course in Zambia, Zimbabwe and Malawi.

dega – A cool climatic region usually above 2,500 m in the Ethiopian Highlands. The vegetation consists of alpine prairies.

fadama – Hausa word for seasonal marsh in areas of low topography with clayey soils. Often found along river floodplains.

frontier – A long narrow zone which 'fronts', that is faces a neighbouring country. It is sometimes called a border, and is different from a boundary which is the actual line separating two countries.

gallery forest – Belt of forest trees along the course of a river or stream in the grass-woodland savanna zone.

huza – A system of land tenure amongst the Krobo migrant farmers of Southern Ghana, in which some migrants form themselves into a company to purchase land which is then laid out in strips and allocated to each member in proportion to the amount of money he contributed.

inselberg – Literally 'island mountain'. An isolated steep sided hill.

kharaj land – Conquered land on which tribute or *kharaj* is payable under Islamic land law. Two forms of *kharaj* land exist and these are *wakf* and *sulh*. *Wakf* land was conquered by force and *kharaj* is payable as rent. *Sulh* land consists of areas that accepted Islam peacefully and under treaty. The inhabitants pay *kharaj* as tribute.

kilowatt – 1,000 watts.

kilowatt-hour – The unit in which electric power consumption is billed. Two 60 watt electric bulbs kept switched on for 24 hours will produce a total consumption of $2 \times 60 \times 24$ or 2,880 watt-hours which is the same as 2·88 kilowatt-hours (Kwh).

kurmi – Hausa word for an island of woodland in an open savanna landscape.

kwashiorkor – A word which literally means 'disease of the deposed baby'. It is a serious disease which affects children of one to three years, and is caused by protein deficiency in food. Kwashiorkor may result in delayed growth of the child, swelling of the face and limbs and even death.

laterite – A red, ferruginous soil which hardens on exposure. It is found in tropical regions and may be rich enough in iron to be used as iron ore.

marasmus – A disease which affects children and is caused by calorie deficiency.

megawatt – A system of units for measuring power. I megawatt = 1,000 kilowatts or 1,000,000 watts.

mesas – Flat-topped hills with steep sides in a desert or semi-desert environment. The word *mesa* in Spanish means 'table'.

miombo woodland – Tree savanna vegetation in Eastern and southern Africa in which the dominant species are *Isoberlinia* and *Brachystegia*.

nation – A group of people associated with one another by ties of history, descent and sometimes language. A nation may be organized into a separate country or state, but usually a state or a country contains two or more national groups.

navetanes – Strange farmers or seasonal migrant farmers to the groundnut growing districts of Senegal and the Gambia. Most of these migrant farmers originate from Mali and Guinea.

quolla – The hot and wet climatic zone which extends to a height of 1,830 m on the Ethiopian Highlands. It is covered with dense forest of juniper and euphorbia.

seyane – Lagoons and marshes formed behind coastal sand dunes in the St Louis area of Senegal.

suq – A traditional weekly periodic market in Morocco.

watt – The basic unit of electric power, expressing the rate at which electric energy is being expended. Note that 1 horsepower (HP) = 746 watts.

woina dega – A warm or temperate climatic zone in the Ethiopian Highlands which lies between 1,830–2,500 m above sea level. It has a mountain grassland vegetation.

Further Reading List

(A) Books

Allan, W. (1965), *The African Husbandman*, Oliver & Boyd, Edinburgh.

Baldwin, K. D. C. (1957), *The Niger Agricultural Project*, Blackwell, Oxford.

Barbour, K. M. (1961), *The Republic of the Sudan*, University of London Press, London.

Batten, T. R. (1953), *Problems of African Development*, Oxford University Press, Oxford.

Bauer, P. T. (1954), *West African Trade*, Cambridge, Cambridge University Press.

Bohannan, P. (1954), *Tiv Farm and Settlement*, Colonial Research Series, London.

Bohannan, L. and Bohannan, P. (1962), *The Tiv of Central Nigeria*, International African Institute, London.

Bohannan, P. and Dalton, G. (1962), *Markets in Africa*, Northwestern University Press, Evanston.

Buchanan, K. M. and Pugh, J. C. (1955), *Land and People in Nigeria*, University of London Press, London.

Buckle, C. (1978), *Landforms in Africa: An Introduction to Geomorphology*, Longman, London.

Caldwell, J. C. and Okonjo, C. (eds.) (1968), *The Population of Tropical Africa*, Longman, London.

Chambers, R. (1969), *Settlement Schemes in Tropical Africa: A Study of Organization and Development*, Routledge and Kegan Paul, London.

Chubb, L. T. (1961), *Ibo Land Tenure*, Ibadan University Press, Ibadan.

Clarke, J. I. (ed.) (1966), *Sierra Leone in Maps*, University of London Press, London.

Coleman, J. S. and Rosberg, C. G. (eds.) (1970), *Political Parties and National Integration in Tropical Africa*, University of California Press, Berkeley.

Crowder, M. (1962), *The Story of Nigeria*, Faber and Faber, London.

Culwick, G. M. (1951), *Diet in the Gezira Irrigated Area, Sudan*, Government Printing Press, Khartoum.

Dike, K. O. (1956), *Trade and Politics in the Niger Delta 1830–85*, Oxford University Press, Oxford.

Duffy, J. (1962), *Portugal in Africa*, Penguin Books, Harmondsworth.

Europa Editorial Board (1971–80, 10 edns.), *Africa South of the Sahara*, yearbook, Europa Publications, London.

Fage, J. D. (1962), *An Introduction to the History of West Africa*, Cambridge University Press, Cambridge.

Fitzgerald, W. (1957), *Africa: A Social, Economic and Political Geography of Its Major Regions*, Methuen and Co, London.

Galletti, R., Baldwin, K. D. S. and Dina, I. O. (1956), *Nigerian Cocoa Farmers*, Oxford University Press, Oxford.

Gann, L. H. (1958), *The Birth of a Plural Society*, Manchester University Press, Manchester.

Gleave, M. B. and White, H. P. (1971), *An Economic Geography of West Africa*, Bell, London.

Gnielinski, S. V. (1972), *Liberia in Maps*, University of London Press, London.

Gourou, P. (1955, 5th ed. 1980), *The Tropical World*, translated by E. D. Laborde, Longman, Harlow.

Green, L. P. and Fair, T. J. D. (1962), *Development in Africa*, Witwatersrand University Press, Johannesburg.

Grove, A. T. (1970, 2nd ed.), *Africa South of the Sahara*, Oxford University Press, Oxford.

Gusten, R. (1968), *Studies in the Staple Food Economy of Western Nigeria*, Weltforum-Verlag, Munich.

Hailey, Lord (1957), *An African Survey: A Study of Problems Arising in Africa South of the Sahara*, Oxford University Press, Oxford.

Hance, W. A. (1967), *African Economic Development*, Praeger, New York.

Hance, W. A. (1970), *Population, Migration and Urbanization in Africa*, Praeger, New York.

Hance, W. A. (1975), *The Geography of Modern Africa*, Columbia University Press, New York.

Harrison Church, R. J. (1956), 'The Transport Pattern of British West Africa', in R. W. Steel and C. A. Fisher (eds.) *Geographical Essays on British Tropical Lands*, Philip (George) & Son, London, pp. 53–76.

Harrison Church, R. J. (1971), Africa and the Islands, John Wiley, New York.

Harrison Church, R. J. (1974 ed.), *West Africa: A Study of the Environment and Man's Use of It*, Longman, Harlow.

Hay, A. and Smith, R. H. T. (1970), *Inter-regional Trade and Money Flows in Nigeria*, Oxford University Press, Ibadan.

Hill, P. (1970), *Studies in Rural Capitalism in West Africa*, Cambridge University Press, Cambridge.

Hodder, B. W. (1968), *Economic Development in the Tropics*, Methuen & Co., London.

Hodder, B. W. and Ukwu, U. I. (1969), *Markets in West Africa*, Ibadan University Press, Ibadan.

Hopkins, B. (1965), *Forest and Savanna*, Heinemann, London.

Hoyle, B. S. and Hilling, D. (eds.) (1970), *Seaports and Development in Tropical Africa*, Macmillan, London.

Irvine, F. R. (1970), *West African Agriculture*, Oxford University Press, Oxford.

Johnson, B. F. (1958), *The Staple Food Economies of Western Tropical Africa*, Stanford University Press, Stanford.

Kamarck, A. M. (1971), *The Economics of African Development*, Praeger, New York.

Kay, G. (1967), *A Social Geography of Zambia*, London University Press, London.

Kimble, G. H. T. (1960), *Tropical Africa*, (2 vols.), Johns Hopkins Press, Baltimore.

Knight, C. G. and Newman, J. L. (eds.) (1976), *Contemporary Africa: Geography and Change*, Prentice Hall, Englewood

Cliffs, NJ.

Kuper, H. (1965), *Urbanization and Migration in West Africa*, University of California Press, Berkeley.

Latham, M. (1965), *Human Nutrition in Tropical Africa*, FAO, Rome.

Lee, D. H. K. (1957), *Climate and Economic Development in the Tropics*, Harper & Row, New York.

Lloyd, P. C. (1962), *Yoruba Land Law*, Oxford University Press, Oxford.

Lugard, Lord (1965, 5th ed.), *The Dual Mandate in British Tropical Africa*, Frank Cass, London.

Mabogunje, A. L. (1968), *Urbanization in Nigeria*, University of London Press, London.

Mabogunje, A. L. (1972), *Regional Mobility and Resource Development in West Africa*, McGill-Queen's University Press, Montreal.

Mabogunje, A. L. and Faniran, A. (eds.) (1977), *Regional Planning and National Development in Tropical Africa*, Ibadan University Press, Ibadan.

Morgan, W. B. and Pugh, J. C. (1973), *West Africa*, Methuen & Co., London.

Morgan, W. T. W. (1973), *East Africa*, Longman, London.

Mortimore, M. J. and Wilson, J. (1965), *Land and People in the Kano Close-Settled Zone*, Ahmadu Bello University, Zaria, Department of Geography, *Occasional Paper* no. 1.

Mountjoy, A. B. and Embleton, C. (1965), *Africa – A Geographical Study*, Hutchinson, London.

O'Connor, A. M. (1966), *An Economic Geography of East Africa*, G. Bell & Sons, London.

O'Connor, A. M. (1971), *The Geography of Tropical Development*, Pergamon Press, Oxford.

Oguntoyinbo, J. S., Areola, O. O. and Filani, M. (1978), *A Geography of Nigerian Development*, Heinemann, Ibadan.

Ojo, G. J. A. (1966), *Yoruba Culture*, University of London Press, London.

Ominde, S. (1968), *Land and Population Movements in Kenya*, Heinemann, London.

Ominde, S. (ed.) (1971), *Studies in East African Geography and Development*, Heinemann, London.

Ominde, S. and Ejiogu, C. H. (eds.) (1972), *Population Growth and Economic Development in Africa*, Heinemann, London.

Pike, J. G. and Rimmington, G. T. (1965), *Malawi – A Geographical Study*, Oxford University Press, London.

Post, K. W. (1964), *The New States of West Africa*, Penguin Books, Harmondsworth.

Prothero, R. M. (1965), *Migrants and Malaria*, Longman, Harlow.

Prothero, R. M. (ed.) (1969), *A Geography of Africa*, Routledge and Kegan Paul, London.

Richards, A. I. (ed.) (1954), *Economic Development and Tribal Change*, Cambridge University Press, Cambridge.

Roper, J. I. (1958), *Labour Problems in West Africa*, Penguin Books, Harmondsworth.

Russell, E. W. (ed.) (1962), *The Natural Resources of East Africa*, East African Literature Bureau, Nairobi.

Senior, M. (1979), *Tropical Lands: A Human Geography*, Longman, Harlow.

Soja, E. W. (1968), *The Geography of Modernization in Kenya*, Syracuse University Press, Syracuse.

Stamp, L. D. (1953), *Africa: A Study in Tropical Development*, John Wiley, New York.

Udo, R. K. (1970), *Geographical Regions of Nigeria*, Heinemann, London.

Udo, R. K. (1975), *Migrant Tenant Farmers of Nigeria*, African Universities Press, Lagos.

Udo, R. K. (1978), *A Comprehensive Geography of West Africa*, Heinemann, London & Ibadan.

Varley, W. J. and White, H. P. (1958), *The Geography of Ghana*, Longman, London.

Warren, W. M. and Rubin, N. (eds.) (1968), *Dams in Africa*, Frank Cass, London.

White, H. P. and Gleave, M. B. (1971), *An Economic Geography of West Africa*, Bell, London.

Worthington, E. B. (1958), *Science in the Development of Africa*, prepared for Commission for Technical Co-operation in Africa South of the Sahara (CCTA) and the Scientific Council for Africa South of the Sahara (CSA), London.

(B) Articles in journals and periodicals

Adalemo, I. A. (1968), 'Resettlement of Population Displaced by the Kainji Lake', *Nigerian Geographical Journal*, II, pp. 175–88.

Adejuyigbe, O. (1968), 'The Problems of Unity and the Creation of States in Nigeria', *Nigerian Geographical Journal*, II, pp. 39–60.

Ajaegbu, H. I. (1970), 'Food Crop Farming in the Coastal Area of South-western Nigeria', *Journal of Tropical Geography*, 31, pp. 1–9.

Baldwin, M. and Thorp, J. (1940), 'Laterite in Relation to Soils of the Tropics', *Annals of the Association of American Geographers*, 30, pp. 163–83.

Baker, S. J. K. (1963), 'The Population Geography of East Africa', *East African Geographical Review*, I, pp. 1–6.

Barbour, K. M. (1959), 'Irrigation in the Sudan', *Transactions of the Institute of British Geographers*, 26, pp. 243–63.

Benneh, G. (1972), 'Systems of Agriculture in Tropical Africa', *Economic Geography*, 48, pp. 244–57.

Bowden, B. N. (1964), 'The Dry Seasons of Inter-Tropical Africa and Madagascar', *Journal of Tropical Geography*, 19, pp. 1–3.

Brooke, C. (1959), 'The Rural Village in the Ethiopian Highlands', *Geographical Reviews*, 49, pp. 58–75.

Brookfield, H. C. (1955), 'New Railroad and Port Development in East and Central Africa', *Economic Geography*, 31, pp. 60–70.

Buchanan, K. (1954), 'Livestock in Tropical Africa', *Geographical Review*, 44, pp. 593–4.

Bunting, A. H. (1961), 'Some Problems of Agricultural Climatology in Tropical Africa', *Geography*, 46, pp. 283–94.

Cohen, A. (1966), 'Politics of the Kola Trade', *Africa*, 36, p. 19.

Cole, M. M. (1960), 'The Kariba Project', *Geography*, 45, pp. 98–105.

Cole, M. M. (1962), 'The Rhodesian Economy in Transition and the Role of Kariba', *Geography*, 47, pp. 15–40.

Cole, M. M. (1963), 'Vegetation and Geomorphology in Northern Rhodesia', *Geographical Journal*, 129, pp. 290–310.

Dale, E. H. (1968), 'Some Geographical Aspects of African Land-locked States', *Annals of the Association of American Geographers*, 58, pp. 485–505.

Darkoh, M. B. K. (1971), 'The Distribution of Manufacturing in Ghana: A Case Study of Industrial Location in a Developing Country', *Scottish Geographical Magazine*, 87, pp. 38–57.

Davis, H. R. J. (1964), 'The West African in the Economic Geography of the Sudan', *Geography*, 49, pp. 222–35.

Debenham, F. (1948), 'The Water Resources of Central Africa', *Geographical Journal*, 111, pp. 222–34.

Deshler, W. W. (1960), 'Livestock Trypanosomiasis and Human Settlement in Northeastern Uganda', *Geographical Review*, 50, pp. 541–54.

Deshler, W. W. (1963), 'Cattle in Africa', *Geographical Review*, 53, pp. 52–8.

Finck, A. (1973), 'The Fertility of Tropical Soils Under the Influence of Agricultural Land Use', *Applied Science and Development*, 1, pp. 7–31.

Floyd, B. N. (1962), 'Land Apportionment in Southern Rhodesia', *Geographical Review*, 52, pp. 566–82.

Floyd, B. N. (1964), 'Terrace Agriculture in Eastern Nigeria: The Case of Maku', *Nigerian Geographical Journal*, 7, pp. 33–44.

Floyd B. N. and Adinde, M. (1967), 'Farm Settlements in Eastern Nigeria: A Geographical Appraisal', *Economic Geography*, 43, pp. 189–230.

Forde, C. D. (1953), 'The Cultural Map of West Africa: Successive Adaptations to Tropical Forests and Grasslands', *Transactions of the New York Academy of Sciences*, 15, pp. 206–19.

Gleave, M. B. and White, H. P. (1969), 'The West African Middle Belt: Environmental Fact or Geographer's Fiction?', *Geographical Review*, 59, pp. 123–39.

Goddard, S. (1965), 'Town–Farm Relations in Yorubaland', *Africa*, 35, pp. 21–9.

Good, C. M. (1975), 'Periodic Markets and Travelling Traders in Uganda', *Geographical Review*, 65, pp. 49–72.

Grove, A. T. (1951), 'Land Use and Soil Conservation in Parts of Onitsha and Owerri Provinces', *Geological Survey of Nigeria*, 21.

Hance, W. A., Kotschar, V. and Peterec, R. J. (1961), 'Source Areas of Export Production in Tropical Africa', *Geographical Review*, 51, pp. 487–99.

Harrison Church, R. J. (1961), 'Problems and Development of the Dry Zone of West Africa', *Geographical Journal*, 127, pp. 187–204.

Hay, A. M. (1971), 'Notes on the Economic Basis for Periodic Marketing in Developing Countries', *Geographical Analysis*, 3, pp. 393–401.

Hill, P. (1966), 'Notes on Traditional Market Authority and Market Periodicity in West Africa', *Journal of African History*, 7, pp. 295–311.

Hilling, D. (1963), 'The Changing Economy of Gabon', *Geography*, 48, pp. 155–65.

Hilling, D. (1965), 'The Volta River Project', *Geographical Magazine*, 37, pp. 830–41.

Hilton, T. E. (1959), 'Land Planning and Resettlement in Northern Ghana', *Geography*, 44, pp. 227–40.

Hodder, B. W. (1959), 'Tin Mining on the Jos Plateau of Nigeria', *Economic Geography*, 35, pp. 109–22.

Hunter, J. M. (1961), 'Akotuadrom: A Devastated Cocoa Village in Ghana', *Transactions of the Institute of British Geographers*, 24, pp. 161–86.

Hunter, J. M. (1966), 'River Blindness in Nangodi, Northern Ghana', *Geographical Review*, 56, pp. 398–416.

Hunter, J. M. (1967), 'Seasonal Hunger in a Part of the West African Savanna', *Transactions of the Institute of British Geographers*, 41, pp. 167–85.

Hunter, J. M. (1967), 'The Social Roots of Dispersed Settlement in Northern Ghana', *Annals of the Association of American Geographers*, 57, pp. 339–49.

Ireland, A. W. (1962), 'The Little Dry Season of Southern Nigeria', *Nigerian Geographical Journal*, 5, pp. 7–20.

Jackson, R. T. (1971), 'Periodic Markets in Southern Ethiopia', *Transactions of the Institute of British Geographers*, 53, pp. 31–42.

Jarrett, H. R. (1949), 'The Strange Farmers of the Gambia', *Geographical Review*, 39, pp. 649–57.

Johnson, H. B. (1967), 'The Location of Christian Missions in Africa', *Geographical Review*, 57, pp. 168–202.

Jones, Bryamor (1938), 'Desiccation and the West African Colonies', *Geographical Journal*, 95, pp. 401–23.

Jones, W. O. (1965), 'Environment, Technical Knowledge, and Economic Development in Tropical Africa', *Food Research Institute Studies*, 5, pp. 101–116.

Jurgens, H. W., Tracey, K. A. and Mitchell, P. K. (1966), 'Internal Migration in Liberia', *Bulletin, Sierra Leone Geographical Association*, 10, pp. 39–59.

Kampfe, I. K. (1973), 'Unification of African Railways', *Applied Science and Development*, Institute for Scientific Co-operation, Federal Republic of Germany, 2, pp. 96–121.

Keay, R. W. J. (1959), 'Derived Savanna: Derived from What?', *Bulletin de l'Ifan*, 21, pp. 427–38.

Khuri, F. I. (1965), 'Kinship, Emigration and Trade Partnership Among the Lebanese of West Africa', *Africa*, 35, pp. 385–95.

Knight, C. G. (1971), 'The Ecology of African Sleeping Sickness', *Annals of the Association of American Geographers*, 61, pp. 23–44.

Lebon, J. H. G. (1956), 'Rural Water Supplies and the Development of the Economy in the Central Sudan', *Geografiska Annaler*, 38, pp. 78–101.

Ledger, D. C. (1961), 'Recent Hydrological Changes in the Rima Basin, Northern Nigeria', *Geographical Journal*, 127, pp. 477–87.

Logan, M. I. (1970), 'The Process of Regional Development and its Implications for Planning', *Nigeria Geographical Journal*, 13, pp. 109–20.

Mabogunje, A. L. (1962), 'The Growth of Residential Districts in Ibadan', *Geographical Review*, 52, pp. 56–77.

Mabogunje, A. L. (1974), 'Manufacturing and the Geography of Development in Tropical Africa', *Economic Geography*, 49, pp. 1–20.

Manshard, W. (1974), 'The Large African Reservoirs', *Applied Sciences and Development* (W. Germany), 3, pp. 53–62.

Mason, M. (1969), 'Population Density and "Slave Raiding" – the Case of the Middle Belt of Nigeria', *Journal of African History*, 10, pp. 551–64.

Morgan, W. B. (1959), 'Agriculture in Southern Nigeria', *Economic Geography*, 35, pp. 138–50.

Morgan, W. B. (1959), 'The Influence of European Contacts on the Landscape of Southern Nigeria', *Geography*, 125, pp. 48–64.

Morgan, W. B. (1963), 'Food Imports of West Africa', *Economic Geography*, 39, pp. 351–62.

Morgan, W. B. (1977), 'Food Supply and Staple Food Imports of Tropical Africa', *African Affairs*, 76, pp. 167–76.

Morgan, W. T. W. (1963), 'The "White Highlands" of Kenya', *Geographical Journal*, 129, pp. 140–55.

Murdock, G. P. (1960), 'Staple Subsistence Crops of Africa', *Geographical Review*, 50, pp. 523–40.

O'Connor, A. M. (1963), 'Regional Inequalities in Economic Development in Uganda', *East African Geographical Review*, 1, pp. 33–44.

Ofomata, G. (1967), 'Landforms of the Nsukka Plateau of Eastern Nigeria', *Nigerian Geographical Journal*, 10, pp. 3–10.

Ojo, G. J. A. (1970), 'Some Observations on the Journey to Agricultural Work in Yorubaland, Southwestern Nigeria', *Economic Geography*, 46, pp. 459–71.

Pendleton, R. L. (1949), 'The Belgian Congo: Impressions of a Changing Region', *Geographical Review*, 39, pp. 371–400.

Pool, D. I. (1971), 'Urbanization and Fertility in Africa', *African Urban Notes*, 6, pp. 25–32.

Prescott, J. R. V. (1959), 'Migrant Labour in the Central African Federation', *Geographical Review*, 49, pp. 424–7. *Geographers*, 54, pp. 41–58.

Prescott, J. R. V. (1959), 'Nigeria's Regional Boundary Problems', *Geographical Review*, 49, pp. 485–505.

Prescott, J. R. V. (1962), 'Population Distribution in Southern Rhodesia', *Geographical Review*, 52, pp. 559–65.

Prothero, R. M. (1957), 'Migratory Labour from Sokoto Province', *Africa*, 27, pp. 251–61.

Reeve, W. H. (1960), 'Progress and Geographical Significance of the Kariba Dam', *Geographical Journal*, 126, pp. 140–6.

Rempel, H. (1971), 'The Rural-to-Urban Migrant in Kenya', *African Urban Notes*, 6, pp. 53–72.

Richards, A. L. (1958), 'A Changing Pattern of Agriculture in East Africa: the Beinba of Northern Rhodesia', *Geographical Journal*, 124, pp. 302–14.

Riddell, J. B. and Harvey, M. E. (1972), 'The Urban System in the Migration Process: An Evaluation of Stepwise Migration in Sierra Leone', *Economic Geography*, 48, pp. 270–83.

Roder, W. (1964), 'The Division of Land Resources in Southern Rhodesia', *Annals of the Association of American Geographers*, 54, pp. 41–58.

Scott, E. P. (1972), 'The Spatial Structure of Rural Northern Nigeria: Farmers, Periodic Markets and Villages', *Economic Geography*, 48, pp. 316–32.

Scott, P. (1954), 'Migrant Labour in Southern Rhodesia', *Geographical Review*, 44, pp. 29–48.

Stanley, W. R. (1970), 'Transport Expansion in Liberia', *Geographical Review*, 60, pp. 529–47.

Stanz, D. (1978), 'Rain in Africa and the Drought of Recent Years', *Applied Sciences and Development* (W. Germany), 11, pp. 49–77.

Steel, R. W. (1955), 'Land and Population in British Tropical Africa', *Geography*, 40, pp. 1–17.

Steel, R. W. (1957), 'The Copperbelt of Northern Rhodesia', *Geography*, 42, pp. 83–92.

Stern, R. (1972), 'Urban Policy in Africa: A Political Analysis', *African Studies Review*, 15, pp. 485–516.

Swindell, K. (1969), 'Industrialization in Guinea', *Geography*, 54, pp. 456–8.

Taaffe, E. J., Morrill, R. L. and Gould, P. R. (1963), 'Transport Expansion in Underdeveloped Countries: A Comparative Analysis', *Geographical Review*, 53, pp. 503–29.

Thomas, B. (1957), 'Railways and Ports in French West Africa', *Economic Geography*, 33, pp. 1–15.

Trewartha, G. T. and Zelinsky, W. (1954), 'The Population Geography of Belgian Africa', *Annals of the Association of American Geographers*, 44, pp. 163–93.

Udo, R. K. (1965), 'Disintegration of Nucleated Settlement in Eastern Nigeria', *Geographical Review*, 55, pp. 53–67.

Udo, R. K. (1965), 'Sixty Years of Plantation Agriculture in Southern Nigeria 1902–1962', *Economic Geography*, 41, pp. 356–68.

Udo, R. K. (1971), 'Food Deficit Areas of Nigeria', *Geographical Review*, 61, pp. 415–30.

Van Dongen, I. S. (1961), 'Coffee Trade, Coffee Regions and Coffe Ports in Angola', *Economic Geography*, 37, pp. 320–46.

Varian, H. F. (1931), 'The Geography of the Benguela Railway', *Geographical Journal*, 78, pp. 497–523.

Weigend, G. C. (1954), 'River Ports and Outports: Matadi and Banana', *Geographical Review*, 44, pp. 430–2.

Wells, F. B. (1957), 'Transport in the Rhodesian Copperbelt', *Geography*, 42, pp. 93–5.

White, H. P. (1959), 'Ports of West Africa', *Tijdschrift voor Economigos en Sociate Geographie*, 50, pp. 1–8.

Whittington, G. (1964), 'Iron Mining in Angola', *Geography*, 49, pp. 418–19.

Whittlesey, D. S. (1924), 'Geographic Provinces of Angola', *Geographical Review*, 14, pp. 113–26.

Sample Examination Questions

Section A   The Physical Environment

1. Describe and explain the main features of the relief and drainage of *either* the East African Plateau *or* the Zaïre Basin.

2. Discuss, with reference to tropical Africa, the current theories concerning the origins of savanna vegetation.

3. To what extent does a knowledge of surface geology and climatic features assist in the recognition and definition of major natural regions in tropical Africa?

4. Discuss the nature and causes of soil erosion in any one sub-region of tropical Africa.

5. What is derived savanna and how extensive is this type of vegetation in tropical Africa?

6. It is relative humidity, more than any other factor, which has given the climates of tropical Africa a bad name. Comment.

7. Discuss the characteristics of the air masses which influence the climate of *either* West Africa *or* Central Africa.

8. Laterite is utterly infertile and hostile to agriculture owing to its sterility and compactness. Comment with respect to the situation in any one sub-region of tropical Africa.

9. Write a brief account of two of the following:
a. the effect of bush burning on soil fertility;
b. the length of the rainy season in West Africa;
c. the drainage characteristics of southern Uganda.

10. With reference to specific examples, discuss the uses that are made of the principal rivers of tropical Africa. What factors limit the extent to which they can be used?

11. Compare and contrast the equatorial climate of central Zaïre with that of central Kenya.

12. Discuss the various ways in which pests and diseases have affected the economic and social development of tropical Africa.

13. Primitive living conditions, rather than climate, have been largely responsible for many diseases which are still rampant in tropical Africa. Discuss.

14. Discuss the possibilities and problems of developing the semi-arid lands of tropical Africa as a major source of food for man.

Section B   Peoples, Societies and Social Change

1. Drawing examples from West and Central Africa, discuss how an increase in population may provoke or prevent economic development.

2. Account for the increasing drift of population from the interior to the coastal areas of West Africa.

3. Write an essay on the shanty towns of tropical African cities.

4. Comment on the view that the traditional land tenure systems constitute one of the major problems facing agricultural development in western tropical Africa.

5. Account for the rapid growth in the population of tropical Africa since about 1950.

6. Examine the developmental implications of the primate-city structure in the urban systems of many tropical African countries.

7. Discuss the view that internal migrations within Nigeria share many of the characteristics of international migrations in tropical Africa.

8. In what ways are the factors which led to the expansion of cities in western Europe since the industrial revolution different from those operating in tropical Africa today?

9. Account for the major changes affecting the distribution and internal structure of rural settlements in tropical Africa since about 1900.

10. 'Large-scale urbanization is costly for transitional societies not only in economic but also in social and political terms.' Discuss with reference to any one sub-region of tropical Africa.

11. The death rate is still the decisive factor in determining the rate of population increase in tropical Africa. Comment.

12. Compare and contrast the pre-colonial cities of tropical Africa with the new towns of the colonial and post-colonial periods.

13. Outline and discuss the major problems associated with the increasing influx of people into the major cities of tropical Africa.

14. Discuss the major population problems of any two tropical African countries and suggest ways for solving them.

15. Drawing examples from at least two countries, discuss how the migrations of nomadic herders are adjusted to the physical environment in which they live.

16. Explain how the people of tropical Africa react to the uneven distribution of resources and opportunities in the region.

17. Discuss the origins, distribution and internal structure of the pre-colonial cities of tropical Africa.

18. Discuss the relevance to tropical Africa of the

arguments for and against fertility control and family planning.

19. Although the Ivory Coast is a labour-deficient country, it has a large and increasing number of urban unemployed. Discuss.

20. Describe the traditional systems of land tenure in your home district and account for the changes (if any) which have occurred during the last sixty years.

Section C   Primary Economic Activities

1. Discuss the similarities and contrasts between African and white settler farming in Zimbabwe.

2. Locate on a sketch map the chief crude-oil producing areas of tropical Africa and discuss the relative importance of oil as a source of power in the region.

3. Describe the main features of plantation agriculture and examine the advantages and disadvantages of the plantation system over peasant-type agriculture.

4. Compare African farming in the Kikuyu highlands of Kenya with that in the Kano district of Nigeria.

5. Examine the main features of pastoral nomadism in northern tropical Africa.

6. Discuss the importance of irrigation in the agricultural development of the grasslands of western tropical Africa.

7. Regional differences in tropical African agriculture are primarily due to differences in climate. Discuss.

8. Natural conditions in tropical Africa are generally unfavourable for agriculture. Comment.

9. Discuss the importance of mining to the economy of any two countries in tropical Africa.

10. Write briefly on two of the following:
a. rice production in West Africa;
b. mixed farming in the Kenya Highlands;
c. floodland cultivation in Mali.

11. Compare the role of peasant farmers in the production of agricultural exports in Nigeria and Zaïre.

12. Mining has been instrumental to the development of power installations and railways in tropical Africa. Comment.

13. The traditional agricultural system of the Tswana of Botswana is one in which each family keeps three homes consisting of the main or permanent home in the village, a crude home in the distant farmland, and another crude home at the cattle post. Elaborate.

14. As a form of agriculture, livestock ranching is not usually associated with tropical Africa. Explain.

15. Discuss the development of modern poultry farming in any country of tropical Africa and assess its importance to the animal protein supply of that country.

16. Discuss the development of sea fishing along the Atlantic coast of tropical Africa.

17. If you give a man a fish he will have food for a day, if you teach him to raise fish he will have food for a lifetime. Discuss.

18. One major problem for agriculture in tropical Africa is that in areas of commercial cropping for export there is a shortage of labour. Comment.

19. Discuss the main features and the problems of increasing food-crop production in either West Africa or the Zaïre Basin.

20. Consider the factors which have made the Gezira one of the most successful agricultural projects in tropical Africa.

21. Examine the relationships between population density and agricultural systems in either West Africa or East Africa.

22. Write an essay on either copper in Zambia or petroleum in Nigeria.

Section D   Manufacturing and Service Industries

1. Write an explanatory account of the competition between road and rail transport in any one country of tropical Africa.

2. The railway network of western tropical Africa reflects national rather than purely economic requirements. Discuss.

3. Outline the major problems of industrialization in any sub-region of tropical Africa.

4. Discuss the relative importance of raw materials and markets as factors in the location of manufacturing industries in tropical Africa.

5. In spite of the relative cheapness of river transport, the River Zaïre now accounts for only a small proportion of freight movement in Zaïre. Discuss.

6. Comment on the view that in tropical Africa, the railway came before the road.

7. Transportation is the key to African development. Discuss.

8. Discuss the importance of hydro-electric power in the development of manufacturing in tropical Africa.

9. Account for the fact that in tropical Africa the textile industry is more common than the iron and steel industry.

10. Describe the role of rural periodic markets in the internal exchange economy of West Africa.

11. Account for the concentration of manufacturing industries along the coastal areas of West Africa.

12. Discuss the factors inhibiting the development of trans-continental railways in tropical Africa.

13. Consider why the development of port facilities has been restricted to a few port-towns since about 1950.

14. Describe the industries of either the Kano Industrial Area or the Nairobi Industrial Area. Account for the geographical circumstances which have encouraged industrial development in either of these two areas.

15. Give a critical appraisal of the reasons why developing countries, including those of tropical Africa, have become seriously committed to ensuring

rapid industrial development since independence.

16. Account for the slow pace of development of the manufacturing sector in colonial Africa.

17. Almost every country in tropical Africa has a weak industrial structure. Elaborate.

18. By laying great emphasis on the manufacture of consumer goods, the countries of tropical Africa are inadvertently slowing down the pace of industrial development. Discuss.

19. Account for the fact that most import-substitution industries are located in the port-towns of tropical Africa.

20. Assess the role of government policy in the location and distribution of industries in African countries.

21. Consider the relevance of the Taaffe model of transport network development to transport planning in *either* Gabon *or* Tanzania *or* the Ivory Coast.

Section E   Aspects of Change in the Political Process

1. Discuss the special problems of the land-locked states of tropical Africa and suggest ways for solving them.

2. In its political geography, Nigeria is the epitome of tropical Africa. Comment.

3. Conditions for regional economic integration are less favourable in West Africa than in East Africa. Discuss.

4. Examine the case for and against a continental government in Africa.

5. Describe the structure and pattern of inter-state trade in tropical Africa.

6. The period of the slave trade and the colonial period constituted a political and economic accident in the historical evolution of the region. Discuss.

7. Discuss the effects of the slave trade on the size and distribution of the population of Africa at the beginning of the twentieth century.

8. Examine the manpower situation at independence in Nigeria and Zaïre.

9. What was the colonial pact? Compare its implementation in French and British colonial Africa.

10. Explain why independent African countries have been unable to alter the so-called artificial boundaries of the colonial period.

11. All political boundaries are artificial. Discuss with reference to the situation in any sub-region of tropical Africa.

12. Explain how political considerations have so far thwarted government efforts to obtain an accurate population census in Nigeria.

Index